Automated Web Testing

(Step by Step Automation Guide)

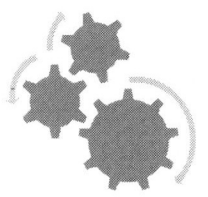

G. Suden

Copyright © 2016 by Gurwinder Suden. All rights reserved. First Edition.
Visit http://www.arkenstone-ltd.com   Email: info@arkenstone-ltd.com

No part of this publication may be reproduced, stored in a retrieval system, or transmitted in any form or by any means, electronic, mechanical, photocopying, recording, scanning, or otherwise, without the written permission of the author.

Microsoft® Visual Studio Express 2015 for Web, Microsoft® SQL Server® 2012 Express and Microsoft® Excel® are trademarks of Microsoft Corporation. © 2010 Microsoft Corporation. All rights reserved. Visit http://www.microsoft.com

All Selenium projects are licensed under the Apache 2.0 License. All rights reserved.
Visit http://www.apache.org/licenses/LICENSE-2.0

Apache log4net™ and log4net™ are trademarks of the Apache Software Foundation. Copyright © 1999-2016 Apache Software Foundation. All Rights Reserved. Visit https://logging.apache.org

Apache NPOI and NPOI are trademarks of the Apache Software Foundation. Copyright © 1999-2016 Apache Software Foundation. All Rights Reserved. Visit https://npoi.codeplex.com

NUnit Copyright © 2002-2015 Charlie Poole
Copyright © 2002-2004 James W. Newkirk, Michael C. Two, Alexei A. Vorontsov
Copyright © 2000-2002 Philip A. Craig
Visit http://nunit.org

Mozilla® and Firefox® are trademarks of The Mozilla Foundation. All rights reserved.
Visit https://www.mozilla.org

Google Chrome Copyright © 2016 Google Inc. All rights reserved. Visit http://www.google.com

Windows® Internet Explorer and Microsoft® Edge Copyright © 2015 are trademarks of Microsoft Corporation. All rights reserved. Visit http://www.microsoft.com

Safari Copyright © 2007-2012 Apple Inc. All rights reserved. Visit http://www.apple.com/safari/

Opera Copyright © 1995-2016 Opera Software ASA. All rights reserved.

Limit of Liability/Disclaimer of Warranty: While the author has used his best efforts in preparing this book, he makes no representations or warranties with respect to the accuracy or completeness of the contents of this book and specifically disclaims any implied warranties of merchantability or fitness for a particular purpose. No warranty may be created or extended by sales representatives or written sales materials. The advice and strategies contained herein may not be suitable for your situation. You should consult with a professional where appropriate. Neither the publisher nor author shall be liable for any loss of profit or any other commercial damages, including but not limited to special, incidental, consequential, or other damages.

Every effort has been made to acknowledge the copyrights. If any copyright holder would like us to make an amendment to the acknowledgement, please notify us and we will gladly update the book at the next reprint. Thank you.

ISBN-13:   978-1535285988
ISBN-10:   1535285982

Printed by CreateSpace, An Amazon.com Company
Order online at https://www.createspace.com/6422746

Available from Amazon.com, Amazon Europe, other online stores and retail outlets.

To my parents, wife and my amazing kids for giving me the support and drive to finish this book. I love you all!

Acknowledgements

The author is thankful to Lovleen, Simran and Kanwal for copy editing the manuscript.

Contents

Dedication		i
Acknowledgements		iii
List of Figures		1
Overview		5

1 Getting Started — 9
- 1.1 Why Automate? — 11
- 1.2 How Not To Automate? — 12
- 1.3 Golden Automation Rules — 14
- 1.4 Typical 3-Tier Web Application Architecture — 15

2 Automation Approach — 17
- 2.1 Automation Environment And Software — 19
- 2.2 About The Website Under Test — 20
    - 2.2.1 Site Map — 21
- 2.3 Identifying Objects or Elements — 23
    - 2.3.1 Identifying Element By Name — 23
    - 2.3.2 Identifying Element By ID — 25
    - 2.3.3 Identifying Element By Link Text — 28
    - 2.3.4 Identifying Element By XPATH — 29
    - 2.3.5 Identifying Element By CSS Selectors — 31
- 2.4 Automation Framework — 33
    - 2.4.1 Configuration File — 33
    - 2.4.2 Utility File — 33
    - 2.4.3 Reference Files — 34
    - 2.4.4 Repository File — 34
    - 2.4.5 Page Files — 34
    - 2.4.6 Test Files — 34
- 2.5 Creating The Project Structure — 36
- 2.6 Adding Necessary References — 41

3 Let's Automate — 45
- 3.1 Your First Automated Test — 46
    - 3.1.1 Creating The Configuration Parameters — 46
    - 3.1.2 Building The Object Repository — 47
    - 3.1.3 Creating The Utility Functions — 51

		3.1.4	Creating The Page Logic	55
			3.1.4.1 Base Page	55
			3.1.4.2 Home Page	57
			3.1.4.3 Login Page	59
		3.1.5	Creating Tests	61
		3.1.6	Building Tests	63
		3.1.7	Executing Tests	64
	3.2	Reporting Expected Vs. Actual		66
		3.2.1	Utility Functions	66
		3.2.2	Updating Page Logic	69
		3.2.3	Updating Tests	69
		3.2.4	Executing Tests	70
	3.3	Logging Information		71
		3.3.1	Logging To Console Via Logger	73
			3.3.1.1 Updating Utility Functions	73
			3.3.1.2 Updating Tests	76
			3.3.1.3 Creating Configuration File	79
			3.3.1.4 Updating Assembly	80
			3.3.1.5 Executing Tests	80
		3.3.2	Logging To A File	81
			3.3.2.1 Updating Configuration File	81
			3.3.2.2 Detail Log File	82
			3.3.2.3 Configuration Parameters	83
			3.3.2.4 Utility Functions	84
			3.3.2.5 Updating Tests	85
			3.3.2.6 Executing Tests	86
	3.4	Negative Tests - Login		87
		3.4.1	Object Repository	88
		3.4.2	Configuration Parameters	89
		3.4.3	Utility Functions	90
		3.4.4	Page Logic	91
		3.4.5	Creating Tests	92
		3.4.6	Executing Tests	96
	3.5	Saving Screenshots		97
		3.5.1	Configuration Parameters	97
		3.5.2	Utility Functions	97
		3.5.3	Capturing A Test Failure	99
		3.5.4	Capturing A Test Step Failure	100
		3.5.5	Capture An Event	101
		3.5.6	Executing Tests	101
	3.6	Data Entry - Add Employee		102
		3.6.1	Object Repository	103
		3.6.2	Configuration Parameters	104
		3.6.3	Utility Functions	105
		3.6.4	Page Logic	106

			3.6.4.1	Home Page - Tester	106
			3.6.4.2	Add Employee Page	108
		3.6.5	Creating Tests	110
		3.6.6	Executing Tests	112
	3.7	Data Verification - View Employee	113
		3.7.1	Object Repository	113
		3.7.2	Configuration Parameters	115
		3.7.3	Utility Functions	115
		3.7.4	Page Logic	118
		3.7.5	Creating Tests	120
		3.7.6	Executing Test	121

4 Automate With Databases — 123

	4.1	Setting up Testing Database	125
		4.1.1 Creating The Database	125
		4.1.2 Creating Employees Table	127
		4.1.3 Creating The Test Data	128
		4.1.4 Loading The Test Data	128
	4.2	Table Handling - Summary Reports	128
		4.2.1 Object Repository	129
		4.2.2 Configuration Parameters	130
		4.2.3 Utility Functions	131
		4.2.4 Page Logic	132
		4.2.4.1 Home Page - Admin	132
		4.2.4.2 Reports Page - Admin	134
		4.2.5 Creating Tests	137
		4.2.6 Executing Tests	139
	4.3	Table Handling - Tabular Reports	140
		4.3.1 Object Repository	141
		4.3.2 Configuration Parameters	142
		4.3.3 Utility Functions	142
		4.3.4 Page Logic	143
		4.3.5 Creating Tests	152
		4.3.6 Executing Tests	154
	4.4	Creating Test Result Summary	155
		4.4.1 Configuration Parameters	155
		4.4.2 Utility Functions	156
		4.4.3 Updating Page Logic	157
		4.4.4 Updating Tests	158
		4.4.5 Executing Tests	159

5 Data Driven Testing — 161

	5.1	Adding Necessary References	163
	5.2	Configuration Parameters	164
	5.3	Excel XLS Format	164

		5.3.1	Utility Functions	164
		5.3.2	Data Driven - Login	168
			5.3.2.1 Test Data File	168
			5.3.2.2 Creating Test	169
			5.3.2.3 Executing Test	170
		5.3.3	Data Driven - Add Employee	170
			5.3.3.1 Test Data File	171
			5.3.3.2 Page Logic	171
			5.3.3.3 Creating Test	173
			5.3.3.4 Executing Test	174
		5.3.4	Data Driven - View Employee Verification	174
			5.3.4.1 Page Logic	175
			5.3.4.2 Creating Test	176
			5.3.4.3 Executing Test	177
	5.4	Excel XLSX Format	178
		5.4.1	Utility Functions	178
		5.4.2	Data Driven - Employee List Verification	181
			5.4.2.1 Test Data File	181
			5.4.2.2 Page Logic	183
			5.4.2.3 Creating Test	185
			5.4.2.4 Executing Test	186
	5.5	Automation Framework - Adding More Features	186
		5.5.1	Test Step Failure Threshold	186
			5.5.1.1 Configuration Parameters	187
			5.5.1.2 Utility Functions	187
			5.5.1.3 Page Logic	189
			5.5.1.4 Creating Test	191
			5.5.1.5 Executing Test	192
		5.5.2	Log Failed Test Steps Only	192
			5.5.2.1 Configuration Parameters	193
			5.5.2.2 Utility Functions	193
			5.5.2.3 Executing Test	194
		5.5.3	Comparing Decimals With Tolerance	194
			5.5.3.1 Configuration Parameters	195
			5.5.3.2 Utility Functions	195
			5.5.3.3 Creating Test	197
			5.5.3.4 Executing Test	197
6	**Cross Browser Testing**			**199**
	6.1	Mozilla Firefox	201
		6.1.1	Firefox WebDriver	201
		6.1.2	Configuration Parameters	201
		6.1.3	Utility Functions	201
		6.1.4	Executing Tests	202
		6.1.5	Loading Firefox Add-ons	203

		6.1.5.1 Creating Test	204
		6.1.5.2 Executing Test	207
	6.1.6	Loading Default Firefox Profile	207
		6.1.6.1 Creating Test	208
		6.1.6.2 Executing Test	209
	6.1.7	Loading Specific Firefox Profile	210
		6.1.7.1 Creating Test	213
		6.1.7.2 Executing Test	214
	6.1.8	Setting Firefox Preferences	215
		6.1.8.1 Creating Test	217
		6.1.8.2 Executing Test	219
6.2	Google Chrome		221
	6.2.1	Chrome Driver	221
	6.2.2	Configuration Parameters	221
	6.2.3	Utility Functions	221
	6.2.4	Executing Tests	222
	6.2.5	Adding Chrome Options - Disable Extensions	222
		6.2.5.1 Creating Tests	223
		6.2.5.2 Executing Tests	226
	6.2.6	Adding Chrome Options - Allow File Access	226
		6.2.6.1 Creating Tests	227
		6.2.6.2 Executing Tests	228
	6.2.7	Adding Chrome Extensions	229
		6.2.7.1 Creating Test	230
		6.2.7.2 Executing Test	231
6.3	Internet Explorer		231
	6.3.1	Internet Explorer Driver	231
	6.3.2	Configuration Parameters	231
	6.3.3	Utility Functions	232
	6.3.4	Executing Tests	232
	6.3.5	Internet Explorer Options	233
		6.3.5.1 Creating Tests	233
		6.3.5.2 Executing Test	236
6.4	Microsoft Edge		237
	6.4.1	Microsoft Edge WebDriver	237
	6.4.2	Configuration Parameters	237
	6.4.3	Utility Functions	238
	6.4.4	Executing Tests	238
	6.4.5	Edge Options	239
		6.4.5.1 Creating Tests	239
		6.4.5.2 Executing Test	242
6.5	Safari		243
	6.5.1	SafariDriver	243
	6.5.2	Configuration Parameters	243
	6.5.3	Utility Functions	243

		6.5.4	Executing Tests	244
		6.5.5	Safari Options	244
			6.5.5.1 Creating Tests	244
			6.5.5.2 Executing Test	247
	6.6	Opera		248
		6.6.1	Opera WebDriver	248
		6.6.2	Configuration Parameters	248
		6.6.3	Utility Functions	248
		6.6.4	Executing Tests	249
		6.6.5	Opera Options	249
			6.6.5.1 Creating Tests	249
			6.6.5.2 Executing Test	252
	6.7	Automation Framework - Adding More Features		253
		6.7.1	Testing On Different Environments	253
		6.7.2	Logging Environment and Browser Name	258
		6.7.3	Logging System Info	259
			6.7.3.1 Configuration Parameters	259
			6.7.3.2 Utility Functions	259
			6.7.3.3 Updating Page Logic	261
			6.7.3.4 Executing Tests	262

7 Web Services Testing — 265

	7.1	Demo Web Service	267
		7.1.1 Creating The Web Service	270
		7.1.2 Running The Web Service	273
		7.1.3 Invoking The Web Service	276
	7.2	Testing The Web Service via WebRequest	278
		7.2.1 Utility Functions	278
		7.2.2 Creating Test	282
		7.2.3 Executing Tests	284
	7.3	Testing The Web Service via HttpWebRequest SOAP	285
		7.3.1 Utility Functions	285
		7.3.2 Creating Test	289
		7.3.3 Executing Tests	290
	7.4	Testing The Web Service via Service Reference	291
		7.4.1 Adding Service Reference	291
		7.4.2 Utility Functions	292
		7.4.3 Creating Test	293
		7.4.4 Executing Tests	294

8 Miscellaneous — 297

	8.1	Finding Missing Images	299
		8.1.1 Utility Functions	299
		8.1.2 Creating Tests	301
		8.1.3 Executing Tests	302

- 8.2 Finding Broken Links 303
  - 8.2.1 Utility Functions 303
  - 8.2.2 Creating Tests 306
  - 8.2.3 Executing Tests 307
- 8.3 Finding Tooltips 308
  - 8.3.1 Configuration Parameters 308
  - 8.3.2 Utility Functions 309
  - 8.3.3 Page Logic 310
  - 8.3.4 Creating Tests 311
  - 8.3.5 Executing Tests 312
- 8.4 Drag And Drop 312
  - 8.4.1 Object Repository 313
  - 8.4.2 Creating Test - DragAndDrop 313
  - 8.4.3 Executing Test - DragAndDrop 315
  - 8.4.4 Creating Test - Mouse In Action 315
  - 8.4.5 Creating Test - DragAndDropToOffset 317
- 8.5 Context Click 318
  - 8.5.1 Adding Necessary Reference 318
  - 8.5.2 Creating Tests 319
  - 8.5.3 Executing Test 321
- 8.6 Executing JavaScript 321
  - 8.6.1 Utility Functions 322
  - 8.6.2 Creating Page Logic 323
  - 8.6.3 Creating Tests 324
  - 8.6.4 Executing Tests 325

Appendices   327
- A.1 Automation Portal 329

Index   341

List of Figures

1.1	Typical Web Application Architecture	15
2.1	Demonstration Website - Automation Portal	21
2.2	Demo Portal - Site Map	22
2.3	Element Identification By Name	24
2.4	Element Identification By ID	25
2.5	Element Identification By Name - IE11	26
2.6	Element Identification By Name using Firefox	27
2.7	Element Identification By ID using Firefox - DOM	28
2.8	Element Identification By Link Text	29
2.9	Element Identification By XPath	30
2.10	Element Identification - XPath Checker	30
2.11	Element Identification By CSS Selectors	31
2.12	Element Identification By CSS Selectors - Firefinder	32
2.13	Automation Framework	33
2.14	Automated Test Script Structure	35
2.15	Create New Visual C# Class Library	36
2.16	Add a Class	37
2.17	Add the Configuration Class	38
2.18	Add the Utility Class	38
2.19	Rename to Repository.cs	39
2.20	Rename Class	39
2.21	Add New Folder	40
2.22	Solution Explorer Window	40
2.23	Add Selenium Reference Files	41
2.24	Add NUnit Reference File	42
2.25	Complete Solution Explorer Window	43
3.1	Repository Home Page	48
3.2	Repository Home Page - Version Label	49
3.3	Page Base	56
3.4	Selecting Solution Configuration	63
3.5	Building Test	63
3.6	Output Window	64
3.7	Create Project	64

3.8	Selecting Assembly	65
3.9	Select Test To Run	65
3.10	Test Run Output	66
3.11	Adding Missing Reference	68
3.12	Rebuilding Tests	70
3.13	Rerun Tests	71
3.14	Adding log4net Reference	72
3.15	Logging to Console	80
3.16	Log File - DetailLog.csv	82
3.17	Excel - Format DateTime	83
3.18	The Result Folder	86
3.19	CSV Files in the Result Folder	87
3.20	Invalid Login	88
3.21	Login All Tests	96
3.22	Add System Drawing Reference	99
3.23	Captured Screenshot	102
3.24	Console Output - Add Employee	113
3.25	Console Output - Verify Employee	122
4.1	Console Output - Admin Report By Gender	140
4.2	Console Output - Admin Employee List	155
4.3	Login Tests With Test Summary File	159
4.4	Test Summary File Contents	160
5.1	Adding References to Support Excel Files	163
5.2	XLS Format- Creating Login Test Data	168
5.3	Data Driven Login Output	170
5.4	XLS Format - Creating Employee Data	171
5.5	Data Driven Add Employee Output	174
5.6	Data Driven Verify Employee Output	178
5.7	XLSX Format - Creating Login Test Data	182
5.8	XLSX Format - Creating Employee List Test Data	182
5.9	Data Driven Verify Employee List Output	186
5.10	Step Failure Threshold Output	192
5.11	Log Failed Test Steps Only Output	194
5.12	Compare Decimals With Tolerance	198
6.1	Firefox Browser	203
6.2	Loading Firefox With Firebug	207
6.3	Loading Firefox Default Profile	210
6.4	Open Run Dialog	211
6.5	Choose User Profile	211
6.6	Create User Profile	212
6.7	Start-up User Profile	212
6.8	Loading Specific Firefox Profile	214
6.9	With Search Suggest - Default Profile	215

6.10 About:Config - Default Profile 216
6.11 New Tab - Default Profile 217
6.12 Without Search Suggest - Automation Profile 219
6.13 About:Config - Automation Profile 220
6.14 New Tab - Automation Profile 220
6.15 ChromeDriver Window 222
6.16 Load Extension Failure 222
6.17 Chrome Loaded With Disable Extensions 226
6.18 Chrome Without File Access Option 227
6.19 Chrome With File Access Option 229
6.20 Chrome With Extension 231
6.21 Internet Explorer WebDriver Window 233
6.22 Internet Explorer With Ignore Zoom Level 237
6.23 Microsoft Edge WebDriver Window 238
6.24 Microsoft Edge Load With Options 242
6.25 Safari Load With Options 247
6.26 Opera WebDriver Window 249
6.27 Opera Load With Options 253
6.28 Logging Environment And Browser Name 258
6.29 Logging System Information 262
6.30 Logging Version No 263

7.1 Web Services Overview 267
7.2 Add Web Service Project 268
7.3 My Web Service 268
7.4 Select Empty Template 269
7.5 Web Tools 270
7.6 Employee Web Service 271
7.7 Set StartUp Project 274
7.8 Localhost Web Service 274
7.9 Internet Information Services Error 275
7.10 Internet Information Service Turned On 275
7.11 IIS Express Running 276
7.12 Get Employee Web Service 277
7.13 Get Employee Web Service Result 277
7.14 Web Services WebRequest Output 285
7.15 Web Services HttpWebRequest Output 290
7.16 Add Service Reference 291
7.17 App Config File Properties 292
7.18 Specify Configuration File Name 295
7.19 Web Services Service Reference Output 295

8.1 Find Missing Images On A Page 302
8.2 Find Missing Links On A Page 308
8.3 Verify Tooltips 312

8.4	Drag And Drop Output	315
8.5	Add Windows Forms Dll Reference	319
8.6	Context Click	321
8.7	Login With Highlight	325
A.1	Home Page	329
A.2	Login Page	330
A.3	Help Page	331
A.4	Tester's Home Page	332
A.5	Add An Employee Page	333
A.6	Success Message	333
A.7	View An Employee Page	334
A.8	Other Page	335
A.9	Drag-n-Drop Page	336
A.10	Admin's Home Page	337
A.11	Reports Page	338
A.12	View All Employee Details Page	339

Overview

This book aims to assist QA (Quality Assurance) teams in performing website testing effectively using automation. Over the past two decades, the number of internet users has grown enormously. The importance of automated web testing drives from the increasing reliance on systems for business, social and organisational functions. One major advantage of web applications is their continual availability as they are not restricted by their location or time. Due to economic and time constraints, there is always a pressure on the development team which usually results in a reduced testing phase, especially when it is not automated, hence labour intensive and slow. In these circumstances, the ability to perform automated testing becomes extremely useful as it provides testers and the organisation as a whole, an added level of confidence.

One good thing about automation is that it can be performed unattended i.e. you can initiate your tests before leaving the office and, when you get back in the morning, your test results are ready for review!

"With an automated test in my quiver, I always feel like I have an extra pair of hands."

With each additional automated test that we can create, we have more time to focus on other important tasks while your 'automated buddy' is executing the tests. The help from this 'buddy' becomes even more significant when as a testing team you are given a new build to test at the eleventh hour and in a few hours are asked, "What do you guys think about the new build?" In situations like this, you can feel positive that you have some automated tests that will give you a degree of confidence about the quality of the build.

I have experience working in a Quality Assurance role on a number of web projects and thought it would help other professionals like me who perhaps need a helping hand in automating their web testing. Web automation is a powerful and exciting skill that can benefit any testing team.

This book is aimed at testers who want to try their hands at automated testing. It provides a step by step guide that will teach you how to setup an Automation Framework from scratch. As we will see, the framework is quite generic and as such can be applied to most website projects. This book concentrates on the 'practical side' of automated testing rather than the 'theoretical side'. It also includes the complete listings of the automated code for the demo website that has been set up for you to test against. The code listings explain the logic of individual tests and generic functions.

The book is divided into eight chapters as follows:

- Chapter 1, Getting Started, introduces reasons to use automation in testing. It highlights reasons why to avoid 'Record and Playback' approach. It also summarises the main reasons to automate our testing and provides golden rules for you to follow when automating tests. It goes through a typical 3-Tier Website Architecture.

- Chapter 2, Automation Approach, covers the importance of having a framework, which is the driving force behind a successful automation. It looks at the software you will need to set up the Automation Framework, and one piece of good news is that all of this is freeware! It also discusses the components of an Automation Framework. A demo website has been created to help you go through practical examples listed in the book. We will setup the project structure required to create our Automation Framework.

- Chapter 3, Let's Automate, starts with creating our first automated test. We will expand our Automation Framework to add a number of important features to the framework such as logging to a console, files (so that you can refer back when required), saving a screenshot etc. The chapter also covers how to automate data entry, verification and negative tests.

- Chapter 4, Automate With Databases, covers automating the tabular and summary reports using the demo website. We will also expand our Automation Framework to create a test result summary file at the end of test execution.

- Chapter 5, Data Driven Testing, describes how to perform data driven testing using external data files (instead of using hard-coded data in the test). We will cover both XLS and XLSX Excel formats for automation purpose. Before we finish this chapter, we will add more features to the Automation Framework i.e. adding a test step failure threshold, logging failed test steps only and comparing decimal numbers with a defined tolerance.

- Chapter 6, Cross Browser Testing, covers testing our demo website with different browsers. We will cover Mozilla Firefox, Google Chrome, Internet Explorer, Microsoft Edge, Safari and Opera web browsers. Before we finish this chapter, we will add further features to the Automation Framework e.g. testing on different environments and logging useful system information during the test execution.

- Chapter 7, Web Services Testing, deals with automating the testing of web services. We will write a sample working web service and automate its testing via different methods, namely WebRequest, HttpWebRequest and Service Reference.

- Chapter 8, Miscellaneous, deals with the different aspects of automation (with practical examples using the demo website) - finding missing images on web pages, finding broken links, verifying Tooltips, using Drag-and-Drop functionality, context click and executing JavaScripts through your tests.

Please note that this book aims to teach you how to automate web testing and provides you with a framework to achieve this. It is not about teaching you "how to code effectively". You may find there are another ways to code certain listings shown in the book, so feel free to modify the code and implement this in your framework. In my view, as an experienced automation tester, as long as your code is doing what it is supposed to do and is highlighting bugs or issues in the system you are testing, you are doing a good job. It doesn't need to be a perfectly written piece of code using all the advanced and fancy features of the language. A tester's coding skills do not need to be as comprehensive as a professional programmer to add value. Personally, I don't mind if it takes a few milliseconds, or a few seconds, or for that matter a few minutes to execute an automated test. Once automated, I can add it to my Regression Test Pack and execute it almost without any effort while I'm concentrating on other important tests.

Chapter 1

Getting Started

Getting Started

In this chapter, we will learn:

- *Why we should automate testing*
- *How not to automate testing*
- *Golden rules to keep in mind while automating tests*
- *About a typical 3-tier website architecture*

So let's get on with it...

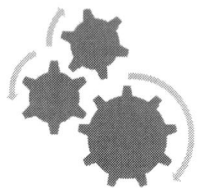

THERE has always been enormous pressure on software organisations to meet delivery deadlines with static or even reduced Quality Assurance (QA) resources. In your time being a QA person, have you ever worked in a project where the development dates have shifted to the right on a project plan? The very first thing that usually happens in such instances is to reduce the testing time! The financial pressures demand cost and resource reductions. This results in an increased risk of software failure. On the other hand, there is always a lot of pressure to deliver new functionalities to keep ahead of the competition. Delivering a bug free system demands good test coverage. Manual software testing with good test coverage is a labour intensive task. This is where the automated testing comes into the picture: *to achieve desired quality goals within the constraints of time and money.* I must emphasise here that the primary goal of automation should be to increase the test coverage and hence the quality, not to cut testing costs.

Once automated tests are created they can easily be repeated to perform frequent regression testing as and when required. Sanity automated tests can be shared with the development team to execute before the builds are made available to the QA team.

You will find a lot of books which go through mainly theoretical aspects of automation and provide just a few examples on how actually automation is performed. There is a famous saying *'In theory, theory and practice are the same. In practice, they are not'*, so I thought I should write a book which explains how automation is *practically* done rather than just explaining it in theory. We shall go through various aspects of automation with a demo website as we progress through the book.

1.1 Why Automate?

The need for speed is practically the mantra of the Information Age. In the real world, automating any part of the testing can pay big dividends. Delivering a product late will result in loss of customers, revenue and market share. However, on the other hand, delivering a defective software product will be even more catastrophic - costing millions or billions and even bringing the entire organisation down. If it doesn't do what it says on the tin then the product may cost you many times more than the entire testing budget!

Thankfully automation usually brings a lot of benefits to the organisation such as:

- **Regression Testing** - Software applications grow in functionality and complexity over time, meaning that the number of tests will also increase. Depending on the impact analysis, even with a very low percentage of code change, the software needs a very high percentage of the regression tests to be repeated. In some cases, 100% regression tests need to be repeated. When testing time is cut-short, regression testing is usually cut-short too to give priority to other important areas. Automation can really help test the new functionality as well as regression test the existing functionality.

- **Test Efficiency and Accuracy** - is usually improved as the comparison of the expected and actual results is performed by computer and thereby eliminating human error. Automated tests are fast and, as we will see later, reuse functions & modules within different tests or on different versions of the software.

- **Test Coverage** - We can achieve better test coverage using automation. We can randomly select records each time we execute a test and thus providing more coverage. Similarly the same tests can be executed when new data arrives.

- **Saves Time and Money** - Automation initially is associated with increased effort however; its benefits will pay off in the long run! Regression testing becomes effortless and is highly beneficial for software products with a long maintenance life.

- **Tester's Motivation** - Manual testing can be error-prone and mundane. Automated testing on the other hand is repeatable, leaving testers to concentrate on other important tasks.

- **Reliable** - Automated testing is reliable. When a tester writes a test for a defect he or she has found, and adds it to the Regression Test Pack; the test just cannot be forgotten. It automatically executes and checks for that peculiar condition where it failed once. A manual tester on the other hand can simply forget to perform this test or may even choose not to perform it due to time pressure or a number of other reasons.

- **Quicker Time to Market** - In today's competitive environment, time to market is usually the key driver for a number of projects, particularly for the revenue generating products. Automation can help reduce time to market by not only shortening the test cycle but also helps you meet the deadlines with a reliable product.

1.2 How Not To Automate?

There are many ways to approach the test automation and it is highly important to develop an overall approach which suits your project. If you approach automation purely from a Record and Playback perspective, you are due for a big surprise later on. In a Record and Playback approach, tests are performed manually while the inputs and outputs are recorded in the background. During a subsequent execution, same steps are played back with the same input values and the actual outputs are compared with the stored ones. Any differences are reported as errors.

Although the Record and Playback approach will get you on-board with a very little learning curve, there are several disadvantages in using this approach. We shall cover some main ones here:

- It requires all the actions to be recorded manually. For example, if you have an employee data entry system, all the steps have to be repeated for each employee to be added, updated and deleted.

- The application under test must be stable enough for business transactions to be recorded, leaving very little opportunity for early detection of errors.

- For a highly agile development environment, an object's recognition properties may change which would result in the object being not identified successfully during a playback and subsequently failing the test. This causes scripts to be re-recorded, which is often very costly and time consuming.

- There is no decision making logic in the recorded scripts. For example, if you need to perform different actions based on employee's age group then you would need to record separate scripts because the data is hard-coded in scripts. Moreover, if for some reason you have to re-record a script due to change in age group logic then you would most likely need to re-record all age group logic scripts.

- Web browsers continue to be the primary gateway, channelling the end-user's interactions with the web applications. However different web browsers render the web contents differently and for that reason, web based applications need to be tested on a number of different browsers. If you have recorded a script against one browser, it may not work on some other browser.

- For large applications, test execution performance may decrease due to the duplication of objects and hence resulting in a very large repository. This is because the same object may be recorded multiple times in different scripts.

- Recording may not playback successfully because of synchronisation problems, which is a significant issue in automated web testing. The script may be waiting for an object or element to appear on the web page but if it doesn't appear in time, the script may just try to perform action on it resulting in the test failure. This kind of synchronisation points need to be *programmed* into the script via your Automation Framework.

- Recording produces scripts that are difficult to maintain. Amending a recorded script and getting it to replay correctly requires a lot of time and effort. Moreover, as the application's functionality grows, the more tests you record. You will have to re-record scripts due to functionality changes e.g. screens/objects added, modified or removed. Maintenance of these recorded scripts will become an immense burden at some point costing you even more time and money. Maintenance is very important in test automation and this in fact, is one of the main motivation factors to build a robust Automation Framework.

- Record and Playback scripts hardly take advantage of code re-use from one test to another. A good Automation Framework, on the other hand, would facilitate code organisation, minimise duplication and make it easier to re-use the existing code. Moreover, with an Automation Framework you can provide meaningful names to the objects instead of auto-generated names which were given to them at the time of recording the script.

- With a basic Record and Playback, if something unexpected happens during test execution, the test will fail. An automated test however, should cope with different events that may happen and not just 'what happened' when the script was recorded. Again this should be *programmed* into the automation script. During a verification test, I may want to continue the test until it has hit a predefined threshold of failures. A basic Record and Playback tool may not offer this facility.

Record and Playback is one of the earliest automation approaches but I avoid it being my main automation approach for any project. However, this doesn't mean that I don't use it. Record and Playback really has helped me a number of times to identify the code and objects when I didn't know how to start automating a piece of functionality! However, in this book we shall develop an Automation Framework which doesn't use Record and Playback at all. You will be able to write scripts which are modular and easily maintainable. The Automation Framework in this book is quite generic and can be applied to almost all types of web testing projects.

1.3 Golden Automation Rules

Here are some golden automation rules to keep in mind that I have learnt through experience:

1. Start small and simple first. Don't try to automate the complicated scenarios first if you are just starting off with automated testing. Take smaller steps before you start walking and then finally running.

2. An effective automated test design principle - *always* start the test with a known state.

3. Don't try to automate everything. This may not be practical in your project, so set realistic expectations.

4. It is typically not a single complex test that uncovers a bug. You may need to perform a combination of simple tests to highlight a bug.

5. Once you are confident with the Automation Framework, test cases with high value and low effort should be automated first.

6. Run your automated tests regularly, if possible, with every build. Machines can find flaws.

7. Test your *Test* - make sure you have seen the test case failing at least once - force the failure condition so that you know the coded logic works.

8. No matter how much you automate, you still can't replace manual testing or testers. The purpose of automation is not to eliminate testers but to make better use of their time.

9. Ensure that each test has a specific purpose and identifiable result(s).

10. Log your expected and actual result values during comparison. You never know when you are going to need to look into your test results.

11. All things done well can be done even better. Revising and striving to improve your Automation Framework is a way of improving your skills and driving you on to new heights.

12. Use an Automation Framework that is easy to manage and allows new tests to be added easily.

13. Focus on modularity and re-usability. Build libraries of functions that you can reuse in other projects.

14. Test automation is a long term strategic solution and not a quick-fix to testing. Buying an automation tool is just like buying a treadmill - to lose weight. However if you never use it, the only thing you have lost is the weight of your purse! You must really invest your time and effort to get the real benefits in both cases.

15. Code coverage is not a reliable metric for ensuring end-to-end quality, but should be used as a measure to gauge the effectiveness of test automation.

1.4 Typical 3-Tier Web Application Architecture

A Web Application is an application that can be accessed by the users through a Web Browser. Figure 1.1 shows the implementation of a typical 3-Tier Web Application Architecture. Here is the sequence of events that take place when you want to access a website:

- You will be using a *Web Browser* such as Chrome or Firefox on your workstation.

- The *Page Request* of your entered web address is sent to the *Web Server* via your internet service provider.

- The *Web Server* fetches the required data from the *Database Server* e.g. fetch employee details.

- The *Web Server* renders and returns the requested *Web Page* to the *Web Browser* for display.

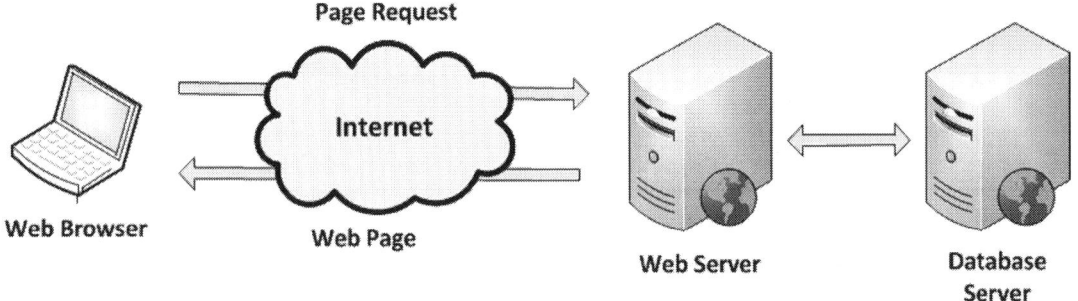

Figure 1.1: Typical Web Application Architecture

Chapter 2

Automation Approach

Automation Approach

In this chapter, we will learn about:

- *The software we need to automate web testing*
- *The strategies to identify objects or elements on the web pages*
- *The Automation Framework that we are going to develop*
- *Setting up the Automation Framework project structure*

So let's get on with it...

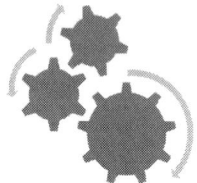

W<span></span>HAT is an Automation Framework? An Automation Framework is an application that allows you to write tests without worrying about the constraints of the underlying test tools. As in the Software Development Life Cycle (SDLC) to develop software applications, framework design plays a vital role in building the test approach for automation. The need for a well-defined and designed test framework is especially important in automated testing. It is the starting point for success with the automated testing.

A well designed Automation Framework makes the test automation more efficient, reduces test automation effort, lowers the cost of maintenance and also provides a higher Return On Investment (ROI). It is very important to have a framework that enhances efficiency in the development of automated test scripts through modular, reusable and maintainable code. The reusable library of functions is much in the same way as any other software system. A good test Automation Framework should ensure a uniformity of design across multiple test scripts and should minimise code maintenance overhead. Easy maintenance of automation code is crucial to test automation. If we cannot maintain the automation code and bring it up-to-date quickly enough with the changes in the Application Under Test (AUT), we will not get payback. Adding more features to the framework should not disturb the existing tests.

Effective test reporting is another important feature and enhances the value of framework. The framework should support the production of both, a summary report - a high level view of all the tests executed as well as a detailed report - providing a step by step view of various steps in the test.

Similarly, log generation is another important part of the test execution. The framework should provide the means to create debug logs which can help find a problem quickly. Execution reports and logs are important for any automation execution and should be stored for future reference.

2.1 Automation Environment And Software

First of all let's start identify the environment and software we will need to automate the testing.

I work on Windows 10 and Windows 7 workstations with the following software on it (with installation/download links):

1. Microsoft® Visual Studio Express 2015 for Web - an Integrated Development Environment we will use to write our automated tests.
   `https://www.visualstudio.com/en-us/products/visual-studio-express-vs.aspx`

2. Selenium - WebDriver to make calls to the browser.
   `http://www.seleniumhq.org/download/`

   Extract to 'C:\Selenium'

3. Mozilla Firefox - internet browser.
   `https://www.mozilla.org`

4. Firebug - tool to find objects (elements) on a web page.
   `https://addons.mozilla.org`

   Within Firefox, open menu Add-on, search for Firebug and install.

5. Firefinder - tool to find HTML objects (elements) matching chosen CSS selector or XPath expression.
   `https://addons.mozilla.org`

   Search for add-on - 'Firefinder for Firebug' and install.

6. XPath Checker - tool to find HTML objects (elements) matching chosen XPath expression.
   `https://addons.mozilla.org`

   Search for add-on - 'XPath Checker' and install.

7. NUnit - an open source testing framework we will use to execute tests.
   `http://nunit.org/index.php?p=download`

8. NPOI - the .NET version of POI Java project to help you read/write Microsoft® Excel files.
   `https://npoi.codeplex.com/releases`

   Extract to 'C:\NPOI'

9. Apache Log4net - a logging library for Microsoft® .NET.
   `https://logging.apache.org/log4net/download_log4net.cgi`

   Extract to 'C:\log4net'

10. Microsoft® SQL Server® 2008 R2 RTM - Express with Management Tools – for the database.
    `http://www.microsoft.com/en-us/download/details.aspx?id=23650`

You will need the corresponding software on your workstation, according to the operating system you are using.

2.2 About The Website Under Test

This book is about less theory and more practical. The more automation you perform, the more confident you become in automating different web applications. For the purposes of automation, we will use a demonstration website at `http://testing.arkenstone-ltd.com` as shown in Figure 2.1. The demo website uses a number of elements that are used in most of the websites these days e.g. data entry fields, command buttons, radio buttons, check boxes, tables, static text, images, links etc. We will learn how to automate the testing of these elements throughout this book.

☞ If you are facing any issue accessing the demo website, please email the 'Book Support Team' at autoweb.testing@gmail.com. Please specify "AutoWeb Demo Portal" in the subject/title of the email.

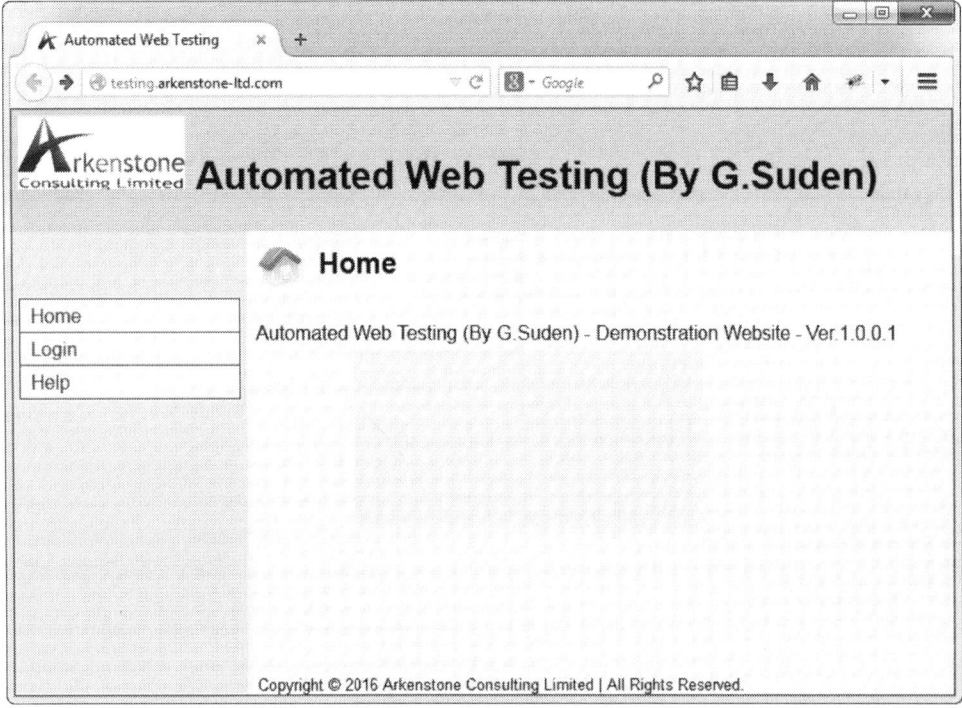

Figure 2.1: Demonstration Website - Automation Portal

There are two types of users that exist in the demo website:

- A general or normal user whose credentials are:

    User: Tester

    Password: Tester123

- An administrator user whose credentials are:

    Admin User: Admin

    Password: Admin123

The credentials are case-sensitive.

2.2.1 Site Map

Figure 2.2 shows the Site Map of the demo website. Each of the two user types (i.e. Tester and Admin), has a home page with the functionality they have access to. Appendix A contains the details of functionalities that are provided by this website. Please spend some time to familiarise yourself with the screens in appendix as you will see them more regularly in the next few chapters.

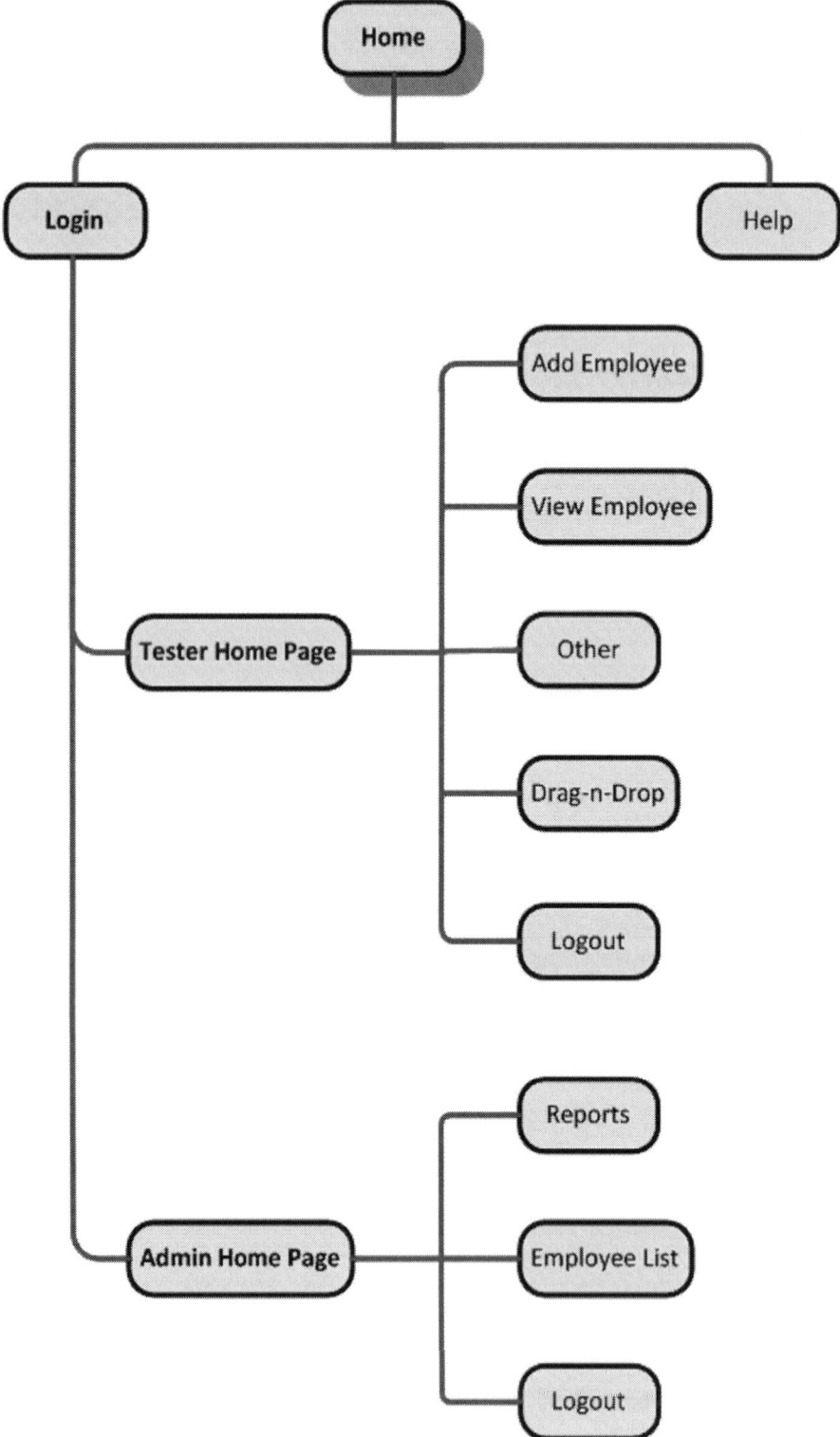

Figure 2.2: Demo Portal - Site Map

2.3 Identifying Objects or Elements

As an Automation Tester, one of the important tasks that you have to perform is to identify objects (also called elements) in the Application Under Test. Why do we need to identify objects?

If you are the developer - you need to know which objects in the browser screen have been filled with data, interacted with so that you can take appropriate action e.g. validate data entry, save data to the database tables etc.

If you are the tester - you need to know which objects need to be interacted with (as part of the Test Scenario) so that you can verify the outcome e.g. enter wrong credentials in the login screen and verify that an error response is generated.

In order to carry out these actions, the objects in the browser are given identification attributes. There are a number of methods to provide such identification however, sometimes a few objects in the website don't have an easy means to identify them and there could be a number of reasons for this e.g. the developer didn't need to interact with the object (hence provided no identification but the tester has to verify its value or state), poor coding standards deployed in the project, website was developed long back when automation wasn't in the scope, testing tool limitations etc. From automated testing perspective, if we can't identify the object on the screen it becomes cumbersome to automate its testing. A close interaction with the developers can make the life of an automated tester a lot easier. Sometimes, for a developer, it just takes a few seconds to add an *id* (an attribute to identify the element) to the object whereas an automated tester may spend hours or days to figure out how to uniquely identify such element on the screen and automate the scenario! Remember the rule that the Application Under Test has to be *Automation Friendly* otherwise the time and effort spent on automation may outweigh any benefits.

We will cover a number of object identification strategies in this chapter which later on will help us build the object repository of our demo website. Various browsers offer different ways to identify elements. Let's initially see how Internet Explorer helps us to identify these elements.

2.3.1 Identifying Element By Name

In general, all the elements on a web page should have an identification attribute. This is normally true for all the elements which a user can interact with. However, some static text may also need some form of identification attribute (as we will see in later chapters) to facilitate automation.

Let me first of all show you how to find an element in our demo website by its *Name* attribute using Internet Explorer (IE 10).

- Launch the Internet Explorer 10

Automated Web Testing

- Navigate to the Automation Portal URL `http://testing.arkenstone-ltd.com`.

- Click Login link on the left hand side.

- Press `F12` or go to Tools ⇒ Developer Tools. You will see a window as shown in Figure 2.3

- Click on the Arrow icon as shown in ①

- Click on the User ID data entry edit box as shown in ②

- Click on the Attributes tab as shown in ③

- This control has an attribute called 'name' with value 'TxtUserId' as shown in ④

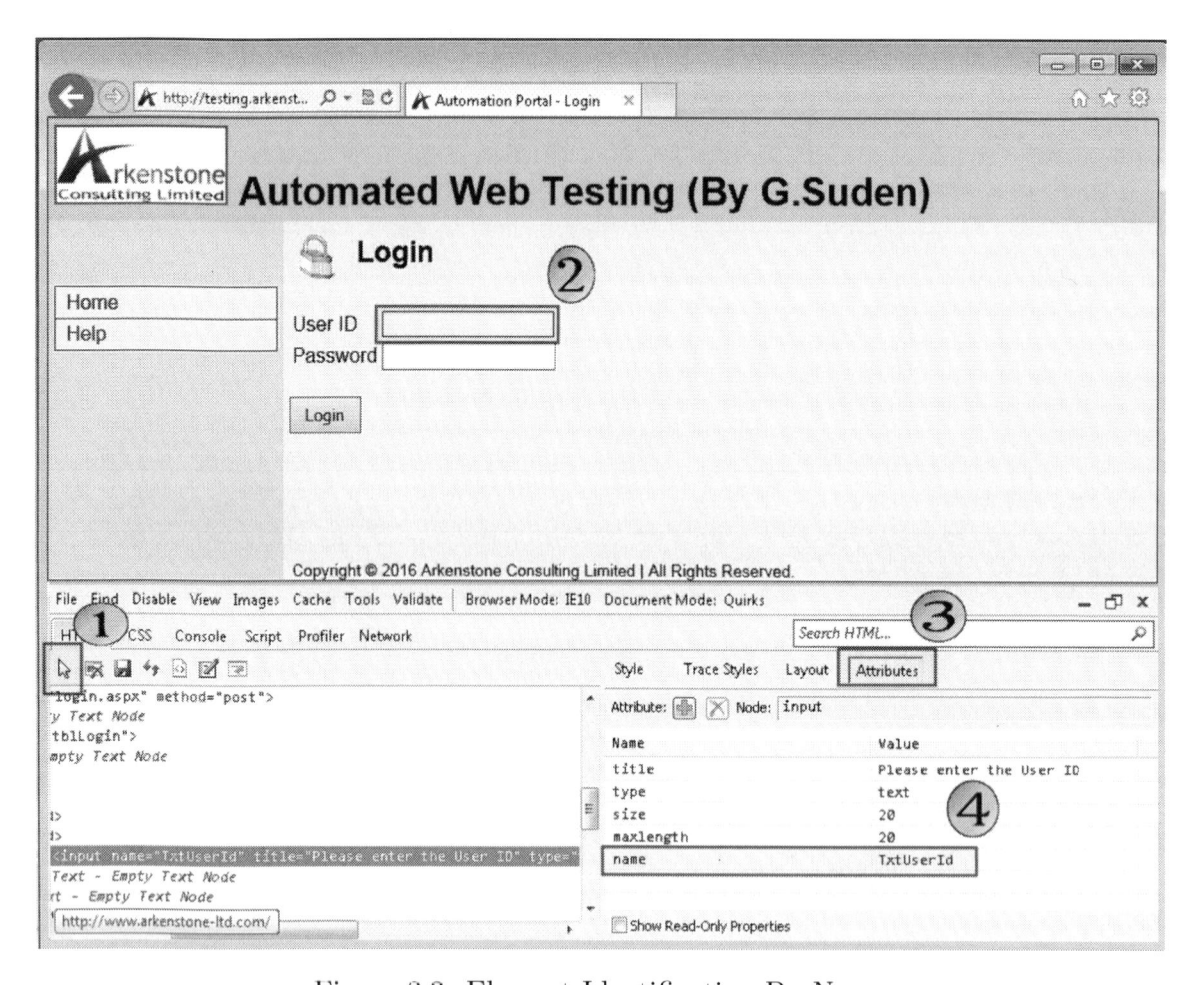

Figure 2.3: Element Identification By Name

So far we have successfully identified a data entry field User ID which has an attribute called 'name' whose value is 'TxtUserId'. In later chapters, we will build our object repository which helps us access this element by *name*.

2.3.2 Identifying Element By ID

Identifying elements by ID is another method which is most commonly used as shown in 2.4. Follow the similar steps as we did earlier i.e.

- Click on the Arrow icon as shown in ①

- Click on the Login button as shown in ②

- Click on the Attributes tab as shown in ③

- This control has an attribute called 'id' with value 'btnLogin' as shown in ④

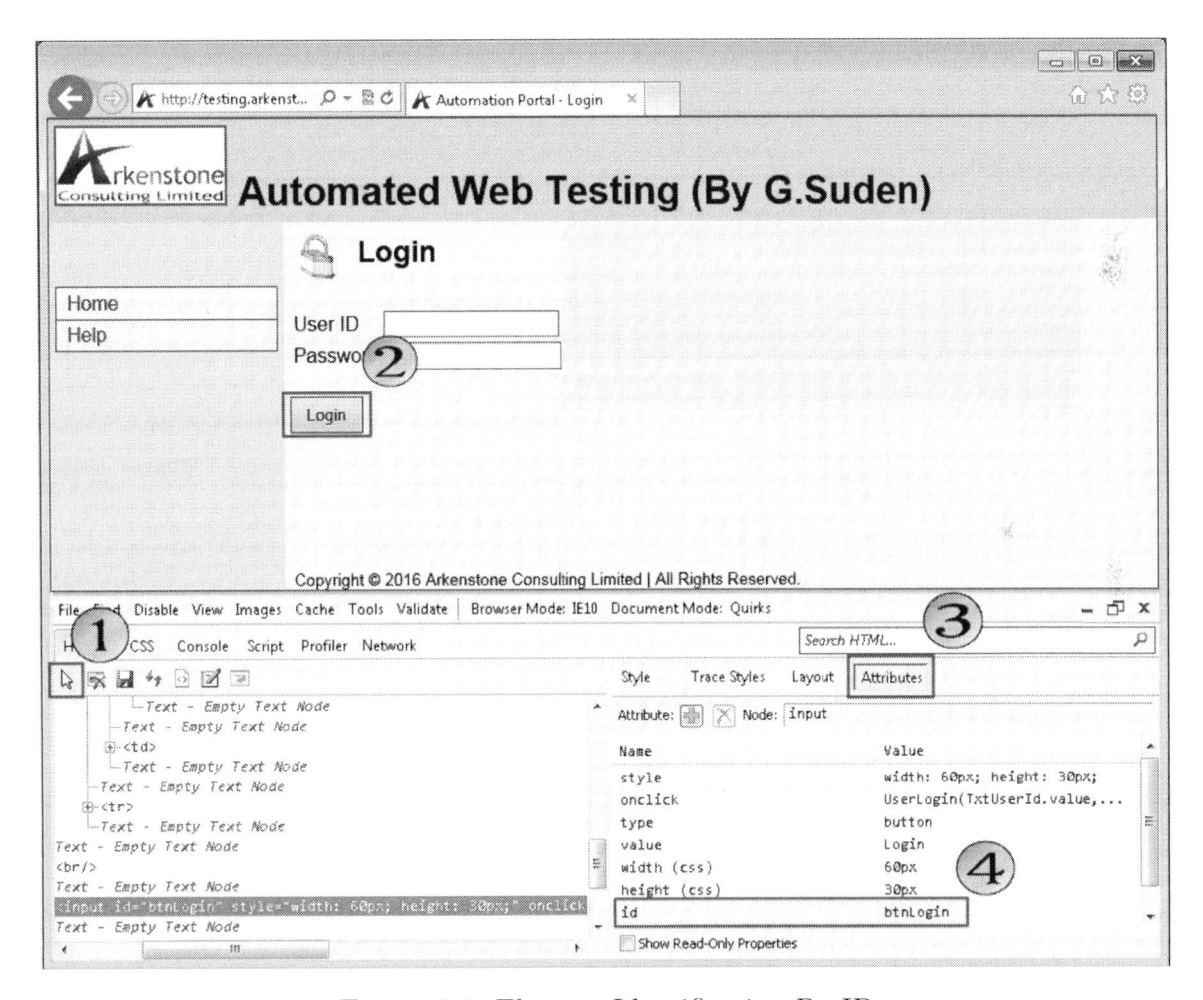

Figure 2.4: Element Identification By ID

If we were using Internet Explorer 11 then this is how we would identify the User ID element.

- Launch Internet Explorer 11

- Navigate to the Automation Portal URL http://testing.arkenstone-ltd.com.

Automated Web Testing

- Click the Login link on the left hand side.

- Press [F12] or go to Tools ⇒ Developer Tools as shown in Figure 2.5.

- Click on the Arrow icon as shown in ①

- Click on the User ID data entry edit box as shown in ②

- In the 'DOM Explorer' tab, this control has an attribute called 'name' with value 'TxtUserId' as shown in ③

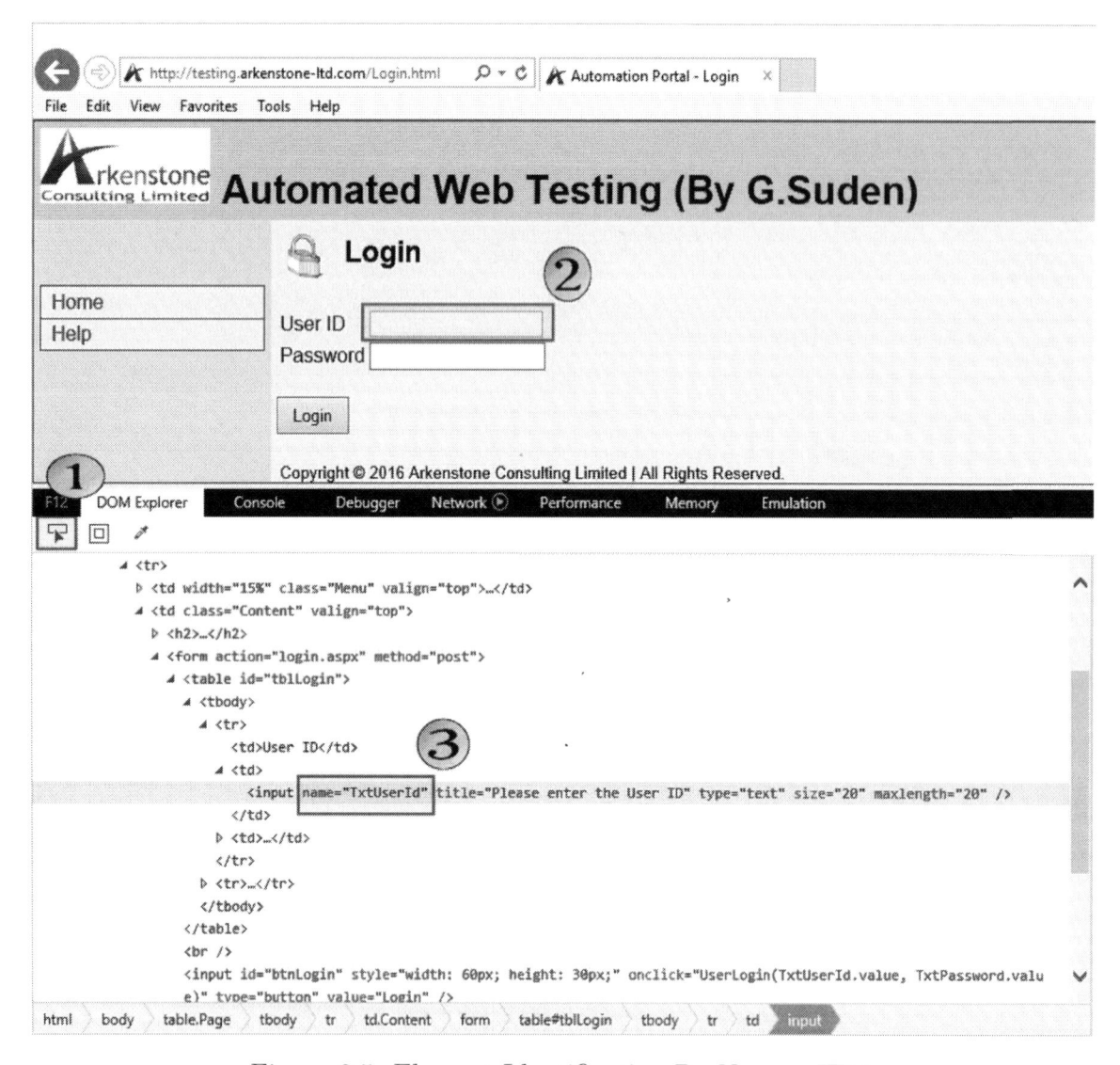

Figure 2.5: Element Identification By Name - IE11

Let's now see how we can identify elements using the Firefox browser as shown in Figure 2.6. We will use Firebug add-on in Firefox to achieve the same.

- Launch Firefox

26 Chapter 2

Automated Web Testing

- Navigate to the Automation Portal URL http://testing.arkenstone-ltd.com.
- Click on the Login link on the left hand side.
- Click on the Firebug icon ① on the tool bar.
- Click on the Arrow icon as shown in ②
- Click on the User ID data entry edit box as shown in ③
- In the 'HTML' tab, this control has an attribute called 'name' with value 'TxtUserId' as shown in ④

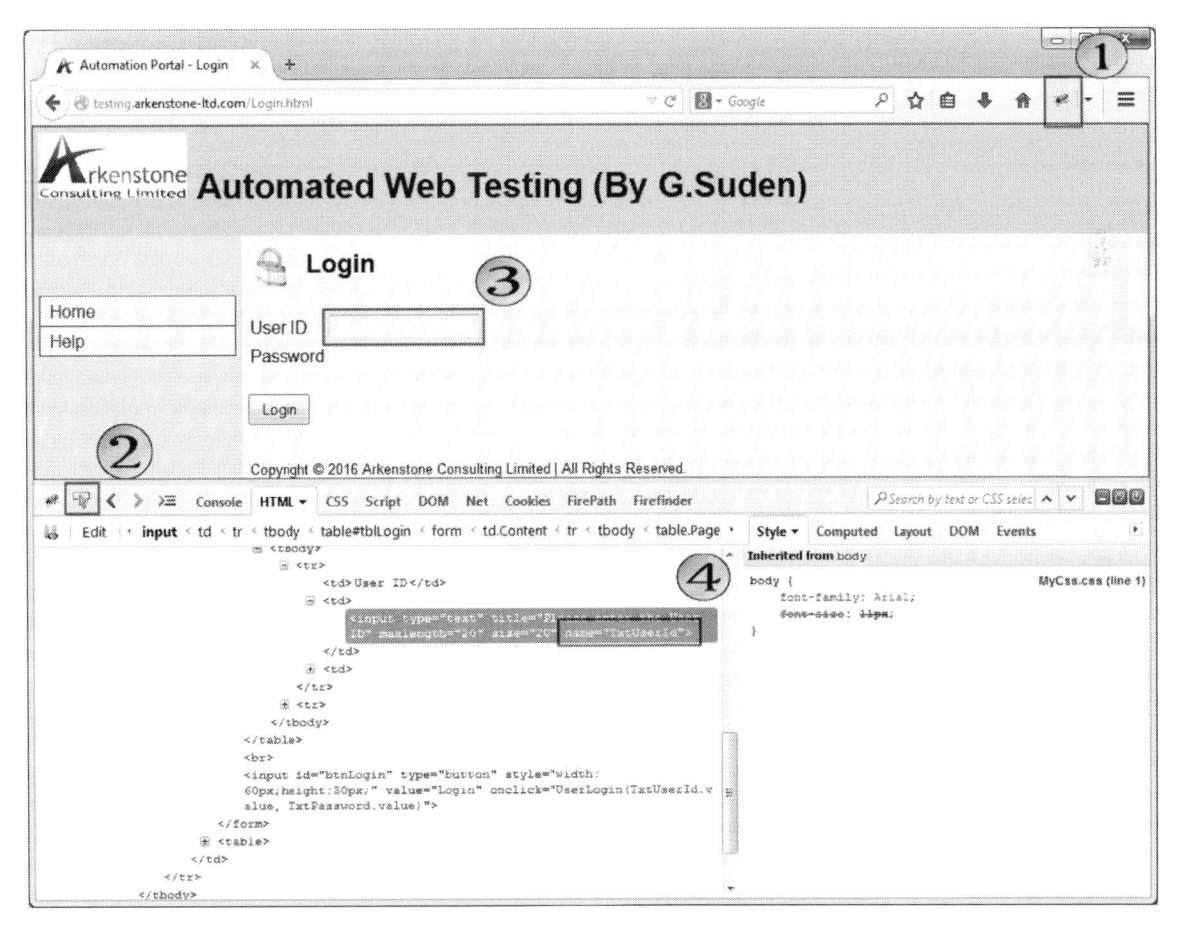

Figure 2.6: Element Identification By Name using Firefox

You can also locate the same element using the 'DOM' tab as shown in Figure2.7.

- Click on the 'DOM' tab as shown in ⑤
- Scroll down to the attribute 'name' as shown in ⑥ which has value "TxtUserId"

Chapter 2

Automated Web Testing

Figure 2.7: Element Identification By ID using Firefox - DOM

Now using Firebug, try to identify the Login button and see if you can locate its 'id'.

> In my demo website, I deliberately used different attributes i.e. 'name' for the User ID and 'id' for the Login button, to show you different attributes for identification. In your application you may have both of these attributes present giving you flexibility to access it via *name* or *id*.

2.3.3 Identifying Element By Link Text

Identifying elements by Link Text is another method which is most commonly used as shown in Figure 2.4. Here we are identifying the Home link by its attribute 'text' whose value is "Home".

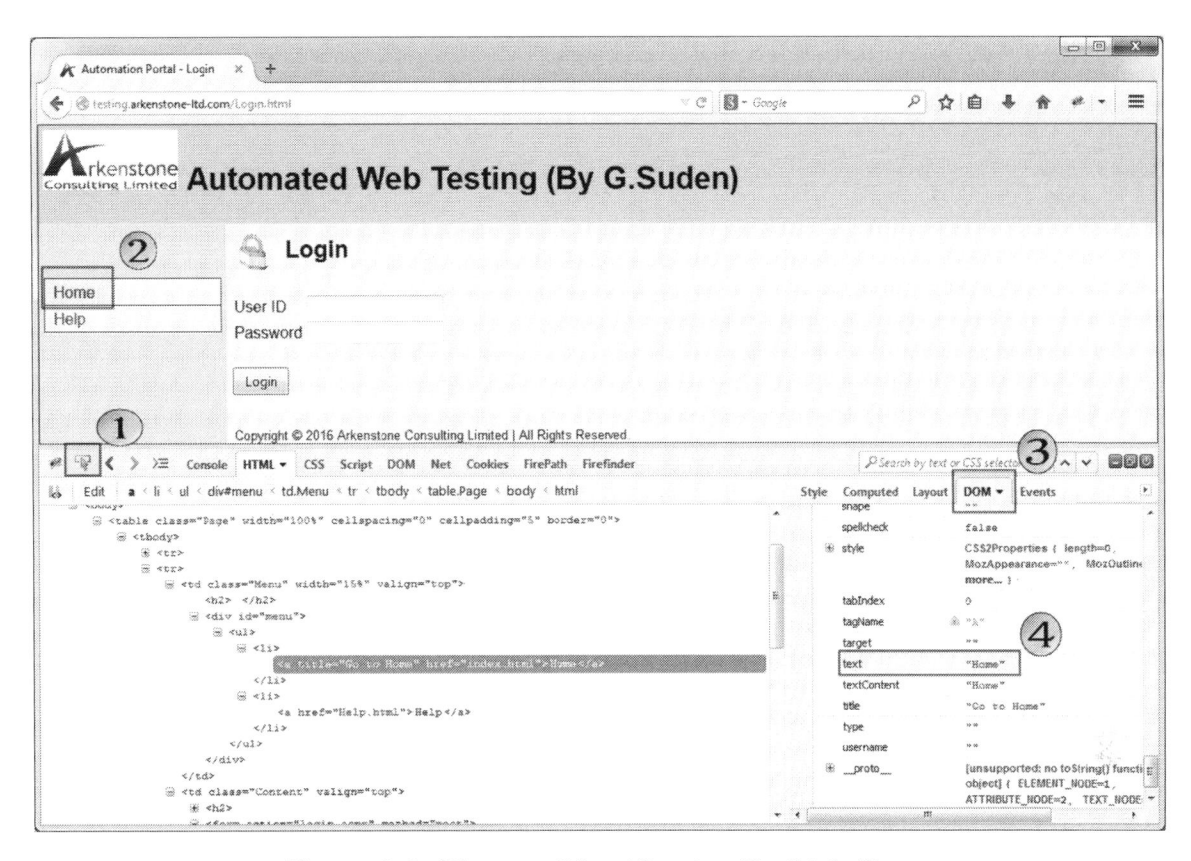

Figure 2.8: Element Identification By Link Text

2.3.4 Identifying Element By XPATH

Sometimes there is no 'name' or 'id' attribute defined for the particular element you wish to locate. In such cases, we need to use a different strategy to identify these elements. XPath is designed to allow the navigation of XML documents and helps in locating elements. Let me show you how to identify the XPath of an element in our demo website.

- Launch Firefox

- Navigate to the Automation Portal URL http://testing.arkenstone-ltd.com.

- Click the Login link on the left hand side

- Login as the Admin user

- Click the Employee List menu item on the left hand side. Let's find the XPath of the cell containing EmployeeId 10004.

- Right click on the cell containing value 10004 and select 'View XPath' as shown in Figure 2.9

- A new window XPath Checker will open showing the XPath as shown in Figure 2.10

- The XPath of the selected cell element is "id('TblEmployees')/x:tbody/x:tr[5]/x:td[1]". It also displays the number of matches found.

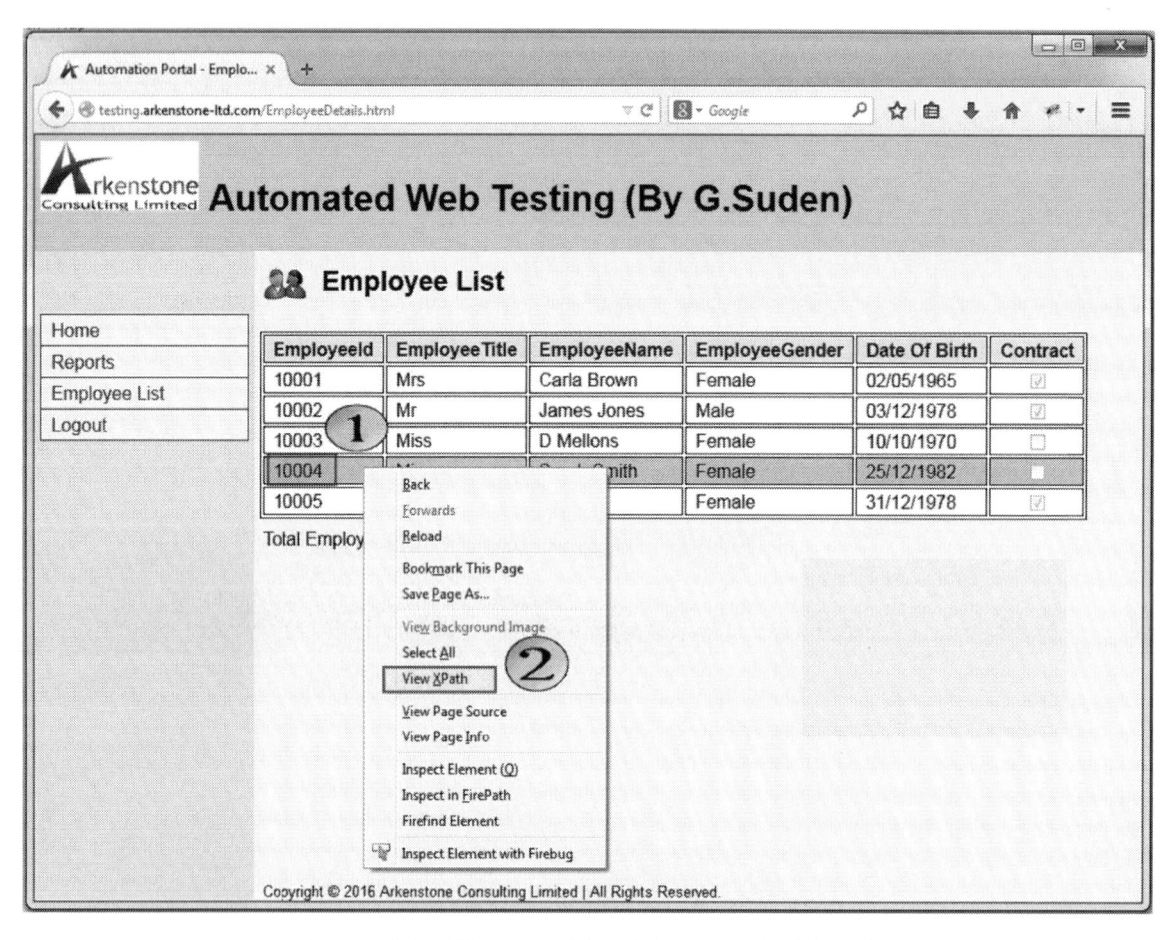

Figure 2.9: Element Identification By XPath

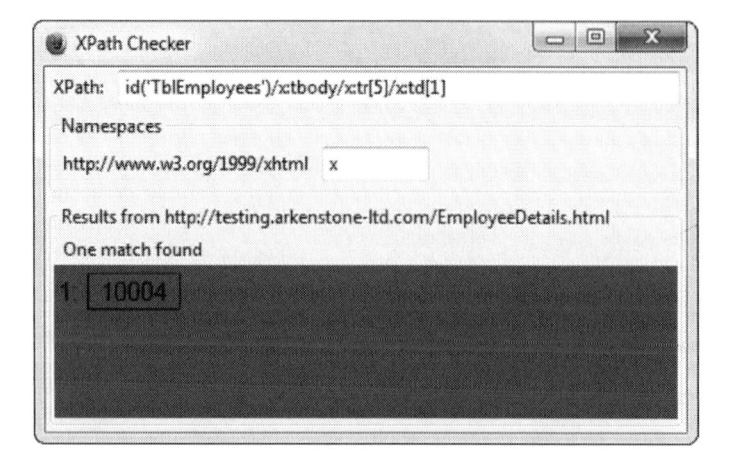

Figure 2.10: Element Identification - XPath Checker

In later chapters, we will learn how to manipulate this XPath to retrieve values of different cells.

2.3.5 Identifying Element By CSS Selectors

Sometimes we don't have an option to identify an element by 'id' or 'name' or by any other means we have learnt so far. If so, we can then use CSS locators to identify such elements. The Close button on the View Employee page doesn't have any 'id' or 'name' attribute as shown in Figure 2.11. However, it has an attribute called 'value', whose value is "Close".

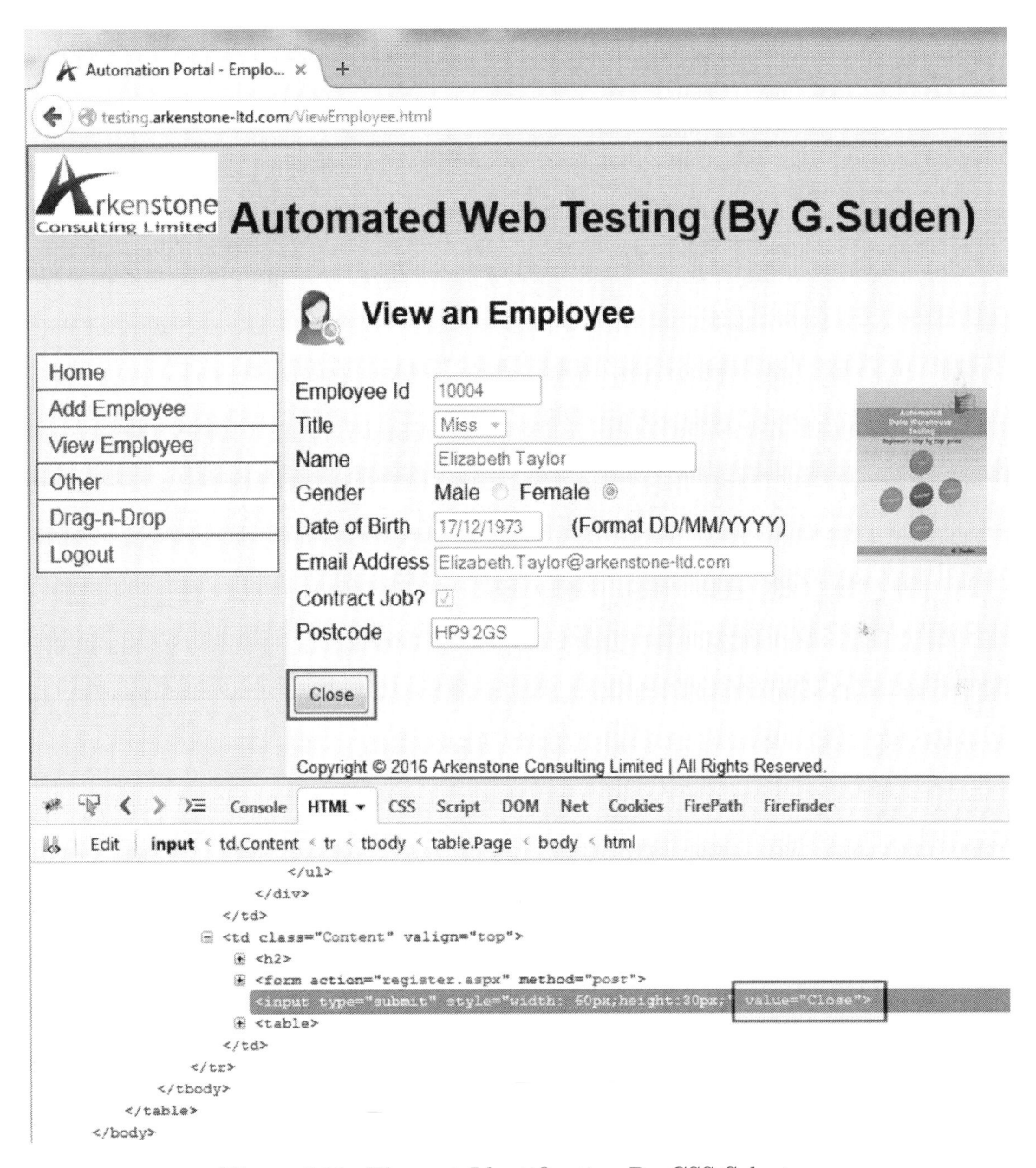

Figure 2.11: Element Identification By CSS Selectors

Let's learn how we can use CSS Selectors to identify the Close button using Firefinder.

Automated Web Testing

- Click on the Firefinder as shown in ①.

- Type 'input[value=Close]' in the entry box as shown in ②. Click on the Filter button.

- Firefinder highlights the Close button ③, and shows number of matching elements found using criteria 'input[value=Close]' as shown in ④.

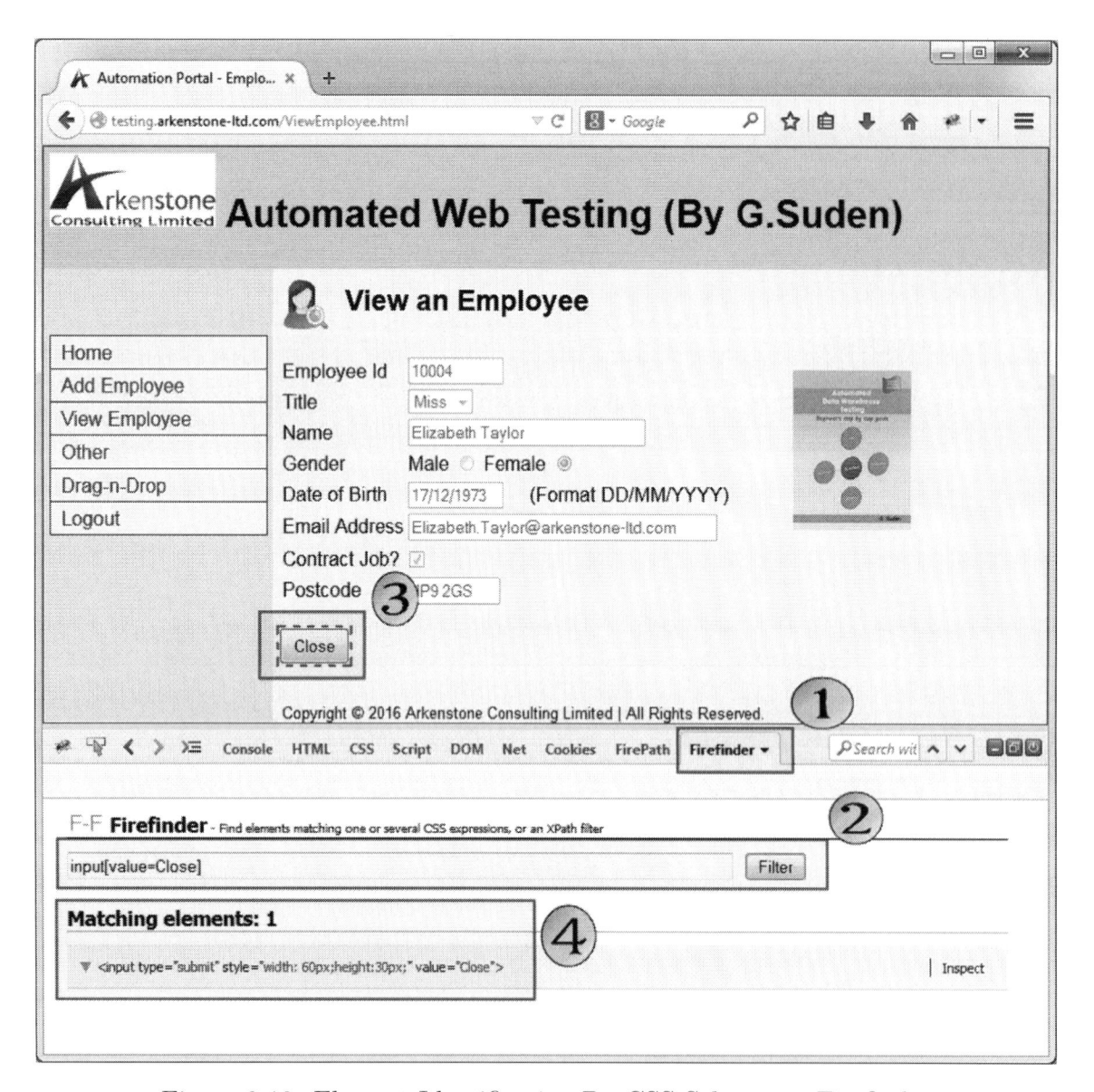

Figure 2.12: Element Identification By CSS Selectors - Firefinder

☞ In order to close the Firebug or Developer Tools window press [F12] on your keyboard which is a toggle switch.

In a later chapter, when we build our repository, we will use the CSS Selector to identify the Close button on this page.

2.4 Automation Framework

We will develop our Automation Framework as we progress through this book. Figure 2.13 shows the Automation Framework in its simplest form. We will add more components to the framework as we progress through its development.

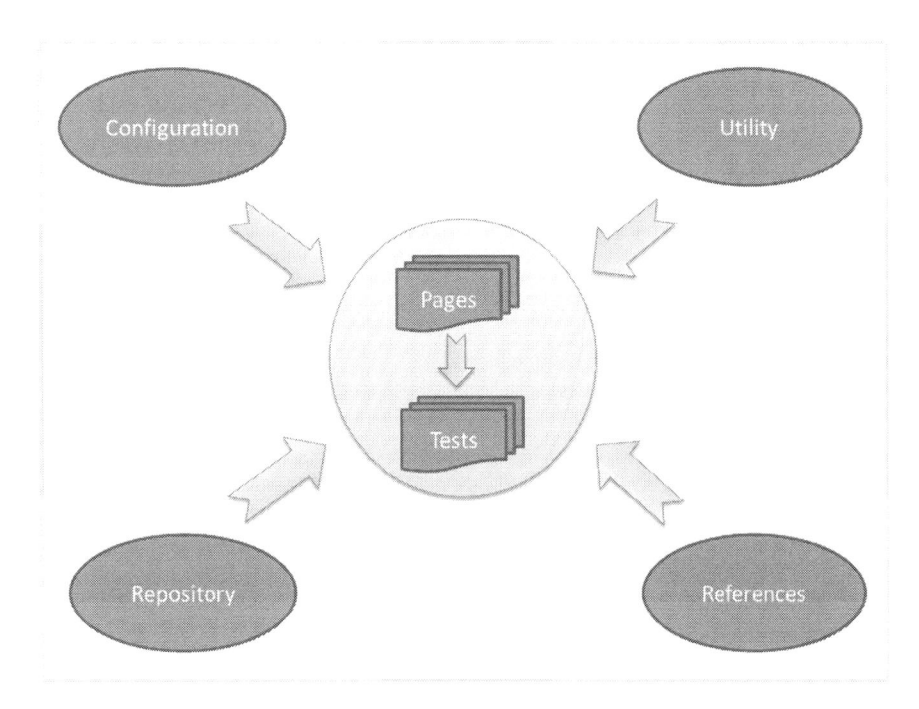

Figure 2.13: Automation Framework

Let me start by explaining the framework components.

2.4.1 Configuration File

The Configuration File is used to store a number of configurable parameters of your framework that are used throughout your testing. Some examples of these parameters are:

```
public const string PASS = "Pass";
public const string FAIL = "Fail";
```

2.4.2 Utility File

The Utility File holds a number of general purpose functions that are to be used throughout your testing. An example of such a function is:

```
public static void ReportExpectedVsActual(String exp, String act)
```

This function accepts two arguments, the expected outcome and the actual outcome, and reports the result. If the expected and actual outcomes are the same, it will pass the test step, otherwise will fail it.

2.4.3 Reference Files

The Automation Framework uses a number of reference files and libraries. You will learn how to attach these to the framework in later chapters.

2.4.4 Repository File

The Repository File contains the repository of all the objects in the Website Under Test. This repository is shared by all the tests.

2.4.5 Page Files

The Page Files contain the testing logic for individual web pages (screens). In a page file, we write functions which accomplish business processes for that web page. For example, the page file for a login page will have functions
- to login a user with the given credentials or
- to perform an individual action on the login page e.g. click the OK button.

2.4.6 Test Files

The Test Files contain all of your Test Scenarios (tests). One test file may contain one or more Test Scenarios. Each Test Scenario completes a business process end-to-end. Figure 2.14 shows the structure of an automated test script file. As you can see, each test script file has a number of important parts:

- Setup Before Each Test - this is the code that is executed before a test is executed e.g. setting up the browser driver.

- Teardown After Each Test - this is the code that is executed after a test completes execution e.g. saving log file, closing the browser driver etc.

- Each test will have its own logic to verify. For each test step, once we have derived the expected and actual results, we will make a call to a generic function 'ReportExpectedVsActual' to report the outcome of the test step.

- Report Overall Test Result will report the final result of the current test. If any test step has failed, the overall result of that test will be Fail.

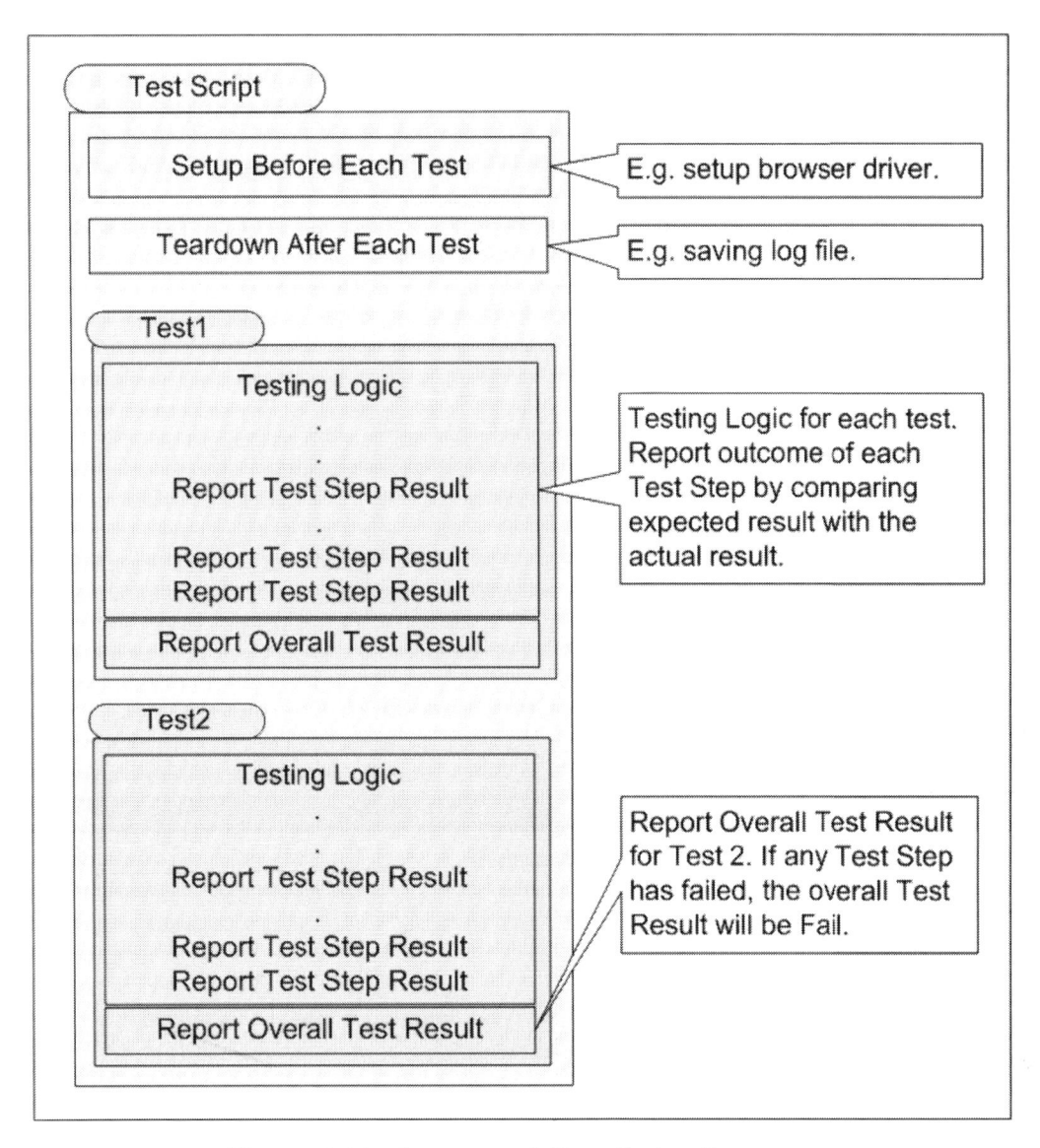

Figure 2.14: Automated Test Script Structure

The above structure will be followed for all the tests. This gives us a consistent approach to writing tests. Don't worry if you don't understand the flow at this stage. Just keep the script structure in mind for the time being. Things will be clearer when we start writing our first test in the next chapter!

At this stage, this book assumes that you have successfully downloaded and installed the required software as stated in the beginning of this chapter.

Automated Web Testing

2.5 Creating The Project Structure

Let's now setup the project structure of the Automation Framework using the following steps.

Step 1: Launch 'Visual Studio Express for Web' from its installed location or from the desktop shortcut.

Step 2: Create a new project.

- Go to File ⇒ New Project...

- Select 'Visual C#' - 'Class Library' as shown in Figure 2.15.

- Type 'Name:' as WebTesting

- Select 'Location:' as C:\. You can select a different location; however this book assumes you have chosen C:\.

- Leave everything else as default and click the OK button.

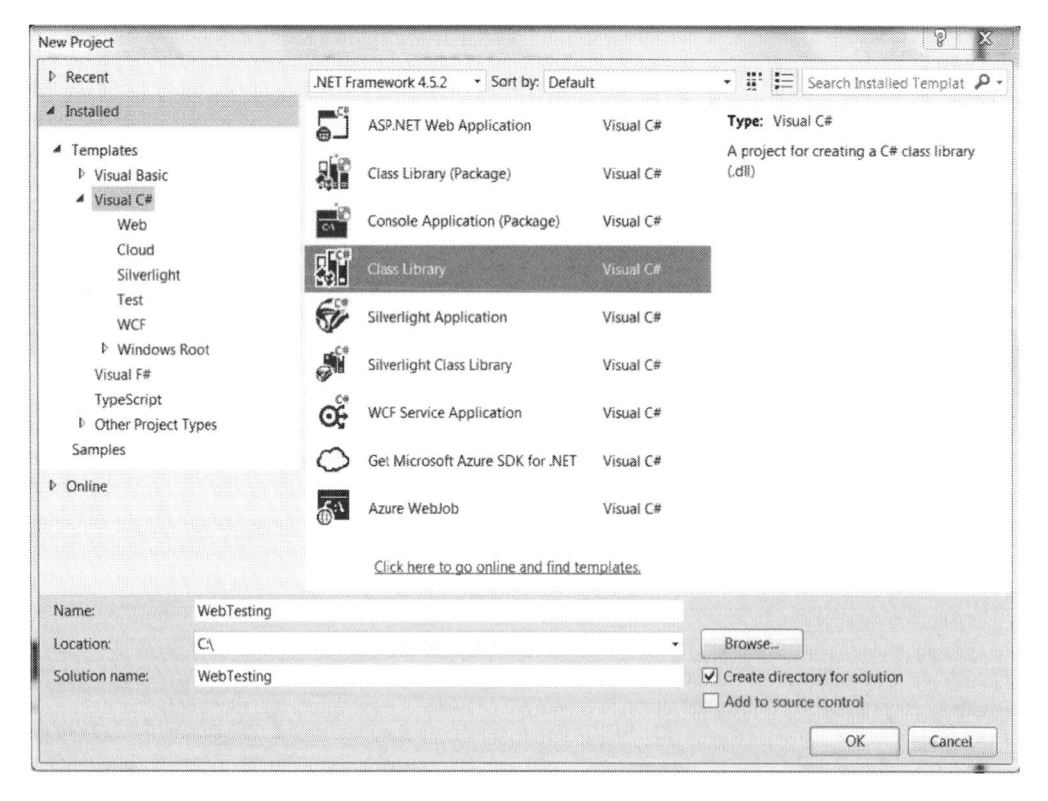

Figure 2.15: Create New Visual C# Class Library

Step 3: Now let's setup the Configuration File.

- In the 'Solution Explorer' on the right hand side (it may be left hand side on your workstation depending on your setup), right click on 'WebTesting' and select Add ⇒ Class as shown in Figure 2.16.

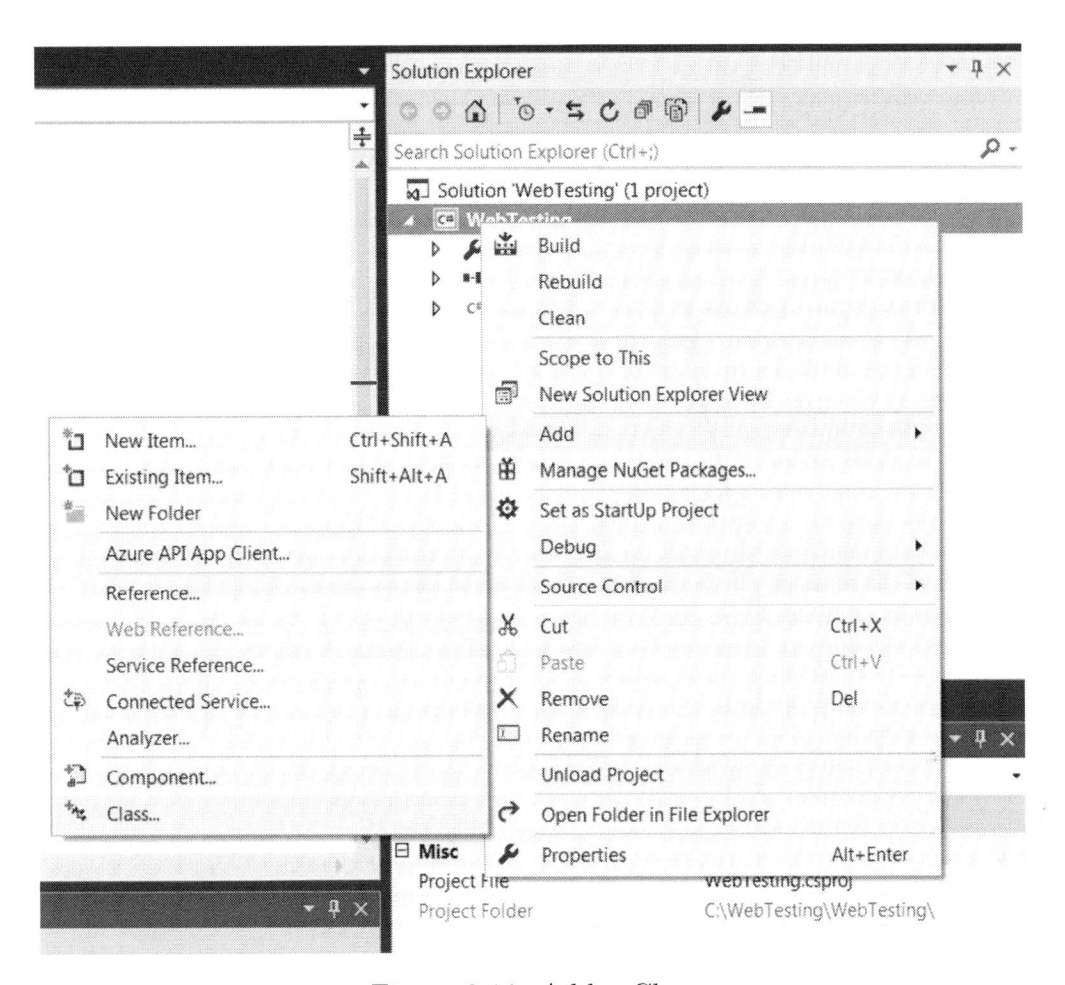

Figure 2.16: Add a Class

- Type Config.cs in the 'Name' edit box as shown in Figure 2.17.
- Click the Add button.

Automated Web Testing

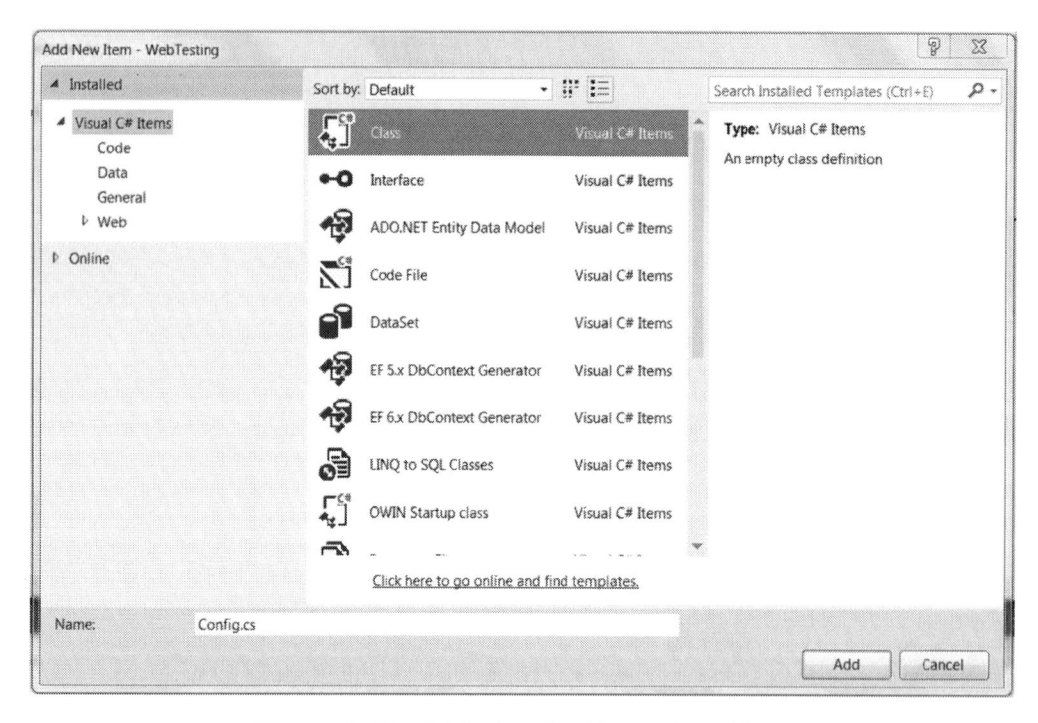

Figure 2.17: Add the Configuration Class

Step 4: Setup the Utility File.

- Similarly add the Utility class as shown in Figure 2.18.
- Click the Add button.

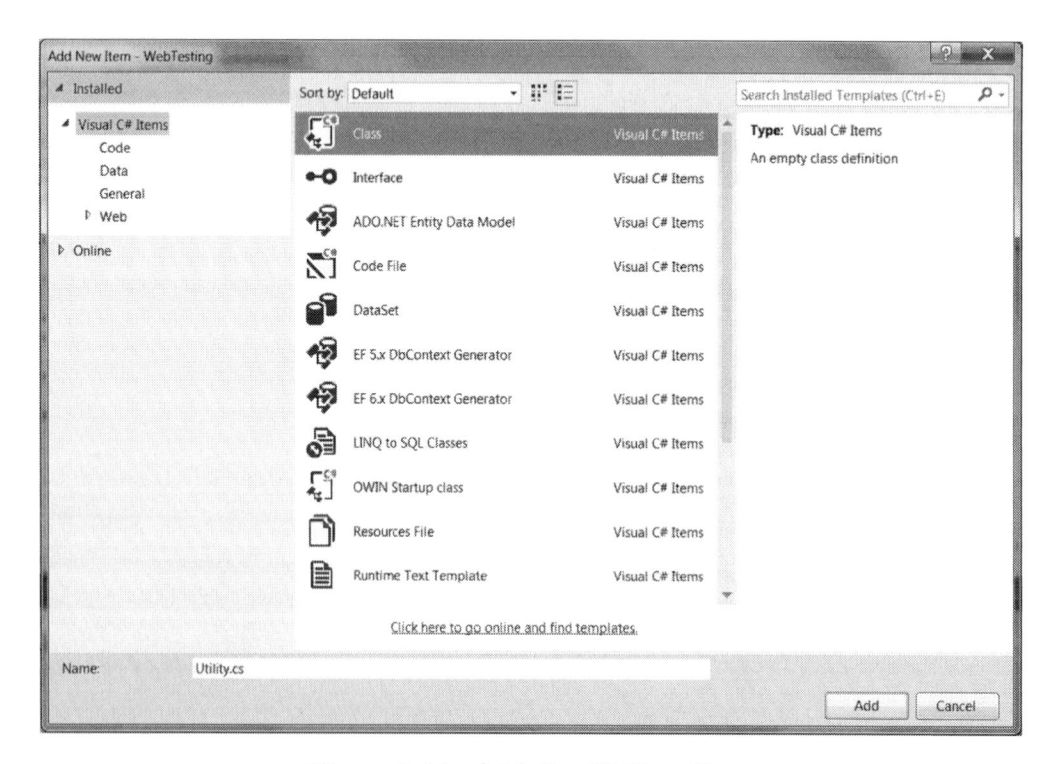

Figure 2.18: Add the Utility Class

Step 5: Setup the Repository file.

- In the 'Solution Explorer', right click on 'Class1.cs' and select Rename as shown in Figure 2.19.

- Type Repository.cs and press the [Enter] key.

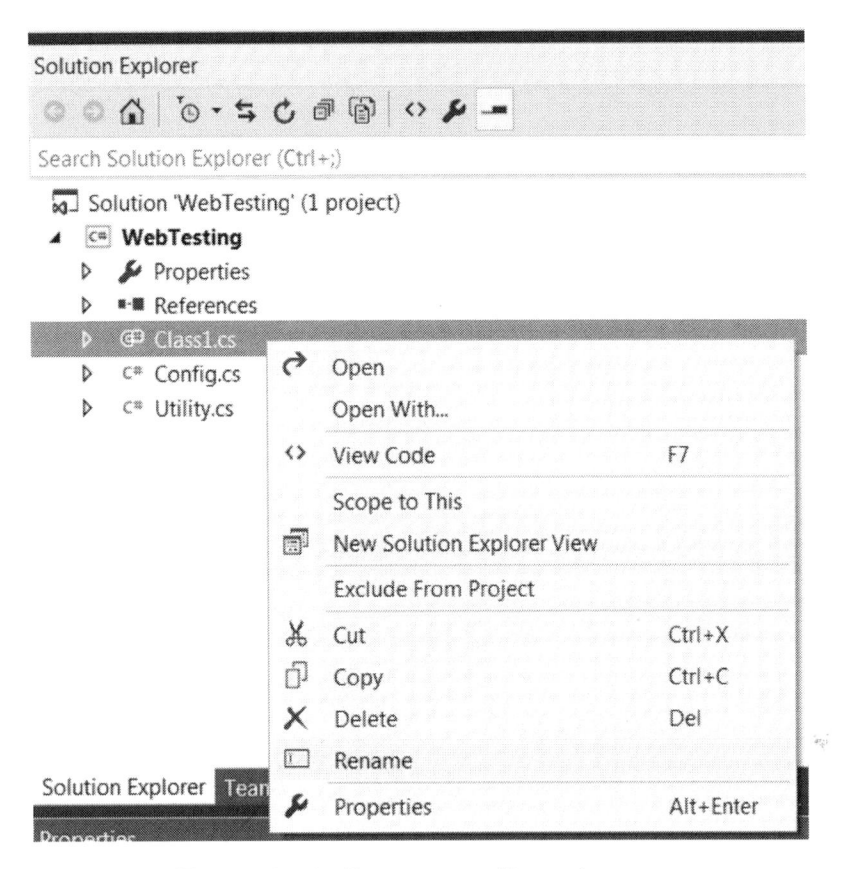

Figure 2.19: Rename to Repository.cs

- Select Yes in the dialog box as shown in Figure 2.20.

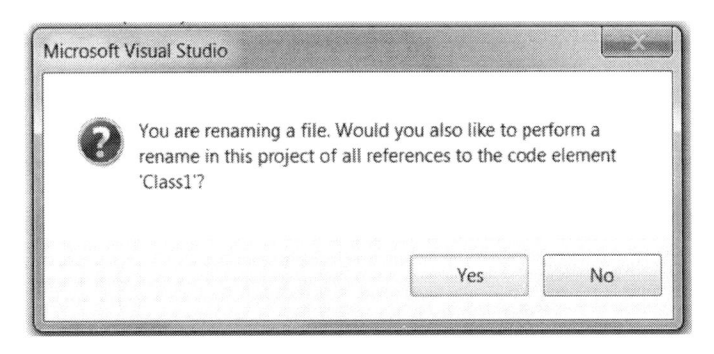

Figure 2.20: Rename Class

Step 6: Now let's setup the Pages and Tests folders.

Automated Web Testing

- In the 'Solution Explorer' window, right click on 'WebTesting' and select Add ⇒ New Folder as shown in Figure 2.21.

- Type Pages and press the Enter key.

- Similarly Add a New Folder named Tests.

- Select File ⇒ Save All.

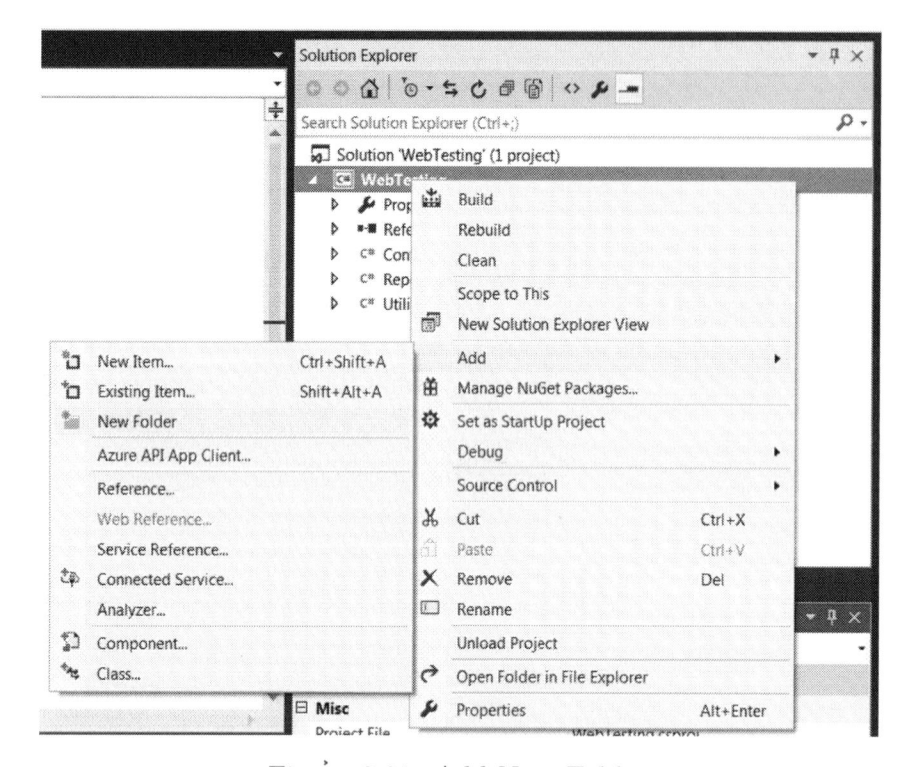

Figure 2.21: Add New Folder

The 'Solution Explorer' window should now look like as shown in Figure 2.22.

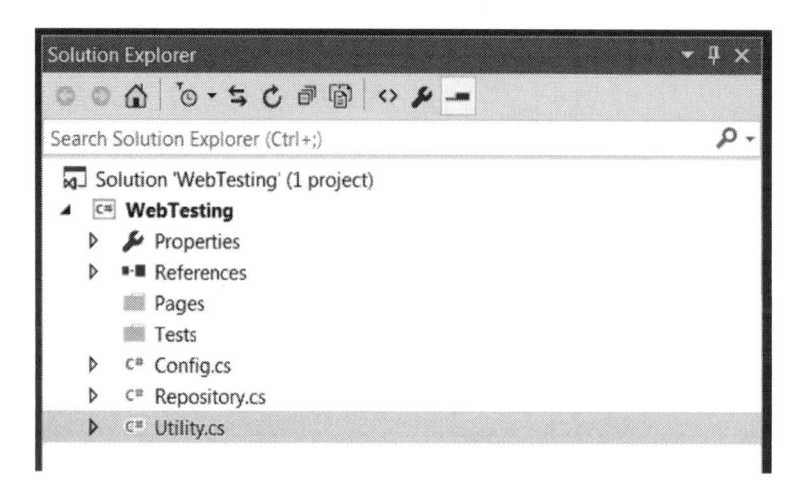

Figure 2.22: Solution Explorer Window

☞ While working in Visual Studio it is always a good practice to keep saving your work. Use `Ctrl`+`S` to Save the current file or use `Ctrl`+`Shift`+`S` to Save All.

2.6 Adding Necessary References

Now let's add the necessary Selenium reference files to our Automation Framework.

- In the 'Solution Explorer' window, right click on 'References' and select Add Reference.

- Click the 'Browse...' button.

- Navigate to folder 'C:\Selenium\selenium-dotnet-2.53.0\net40'. Remember this book assumes you have extracted Selenium files in 'C:\Selenium' folder.

- Select files 'WebDriver.dll' and 'WebDriver.Support.dll' as shown in Figure 2.23. Use the `Ctrl` button and click on the files to select multiple files.

- Click the Add button and then press OK.

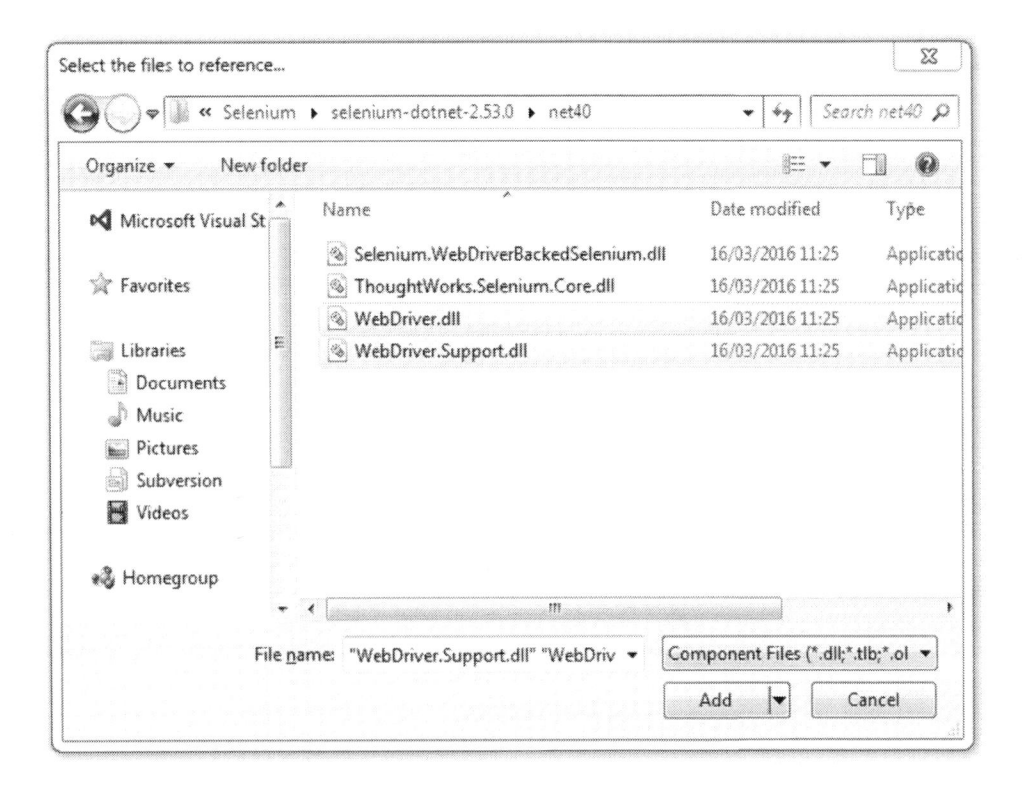

Figure 2.23: Add Selenium Reference Files

Now let's add the necessary NUnit reference file to our Automation Framework.

Automated Web Testing

- In the 'Solution Explorer' window, right click on 'References' and select Add Reference.

- Click the 'Browse...' button

- Navigate to folder 'C:\Program Files (x86)\NUnit 2.6.4\bin\framework. Your location may differ depending on where you installed NUnit.

- Select file 'nunit.framework.dll' as shown in Figure 2.24.

- Click the Add button and then press OK.

- Select File ⇒ Save All.

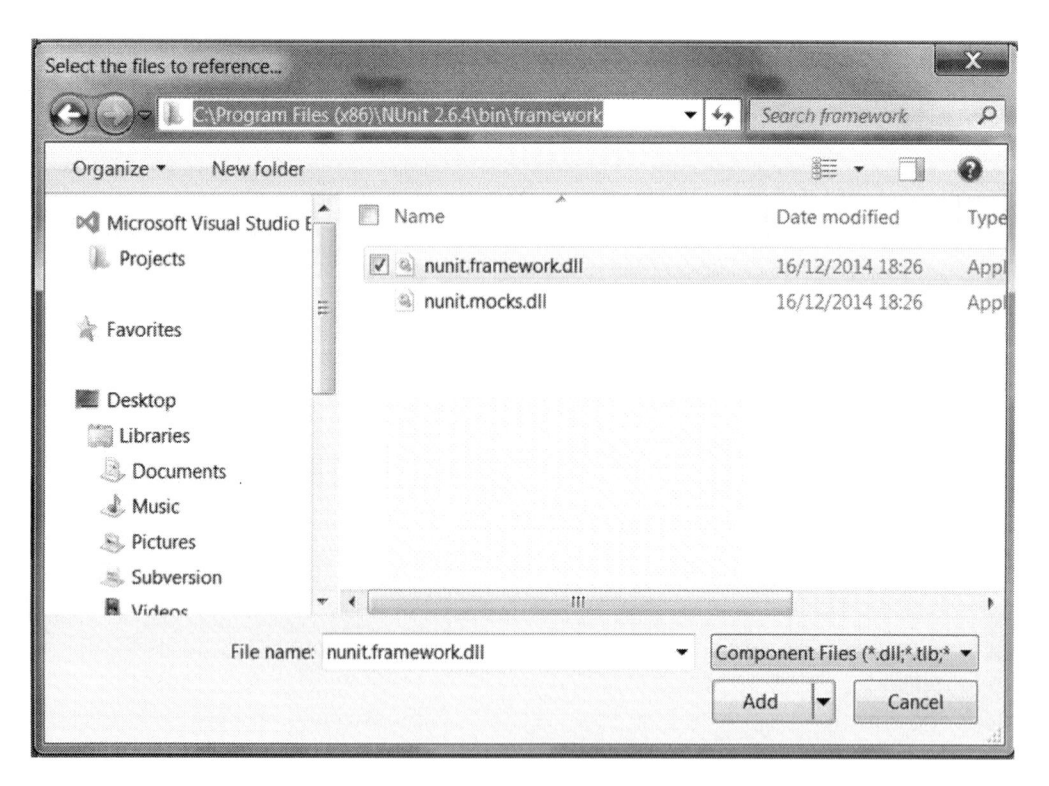

Figure 2.24: Add NUnit Reference File

The 'Solution Explorer' window should now look like as shown in Figure 2.25.

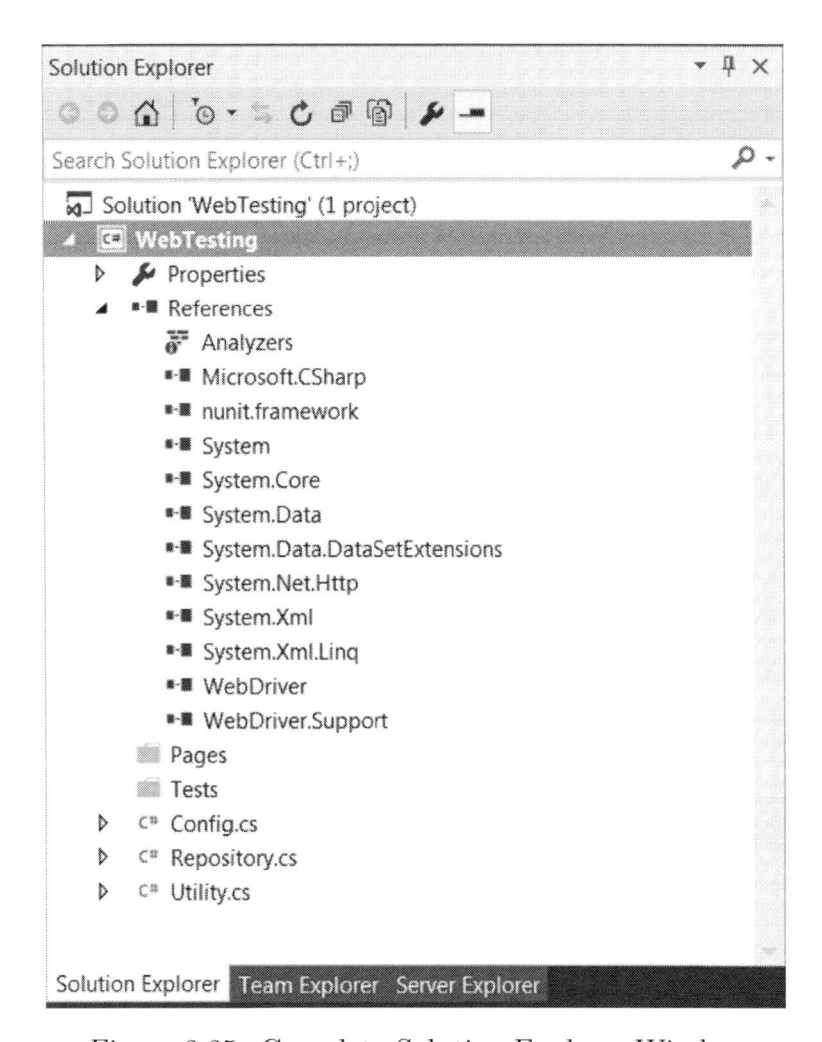

Figure 2.25: Complete Solution Explorer Window

By now we have created the required project structure for our Automation Framework and we are all set to write our first automated test in the next chapter.

Chapter 3

Let's Automate

Let's Automate

In this chapter, we will learn about how to:

- *Write our first automated test*
- *Log useful information to console and files during test execution*
- *Perform negative automated testing*
- *Save screenshots during test execution*
- *Perform data entry and verification tasks on various type of elements on a web page*

So let's get on with it...

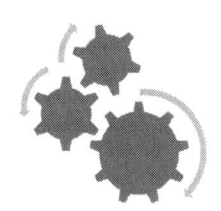

As per the famous saying *'An ounce of practice is worth more than tons of theory'*; so without delving into anything else, let's jump straight into writing our first automated test and see the automation in action!

3.1 Your First Automated Test

3.1.1 Creating The Configuration Parameters

First of all, let's add some configuration variables which we will need throughout our Automation Framework. Double click the 'Config.cs' file in 'Solution Explorer' and add the Listing 3.1 code to it.

Listing 3.1: 'Config.cs' - Parameters file

```csharp
/***************************************************************
 * All rights reserved. Copyright 2016 Arkenstone-ltd.com       *
 ***************************************************************/
using System;

namespace WebTesting
{
    public static class Config
    {
        public const string PASS = "Pass";
        public const string FAIL = "Fail";

        public const string URL = ↵
            ↪ "http://testing.arkenstone-ltd.com/";

        public static int OBJECT_TIMEOUT_SECS = 30;
    }
}
```

Let me explain the code:

Line 4: The `using` keyword states that we are using the `System` namespace in our program.
Line 6: The name of our namespace i.e. `WebTesting`.
Line 8: Name of the class i.e. `Config`.
Line 10: and 11: Define the PASS and FAIL configuration variables used throughout in the framework.

☞ It is a good practice to define such values as string constants because if you need to change their value later on, you just change them at one place i.e. 'Config.cs' file and all the other automation code is automatically taken care of.

Line 13: The URL of the Website Under Test.
Line 15: Timeout in seconds when searching for objects on a web page.

3.1.2 Building The Object Repository

Let's start building our object repository. The home page of our demo website has a number of links. Within Firefox, launch Firebug and navigate to the *Home* link and note down its 'text' attribute as shown in Figure 3.1

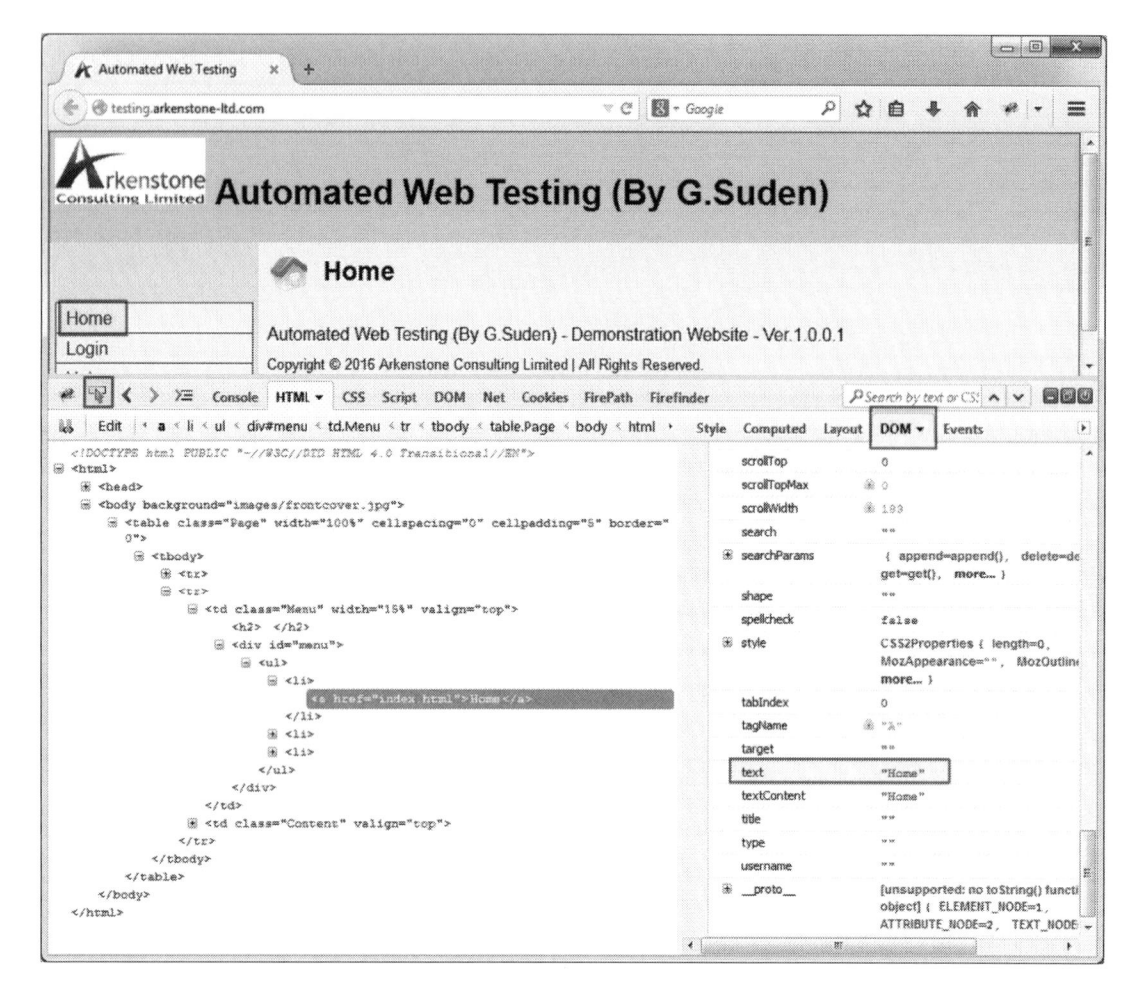

Figure 3.1: Repository Home Page

Similarly note down the attributes of other objects as shown in the following table. Identification of Version Label is shown in Figure 3.2.

Home Page Elements			
Element	*Type*	*Attribute*	*Value*
Home	Link	text	Home
Login	Link	text	Login
Help	Link	text	Help
Version	Label	id	sysVer

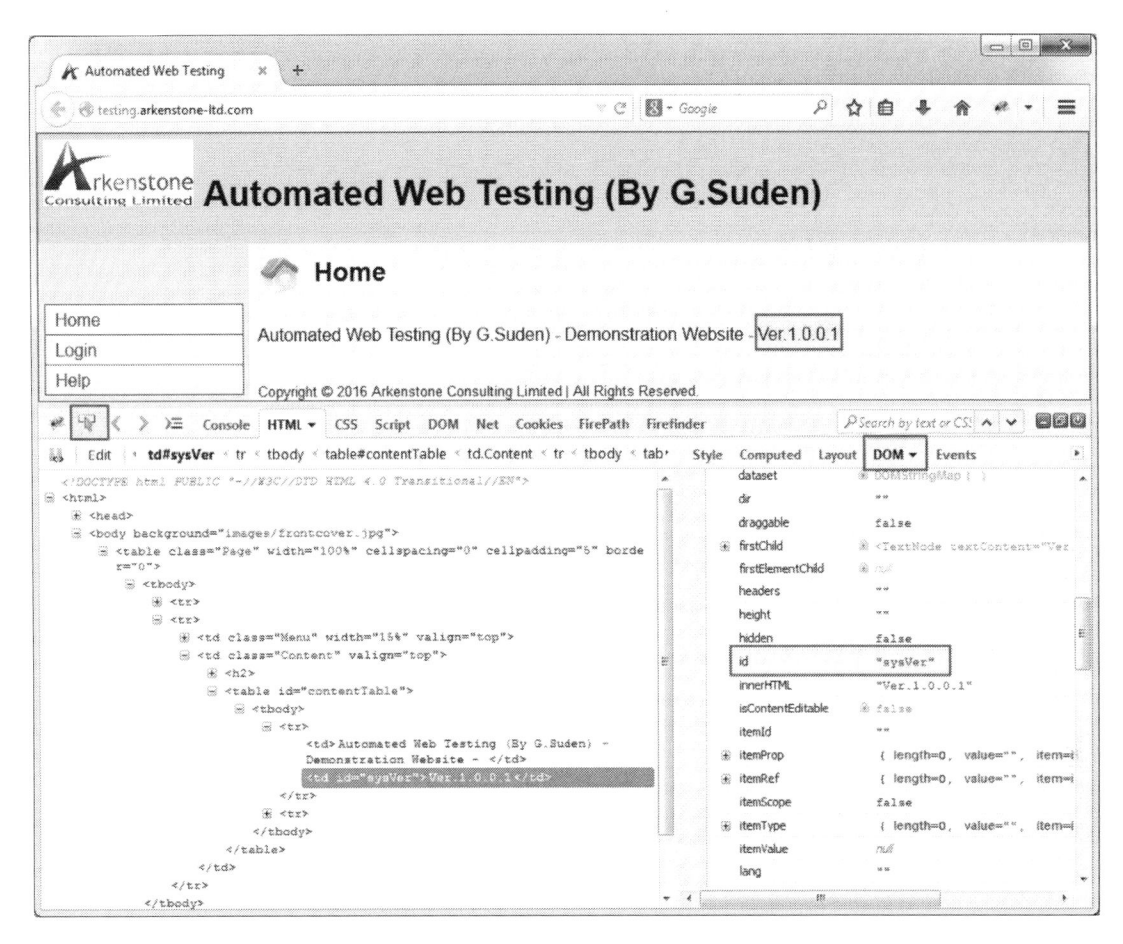

Figure 3.2: Repository Home Page - Version Label

Now double click the 'Repository.cs' file in 'Solution Explorer' and add the Listing 3.2 code to it.

Listing 3.2: 'Repository.cs' - Home page repository

```
/*************************************************************
 * All rights reserved. Copyright 2016 Arkenstone-ltd.com     *
 *************************************************************/
namespace WebTesting
{
    public static class Repository
    {
        public static class Home
        {
            public static string lnkHome_ByLinkText { get
                { return "Home"; } }
            public static string lnkLogin_ByLinkText {
                get { return "Login"; } }
            public static string lnkHelp_ByLinkText { get
                { return "Help"; } }
```

```
13                public static string lblSysVersion_ById { get ↵
                  ↪ { return "sysVer"; } }
14            }
15        }
16 }
```

Line 8: The screen name these elements belong to i.e. the *Home* page.
Line 10: Returns the attribute's value "Home" for the *Home* link. Please note the suffix '`_ByLinkText`' at the end of the variable name. This will be a reminder for us on how to find this element on a page as we will see later in this chapter.
Line 11: Returns the attribute's value "Login" for the *Login* link.
Line 12: Returns the attribute's value "Help" for the *Help* link.
Line 13: Please note the suffix '`_ById`' at the end of the variable name.

Now navigate to the *Login* page and note down the properties of the objects as follows:

Login Page Elements			
Element	**Type**	**Attribute**	**Value**
User ID	Edit Box	name	TxtUserId
Password	Edit Box	name	TxtPassword
Login	Button	id	btnLogin

Add the *Login* page's objects to the 'Repository.cs' file, as shown in Listing 3.3

Listing 3.3: 'Repository.cs' - Login and Home page repository

```
1  /****************************************************************
2   * All rights reserved. Copyright 2016 Arkenstone-ltd.com        *
3   ****************************************************************/
4  namespace WebTesting
5  {
6      public static class Repository
7      {
8          public static class Home
9          {
10             public static string lnkHome_ByLinkText { get ↵
                  ↪ { return "Home"; } }
11             public static string lnkLogin_ByLinkText { ↵
                  ↪ get { return "Login"; } }
12             public static string lnkHelp_ByLinkText { get ↵
                  ↪ { return "Help"; } }
13             public static string lblSysVersion_ById { get ↵
                  ↪ { return "sysVer"; } }
```

```
14          }
15
16          public static class Login
17          {
18              public static string txtUserId_ByName { get { ↵
                 ↪ return "TxtUserId"; } }
19              public static string txtPassword_ByName { get ↵
                 ↪ { return "TxtPassword"; } }
20              public static string btnLogin_ById { get { ↵
                 ↪ return "btnLogin"; } }
21          }
22      }
23  }
```

Line 16: The screen name these elements belong to i.e. the *Login* Page.
Line 18: Returns the attribute's value "TxtUserId" for the User ID data entry field. Please note the suffix '`_ByName`' at the end of the variable name.
Line 19: Returns the attribute's value "TxtPassword" for the Password data entry field.
Line 20: Returns the attribute's value "btnLogin" for the Login button. Please note the suffix '`_ById`' at the end of the variable name.

3.1.3 Creating The Utility Functions

Let's now start creating some generic functions which will be used throughout the Automation Framework. The very first of such functions is to setup the browser driver.

SetupDriver - Sets up the web browser driver		
Input Parameters	*driver*	Object driver to control the browser
Return Value	*driver*	Returns the driver object

Let's now define another generic function which will find any kind of element on the web page. This function will be used by a number of wrapper functions which we will define later on. Don't worry if you don't understand these functions at this stage. Things will be clearer as we will progress through the book!

FindElementEx - Core function that finds any type of element		
Input Parameters	*driver*	Object driver to control the browser
	by	Mechanism by which to find the element within the browser
	timeoutInSeconds	Timeout in seconds to wait for the object to appear in the browser
Return Value	*element*	Returns the element found

Now let's define a function which will find an element on the browser window and click it e.g. find the 'Login' button and click it. We will see how it uses the generic function 'FindElementEx' we defined previously.

FindElementAndClick - Finds an element in the browser and clicks it		
Input Parameters	*driver*	Object driver to control the browser
	by	Mechanism by which to find the element within the browser
Return Value	*void*	Returns nothing

Listing 3.4 shows the complete code of 'Utility.cs' file created so far.

Listing 3.4: 'Utility.cs' - Complete code so far

```
/****************************************************************
 * All rights reserved. Copyright 2016 Arkenstone-ltd.com *
 ****************************************************************/
using System;
using OpenQA.Selenium;
using OpenQA.Selenium.Firefox;
using OpenQA.Selenium.Support.UI;

namespace WebTesting
{
    public static class Utility
    {
        public static string TestResult;

        public static IWebDriver SetupDriver(this
            IWebDriver driver)
        {
            try
            {
                driver = new FirefoxDriver();
                return driver;
            }
            catch (Exception ex)
            {
                Console.WriteLine("SetupDriver Exception: 
                    " + ex.ToString());
                throw ex;
            }
        }
```

```csharp
        private static IWebElement FindElementEx(this
            IWebDriver driver, By by, int timeoutInSeconds)
        {
            string ex = "";

            try
            {
                if (timeoutInSeconds > 0)
                {
                    var wait = new WebDriverWait(driver,
                        TimeSpan.FromSeconds
                        (timeoutInSeconds));
                    Console.WriteLine("Find Element: " +
                        by + "   timeoutInSeconds: " +
                        timeoutInSeconds);
                    return wait.Until(drv =>
                        drv.FindElement(by));
                }

                Console.WriteLine("Find Element: " + by +
                    "   timeoutInSeconds: " +
                    timeoutInSeconds);
                return driver.FindElement(by);
            }
            catch (NoSuchElementException)
            {
                ex += "Object not found " + by.ToString();
                Console.WriteLine(ex);
                throw new NoSuchElementException(ex);
            }
        }

        public static void FindElementAndClick(this
            IWebDriver driver, By by)
        {
            string ex = "";

            try
            {
                FindElementEx(driver, by,
                    Config.OBJECT_TIMEOUT_SECS).Click();
                Console.WriteLine("Clicking : " + by);
                return;
            }
```

```
63                catch (NoSuchElementException)
64                {
65                    ex += "Unable to Click " + by;
66                    Console.WriteLine(ex);
67                    throw new NoSuchElementException(ex);
68                }
69            }
70        }
71 }
```

Line 13: Defines the global 'TestResult' variable to store the outcome of the test.
Line 19: Initialises the Firefox driver.
Line 20: Returns the driver object.
Line 22: Catches any exception.
Line 25: Throws exception in case of error.
Line 35: Keeps looking for the element until the timeout period.
Line 43: Returns the element.
Line 59: Calls the core function 'FindElementEx' to find the element and click it.
Line 61: Returns nothing.

Before we proceed further, let's define another function which will find an element in the browser window and also enters data in it e.g. enter value "Tester" in the User ID edit box. This function again uses our generic function 'FindElementEx' we wrote previously.

FindElementAndSendKeys - Finds an element in the browser window and sends keys to it		
Input Parameters	*driver*	Object driver to control the browser
	by	Mechanism by which to find the element within the browser
	val	Data string to be sent to the element
Return Value	*void*	Returns nothing

Add Listing 3.5 code to the 'Utility.cs' file.

Listing 3.5: 'Utility.cs' - Code for FindElementAndSendKeys

```
1 public static void FindElementAndSendKeys(this IWebDriver ↵
       ↪ driver, By by, string val)
2 {
3     string ex = "";
4
5     try
6     {
```

```
 7          FindElementEx(driver, by, ↵
                ↪ Config.OBJECT_TIMEOUT_SECS).SendKeys(val);
 8          Console.WriteLine("SendKeys Value: " + val);
 9          return;
10      }
11      catch (NoSuchElementException)
12      {
13          ex += "Unable to Sendkeys " + val;
14          Console.WriteLine(ex);
15          throw new NoSuchElementException(ex);
16      }
17  }
```

Line 7: Calls the core function 'FindElementEx' to find the element and sends keys to it.

3.1.4 Creating The Page Logic

A website may contain a number of webpages. Each page serves its own purpose and carries a certain amount of functionality e.g. a login page usually presents the user with a set of controls to enter his/her login credentials. Once the login credentials are verified, the user will be presented with another webpage depending on access rights e.g. the Admin user in our demo website will be presented with a new webpage that has access to the employee list and report by gender.

3.1.4.1 Base Page

In our Automation Framework, each web page's logic will be built into a separate page e.g. the home page's logic will present the *Home* screen to the user and provide a mechanism to click various links to navigate around. First of all, we will create a 'generic' page from which each page will inherit. This page is called 'pageBase'.

- In the 'Solution Explorer', right click on the 'Pages' folder
- Click Add ⇒ Class as shown in Figure 3.3
- Type the 'name' as pageBase.cs
- Click Add

Automated Web Testing

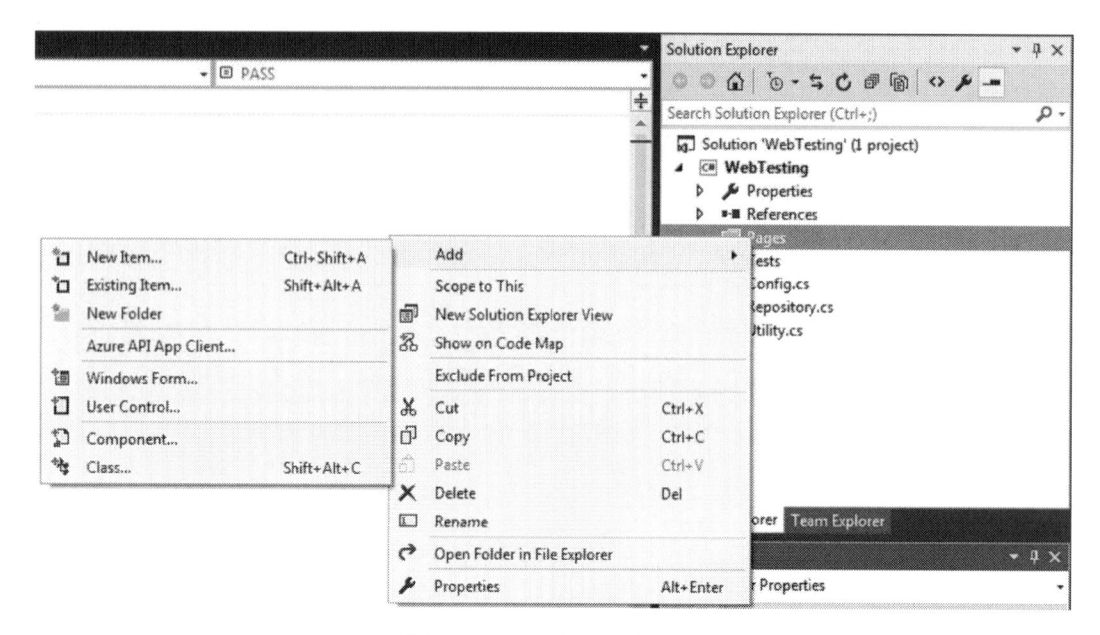

Figure 3.3: Page Base

Add Listing 3.6 code to it.

Listing 3.6: 'pageBase.cs' - Code for Base page

```
/****************************************************************
 * All rights reserved. Copyright 2016 Arkenstone-ltd.com        *
 ****************************************************************/
using System;
using OpenQA.Selenium;

namespace WebTesting.Pages
{
    class pageBase
    {
        public IWebDriver driver;
        public readonly string WebUrl;

        protected pageBase(IWebDriver driver, String ↵
           ↪ loadUrl = "")
        {
            this.driver = driver;
            WebUrl = loadUrl;
        }

        protected void GoToSite()
        {
            driver.Navigate().GoToUrl(WebUrl);
```

```
23          }
24      }
25  }
```

Line 11: Defines the driver variable through which the browser is controlled.
Line 12: Defines the variable to store the URL name.
Line 16: Initialises the driver.
Line 17: Initialises the URL.
Line 22: Instructs the driver to navigate the browser to the URL.

3.1.4.2 Home Page

The *Home* page of our demo website will have the following actions:

Action	Description
Visit()	This action will launch the browser and display the *Home* page of our demo website.
ClickHome()	This action will navigate to the *Home* page.
ClickLogin()	This action will navigate to the *Login* page.
ClickHelp()	This action will navigate to the *Help* page.

Let's now add the page logic for the *Home* page. In the 'Solution Explorer', right click on the 'Pages' folder, click Add ⇒ Class. Type the name as 'pageHome.cs' and click the Add button. Add Listing 3.7 code to it.

Listing 3.7: 'pageHome.cs' - Code for Home page

```
1  /*****************************************************************
2   * All rights reserved. Copyright 2016 Arkenstone-ltd.com *
3   *****************************************************************/
4  using System;
5  using OpenQA.Selenium;
6
7  namespace WebTesting.Pages
8  {
9      class pageHome : pageBase
10     {
11         private static readonly String Url = Config.URL; ↵
                ↪
```

```
12
13              public pageHome(IWebDriver driver) : base(driver, ↵
                    ↪ Url)
14              {
15              }
16
17              public void Visit()
18              {
19                  GoToSite();
20              }
21
22              public void ClickHome()
23              {
24                  Utility.FindElementAndClick(driver, ↵
                        ↪ By.LinkText( ↵
                        ↪ Repository.Home.lnkHome_ByLinkText));
25              }
26
27              public void ClickLogin()
28              {
29                  Utility.FindElementAndClick(driver, ↵
                        ↪ By.LinkText( ↵
                        ↪ Repository.Home.lnkLogin_ByLinkText));
30              }
31
32              public void ClickHelp()
33              {
34                  Utility.FindElementAndClick(driver, ↵
                        ↪ By.LinkText( ↵
                        ↪ Repository.Home.lnkHelp_ByLinkText));
35              }
36          }
37 }
```

Line 9: The derived class (pageHome) inherits the base class (pageBase) member variables and member methods.

Line 11: Assigns the URL variable defined in the configuration file to a private read-only member.

Line 13: Constructor to re-use the driver.

Line 17: Defines the member method `Visit()`.

Line 19: Note the call to the `GoToSite()` method of the 'pageBase'.

Line 22: Defines the member method `ClickHome()`.

Line 24: Calls the Utility function 'FindElementAndClick' with the repository element for the home link i.e. 'Repository.Home.lnkHome_ByLinkText'. Remember when we defined the repository element for the home link, we suffixed it with '_ByLinkText'.

This reminded us how to use it in the 'By' parameter .i.e. 'By.LinkText'.
Line 27: Defines the member method `ClickLogin()`.
Line 29: Passes the repository element for the login link i.e.
'Repository.Home.lnkLogin_ByLinkText'.
Line 32: Defines the member method `ClickHelp()`.
Line 34: Passes the repository element for the help link i.e.
'Repository.Home.lnkHelp_ByLinkText'.

3.1.4.3 Login Page

The *Login* page of our demo website will have the following actions:

Action	Description
Login()	This action will perform user login with the given credentials.
ClickHome()	This action will navigate to the *Home* page.
ClickHelp()	This action will navigate to the *Help* page.

Let's now add the page logic for *Login* page. In the 'Solution Explorer', right click on the 'Pages' folder, click Add ⇒ Class. Type the name as 'pageLogin.cs' and click the Add button. Add Listing 3.8 code to it.

Listing 3.8: 'pageLogin.cs' - Code for Login page

```
1  /***************************************************************
2   * All rights reserved. Copyright 2016 Arkenstone-ltd.com *
3   ***************************************************************/
4  using System;
5  using OpenQA.Selenium;
6  
7  namespace WebTesting.Pages
8  {
9      class pageLogin : pageBase
10     {
11         private static readonly String Url = Config.URL;
12 
13         public pageLogin(IWebDriver driver) : ↵
                base(driver, Url)
14         {
15         }
16 
17         public void Login(string uid, string pwd)
```

```
18              {
19                      Utility.FindElementAndSendKeys(driver, ↵
                        ↪ By.Name(Repository.Login. ↵
                        ↪ txtUserId_ByName), uid);
20                      Utility.FindElementAndSendKeys(driver, ↵
                        ↪ By.Name(Repository.Login. ↵
                        ↪ txtPassword_ByName), pwd);
21                      Utility.FindElementAndClick(driver, ↵
                        ↪ By.Id(Repository.Login.btnLogin_ById));
22              }
23
24              public void ClickHome()
25              {
26                      Utility.FindElementAndClick(driver, ↵
                        ↪ By.LinkText( ↵
                        ↪ Repository.Home.lnkHome_ByLinkText));
27              }
28
29              public void ClickHelp()
30              {
31                      Utility.FindElementAndClick(driver, ↵
                        ↪ By.LinkText( ↵
                        ↪ Repository.Home.lnkLogin_ByLinkText));
32              }
33      }
34 }
```

Line 9: The derived class (pageLogin) inherits the base class (pageBase) member variables and member methods.

Line 11: Assigns the URL variable defined in the configuration file to a private read-only member.

Line 13: Constructor to re-use the driver.

Line 17: Defines the member method Login(). Note that it has two parameters i.e. user id 'uid' and password 'pwd'.

Line 19: Note the definition of the user id repository element with suffix '_ByName' and the 'By' parameter's usage in the call .i.e. 'By.Name'.

Line 20: Passes the repository element for the password entry field i.e. 'Repository.Login.txtPassword_ByName'.

Line 21: Passes the repository element for the login button i.e. 'Repository.Login.btnLogin_ById' and note the call 'By.Id'.

Line 24: Defines the member method ClickHome().

Line 26: Please note the reuse of 'Repository.Home.lnkHome_ByLinkText'. If the attribute's value differs in the test you are creating then you would need to define a new variable.

Line 29: Defines the member method ClickHelp().

Line 31: Please note the reuse of 'Repository.Home.lnkLogin_ByLinkText'. If the attribute's value differs in the test you are creating then you would need to define a new variable.

3.1.5 Creating Tests

Let's verify the following Test Scenario:

- Launch the Firefox browser with our demo website.
- Click on the *Login* link.
- Login with the user 'Tester'.

In the 'Solution Explorer', right click on the 'Tests' folder, click Add ⇒ Class. Type the name as 'TestLogins.cs' and click the Add button.

Add the Listing 3.9 code to it.

Listing 3.9: 'TestLogins.cs' - Code for login tests

```csharp
/***************************************************************
 * All rights reserved. Copyright 2016 Arkenstone-ltd.com       *
 ***************************************************************/
using System;
using OpenQA.Selenium;
using NUnit.Framework;
using WebTesting.Pages;

namespace WebTesting.Tests
{
    public class TestLogins
    {
        IWebDriver driver;

        [SetUp]
        public void Setup()
        {
            driver = Utility.SetupDriver(driver);
            Utility.TestResult = Config.PASS;
        }

        [TearDown]
        public void Teardown()
        {
```

```
25                 if (TestContext.CurrentContext.Result.Status ↵
                       == TestStatus.Failed)
26                 {
27                     Console.WriteLine("***** Teardown ==> ↵
                           Test FAILED ***** =>" + ↵
                           TestContext.CurrentContext.Test.FullName);
28                 }
29                 else if ↵
                       (TestContext.CurrentContext.Result.Status ↵
                       == TestStatus.Passed)
30                 {
31                     Console.WriteLine("PASS => " + ↵
                           TestContext.CurrentContext.Test.FullName);
32                 }
33
34                 driver.Quit();
35             }
36
37             [Test]
38             public void LoginUser()
39             {
40                 var home = new pageHome(driver);
41                 home.Visit();
42                 home.ClickLogin();
43
44                 var login = new pageLogin(driver);
45                 login.Login("Tester", "Tester123");
46             }
47         }
48 }
```

Line 15: The '[SetUp]' attribute is used to provide a function that is performed just before each test method is executed.

Line 18: Calls the generic function 'SetupDriver' to setup the web browser.

Line 19: Sets the initial value of the test to 'Config.PASS'.

Line 22: The '[TearDown]' attribute is used to provide a function that is performed after each test method is executed.

Line 25: If the test has failed then displays a failure message in the console.

Line 29: If the test has passed then displays a pass message in the console.

Line 34: Closes the browser window after the test finishes.

Line 37: The '[Test]' attribute marks a specific method inside a class as a test method. In other words, this is our Test Scenario to be executed.

Line 40: Initialises the 'home' variable by creating a new instance of the 'pageHome'.

Line 41: Calls the member function 'Visit()' to visit the *Home* page.

Line 42: Calls the member function 'ClickLogin()' to click the *Login* link.

Line 44: Initialises the '`login`' page variable by creating a new instance of the '`pageLogin`'.
Line 45: Calls the member function '`Login()`' to allow user login. Note the two parameters supplied i.e. user id and password.

3.1.6 Building Tests

By now you have completed all the code required for your first automated test. In Visual Studio's Toolbar, select the 'Release' Solution Configuration as shown in Figure 3.4.

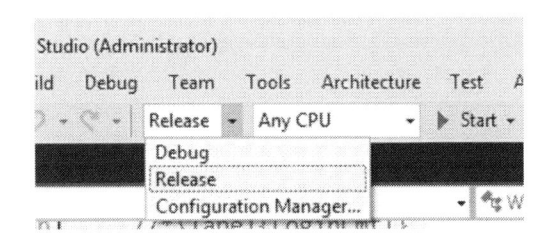

Figure 3.4: Selecting Solution Configuration

In the 'Solution Explorer', right click on 'WebTesting', click Build as shown in Figure 3.5.

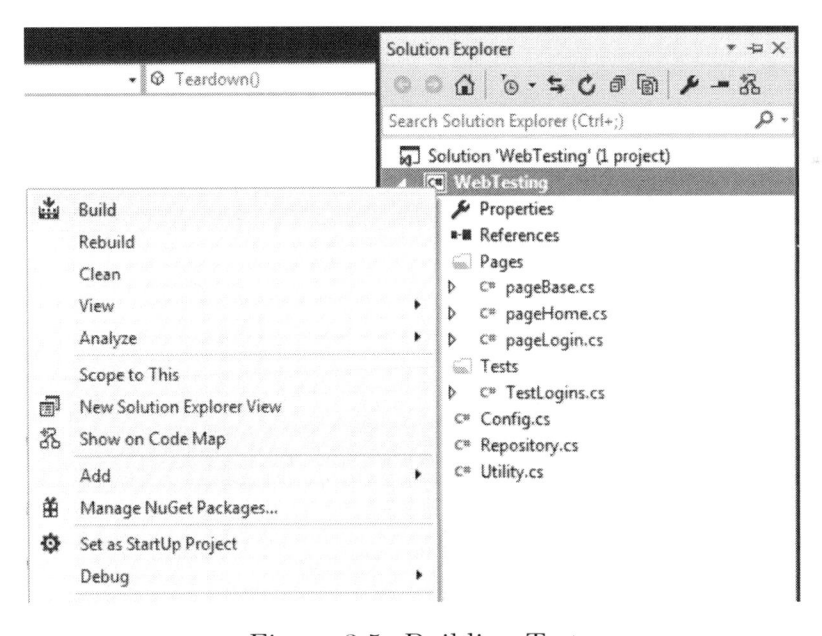

Figure 3.5: Building Test

Click View $\Rightarrow$ Output to view the Output Window as shown in Figure 3.6 which shows a successful build.

Automated Web Testing

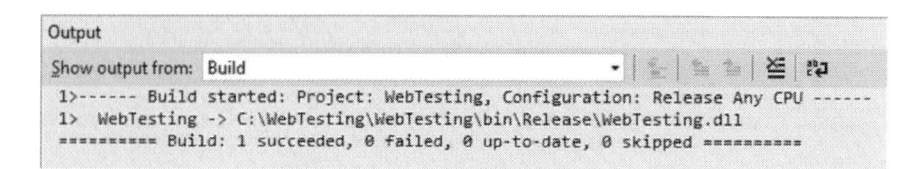

Figure 3.6: Output Window

3.1.7 Executing Tests

We are almost there! We will use NUnit to execute our first test we just compiled. Launch NUnit from the location you installed. On my workstation it is at "C:\Program Files\NUnit-2.6.4\bin\nunit.exe".

- Go to File ⇒ New Project...
- Navigate to the 'C:\WebTesting\WebTesting' folder as shown in Figure3.7.
- Type the 'File Name:' as DemoPortal.nunit
- Click the Save button.

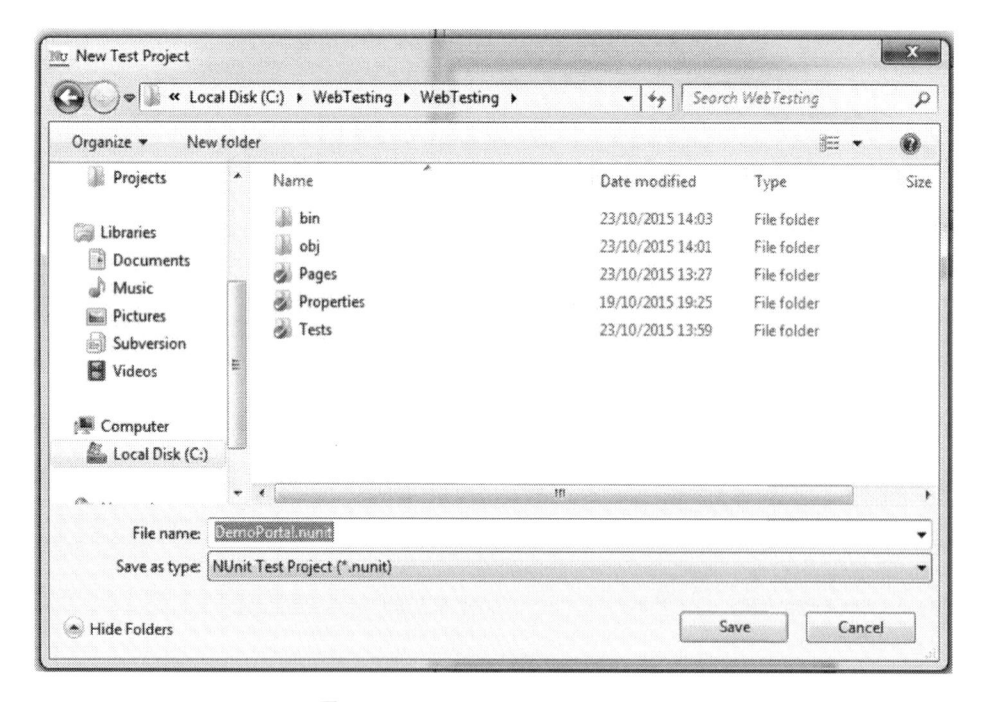

Figure 3.7: Create Project

- Now go to Project ⇒ Add Assembly...
- Navigate to the 'C:\WebTesting\WebTesting\bin\Release' folder and select WebTesting.dll as shown in Figure3.8.
- Click the Open button.

64   Chapter 3

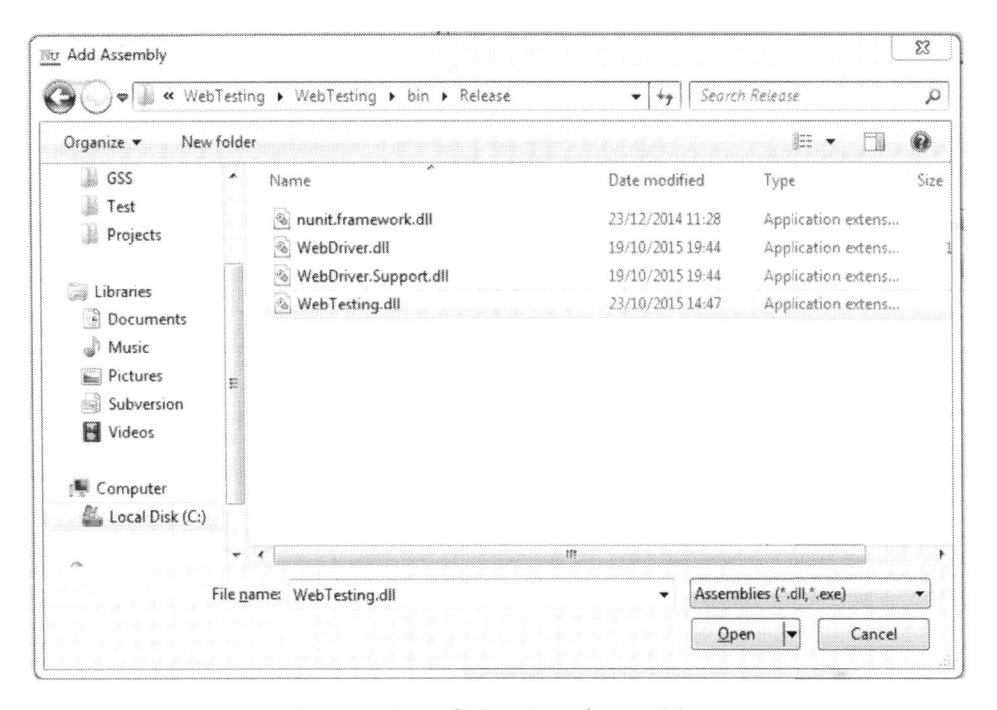

Figure 3.8: Selecting Assembly

- Go to File ⇒ Save

- Click on the 'LoginUser' checkbox and click the run button as shown in Figure 3.9. Or right click the test 'LoginUser' and select Run.

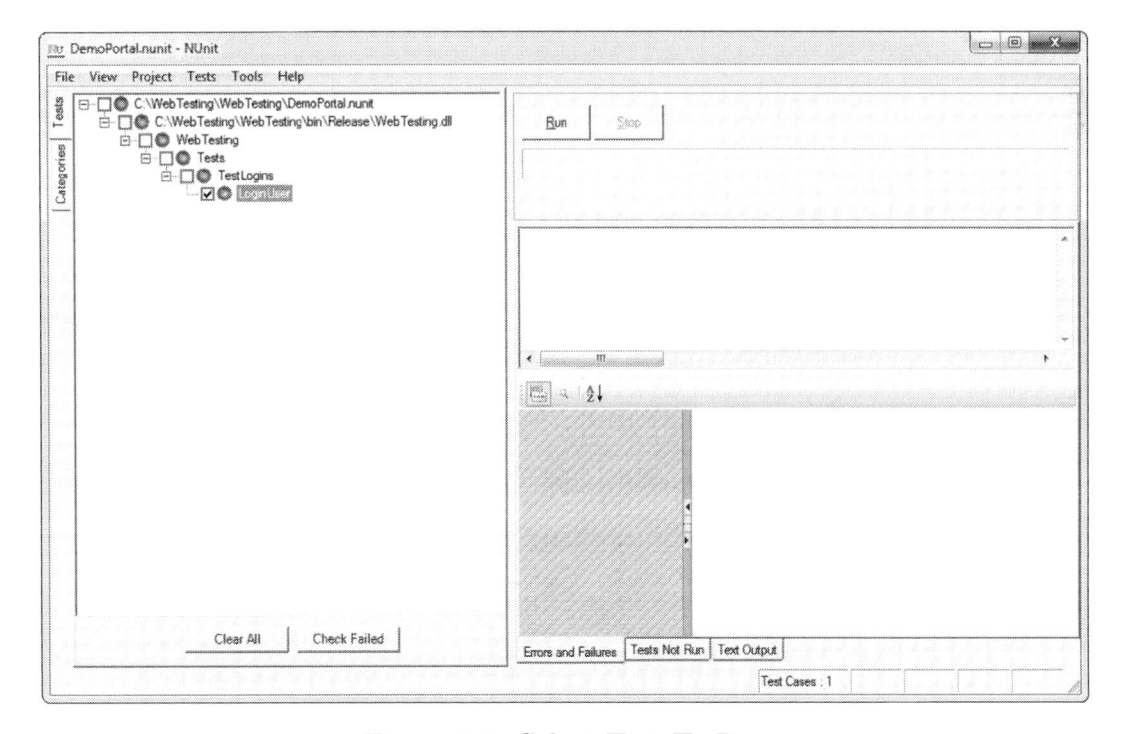

Figure 3.9: Select Test To Run

You will see a Firefox browser window launching and executing our first automated test! Once the test execution is finished, click the 'Text Output' Tab in the NUnit and you will see an output as shown in Figure 3.10.

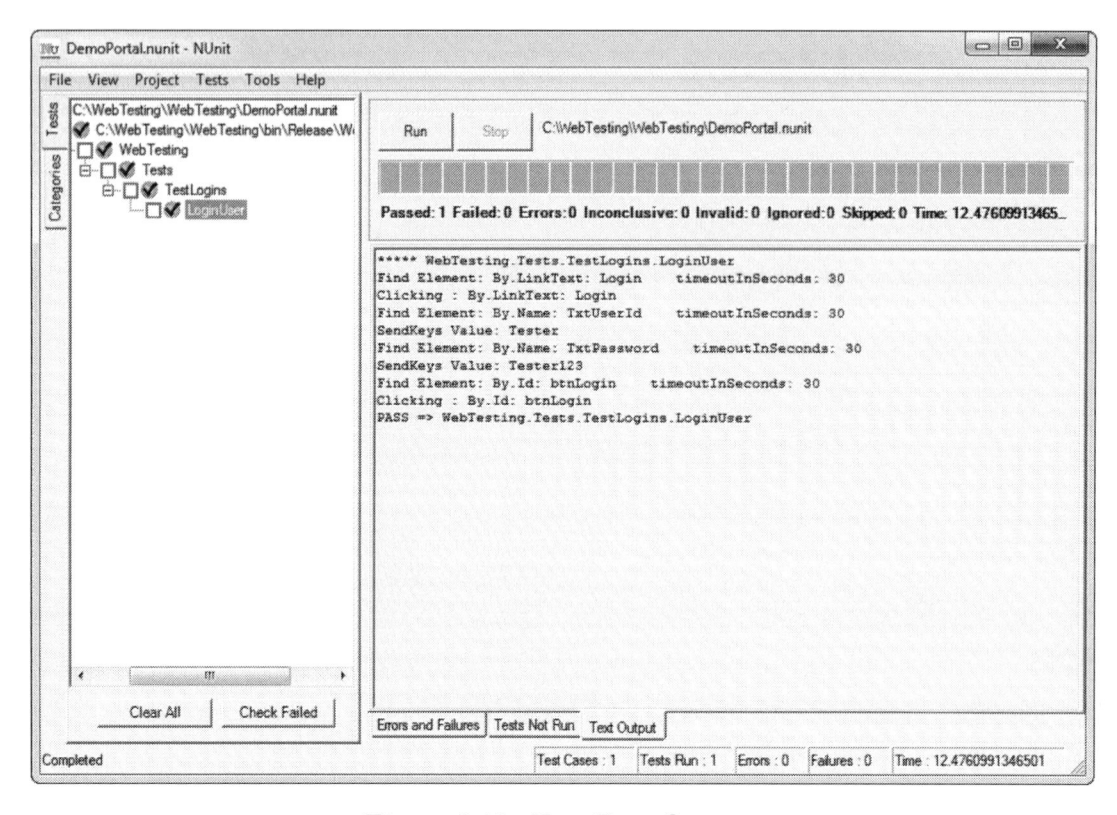

Figure 3.10: Test Run Output

The output tab shows that its final outcome is a "PASS", the logic of which we coded earlier in the `Teardown()` function.

3.2 Reporting Expected Vs. Actual

The Automation Framework we are writing should perform two important tasks:

- Compare the Expected and Actual Result of a *Test Step* and report the outcome - either Pass or Fail.

- Report the final outcome of the *Test* - again either Pass or Fail.

So before we proceed further, let's add these features to our Automation Framework.

3.2.1 Utility Functions

We need to define a new function in the Utility file as follows:

ReportExpectedVsActual - Reports the outcome of expected verses actual result comparison		
Input Parameters	*driver*	Object driver to control the browser
	expResult	Expected result
	actResult	Actual result
Return Value	*void*	Returns nothing

Now add Listing 3.10 code to the 'Utility.cs' file.

Listing 3.10: 'Utility.cs' - Code for ReportExpectedVsActual

```
1  public static void ReportExpectedVsActual(this IWebDriver ↵
       ↪ driver, string expected, string actual)
2  {
3      if (expected.Trim() == actual.Trim())
4      {
5          Console.WriteLine("[Expected: ]" + expected + " ↵
              ↪      [Actual: ]" + actual + "        [Step ↵
              ↪ Passed]");
6      }
7      else
8      {
9          Console.WriteLine("[Expected: ]" + expected + " ↵
              ↪      [Actual: ]" + actual + "        [Step ↵
              ↪ Failed]");
10         TestResult = Config.FAIL;
11     }
12 }
```

Line 3: Compares the expected result with the actual result which are passed as parameters to this function. Note the removal of leading and trailing spaces before the compare is performed by using the "Trim()" function.

Line 5: If the expected value matches the actual value, logs a Pass message with the matching values.

Line 9: If the expected value doesn't match the actual value, logs a Fail message with the mismatched values.

Line 10: Sets the `TestResult` configuration parameter's value to 'Config.FAIL'.

Let's now add another function to the Utility file which reports the final outcome of the test.

Automated Web Testing

ReportResult - Reports the final outcome of the test		
Input Parameters	*void*	No parameters
Return Value	*void*	Returns nothing

Listing 3.11: 'Utility.cs' - Code to report the test outcome

```
1  public static void ReportResult()
2  {
3      if (TestResult == Config.FAIL)
4      {
5          Assert.Fail("Test failed, please check error log.");
6      }
7  }
```

Line 3: If the configuration parameter `'TestResult'` was set to fail in any of the *Test Step* comparison then report the final outcome of the *Test* as fail.

☞ Sometimes when you add additional code to the files, it may show an erroneous statement due to a missing reference (as happened just now when we added the new code). Just by clicking on the dropdown and selecting the required reference will resolve the error. For example, by selecting *'using NUnit.Framework;'*, the missing reference will be added to our Utility.cs file as shown in Figure 3.11. Alternatively you can manually add 'using NUnit.Framework;' at the top of the 'Utility.cs' file to resolve the issue.

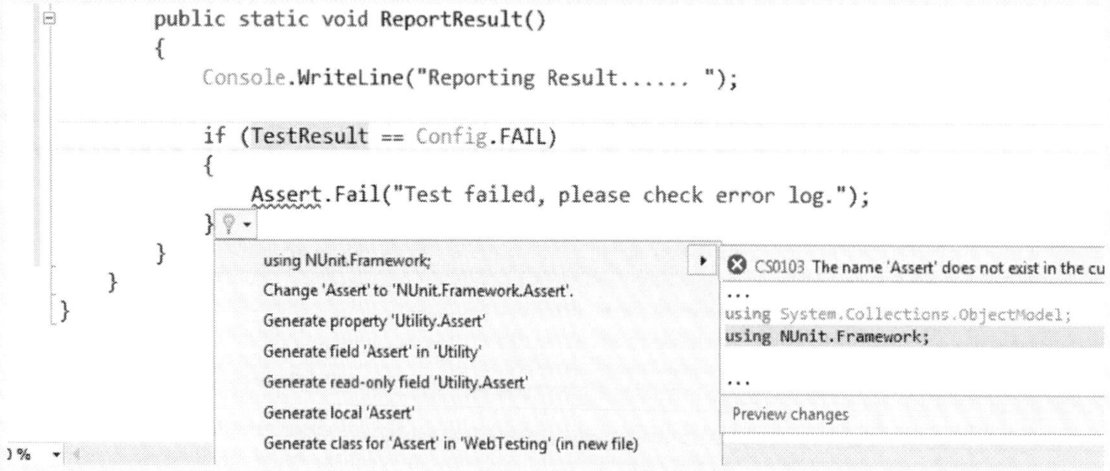

Figure 3.11: Adding Missing Reference

3.2.2 Updating Page Logic

Let's now use these functions. First of all let's verify a *Test Step* i.e. confirm that the Title of the website being launched is "Automated Web Testing". Update the `Visit()` code in 'pageHome.cs' as shown in Listing 3.12.

Listing 3.12: 'pageHome.cs' - Updated code for Visit

```
1  public void Visit()
2  {
3      GoToSite();
4      Utility.ReportExpectedVsActual(driver, "Automated Web ↵
          ↪ Testing", driver.Title);
5  }
```

Line 5: Note the second parameter to the 'ReportExpectedVsActual' function i.e. `driver.Title` which gives us the actual value of our demo website's Title at runtime.

3.2.3 Updating Tests

Let's now update the 'TestLogins.cs' file to report the final outcome of the *Test* at the end. We will also add another test for Admin user's login as shown in Listing 3.13.

Listing 3.13: 'TestLogins.cs' - Code for test LoginAdminUser

```
1  [Test]
2  public void LoginUser()
3  {
4      var home = new pageHome(driver);
5      home.Visit();
6      home.ClickLogin();
7  
8      var login = new pageLogin(driver);
9      login.Login("Tester", "Tester123");
10     Utility.ReportResult();
11 }
12 
13 [Test]
14 public void LoginAdminUser()
15 {
16     var home = new pageHome(driver);
17     home.Visit();
18     home.ClickLogin();
```

```
19
20        var login = new pageLogin(driver);
21        login.Login("Admin", "Admin123");
22        Utility.ReportResult();
23   }
```

Line 10: Calls the utility function 'ReportResult()' to report the final outcome at the end of *Test*.

Line 13: Specifies the '[Test]' attribute before writing the new test.

Line 14: Note that the new test 'LoginAdminUser' is just a copy-and-paste of the test 'LoginUser' except the values of user id and password which are passed to the login function.

3.2.4 Executing Tests

In the 'Solution Explorer', right click on 'WebTesting', click Rebuild as shown in Figure 3.12. Ensure that the Rebuild is successful.

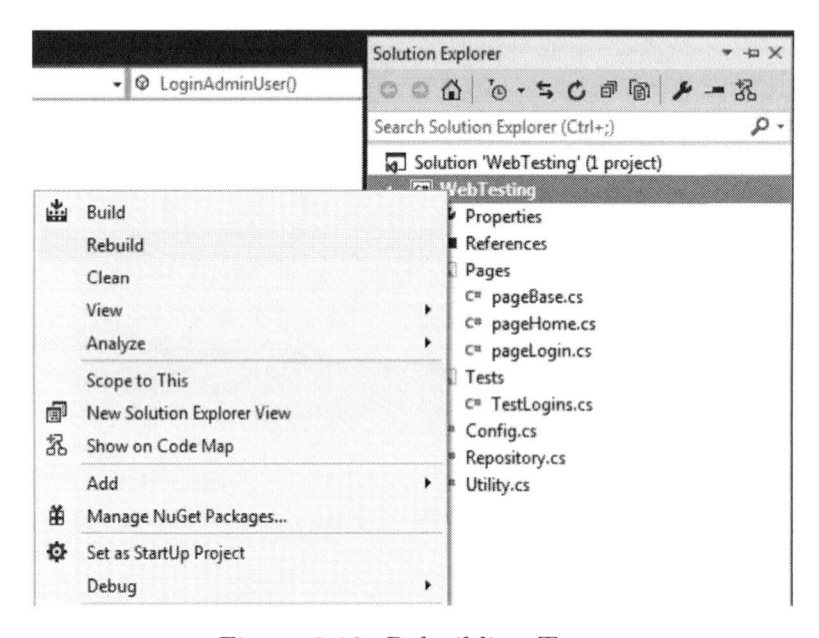

Figure 3.12: Rebuilding Tests

Switch to the NUnit window or relaunch NUnit if you closed it earlier. It should now show two tests - **LoginAdminUser** and **LoginUser** in the Tests Tab. Select both these tests and click the Run button. Both tests should execute successfully and the final output window should look like as shown in Figure 3.13

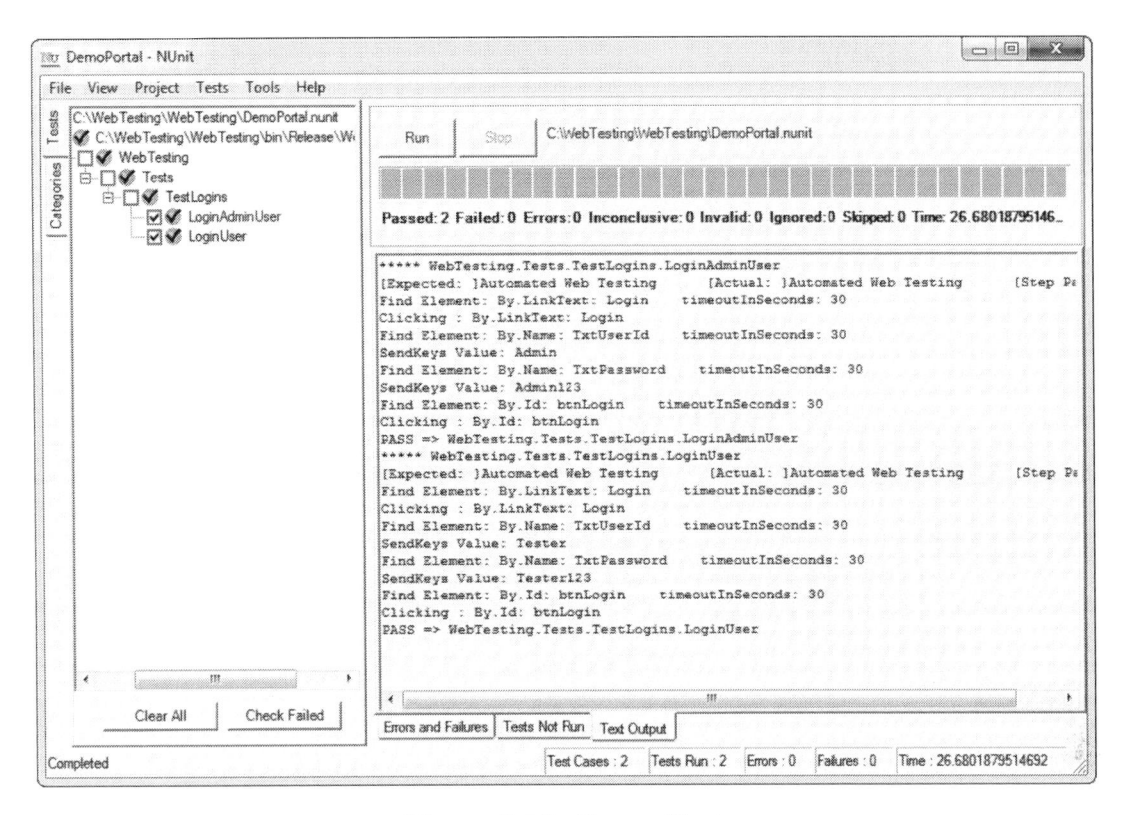

Figure 3.13: Rerun Tests

The output window now shows comparison of the actual website's title with the expected value. It also reports the final outcome of each test - the `LoginUser` and the `LoginAdminUser` in our case.

Our Automation Framework is now capable of performing two more important tasks i.e. has ability to

- compare the Expected and Actual Result of a *Test Step* and report the outcome

- and report the final outcome of the *Test*.

A little exercise for you: Update the code in Listing 3.12 to compare the website's title with the value "Wrong Title" and re-run the tests. Ensure that you rebuild the 'WebTesting.dll'. Confirm that both the tests fail this time.

3.3 Logging Information

So as you saw in the previous section, we developed a simple Automation Framework and it works! Log generation is an important part of the test execution. It is very important to generate debug information at various points in a test. This information can help you identify problematic areas quickly and also reduce the bug fixing time for developers.

In the previous example, the framework used the `Console.WriteLine` function for logging information. However, we need our framework to provide a robust logging mechanism so that we can log different types of messages e.g.

- Info i.e. informational messages
- Error i.e. error messages
- Debug i.e. debug messages

Logging different types of messages provides better control over the flow of the test script. We will use 'Apache log4net' as the mechanism for logging different types of message since it is very easy to use. So let's see how to extend the Automation Framework to include logging.

First of all let's add the required reference to our Automation Framework.

- Right click on the 'References' folder and select Add Reference...
- Click the Browse... button
- Navigate to 'C:\log4net\log4net-1.2.13\bin\net\4.0\release' folder. Remember we extracted the files in 'C:\log4net'.
- Select file 'log4net.dll' as shown in the Figure 3.14.
- Click the Add button and then press OK.

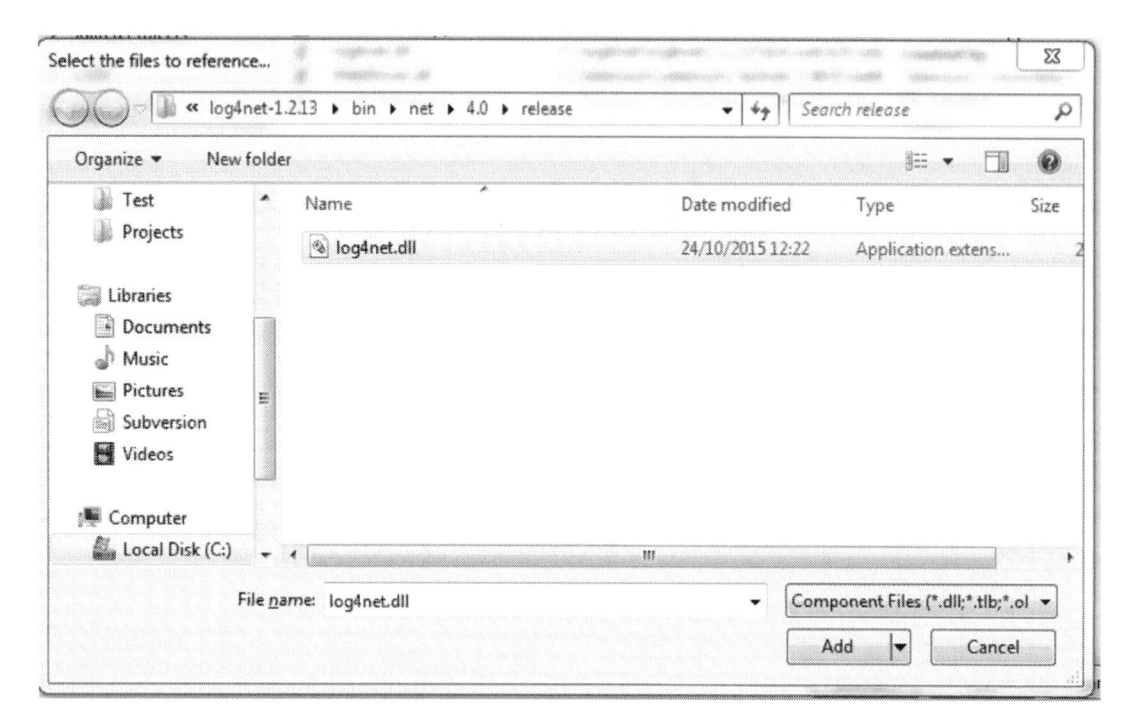

Figure 3.14: Adding log4net Reference

3.3.1 Logging To Console Via Logger

Firstly, let's log our messages to the Console (Text) Output window.

3.3.1.1 Updating Utility Functions

Open the 'Utility.cs' file and make the changes as shown in Listing 3.14.

☞ Note that the listing shows the complete code of 'Utility.cs' file created so far.

Listing 3.14: 'Utility.cs' - Changes for logging to console

```
/****************************************************************
 * All rights reserved. Copyright 2016 Arkenstone-ltd.com *
 *****************************************************************/
using System;
using OpenQA.Selenium;
using OpenQA.Selenium.Firefox;
using OpenQA.Selenium.Support.UI;
using NUnit.Framework;
using log4net;

namespace WebTesting
{
    public static class Utility
    {
        public static string TestResult;
        public static readonly ILog Log = ←
            ↪ LogManager.GetLogger(System.Reflection. ←
            ↪ MethodBase.GetCurrentMethod().DeclaringType);

        public static IWebDriver SetupDriver(this ←
            ↪ IWebDriver driver)
        {
            try
            {
                driver = new FirefoxDriver();
                return driver;
            }
            catch (Exception ex)
            {
                Log.Error("SetupDriver Exception: " + ←
                    ↪ ex.ToString());
                throw ex;
```

```csharp
29                }
30            }
31
32            private static IWebElement FindElementEx(this ↵
                  IWebDriver driver, By by, int timeoutInSeconds)
33            {
34                string ex = "";
35
36                try
37                {
38                    if (timeoutInSeconds > 0)
39                    {
40                        var wait = new WebDriverWait(driver, ↵
                              TimeSpan.FromSeconds ↵
                              (timeoutInSeconds));
41                        Log.Info("Find Element: " + by + "     ↵
                              timeoutInSeconds: " + ↵
                              timeoutInSeconds);
42                        return wait.Until(drv => ↵
                              drv.FindElement(by));
43                    }
44
45                    Log.Info("Find Element: " + by + "     ↵
                          timeoutInSeconds: " + ↵
                          timeoutInSeconds);
46                    return driver.FindElement(by);
47                }
48                catch (NoSuchElementException)
49                {
50                    ex += "Object not found " + by.ToString();
51                    Log.Error(ex);
52                    throw new NoSuchElementException(ex);
53                }
54            }
55
56            public static void FindElementAndClick(this ↵
                  IWebDriver driver, By by)
57            {
58                string ex = "";
59
60                try
61                {
62                    FindElementEx(driver, by, ↵
                          Config.OBJECT_TIMEOUT_SECS).Click();
63                    Log.Info("Clicking : " + by);
```

```
64                    return;
65                }
66                catch (NoSuchElementException)
67                {
68                    ex += "Unable to Click " + by;
69                    Log.Error(ex);
70                    throw new NoSuchElementException(ex);
71                }
72            }
73
74            public static void FindElementAndSendKeys(this ↵
                      ↪ IWebDriver driver, By by, string val)
75            {
76                string ex = "";
77
78                try
79                {
80                    FindElementEx(driver, by, ↵
                          ↪ Config.OBJECT_TIMEOUT_SECS). ↵
                          ↪ SendKeys(val);
81                    Log.Info("SendKeys Value: " + val);
82                    return;
83                }
84                catch (NoSuchElementException)
85                {
86                    ex += "Unable to Sendkeys " + val;
87                    Log.Error(ex);
88                    throw new NoSuchElementException(ex);
89                }
90            }
91
92            public static void ReportExpectedVsActual(this ↵
                      ↪ IWebDriver driver, string expected, string ↵
                      ↪ actual)
93            {
94                if (expected.Trim() == actual.Trim())
95                {
96                    Log.Info("[Expected: ]" + expected + " ↵
                          ↪         [Actual: ]" + actual + "              ↵
                          ↪ [Step Passed]");
97                }
98                else
99                {
100                   Log.Error("[Expected: ]" + expected + " ↵
                          ↪         [Actual: ]" + actual + "              ↵
```

```
                            ↪ [Step Failed]");
101                    TestResult = Config.FAIL;
102                }
103            }
104
105            public static void ReportResult()
106            {
107                if (TestResult == Config.FAIL)
108                {
109                    Assert.Fail("Test failed, please check ↵
                            ↪ error log.");
110                }
111            }
112        }
113 }
```

Line 9: Additional import required to support the logging mechanism.
Line 16: Logger declaration which is used throughout the Automation Framework.
Line 41, 45, 63, 81 and 96: Change the 'Console.WriteLine' calls to the new logger function 'Log.Info' to display an **informational** message.
Line 27, 51, 69, 87 and 100: Change the 'Console.WriteLine' calls to the new logger function 'Log.Error' to log an **error** message.

3.3.1.2 Updating Tests

Now make changes to the 'TestLogins.cs' file as shown in Listing 3.15.

Listing 3.15: 'TestLogins.cs' - Changes for logging to console via logger

```
1  /*****************************************************************
2   * All rights reserved. Copyright 2016 Arkenstone-ltd.com         *
3   *****************************************************************/
4  using System;
5  using OpenQA.Selenium;
6  using NUnit.Framework;
7  using WebTesting.Pages;
8
9  namespace WebTesting.Tests
10 {
11     public class TestLogins
12     {
13         IWebDriver driver;
14
15         [SetUp]
16         public void Setup()
```

```
17          {
18              driver = Utility.SetupDriver(driver);
19              Utility.TestResult = Config.PASS;
20          }
21
22          [TearDown]
23          public void Teardown()
24          {
25              if (TestContext.CurrentContext.Result.Status ↵
                    ↪ == TestStatus.Failed)
26              {
27                  Utility.Log.Error("***** Teardown ==> ↵
                        ↪ Test FAILED ***** =>" + ↵
                        ↪ TestContext.CurrentContext.Test. ↵
                        ↪ FullName);
28              }
29              else if ↵
                    ↪ (TestContext.CurrentContext.Result.Status ↵
                    ↪ == TestStatus.Passed)
30              {
31                  Utility.Log.Info("PASS => " + ↵
                        ↪ TestContext.CurrentContext.Test. ↵
                        ↪ FullName);
32              }
33
34              driver.Quit();
35          }
36
37          [Test]
38          public void LoginUser()
39          {
40              try
41              {
42                  Utility.Log.Info("Starting test: " + ↵
                        ↪ TestContext.CurrentContext.Test. ↵
                        ↪ FullName);
43
44                  var home = new pageHome(driver);
45                  home.Visit();
46                  home.ClickLogin();
47
48                  var login = new pageLogin(driver);
49                  login.Login("Tester", "Tester123");
50                  Utility.ReportResult();
51              }
```

```
52                catch (Exception exception)
53                {
54                    Utility.Log.Error("exception" + ↵
                         ↪ exception.ToString());
55                    throw exception;
56                }
57    }
58
59        [Test]
60        public void LoginAdminUser()
61        {
62            try
63            {
64                Utility.Log.Info("Starting test: " + ↵
                     ↪ TestContext.CurrentContext.Test. ↵
                     ↪ FullName);
65
66                var home = new pageHome(driver);
67                home.Visit();
68                home.ClickLogin();
69
70                var login = new pageLogin(driver);
71                login.Login("Admin", "Admin123");
72                Utility.ReportResult();
73            }
74            catch (Exception exception)
75            {
76                Utility.Log.Error("exception" + ↵
                     ↪ exception.ToString());
77                throw exception;
78            }
79        }
80    }
81 }
```

Line 27: Changes the 'Console.WriteLine' call to the new logger function 'Log.Error' to log an **error** message.

Line 31: Changes the 'Console.WriteLine' call to the new logger function 'Log.Info' to display an **informational** message.

Line 40 and 52: Adds Try-Catch to capture any errors and logs them.

Line 42 and 64: Adds code to the beginning of each test to announce its start.

Line 62 and 74: Adds Try-Catch to capture any errors and logs them.

3.3.1.3 Creating Configuration File

We now need to create a configuration file for the logger. Open Notepad (or any text editor of your choice) and create a 'log4net.config' file in folder 'C:\WebTesting\WebTesting' as shown in the Listing 3.16.

Listing 3.16: 'log4net.config' - Code for logging to console

```xml
<?xml version="1.0" encoding="utf-8" ?>
<log4net>
  <appender name="Console"
    type="log4net.Appender.ConsoleAppender" >
    <layout type="log4net.Layout.PatternLayout">
      <conversionPattern value="%date{yyyy-MM-dd
        HH:mm:ss.fff} [%thread] %-5level %logger -
        %message%newline" />
    </layout>
  </appender>
  <root>
    <level value="DEBUG" />
    <appender-ref ref="Console" />
  </root>
</log4net>
```

The 'log4net.config' file has three main components:

- **Appender** - is responsible for publishing the logging information to the preferred destination. We define the `appender` first with a name, which in our case is 'Console'. This is the name used to refer to the appender in the rest of the configuration file. The `type` method is used to choose which console stream to print messages to, which in our case is 'ConsoleAppender'.

- **Layout** - is responsible for formatting the logging information in the preferred style. The format of the result depends on the conversion pattern. For example, in our case we use '[%thread]' which outputs the name of the thread that generated the logging event.

- **Logger** - is responsible for capturing the logging information to the desired appender. We have a 'root' logger that is configured to `level` 'DEBUG'. The appender 'Console' is attached to it. Since all loggers inherit from the 'root', all debug or higher messages from all the loggers will be printed to the 'Console' appender.

3.3.1.4 Updating Assembly

In the 'Solution Explorer', under Properties, double click on the 'AssemblyInfo.cs' file and add the following code to the bottom:

Listing 3.17: 'AssemblyInfo.cs' - Changes for logging to console

```
1 [assembly: log4net.Config.XmlConfigurator(ConfigFile = ↵
    @"C:\WebTesting\WebTesting\log4net.config", Watch = ↵
    true)]
```

Line 1: Please note the two parameters:
   Parameter `ConfigFile` - name of the configuration file to be used with log4net.
   Parameter `Watch` - reloads the configuration each time the file is modified.

3.3.1.5 Executing Tests

Now rebuild the 'WebTesting.dll' and re-run both the tests via NUnit. You will see an output as shown in Figure 3.15. The Console window now shows a date and timestamp for each test step. The test steps that were logged as 'Log.Info' are displayed as INFO. Each test also announces its start.

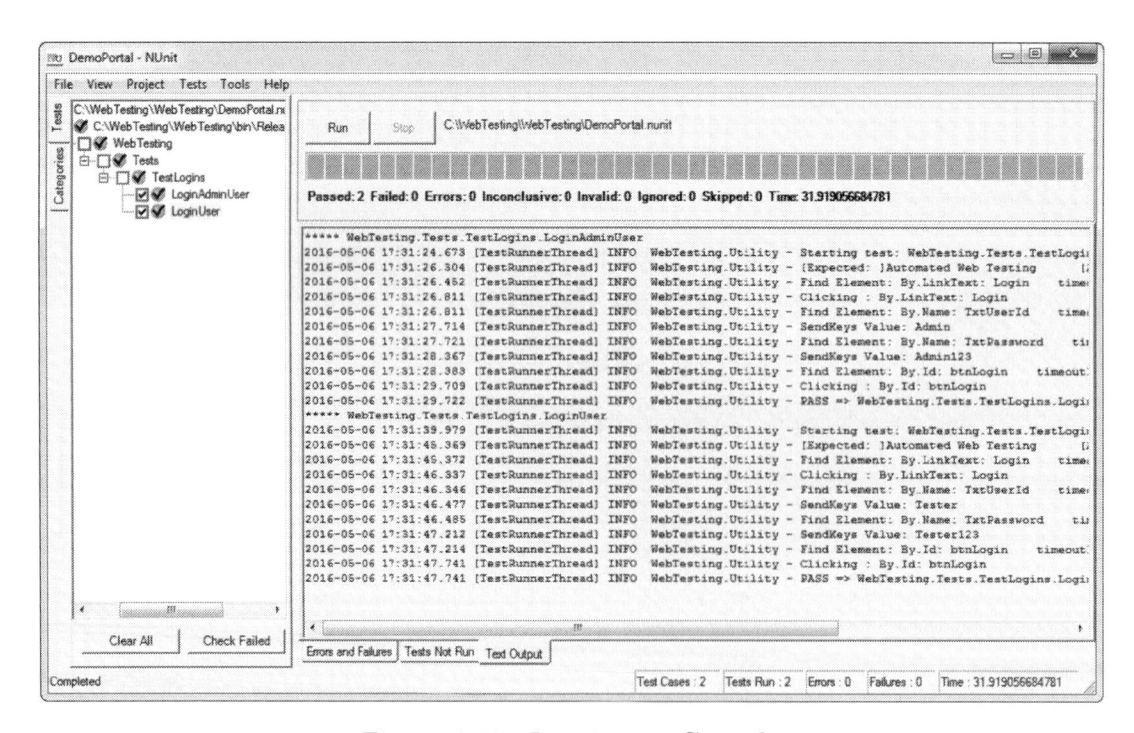

Figure 3.15: Logging to Console

3.3.2 Logging To A File

So far we have extended the Automation Framework to use our own logger to log additional information in the Console window. However, it lacks one important feature which is the ability to save the test results to an output file (because the console is refreshed as soon as you run the next test and all of the information is lost).

We need all the test results to be saved automatically so that we can refer to them at a later stage for investigation purposes. Also, those results are your proof that the test has been executed and can be used as evidence or for audit purposes. I personally log a lot of information for each test execution as it often proves very handy when you need to refer back to logs at a later stage. So, how do we extend our Automation Framework to automatically save logs at the end of the test execution? Here is how to save the console information in a log file.

3.3.2.1 Updating Configuration File

Modify 'log4net.config' which was created previously, as shown in Listing 3.18.

Listing 3.18: 'log4net.config' - Updated code

```
 1  <?xml version="1.0" encoding="utf-8" ?>
 2  <log4net>
 3    <appender name="Console"
          type="log4net.Appender.ConsoleAppender" >
 4      <layout type="log4net.Layout.PatternLayout">
 5        <conversionPattern value="%date{yyyy-MM-dd
            HH:mm:ss.fff} [%thread] %-5level %logger -
            %message%newline" />
 6      </layout>
 7    </appender>
 8    <appender name="CsvFileAppender"
          type="log4net.Appender.FileAppender">
 9      <file value="DetailLog.csv" />
10      <appendToFile value="false" />
11      <lockingModel
          type="log4net.Appender.FileAppender+MinimalLock" />
12      <layout type="log4net.Layout.PatternLayout">
13        <header value="DateTime, Thread, Level, Logger,
            Message&#13;&#10;" />
14        <conversionPattern value="%date{yyyy-MM-dd
            HH:mm:ss.fff}, [%thread], %-5level, %logger,
            %message%newline" />
15      </layout>
16    </appender>
17    <root>
```

```
18      <level value="DEBUG" />
19      <appender-ref ref="Console" />
20      <appender-ref ref="CsvFileAppender" />
21    </root>
22  </log4net>
```

Let's see what changes have been made to the 'log4net.config' file.

- We have defined a new 'Appender' called 'CsvFileAppender' that writes to a file 'DetailLog.csv'.

- We have set the append mode to 'false' so that the file will be cleared before new records are written to it.

- We have created a header row for the log file.

- We are using a similar layout pattern as the Console but with commas inserted after each field to facilitate the CSV file creation.

- Under 'Loggers', we have attached 'CsvFileAppender' appender to the 'root'.

- Since all the loggers inherit from the 'root', all trace or higher messages from our logger will be logged to the file.

3.3.2.2 Detail Log File

Now rebuild the 'WebTesting.dll' and re-run both the tests via NUnit. Go to folder 'C:\WebTesting\WebTesting'. You will see a 'DetailLog.csv' file as shown in Figure 3.16.

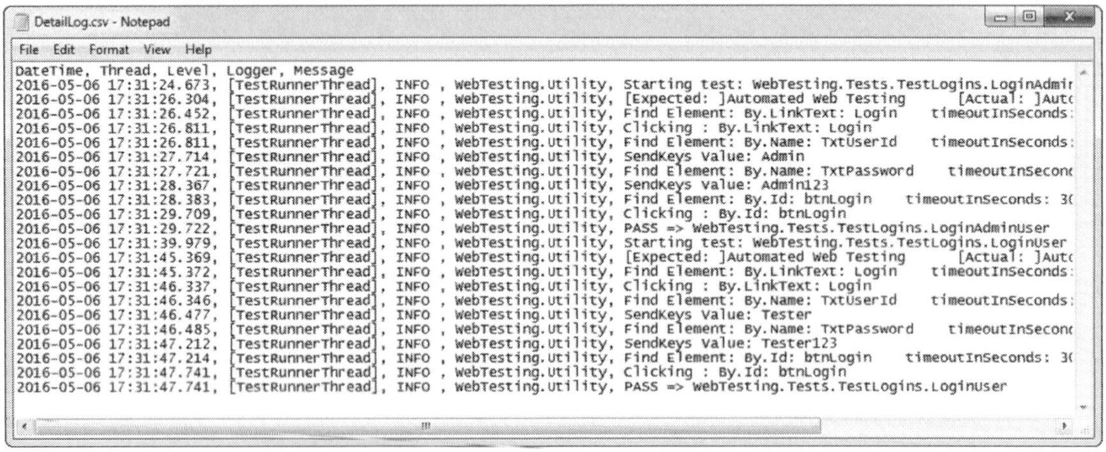

Figure 3.16: Log File - DetailLog.csv

If you are using Excel to open the CSV file, you may need to format the first column i.e. DateTime as **'dd-mmm-yyyy hh:mm:ss.000'** to display it properly. Here are the steps:

- Select the DateTime column in Excel.
- Right click and select Format Cells...
- In the 'Number' Tab select 'Custom' under Category.
- Specify the format under Type as 'dd-mmm-yyyy hh:mm:ss.00' as shown in Figure 3.17
- Click the OK button. The entries should display properly in Excel now!

Figure 3.17: Excel - Format DateTime

Now all of the runtime console information is also available in the 'DetailLog.csv' file. However, we still have the problem of this log file being overwritten every time we run the test. So, we need to save a copy of this file after each test is executed.

3.3.2.3 Configuration Parameters

First of all, add new declarations to the 'Config.cs' file as shown in Listing 3.19.

Listing 3.19: 'Config.cs' - Add new declarations

```
public static string CURRENT_LOGFILE = "";
```

```
2  public static string ResultFolder = ↵
       Environment.CurrentDirectory.Replace(@"bin\Release", ↵
       @"Logs\") + "Results_" + ↵
       DateTime.Now.ToString("dd_MMM_yyyy HH_mm_ss", ↵
       System.Globalization.CultureInfo. ↵
       GetCultureInfo("en-GB"));
```

Line 1: Configuration variable to hold name of the current log file. It has been defaulted to no value but we will construct the file name later on.

Line 2: Configuration variable to hold name of the result folder. We construct the folder name during run-time i.e.

- Get the current directory name - "C:\WebTesting\WebTesting\bin\Release".
- Replace "bin\Release" in it by "Logs\" to give us "C:\WebTesting\WebTesting\Logs\"
- Add folder name "Results_" to it with current date and timestamp to give it a unique name.

3.3.2.4 Utility Functions

Now we define a new generic function in the Utility file as follows:

SaveLogFile - Saves a log file by the name specified in the parameter	
Input Parameters	*fileName*	File name to be used for saving the log file
Return Value	*void*	Returns nothing.

Add Listing 3.20 code to the 'Utility.cs' file.

Listing 3.20: 'Utility.cs' - Code for SaveLogFile

```
1  using System.IO;
2
3  public static void SaveLogFile(string fileName)
4  {
5      Utility.Log.Info("SaveLogFile... ");
6      string logName = "DetailLog.csv";
7      string sourcePath = ↵
           Environment.CurrentDirectory.Replace( ↵
           @"bin\Release", @"");
8
9      var targetPath = Config.ResultFolder;
10     if (!Directory.Exists(targetPath))
11     {
12         Directory.CreateDirectory(targetPath);
```

```
13      }
14
15      string sourceFile = ↵
           ↪ System.IO.Path.Combine(sourcePath, logName);
16      string destFile = System.IO.Path.Combine(targetPath, ↵
           ↪ fileName + DateTime.Now.ToString("_dd_MMM_yyyy ↵
           ↪ HH_mm_ss", System.Globalization.CultureInfo. ↵
           ↪ GetCultureInfo("en-GB")) + ".csv");
17
18      Config.CURRENT_LOGFILE = destFile;
19      System.IO.File.Copy(sourceFile, destFile, true);
20      System.IO.File.Delete(sourceFile);
21  }
```

Line 1: New import required to support the functionality
Line 6: Log file name same as defined in the 'log4net.config' file
Line 7: Path where the file "DetailLog.csv" resides i.e. "C:\WebTesting\WebTesting\"
Line 9: Target folder set to `Config.ResultFolder` as we constructed earlier.
Line 10: Creates the target folder if it doesn't exist.
Line 15: Combines the source path with the file name giving us
"C:\WebTesting\WebTesting\DetailLog.csv".
Line 16: Combines the target path with the file (supplied as an argument) and appends current date timestamp to it.
Line 18: Sets the configuration variable `CURRENT_LOGFILE` to the path filename constructed above.
Line 19: Copies the source path filename to the destination path filename. Note the true parameter which is to overwrite destination file if it exists.
Line 20: Deletes the source file.

3.3.2.5 Updating Tests

Let's make some further modifications to 'TestLogins.cs' as shown in Listing 3.21.

Listing 3.21: 'TestLogins.cs' - changes for saving to a log file

```
1  [TearDown]
2  public void Teardown()
3  {
4      if (TestContext.CurrentContext.Result.Status == ↵
           ↪ TestStatus.Failed)
5      {
6          Utility.Log.Error("***** Teardown ==> Test FAILED ↵
               ↪ ***** =>" + ↵
               ↪ TestContext.CurrentContext.Test.FullName);
```

```
 7      }
 8      else if (TestContext.CurrentContext.Result.Status ==
            ↪ TestStatus.Passed)
 9      {
10          Utility.Log.Info("PASS => " +
                ↪ TestContext.CurrentContext.Test.FullName);
11      }
12
13      driver.Quit();
14
15      Utility.SaveLogFile(TestContext.CurrentContext.Test.
            ↪ FullName.Substring(17) + " (" +
            ↪ TestContext.CurrentContext.Result.Status + ")
            ↪ ");
16 }
```

Line 15: Parameter to the function 'SaveLogFile' identifies the file name to be used for the saving the log file. It also contains the test result status either Pass or Fail.

3.3.2.6 Executing Tests

Now rebuild the 'WebTesting.dll' and re-run both tests via NUnit as we did previously. Navigate to folder 'C:\WebTesting\WebTesting\Logs'. A result folder is created with the Date and Timestamp as shown in Figure 3.18.

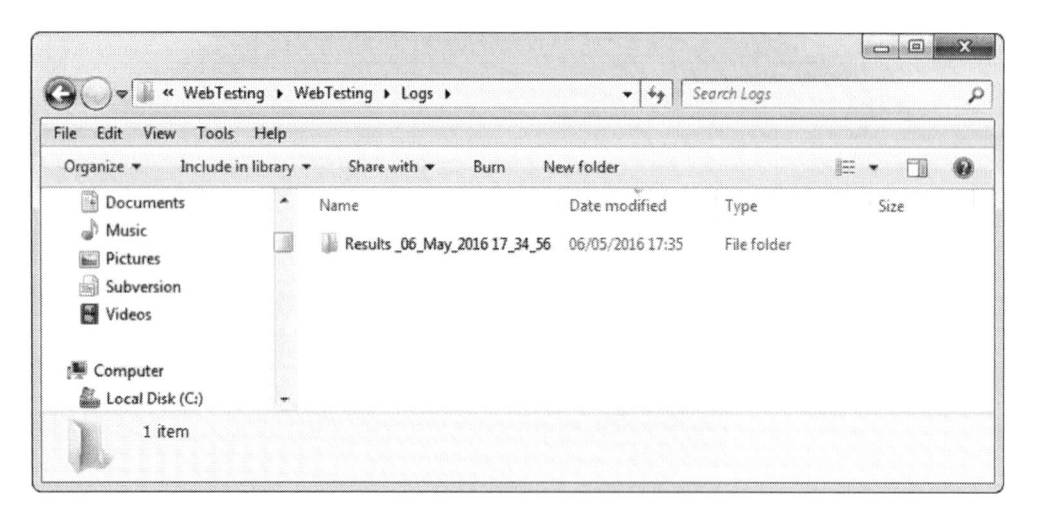

Figure 3.18: The Result Folder

The result folder contains results of each of the individual tests in the CSV format as shown in Figure 3.19. Each file has a Date and Timestamp and also contains the status of the individual test for easy spotting the failures later on.

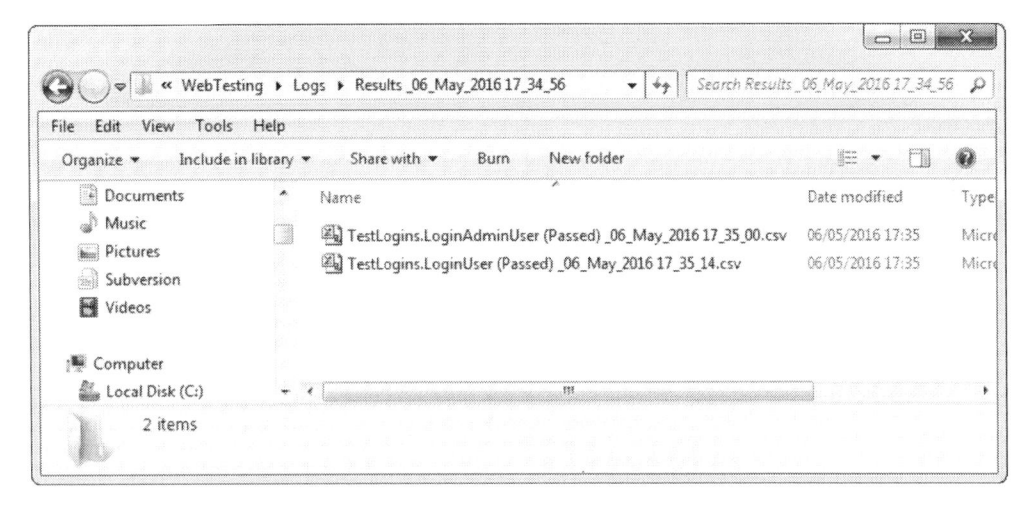

Figure 3.19: CSV Files in the Result Folder

☞ The static string `ResultFolder` is assigned a value when it is used for the first time (i.e. when the first test is executed) in a 'set of tests'. If you have just recompiled the 'WebTesting.dll', NUnit will automatically reload the tests and will create a new result folder during the execution of next 'set of tests'. However, if you want to force a new folder creation at run-time (i.e. assign a new value to the `ResultFolder`) without recompiling the 'WebTesting.dll', just select File ⇒ Reload Tests within the NUnit. This will force creation of a new result folder during the execution of next 'set of tests'.

3.4 Negative Tests - Login

So far we have considered only a positive scenario for the user login i.e. logging in with a valid user id and a valid password. There could be a number of negative scenarios like entering:

- Nothing in the User ID and the Password data entry fields and pressing the Login button.

- A valid User ID but no Password in the data entry fields and pressing the Login button.

- An invalid User ID but no Password in the data entry fields and pressing the Login button.

- Nothing in the User ID and a valid Password in the data entry fields and pressing the Login button.

- Nothing in the User ID and an invalid Password in the data entry fields and pressing the Login button.

- An invalid User ID and Password in the data entry fields and pressing the Login button.

- And so on...

In all these scenarios, the demo website displays the appropriate error messages as shown in Figure 3.20.

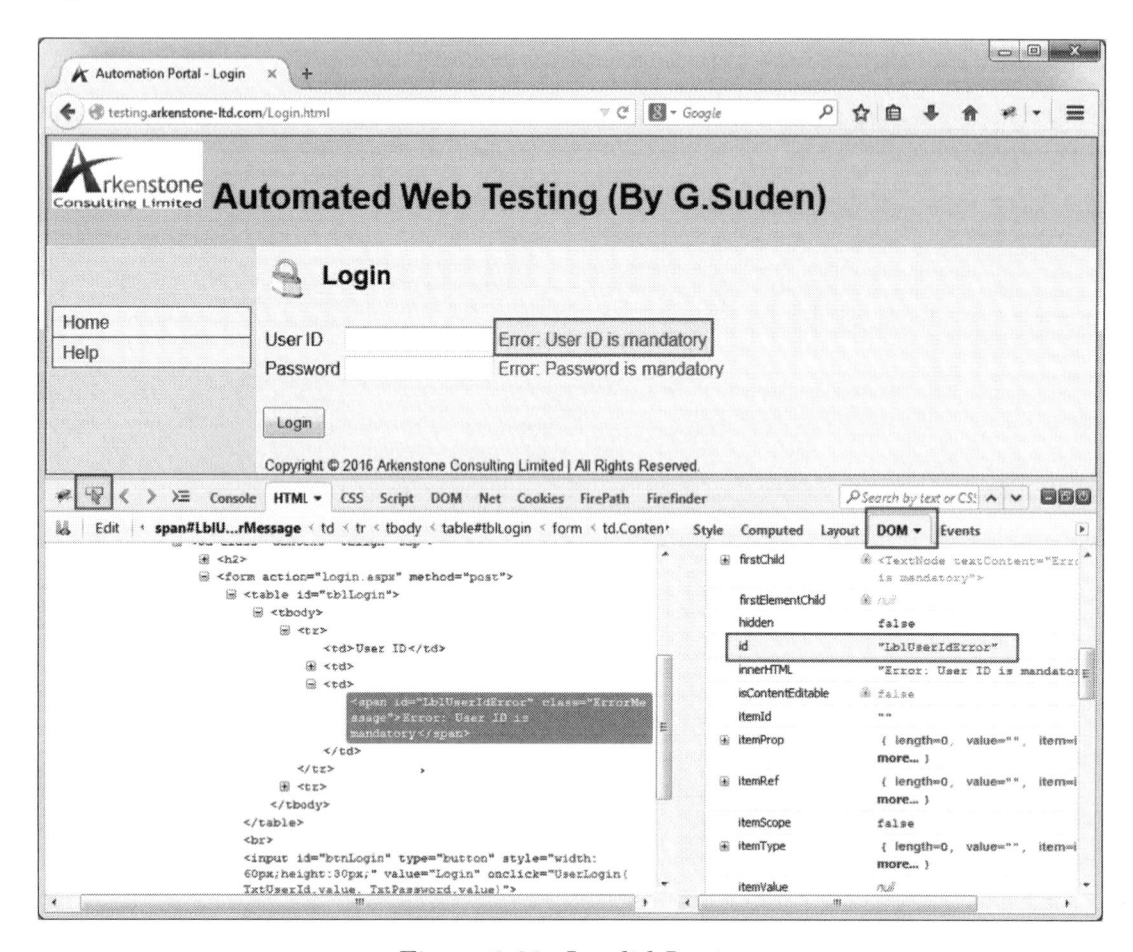

Figure 3.20: Invalid Login

3.4.1 Object Repository

Let us identify additional error message elements in the *Login* screen as shown in the table:

Login Page Elements			
Element	*Type*	*Attribute*	*Value*
User ID	Edit Box	name	TxtUserId
Password	Edit Box	name	TxtPassword
Login	Button	id	btnLogin
User ID Error Msg[†]	Label	id	LblUserIdError
Password Error Msg[†]	Label	id	LblPasswordError

[†]New entries in the table.

Now double click the 'Repository.cs' file in the 'Solution Explorer' and update code for 'LoginScreen' as shown in Listing 3.22.

Listing 3.22: 'Repository.cs' - Repository for Login page

```
1  public static class Login
2  {
3      public static string txtUserId_ByName { get { return 
           "TxtUserId"; } }
4      public static string txtPassword_ByName { get { 
           return "TxtPassword"; } }
5      public static string btnLogin_ById { get { return 
           "btnLogin"; } }
6      public static string lblUserIDError_ById { get { 
           return "LblUserIdError"; } }
7      public static string lblPasswordError_ById { get { 
           return "LblPasswordError"; } }
8  }
```

Line 6: Returns attribute's value "LblUserIdError" for the User ID error message.
Line 7: Returns attribute's value "LblPasswordError" for the Password error message.

3.4.2 Configuration Parameters

Let's add some configuration variables which we will need throughout our Automation Framework. Double click on the 'Config.cs' file in the 'Solution Explorer' and add the Listing 3.23 code to it.

Listing 3.23: 'Config.cs' - Parameters for Error Messages

```
1  public const string USERID_MANDATORY_ERROR = "Error: User 
       ID is mandatory";
```

```
2  public const string PASSWORD_MANDATORY_ERROR = "Error: ↵
      ↪ Password is mandatory";
3  public const string INVALID_USERID_PASSWORD_ERROR = ↵
      ↪ "Error: Invalid User ID or Password";
```

Line 1: Defines a constant string to hold the value of User ID error message.
Line 2: Defines a constant string to hold the value of Password error message.
Line 3: Defines a constant string to hold the value of User ID or Password error message.

3.4.3 Utility Functions

We will now define another generic function as follows:

FindElementAndReturn - Finds an element and returns its reference			
Input Parameters	*driver*	Object driver to control the browser
	by	Mechanism by which to find the element within browser
Return Value	*element*	Returns the element found

Add Listing 3.24 code to the 'Utility.cs' file.

Listing 3.24: 'Utility.cs' - Code for FindElementAndReturn

```
1  public static IWebElement FindElementAndReturn(this ↵
      ↪ IWebDriver driver, By by)
2  {
3      string ex = "";
4  
5      try
6      {
7          Log.Info("Find Element and Return: " + by);
8          return FindElementEx(driver, by, ↵
              ↪ Config.OBJECT_TIMEOUT_SECS);
9      }
10     catch (NoSuchElementException)
11     {
12         ex += "Unable to Find Element and Return: " + by;
13         Log.Error(ex);
14         throw new NoSuchElementException(ex);
15     }
16 }
```

Line 1: Note the return value of type `IWebElement`.
Line 8: Returns the element found.

3.4.4 Page Logic

In order to carry out the negative tests, the following actions will be affected:

Action	Description
`Login()`	Action for user login with given credentials.
`LoginWithInvalidDetails()`	Action for user login with invalid credentials.

Update 'pageLogin.cs' code as shown in Listing 3.25.

Listing 3.25: 'pageLogin.cs' - Updated code

```
1  public void Login(string uid, string pwd)
2  {
3      Utility.FindElementAndSendKeys(driver, ↵
          By.Name(Repository.Login.txtUserId_ByName), ↵
          uid);
4      Utility.FindElementAndSendKeys(driver, ↵
          By.Name(Repository.Login.txtPassword_ByName), ↵
          pwd);
5      Utility.FindElementAndClick(driver, ↵
          By.Id(Repository.Login.btnLogin_ById));
6
7      if (uid.Equals("") && pwd.Equals(""))
8      {
9          Utility.ReportExpectedVsActual(driver, ↵
              Config.USERID_MANDATORY_ERROR, ↵
              Utility.FindElementAndReturn(driver, ↵
              (By.Id(Repository.Login. ↵
              lblUserIDError_ById))).Text);
10         Utility.ReportExpectedVsActual(driver, ↵
              Config.PASSWORD_MANDATORY_ERROR, ↵
              Utility.FindElementAndReturn(driver, ↵
              (By.Id(Repository.Login. ↵
              lblPasswordError_ById))).Text);
11     }
12     else if (uid.Equals(""))
13     {
14         Utility.ReportExpectedVsActual(driver, ↵
              Config.USERID_MANDATORY_ERROR, ↵
              Utility.FindElementAndReturn(driver, ↵
```

```
                    ↪ (By.Id(Repository.Login. ←
                        ↪ lblUserIDError_ById))).Text);
15          }
16          else if (pwd.Equals(""))
17          {
18              Utility.ReportExpectedVsActual(driver, ←
                    ↪ Config.PASSWORD_MANDATORY_ERROR, ←
                    ↪ Utility.FindElementAndReturn(driver, ←
                    ↪ (By.Id(Repository.Login. ←
                        ↪ lblPasswordError_ById))).Text);
19          }
20      }
21
22      public void LoginWithInvalidDetails(string uid, string ←
            ↪ pwd)
23      {
24          Utility.FindElementAndSendKeys(driver, ←
                ↪ By.Name(Repository.Login.txtUserId_ByName), uid);
25          Utility.FindElementAndSendKeys(driver, ←
                ↪ By.Name(Repository.Login.txtPassword_ByName), pwd);
26          Utility.FindElementAndClick(driver, ←
                ↪ By.Id(Repository.Login.btnLogin_ById));
27
28          Utility.ReportExpectedVsActual(driver, ←
                ↪ Config.INVALID_USERID_PASSWORD_ERROR, ←
                ↪ Utility.FindElementAndReturn(driver, ←
                ↪ (By.Id(Repository.Login.lblUserIDError_ById))). ←
                ↪ Text);
29      }
```

Line 7: If the User ID and Password are not entered then ensure that both the messages are displayed i.e. "Error: User ID is mandatory" and "Error: Password is mandatory".
Line 12: Otherwise if the User ID is not entered then ensures that "Error: User ID is mandatory" message is displayed.
Line 16: Otherwise if the Password is not entered then ensures that "Error: Password is mandatory" message is displayed.
Line 22: New function to check login with invalid credentials.
Line 28: Ensures that "Error: Invalid User ID or Password" message is displayed.

3.4.5 Creating Tests

Add the new tests to 'TestLogin.cs' as shown in Listing 3.26.

Listing 3.26: 'TestLogin.cs' - New tests

```csharp
[Test]
public void LoginWithBlankDetails()
{
    try
    {
        Utility.Log.Info("Starting test: " +
            TestContext.CurrentContext.Test.FullName);

        var home = new pageHome(driver);
        home.Visit();
        home.ClickLogin();

        var login = new pageLogin(driver);
        login.Login("", "");
        Utility.ReportResult();
    }
    catch (Exception exception)
    {
        Utility.Log.Error("exception" +
            exception.ToString());
        throw exception;
    }
}

[Test]
public void LoginWithValidUserOnly()
{
    try
    {
        Utility.Log.Info("Starting test: " +
            TestContext.CurrentContext.Test.FullName);

        var home = new pageHome(driver);
        home.Visit();
        home.ClickLogin();

        var login = new pageLogin(driver);
        login.Login("Admin", "");
        Utility.ReportResult();
    }
    catch (Exception exception)
    {
        Utility.Log.Error("exception" +
            exception.ToString());
```

```
41            throw exception;
42        }
43  }
44
45  [Test]
46  public void LoginWithInvalidUserOnly()
47  {
48        try
49        {
50            Utility.Log.Info("Starting test: " + ↵
                  ↪ TestContext.CurrentContext.Test.FullName);
51
52            var home = new pageHome(driver);
53            home.Visit();
54            home.ClickLogin();
55
56            var login = new pageLogin(driver);
57            login.Login("Administrator", "");
58            Utility.ReportResult();
59        }
60        catch (Exception exception)
61        {
62            Utility.Log.Error("exception" + ↵
                  ↪ exception.ToString());
63            throw exception;
64        }
65  }
66
67  [Test]
68  public void LoginWithValidPasswordOnly()
69  {
70        try
71        {
72            Utility.Log.Info("Starting test: " + ↵
                  ↪ TestContext.CurrentContext.Test.FullName);
73
74            var home = new pageHome(driver);
75            home.Visit();
76            home.ClickLogin();
77
78            var login = new pageLogin(driver);
79            login.Login("", "Admin123");
80            Utility.ReportResult();
81        }
82        catch (Exception exception)
```

```
83        {
84            Utility.Log.Error("exception" + ↵
                 ↪ exception.ToString());
85            throw exception;
86        }
87  }
88
89  [Test]
90  public void LoginWithInvalidPasswordOnly()
91  {
92      try
93      {
94          Utility.Log.Info("Starting test: " + ↵
                 ↪ TestContext.CurrentContext.Test.FullName);
95
96          var home = new pageHome(driver);
97          home.Visit();
98          home.ClickLogin();
99
100         var login = new pageLogin(driver);
101         login.Login("", "qqqqq");
102         Utility.ReportResult();
103     }
104     catch (Exception exception)
105     {
106         Utility.Log.Error("exception" + ↵
                 ↪ exception.ToString());
107         throw exception;
108     }
109 }
110
111 [Test]
112 public void LoginWithInvalidUserIdPassword()
113 {
114     try
115     {
116         Utility.Log.Info("Starting test: " + ↵
                 ↪ TestContext.CurrentContext.Test.FullName);
117
118         var home = new pageHome(driver);
119         home.Visit();
120         home.ClickLogin();
121
122         var login = new pageLogin(driver);
123         login.LoginWithInvalidDetails("ABC", "12345");
```

```
124            Utility.ReportResult();
125        }
126        catch (Exception exception)
127        {
128            Utility.Log.Error("exception" + ↵
                ↪ exception.ToString());
129            throw exception;
130        }
131 }
```

Line 2: New test `LoginWithBlankDetails`.
Line 13: Calls the Login function with no values.
Line 24: New test `LoginWithValidUserOnly`.
Line 35: Calls the Login function with a valid user id and no password.
Line 46: New test `LoginWithInvalidUserOnly`.
Line 57: Calls the Login function with an invalid user id and no password.
Line 68: New test `LoginWithValidPasswordOnly`.
Line 79: Calls the Login function with a valid password and no user id.
Line 90: New test `LoginWithInvalidPasswordOnly`.
Line 101: Calls the Login function with an invalid password and no user id.
Line 112: New test `LoginWithInvalidUserIdPassword`.
Line 123: Calls the Login function with an invalid user id and an invalid password.

3.4.6 Executing Tests

Build and execute the tests and you will see a results folder with the outcome as shown in Figure 3.21. The negative login tests written above is not an exhaustive list. You may want to write more negative tests based on the requirements you are testing.

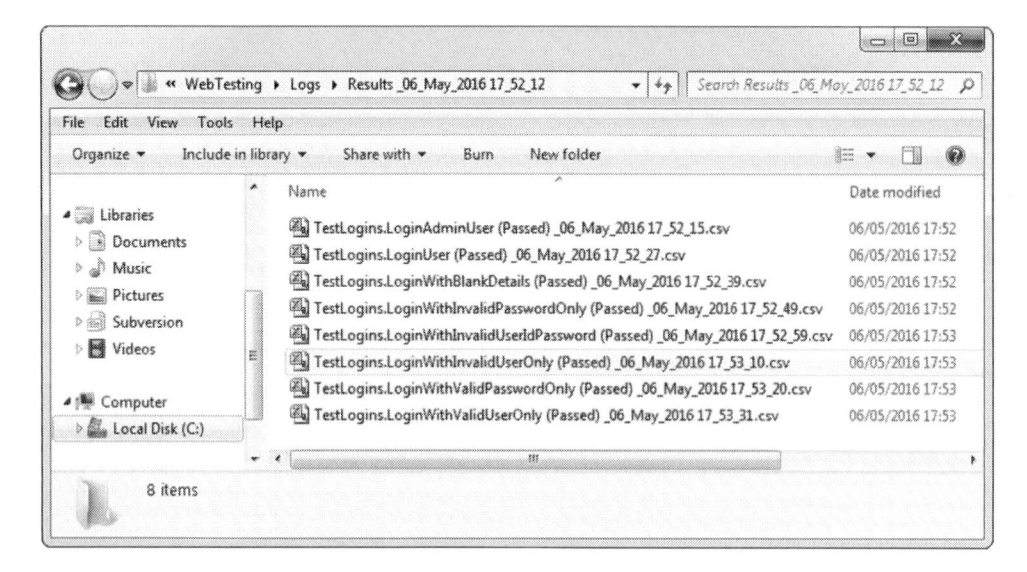

Figure 3.21: Login All Tests

3.5 Saving Screenshots

During the test execution, there may be a number of instances when you may want to save a screenshot of the web page being displayed. For example:
- When a test fails
- When a test step fails
- To capture an event to help you later on

Let's enhance our Automation Framework to save a screenshot of the web page being displayed.

3.5.1 Configuration Parameters

First of all, add a new declaration to the 'Config.cs' file as shown in Listing 3.27.

Listing 3.27: 'Config.cs' - changes for screenshot capture

```
1   public static string ScreenShotFolder = ResultFolder + ↵
    ↪ @"\Screenshots\";
```

Line 1: Defines the screenshot folder which is a subfolder within the result folder.

3.5.2 Utility Functions

Let's now define two new functions in the Utility file as follows:

Wait - Waits for a specified number of seconds		
Input Parameters	*seconds*	Wait time in seconds
Return Value	*void*	Returns nothing.

SaveScreenShot - Saves a screenshot of the web page		
Input Parameters	*driver*	Object driver to control the browser
	screenshotFilename	File name to be used for saving the screenshot
Return Value	*void*	Returns nothing.

Let's make modifications in the 'Utility.cs' file to include new functions as shown in Listing 3.28.

Listing 3.28: 'Utility.cs' - Changes to support the screenshot functionality

```
1   using System.Text;
```

```
2
3   public static void Wait(int seconds)
4   {
5       Log.Info("Waiting: " + seconds + " secs.");
6       System.Threading.Thread.Sleep(seconds * 1000);
7   }
8
9   public static void SaveScreenShot(this IWebDriver driver, ↵
        ↪ string screenshotFilename)
10  {
11      Wait(2);
12
13      var folderLocation = Config.ScreenShotFolder;
14
15      if (!Directory.Exists(folderLocation))
16      {
17          Directory.CreateDirectory(folderLocation);
18      }
19
20      Screenshot screenshot = ↵
            ↪ ((ITakesScreenshot)driver).GetScreenshot();
21      var filename = new StringBuilder(folderLocation);
22      filename.Append(screenshotFilename);
23      filename.Append(DateTime.Now.ToString("_dd_MMM_yyyy ↵
            ↪ HH_mm_ss", System.Globalization.CultureInfo. ↵
            ↪ GetCultureInfo("en-GB")));
24      filename.Append(".png");
25      Utility.Log.Info("Screenshot saved at: " + ↵
            ↪ filename.ToString());
26
27      screenshot.SaveAsFile(filename.ToString(), ↵
            ↪ System.Drawing.Imaging.ImageFormat.Png);
28
29      Wait(2);
30  }
```

Line 1: Additional import required to support the functionality.
Line 6: Suspends the current thread for the specified number of milliseconds.
Line 13: Gets the configured screenshot folder name.
Line 15: Creates the screenshot folder if it doesn't exist.
Line 20: Gets the screenshot.
Line 23: Appends the date and timestamp to the screenshot filename.
Line 27: Saves the screenshot.
Line 29: Waits for 2 seconds to allow the screenshot to be saved.

☞ When you add the above code, Line 27 will show an error as shown in Figure 3.22. Just by clicking on the *Add reference to 'System.Drawing, Version.....'* should add the necessary reference and the error should be resolved.

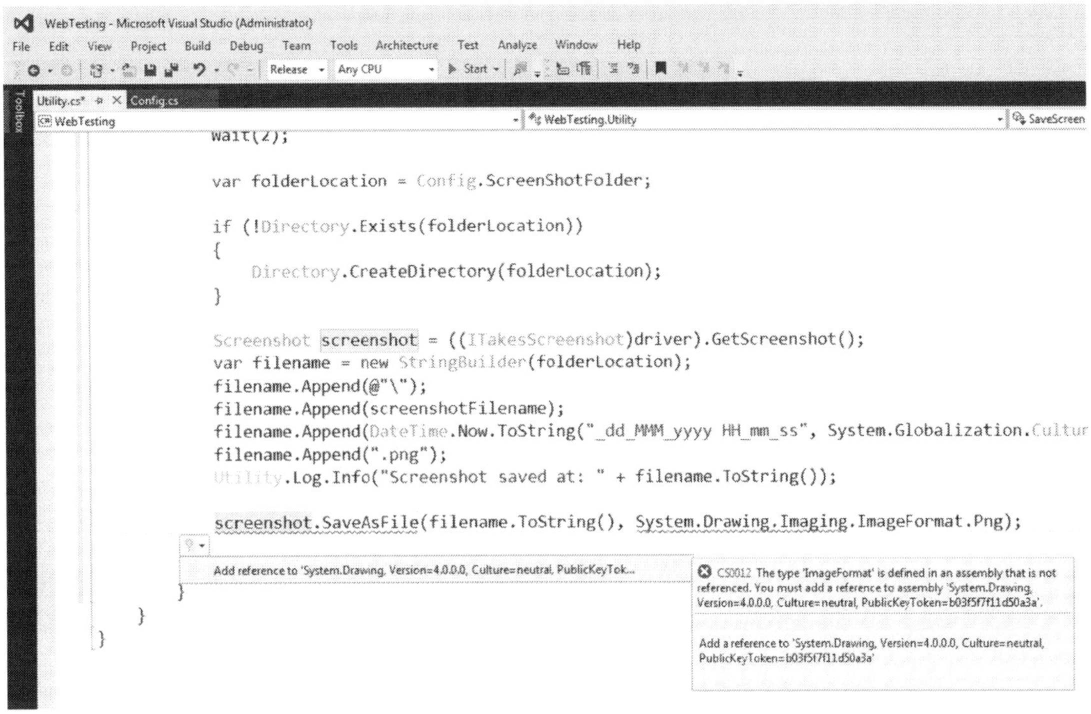

Figure 3.22: Add System Drawing Reference

3.5.3 Capturing A Test Failure

Make changes to the 'TestLogins.cs' file as shown in Listing 3.29 to save a screenshot on `TearDown` in case there is a failure.

Listing 3.29: 'TestLogins.cs' - Changes to support the screenshot functionality

```
1  [TearDown]
2  public void Teardown()
3  {
4      if (TestContext.CurrentContext.Result.Status == ↵
         ↪ TestStatus.Failed)
5      {
6          Utility.Log.Error("***** Teardown ==> Test FAILED ↵
           ↪ ***** =>" + ↵
           ↪ TestContext.CurrentContext.Test.FullName);
7          Utility.SaveScreenShot(driver, ↵
           ↪ TestContext.CurrentContext.Test.Name + "(" + ↵
```

```
                  ↪ TestContext.CurrentContext.Result.Status + ↵
                  ↪ ")");
 8        }
 9        else if (TestContext.CurrentContext.Result.Status == ↵
              ↪ TestStatus.Passed)
10        {
11            Utility.Log.Info("PASS => " + ↵
                  ↪ TestContext.CurrentContext.Test.FullName); ↵
                  ↪
12        }
13
14        driver.Quit();
15
16        Utility.SaveLogFile(TestContext.CurrentContext.Test. ↵
              ↪ FullName.Substring(17) + " (" + ↵
              ↪ TestContext.CurrentContext.Result.Status + ") ↵
              ↪ ");
17 }
```

Line 7: If the test has failed, then calls the function 'SaveScreenShot' to save the screenshot. Note the parameter passed for the screenshot filename which uses the test name and the result status.

Now whenever there is a test failure, a screenshot will be saved in the configured folder.

3.5.4 Capturing A Test Step Failure

Let's make modifications to the 'Utility.cs' file to take a screenshot of the failed test step as shown in Listing 3.30.

Listing 3.30: 'Utility.cs' - Changes to support screenshot functionality

```
1 public static void ReportExpectedVsActual(this IWebDriver ↵
      ↪ driver, string expected, string actual)
2 {
3     if (expected.Trim() == actual.Trim())
4     {
5         Log.Info("[Expected: ]" + expected + "            ↵
              ↪ [Actual: ]" + actual + "          [Step ↵
              ↪ Passed]");
6     }
7     else
8     {
```

```
 9          Log.Error("[Expected: ]" + expected + "        ↵
                ↪ [Actual: ]" + actual + "        [Step ↵
                ↪ Failed]");
10          TestResult = Config.FAIL;
11          SaveScreenShot(driver, ↵
                ↪ TestContext.CurrentContext.Test.FullName + ↵
                ↪ "(Step Failure)");
12      }
13  }
```

Line 11: Saves the screenshot whenever a test step fails.

Now whenever there is a test step failure, a screenshot will be saved in the configured folder.

3.5.5 Capture An Event

Let's enhance the logic of 'pageHome.cs' to capture a screenshot after launching the website. The required changes are shown in Listing 3.31.

Listing 3.31: 'pageHome.cs' - Save screenshot of home page

```
1  using NUnit.Framework;
2
3  public void Visit()
4  {
5      GoToSite();
6      Utility.ReportExpectedVsActual(driver, "Automated Web ↵
             ↪ Testing", driver.Title);
7      Utility.SaveScreenShot(driver, ↵
             ↪ TestContext.CurrentContext.Test.Name);
8  }
```

Line 1: Additional import required to support the functionality.
Line 7: Saves website's *Home* page screenshot.

Now after launching the website, a screenshot of the home page will be saved in the configured folder.

3.5.6 Executing Tests

Now rebuild the 'WebTesting.dll' and execute a test via NUnit. Navigate to the Results folder and you will see a subfolder 'Screenshots' containing the screenshot as shown in Figure 3.23.

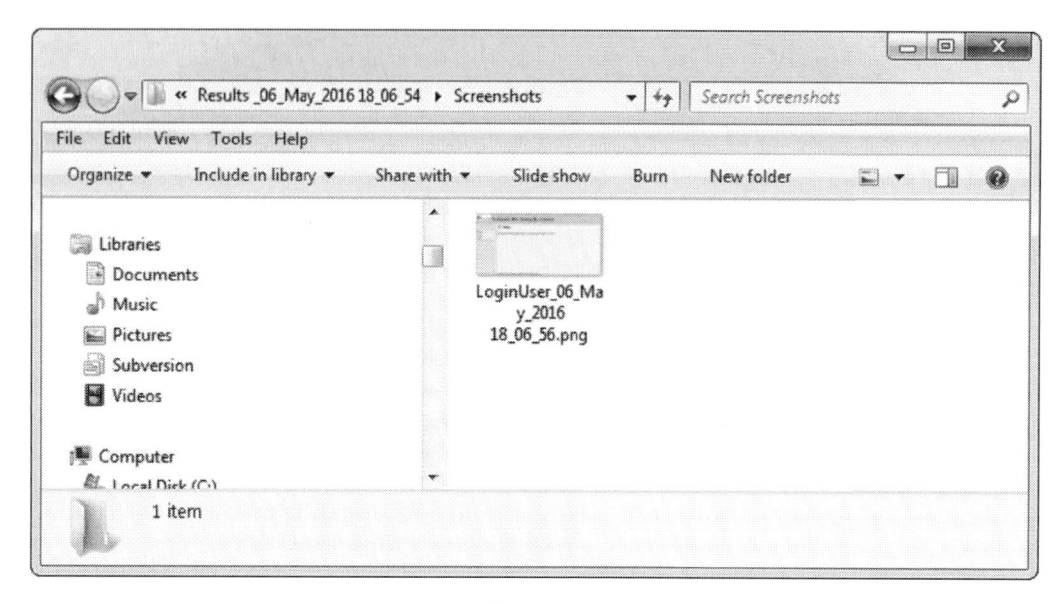

Figure 3.23: Captured Screenshot

3.6 Data Entry - Add Employee

A web page usually contains different types of controls for user interaction. So far we have seen examples on how to interact with Edit Boxes, Command Buttons, Links and Labels (static text). In this section we will learn how to perform data entry tasks on three special types of controls:

- Drop-down ListBox - allows a user to select one item from a predefined list.

- RadioButton - represents a single choice within a limited set of mutually exclusive choices.

- CheckBox - allows a user to pick a combination of options (in contrast, a RadioButton control allows a user to choose from mutually exclusive options.)

We will perform the following Test Scenario to demonstrate the use of above controls:

- Launch the demo website.

- Click on the *Login* link.

- Login with the user 'Tester'.

- Click on the *Add Employee* link.

- Add a new employee.

3.6.1 Object Repository

Let's continue with building the object repository of our demo website. When you login as a Tester user, on successful login, Tester's *Home* Page is displayed as shown in Figure A.4 with the following elements:

\multicolumn{4}{c	}{**Home Page Tester Elements**}
Element	*Type*	*Attribute*	*Value*
Home	Link	text	Home
Add Employee	Link	text	Add Employee
View Employee	Link	text	View Employee
Other	Link	text	Other
Drag-n-Drop	Link	text	Drag-n-Drop
Logout	Link	text	Logout

When you click the *Add Employee* link, the *Add Employee* page is displayed as shown in Figure A.5 with the following elements:

\multicolumn{4}{c	}{**Add Employee Page Elements**}
Element	*Type*	*Attribute*	*Value*
Title	ListBox	name	LbTitle
Name	Edit Box	id	TxtName
Gender	Radio Button	id	RbGender
Date of Birth	Edit Box	name	TxtDOB
Email Address	Edit Box	name	TxtEmail
Contract Job	Checkbox	name	CbContract
Postcode	Edit Box	id	TxtPostcode
Add	Button	id	btnAdd

Now double click the 'Repository.cs' file in the 'Solution Explorer' and add the code for 'HomeTester' and 'EmployeeDetail' as shown in Listing 3.32.

Listing 3.32: 'Repository.cs' - Repository for Tester's Home and Employee Detail pages

```
1  public static class HomeTester
2  {
3      public static string lnkHome_ByLinkText { get {
           return "Home"; } }
4      public static string lnkAddEmployee_ByLinkText { get
           { return "Add Employee"; } }
5      public static string lnkViewEmployee_ByLinkText { get
           { return "View Employee"; } }
```

```
 6       public static string lnkOther_ByLinkText { get { ↵
            ↪ return "Other"; } }
 7       public static string lnkDragnDrop_ByLinkText { get { ↵
            ↪ return "Drag-n-Drop"; } }
 8       public static string lnkLogout_ByLinkText { get { ↵
            ↪ return "Logout"; } }
 9   }
10
11   public static class EmployeeDetail
12   {
13       public static string lbTitle_ByName { get { return ↵
            ↪ "LbTitle"; } }
14       public static string txtName_ById { get { return ↵
            ↪ "TxtName"; } }
15       public static string rbGender_ById { get { return ↵
            ↪ "RbGender"; } }
16       public static string txtDateOfBirth_ByName { get { ↵
            ↪ return "TxtDOB"; } }
17       public static string txtEmail_ByName { get { return ↵
            ↪ "TxtEmail"; } }
18       public static string cbContractJob_ByName { get { ↵
            ↪ return "CbContract"; } }
19       public static string txtPostcode_ById { get { return ↵
            ↪ "TxtPostcode"; } }
20       public static string btnAdd_ById { get { return ↵
            ↪ "btnAdd"; } }
21
22   }
```

Line 1: Elements of the Tester's *Home* Page.
Line 11: Elements of the *Add Employee* Page.

3.6.2 Configuration Parameters

Let's add some configuration parameters which we will need later on. Double click on the 'Config.cs' file in the 'Solution Explorer' and add the Listing 3.33 code to it.

Listing 3.33: 'Config.cs' - Parameters for adding an employee

```
1  public const string RECORD_ADDED_SUCCESSFULLY = "Record ↵
      ↪ added successfully.";
2  public const string MALE = "1";
3  public const string FEMALE = "2";
```

Line 1: Defines a string equivalent of the message displayed in the browser when a record has been added successfully.
Line 2: Defines a string equivalent of the Male gender selection.
Line 3: Defines a string equivalent of the Female gender selection.

3.6.3 Utility Functions

Let's now define some new functions in the Utility file as follows:

SelectOptionInList - Selects an option in the ListBox		
Input Parameters	*driver*	Object driver to control the browser
	by	Mechanism by which to find the element within the browser
	optionText	Option to be selected in the ListBox
Return Value	*void*	Returns nothing.

SelectRadioButton - Selects a RadioButton option		
Input Parameters	*driver*	Object driver to control the browser
	elementId	Id attribute of the RadioButton
	option	RadioButton option to be selected
Return Value	*void*	Returns nothing.

HandleAlert - Handles the alert window displayed on the current web page		
Input Parameters	*driver*	Object driver to control the browser
	msg	Message to be verified on the alert window
Return Value	*void*	Returns nothing.

Add Listing code to the 'Utility.cs' file.

Listing 3.34: 'Utility.cs' - New functions

```
public static void SelectOptionInList(this IWebDriver 
    driver, By by, string optionText)
{
    Log.Info("SelectOptionInList: " + optionText);
    Utility.Wait(1);
    new SelectElement(FindElementEx(driver, by, 
        Config.OBJECT_TIMEOUT_SECS)).
        SelectByText(optionText);
}

```

```
 8  public static void SelectRadioButton(this IWebDriver ↵
        driver, string elementId, string option)
 9  {
10      Log.Info("SelectRadioButton: " + option);
11      FindElementAndClick(driver, By.XPath("(//input[@id='" ↵
          + elementId + "'])[" + option + "]"));
12  }
13
14  public static void HandleAlert(this IWebDriver driver, ↵
        string msg)
15  {
16      Log.Info("HandleAlert: " + msg);
17      String alertText = driver.SwitchTo().Alert().Text;
18      ReportExpectedVsActual(driver, msg, alertText);
19      driver.SwitchTo().Alert().Accept();
20  }
```

Line 5: Selects the ListBox option by its text.
Line 11: Uses XPath to select the element and the option.
Line 17: Gets the text displayed in the alert window.
Line 18: Compares it with the expected text and reports the outcome.
Line 19: Accepts the alert.

3.6.4 Page Logic

3.6.4.1 Home Page - Tester

The Tester's *Home* page of our demo website will have the following actions:

Action	Description
ClickHome()	This action will navigate to the Tester's *Home* page.
ClickAddEmployee()	This action will navigate to the *Add Employee* page.
ClickViewEmployee()	This action will navigate to the *View Employee* page.
ClickOther()	This action will navigate to the *Other* page.
ClickDragnDrop()	This action will navigate to the *Drag-n-Drop* page.
ClickLogout()	This action will log the user out and navigate to the generic *Home* page.

Let's now add the page logic for the Tester's *Home* page. In the 'Solution Explorer', right click on the 'Pages' folder, click Add ⇒ Class. Type name as 'pageTesterHome.cs' and click the Add button. Add Listing 3.35 code to it.

Listing 3.35: 'pageTesterHome.cs' - Code for Tester's Home page

```
/***************************************************************
 * All rights reserved. Copyright 2016 Arkenstone-ltd.com      *
 ***************************************************************/
using System;
using OpenQA.Selenium;

namespace WebTesting.Pages
{
    class pageTesterHome : pageBase
    {
        private static readonly String Url = Config.URL;

        public pageTesterHome(IWebDriver driver) :
            base(driver, Url)
        {
        }

        public void ClickHome()
        {
            Utility.FindElementAndClick(driver,
                By.LinkText(Repository.
                HomeTester.lnkHome_ByLinkText));
        }

        public void ClickAddEmployee()
        {
            Utility.FindElementAndClick(driver,
                By.LinkText(Repository.
                HomeTester.lnkAddEmployee_ByLinkText));
        }

        public void ClickViewEmployee()
        {
            Utility.FindElementAndClick(driver,
                By.LinkText(Repository.
                HomeTester.lnkViewEmployee_ByLinkText));
        }
```

```
31
32          public void ClickOther()
33          {
34              Utility.FindElementAndClick(driver, ↵
                   ↪ By.LinkText(Repository. ↵
                   ↪ HomeTester.lnkOther_ByLinkText));
35          }
36
37          public void ClickDragnDrop()
38          {
39              Utility.FindElementAndClick(driver, ↵
                   ↪ By.LinkText(Repository. ↵
                   ↪ HomeTester.lnkDragnDrop_ByLinkText));
40          }
41
42          public void ClickLogout()
43          {
44              Utility.FindElementAndClick(driver, ↵
                   ↪ By.LinkText(Repository. ↵
                   ↪ HomeTester.lnkLogout_ByLinkText));
45          }
46      }
47 }
```

Ensure that you are using the right repository elements i.e. 'Repository.HomeTester' in all the function calls.

3.6.4.2 Add Employee Page

The *Add Employee* page of our demo website will have the following actions:

Action	Description
AddEmployee()	This action will add a new employee.

Let's now add the page logic for the *Add Employee* page. In the 'Solution Explorer', right click on the 'Pages' folder, click Add ⇒ Class. Type the name as 'pageTesterAddEmployee.cs' and click the Add button. Add Listing 3.36 code to it.

Listing 3.36: 'pageTesterAddEmployee.cs' - Code for the Add Employee page

```
1 /*************************************************************
2  * All rights reserved. Copyright 2016 Arkenstone-ltd.com *
```

```csharp
 ************************************************************/
using System;
using OpenQA.Selenium;

namespace WebTesting.Pages
{
    class pageTesterAddEmployee : pageBase
    {
        private static readonly String Url = Config.URL;

        public pageTesterAddEmployee(IWebDriver driver) :
            base(driver, Url)
        {
        }

        public void AddEmployee()
        {
            Utility.SelectOptionInList(driver,
                By.Name(Repository.EmployeeDetail.
                lbTitle_ByName), "Miss");
            Utility.FindElementAndSendKeys(driver,
                By.Id(Repository.EmployeeDetail.
                txtName_ById), "Nicola");
            Utility.SelectRadioButton(driver,
                Repository.EmployeeDetail.rbGender_ById,
                Config.FEMALE);
            Utility.FindElementAndSendKeys(driver,
                By.Name(Repository.EmployeeDetail.
                txtDateOfBirth_ByName), "01/02/1977");
            Utility.FindElementAndSendKeys(driver,
                By.Name(Repository.EmployeeDetail.
                txtEmail_ByName),
                "Nicola@arkenstone-ltd.com");
            Utility.FindElementAndClick(driver,
                By.Name(Repository.EmployeeDetail.
                cbContractJob_ByName));
            Utility.FindElementAndSendKeys(driver,
                By.Id(Repository.EmployeeDetail.
                txtPostcode_ById), "SN1 5GS");

            Utility.FindElementAndClick(driver,
                By.Id(Repository.EmployeeDetail.
                btnAdd_ById));

            Utility.HandleAlert(driver,
```

```
30                }
31         }
32 }
```
              ↪ Config.RECORD_ADDED_SUCCESSFULLY);

Line 19: Selects ListBox option "Miss".
Line 21: Selects RadioButton option "Female".
Line 24: Selects CheckBox "Contract Job".
Line 29: Handles the alert message and ensures that the message "Record added successfully." is displayed.

3.6.5 Creating Tests

Let's now add a new test which will test the general user's functionality i.e. Tester. In the 'Solution Explorer', right click on the 'Tests' folder, click Add ⇒ Class. Type the name as 'TestGeneralUser.cs' and click the Add button. Add Listing 3.37 code to it.

Listing 3.37: 'TestGeneralUser.cs' - Code to test general user

```
1  /***************************************************************
2   * All rights reserved. Copyright 2016 Arkenstone-ltd.com *
3   ***************************************************************/
4  using System;
5  using OpenQA.Selenium;
6  using NUnit.Framework;
7  using WebTesting.Pages;
8
9  namespace WebTesting.Tests
10 {
11     public class TestGeneralUser
12     {
13         IWebDriver driver;
14
15         [SetUp]
16         public void Setup()
17         {
18             driver = Utility.SetupDriver(driver);
19             Utility.TestResult = Config.PASS;
20         }
21
22         [TearDown]
23         public void Teardown()
24         {
```

```csharp
            if (TestContext.CurrentContext.Result.Status
                == TestStatus.Failed)
            {
                Utility.Log.Error("***** Teardown ==>
                    Test FAILED ***** =>" +
                    TestContext.CurrentContext.Test.
                    FullName);
                Utility.SaveScreenShot(driver,
                    TestContext.CurrentContext.Test.Name
                    + "(" +
                    TestContext.CurrentContext.Result.
                    Status + ")");
            }
            else if
                (TestContext.CurrentContext.Result.Status
                == TestStatus.Passed)
            {
                Utility.Log.Info("PASS => " +
                    TestContext.CurrentContext.Test.
                    FullName);
            }

            driver.Quit();

            Utility.SaveLogFile(TestContext.CurrentContext.
                Test.FullName.Substring(17) + " (" +
                TestContext.CurrentContext.Result.Status
                + ") ");
        }

        [Test]
        public void AddEmployee()
        {
            try
            {
                Utility.Log.Info("Starting test: " +
                    TestContext.CurrentContext.Test.
                    FullName);

                var home = new pageHome(driver);
                home.Visit();
                home.ClickLogin();

                var login = new pageLogin(driver);
                login.Login("Tester", "Tester123");
```

```
53
54                        var homeTester = new pageTesterHome(driver);
55                        homeTester.ClickAddEmployee();
56
57                        var emp = new pageTesterAddEmployee(driver);
58                        emp.AddEmployee();
59
60                        Utility.ReportResult();
61                    }
62                    catch (Exception exception)
63                    {
64                        Utility.Log.Error("exception" + ↵
                            ↪ exception.ToString());
65                        throw exception;
66                    }
67                }
68            }
69 }
```

Line 40: New test **AddEmployee**.

Line 55: Clicks the *Add Employee* link on the Tester's *Home* Page.

Line 58: Calls the **AddEmployee** function in the page logic.

3.6.6 Executing Tests

Execute the test 'AddEmployee' and you will see an output as shown in Figure 3.24. The test should execute successfully.

> Please note that the demo website has no database attached to it. It only mimics the record addition and just gives a success message to facilitate our automated testing.

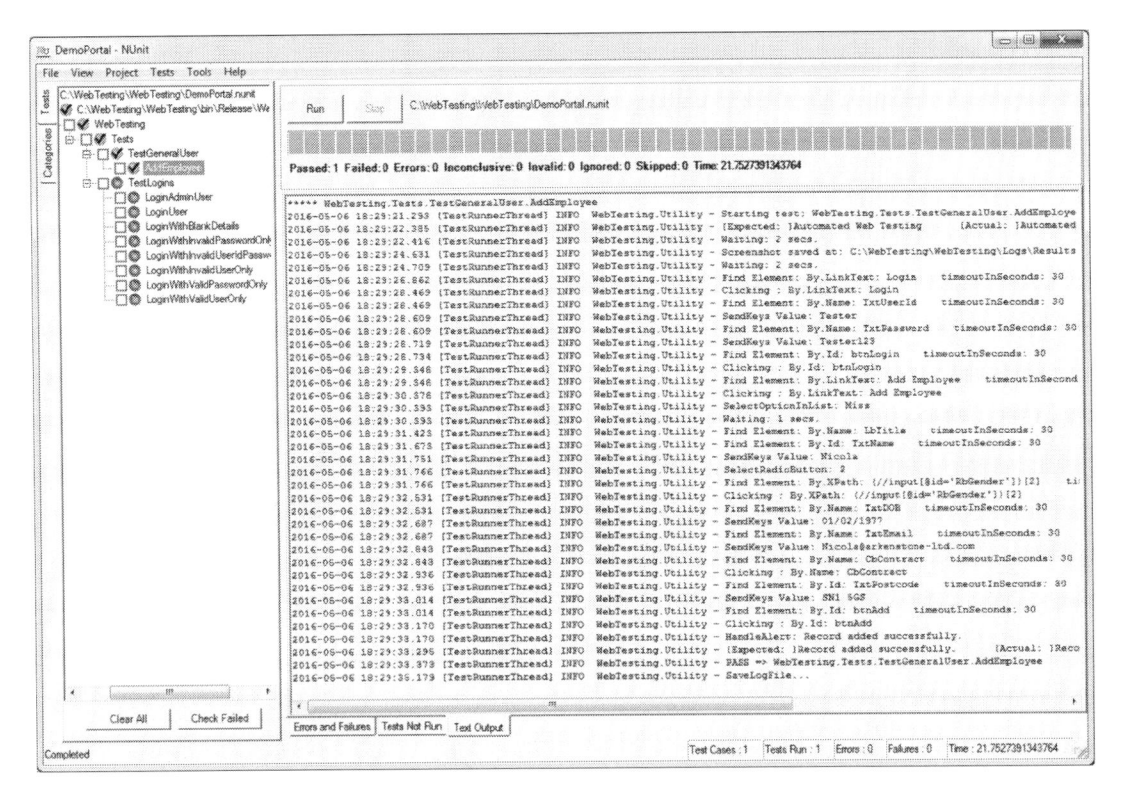

Figure 3.24: Console Output - Add Employee

3.7 Data Verification - View Employee

In this section we will learn how to perform verification tasks on different type of controls that we have used so far. We will perform the following Test Scenario to demonstrate the use of these controls:

- Launch the demo website.

- Click on the *Login* link.

- Login with the user 'Tester'.

- Click on the *View Employee* link.

- Verify the employee's details displayed on the web page.

3.7.1 Object Repository

The *View Employee* page as shown in Figure A.7 has the following screen elements:

| View Employee Page Elements ||||
Element	*Type*	*Attribute*	*Value*
Employee Id	Edit Box	name	TxtEmpId
Title	ListBox	name	LbTitle
Name	Edit Box	id	TxtName
Gender	Radio Button	id	RbGender
Date of Birth	Edit Box	name	TxtDOB
Email Address	Edit Box	name	TxtEmail
Contract Job	Checkbox	name	CbContract
Postcode	Edit Box	id	TxtPostcode
Close	Button	value	Close

You will have noticed that all of these screen elements have same attribute values as the *Add Employee* screen (except Employee Id and Close button which weren't present in the *Add Employee* screen). These elements are displayed in this screen as read-only because it is just for viewing purpose. So what we will do is reuse the repository we already have i.e. reuse the 'EmployeeDetail' repository and add any additional elements to it as shown in Listing 3.38.

Listing 3.38: 'Repository.cs' - Updated code for Employee Detail page

```
1  public static class EmployeeDetail
2  {
3      public static string txtEmployeeId_ByName { get { ↵
            ↪ return "TxtEmpId"; } }
4      public static string lbTitle_ByName { get { return ↵
            ↪ "LbTitle"; } }
5      public static string txtName_ById { get { return ↵
            ↪ "TxtName"; } }
6      public static string rbGender_ById { get { return ↵
            ↪ "RbGender"; } }
7      public static string txtDateOfBirth_ByName { get { ↵
            ↪ return "TxtDOB"; } }
8      public static string txtEmail_ByName { get { return ↵
            ↪ "TxtEmail"; } }
9      public static string cbContractJob_ByName { get { ↵
            ↪ return "CbContract"; } }
10     public static string txtPostcode_ById { get { return ↵
            ↪ "TxtPostcode"; } }
11     public static string btnAdd_ById { get { return ↵
            ↪ "btnAdd"; } }
12     public static string btnClose_ByCSS { get { return ↵
```

```
                ↪ "input[value=Close]"; } }
13 }
```

Line 3: Repository declaration for the Employee Id field.
Line 12: Repository declaration for the Close button. Note that we will access it by CSS Selector as denoted by the suffix _ByCSS.

3.7.2 Configuration Parameters

Let's add some new configuration parameters which we will need later on. Double click on the 'Config.cs' file in the 'Solution Explorer' and add the Listing 3.39 code to it.

Listing 3.39: 'Config.cs' - Parameters to support view employee

```
1 public const string TRUE = "True";
2 public const string FALSE = "False";
```

Line 1: Defines a string constant for the "True" value.
Line 2: Defines a string constant for the "False" value.

3.7.3 Utility Functions

Let's now define some new functions in the Utility file as follows:

FindElementsEx - Core function that finds any type of elements		
Input Parameters	*driver*	Object driver to control the browser
	by	Mechanism by which to find elements within the browser
	timeoutInSeconds	Timeout in seconds
Return Value	*elements*	Returns a collection of the elements found.

FindElementsAndReturn - Find elements and returns its collection		
Input Parameters	*driver*	Object driver to control the browser
	by	Mechanism by which to find elements within the browser
Return Value	*elements*	Returns a collection of the elements found.

GetSelectedRadioButton - Gets the selected RadioButton within a group		
Input Parameters	*driver*	Object driver to control the browser
	elementId	RadioButton group id
Return Value	*rbValue*	Returns the selected RadioButton, -1 otherwise.

Add Listing 3.40 code to the 'Utility.cs' file.

Listing 3.40: 'Utility.cs' - New functions

```
1  using System.Collections.ObjectModel;
2
3  private static ReadOnlyCollection<IWebElement>
       FindElementsEx(this IWebDriver driver, By by, int
       timeoutInSeconds)
4  {
5      string ex = "";
6
7      try
8      {
9          if (timeoutInSeconds > 0)
10         {
11             var wait = new WebDriverWait(driver,
                   TimeSpan.FromSeconds(timeoutInSeconds));
12             Log.Info("Find Objects: " + by + "
                   timeoutInSeconds: " + timeoutInSeconds);
13             return wait.Until(drv =>
                   (drv.FindElements(by).Count > 0) ?
                   drv.FindElements(by) : null);
14         }
15
16         Log.Info("Find Objects: " + by + "
               timeoutInSeconds: " + timeoutInSeconds);
17         return driver.FindElements(by);
18     }
19     catch (NoSuchElementException)
20     {
21         ex += "Elements not found " + by.ToString();
22         Log.Error(ex);
23         throw new NoSuchElementException(ex);
24     }
25 }
```

```
26
27  public static ReadOnlyCollection<IWebElement> ↵
        ↪ FindElementsAndReturn(this IWebDriver driver, By by)
28  {
29      string ex = "";
30
31      try
32      {
33          Log.Info("Find Elements and Return: " + by);
34          return FindElementsEx(driver, by, ↵
                ↪ Config.OBJECT_TIMEOUT_SECS);
35      }
36      catch (NoSuchElementException)
37      {
38          ex += "Unable to Find Elements and Return: " + by;
39          Log.Error(ex);
40          throw new NoSuchElementException(ex);
41      }
42  }
43
44  public static int GetSelectedRadioButton(this IWebDriver ↵
        ↪ driver, string elementId)
45  {
46      Log.Info("GetSelectedRadioButton... ");
47      int rbValue = 0;
48
49      ReadOnlyCollection<IWebElement> rbCollection = ↵
            ↪ FindElementsAndReturn(driver, By.Id(elementId));
50
51      foreach (IWebElement rbElement in rbCollection)
52      {
53          rbValue++;
54          if (rbElement.GetAttribute("checked") == "true")
55              return rbValue;
56      }
57
58      return -1;   //Not found
59  }
```

Line 1: Additional import required to support the functionality.

Line 13: If a timeout was specified then waits until timeout and returns the collection of elements found.

Line 17: Otherwise just returns the collection of elements found without any wait.

Line 34: Calls the core function 'FindElementsEx' to return the collection of elements found.

Line 51: Loops through the collection.
Line 54: Returns value of the selected item.

3.7.4 Page Logic

The *View Employee* page of our demo website will have the following actions:

Action	Description
VerifyEmployee()	This action will verify the employee's details displayed on the web page.

Let's now write the page logic to verify an employee. In the 'Solution Explorer', right click on the 'Pages' folder, click Add ⇒ Class. Type the name as 'pageTesterViewEmployee.cs' and click the Add button. Add Listing 3.41 code to it.

Listing 3.41: 'pageTesterViewEmployee.cs' - Code for View Employee page

```
/***************************************************************
 * All rights reserved. Copyright 2016 Arkenstone-ltd.com       *
 ***************************************************************/
using System;
using OpenQA.Selenium;

namespace WebTesting.Pages
{
    class pageTesterViewEmployee : pageBase
    {
        private static readonly String Url = Config.URL;

        public pageTesterViewEmployee(IWebDriver driver)
            : base(driver, Url)
        {
        }

        public void VerifyEmployee()
        {
            Utility.ReportExpectedVsActual(driver,
                "10004",
                Utility.FindElementAndReturn(driver,
                By.Name(Repository.EmployeeDetail.
                txtEmployeeId_ByName)).
                GetAttribute("Value"));
```

```
20
21              Utility.ReportExpectedVsActual(driver, ↵
                  ↪ "Miss", ↵
                  ↪ Utility.FindElementAndReturn(driver, ↵
                  ↪ By.Name(Repository.EmployeeDetail. ↵
                  ↪ lbTitle_ByName)).Text);
22
23              Utility.ReportExpectedVsActual(driver, "Sarah ↵
                  ↪ Smith", ↵
                  ↪ Utility.FindElementAndReturn(driver, ↵
                  ↪ By.Id(Repository.EmployeeDetail. ↵
                  ↪ txtName_ById)).GetAttribute("Value"));
24
25              Utility.ReportExpectedVsActual(driver, ↵
                  ↪ Config.FEMALE, ↵
                  ↪ Utility.GetSelectedRadioButton(driver, ↵
                  ↪ Repository.EmployeeDetail. ↵
                  ↪ rbGender_ById).ToString());
26
27              Utility.ReportExpectedVsActual(driver, ↵
                  ↪ "25/12/1982", ↵
                  ↪ Utility.FindElementAndReturn(driver, ↵
                  ↪ By.Name(Repository.EmployeeDetail. ↵
                  ↪ txtDateOfBirth_ByName)). ↵
                  ↪ GetAttribute("Value"));
28
29              Utility.ReportExpectedVsActual(driver, ↵
                  ↪ "sarah.smith@arkenstone-ltd.com", ↵
                  ↪ Utility.FindElementAndReturn(driver, ↵
                  ↪ By.Name(Repository.EmployeeDetail. ↵
                  ↪ txtEmail_ByName)). ↵
                  ↪ GetAttribute("Value"));
30
31              Utility.ReportExpectedVsActual(driver, ↵
                  ↪ Config.FALSE, ↵
                  ↪ Utility.FindElementAndReturn(driver, ↵
                  ↪ By.Name(Repository.EmployeeDetail. ↵
                  ↪ cbContractJob_ByName)).Selected. ↵
                  ↪ ToString());
32
33              Utility.ReportExpectedVsActual(driver, "SN1 ↵
                  ↪ 5GS", ↵
                  ↪ Utility.FindElementAndReturn(driver, ↵
                  ↪ By.Id(Repository.EmployeeDetail. ↵
                  ↪ txtPostcode_ById)). ↵
```

```
34                   ↪ GetAttribute("Value"));

35             Utility.FindElementAndClick(driver, ↵
                   ↪ By.CssSelector(Repository.EmployeeDetail. ↵
                   ↪ btnClose_ByCSS));
36         }
37     }
38 }
```

Line 19: Utility function call to 'FindElementAndReturn' returns the reference to the Employee Id element. We retrieve its "Value" attribute and compare it with the expected value of "10004" via the 'ReportExpectedVsActual' function. A similar logic is performed for Line 23, 27, 29 and 33.

Line 21: Utility function call to 'FindElementAndReturn' returns the reference to the ListBox Title element. We retrieve its "Text" and compare it with the expected value of "Miss" via the 'ReportExpectedVsActual' function.

Line 25: Utility function call to 'GetSelectedRadioButton' returns the selected Gender RadioButton. We then compare it with the expected value of Config.FEMALE via the 'ReportExpectedVsActual' function.

Line 31: Utility function call to 'FindElementAndReturn' returns the reference to the CheckBox element. We then retrieve its "Selected" attribute and compare it with the expected value of Config.FALSE via the 'ReportExpectedVsActual' function.

Line 31: Finds the Close button by "CssSelector".

3.7.5 Creating Tests

Let's now add a new test in 'TestGeneralUser.cs' as shown in Listing 3.37 code to it.

Listing 3.42: 'TestGeneralUser.cs' - Additional test to verify an employee

```
1  [Test]
2  public void VerifyEmployee()
3  {
4      try
5      {
6          Utility.Log.Info("Starting test: " + ↵
               ↪ TestContext.CurrentContext.Test.FullName);
7
8          var home = new pageHome(driver);
9          home.Visit();
```

```
10          home.ClickLogin();
11
12          var login = new pageLogin(driver);
13          login.Login("Tester", "Tester123");
14
15          var homeTester = new pageTesterHome(driver);
16          homeTester.ClickViewEmployee();
17
18          var emp = new pageTesterViewEmployee(driver);
19          emp.VerifyEmployee();
20
21          Utility.ReportResult();
22      }
23      catch (Exception exception)
24      {
25          Utility.Log.Error("exception" + ↵
              ↪ exception.ToString());
26          throw exception;
27      }
28 }
```

Line 1: New test `VerifyEmployee`.
Line 16: Clicks the *View Employee* link on Tester's *Home* Page.
Line 19: Calls the `VerifyEmployee` function in the page logic.

3.7.6 Executing Test

Execute the test and you will see an output as shown in Figure 3.25.

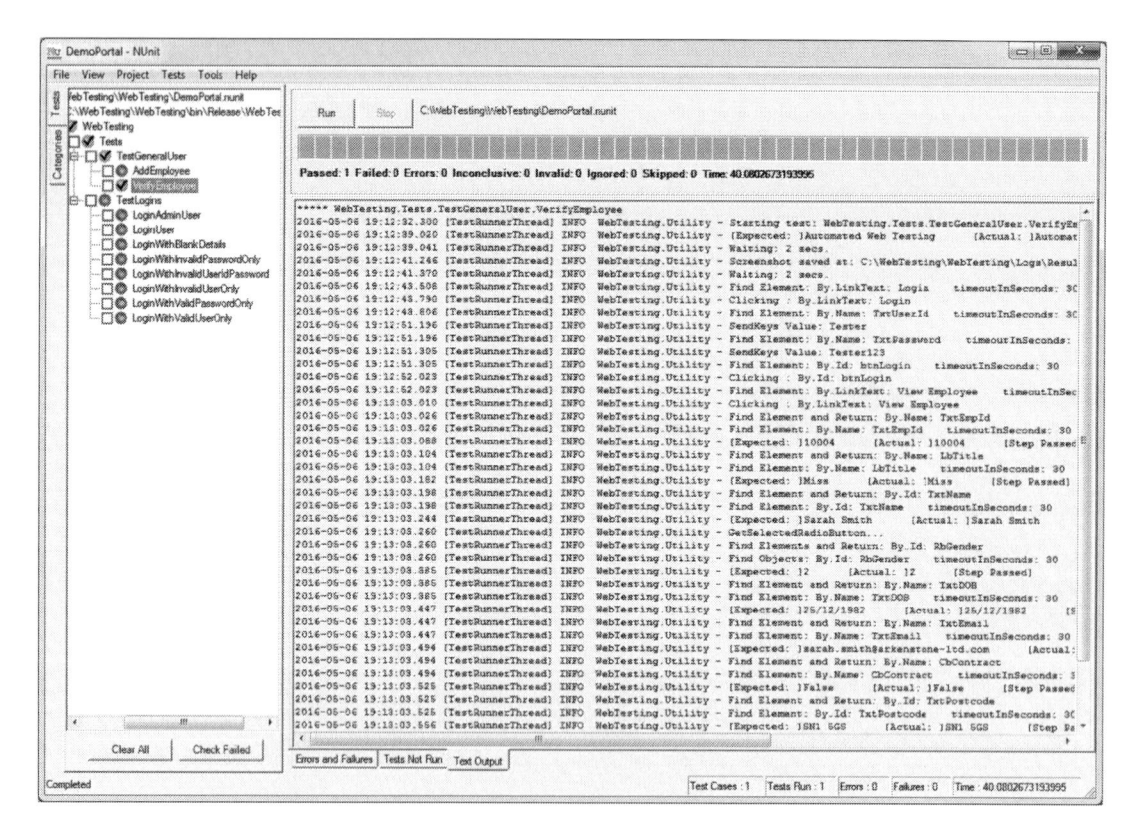

Figure 3.25: Console Output - Verify Employee

Chapter 4

Automate With Databases

Automate With Databases

In this chapter, we will learn about how to:

- *Setup a testing database*
- *Perform verification tasks using data fetched from the testing database tables*
- *Perform verification tasks using random data fetched from the database tables*
- *Create a Test Result Summary file*

So let's get on with it...

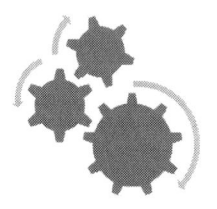

Usually every website is connected to a database which stores information related to it. Various pages in a website provide the means to:

- create new data e.g. add a new employee
- edit existing data e.g. change the employees' details
- view existing data e.g. view employee's details
- delete data e.g. delete an employee's record
- display reports in various formats e.g. employee's details in a tabular form

When performing the testing of a website, a tester has to refer to the database tables to verify that the information displayed in the web page is same as stored in the database tables e.g. if you login as an Admin user in our demo website and go to *Reports* link, an

'Employee Report by Gender' page is displayed as shown in Figure A.11. As a tester, you must ensure that the 'counts by gender' displayed in the web page report match the counts retrieved by the SQL Query executed on the database table. This is a very simple example but in real life testing you may have to deal with more complex reports with database verifications. In this book we will cover how we can perform these verifications via automated testing i.e. retrieve data from the database table and compare it with the contents in the web page.

The demo website has no database attached to it but to demonstrate this kind of automated testing, we will set up a test database on our local workstation and mimic that the demo website is fetching data from your local database. We will essentially create the same data in your local database as is in the static demo website e.g. record level data for the 'Employee Report by Gender' report. The data will then be fetched from your local database in SQL Query and compared with the demo website.

4.1 Setting up Testing Database

You can use 'SQL Server Management Studio', as I have done, to execute the SQL scripts provided in this section. I have used the 'sa' login to execute the scripts but you can use any login that has the database create/update permission. The script creates the required database 'WebTesting' in the 'C:\WebTesting\WebTestingDB' folder. However, you can change the destination folder in the script to your preferred location. Make sure the folder 'C:\WebTesting\WebTestingDB' exists before you execute the first SQL script.

> As a tester in a real environment, you probably wouldn't need to create this database as it should already exist but here we need to create this database as we need something to automate our tests against. If you don't understand any of the code here, don't worry. You are not a database administrator! Just execute these SQL scripts to create the environment you need to be able to start writing your automated tests.

4.1.1 Creating The Database

Use Listing 4.1 SQL to create the 'WebTesting' database.

Listing 4.1: Creating the 'WebTesting' Database

```
1  /**************************************************************
2   * All rights reserved. Copyright 2016 Arkenstone-ltd.com      *
3   **************************************************************/
4  USE [master]
5  GO
```

```
 6
 7  CREATE DATABASE [WebTesting] ON  PRIMARY
 8    ( NAME = N'WebTesting', FILENAME = ↵
         ↪ N'C:\WebTesting\WebTestingDB\WebTesting.mdf' , ↵
         ↪ SIZE = 5504KB , MAXSIZE = UNLIMITED , FILEGROWTH = ↵
         ↪ 10%)
 9     LOG ON
10    ( NAME = N'WebTesting_log', FILENAME = ↵
         ↪ N'C:\WebTesting\WebTestingDB\WebTesting.ldf' , ↵
         ↪ SIZE = 3456KB , MAXSIZE = UNLIMITED , FILEGROWTH = ↵
         ↪ 10%)
11    GO
12
13  ALTER DATABASE [WebTesting] SET COMPATIBILITY_LEVEL = 90
14
15  IF (1 = FULLTEXTSERVICEPROPERTY('IsFullTextInstalled'))
16  begin
17      EXEC [WebTesting].[dbo].[sp_fulltext_database] @action ↵
         ↪ = 'disable'
18  end
19
20  ALTER DATABASE [WebTesting] SET ANSI_NULL_DEFAULT OFF
21  ALTER DATABASE [WebTesting] SET ANSI_NULLS OFF
22  ALTER DATABASE [WebTesting] SET ANSI_PADDING OFF
23  ALTER DATABASE [WebTesting] SET ANSI_WARNINGS OFF
24  ALTER DATABASE [WebTesting] SET ARITHABORT OFF
25  ALTER DATABASE [WebTesting] SET AUTO_CLOSE ON
26  ALTER DATABASE [WebTesting] SET AUTO_CREATE_STATISTICS ON
27  ALTER DATABASE [WebTesting] SET AUTO_SHRINK OFF
28  ALTER DATABASE [WebTesting] SET AUTO_UPDATE_STATISTICS ON
29  ALTER DATABASE [WebTesting] SET CURSOR_CLOSE_ON_COMMIT OFF
30  ALTER DATABASE [WebTesting] SET CURSOR_DEFAULT  GLOBAL
31  ALTER DATABASE [WebTesting] SET CONCAT_NULL_YIELDS_NULL OFF
32  ALTER DATABASE [WebTesting] SET NUMERIC_ROUNDABORT OFF
33  ALTER DATABASE [WebTesting] SET QUOTED_IDENTIFIER OFF
34  ALTER DATABASE [WebTesting] SET RECURSIVE_TRIGGERS OFF
35  ALTER DATABASE [WebTesting] SET ENABLE_BROKER
36  ALTER DATABASE [WebTesting] SET ↵
         ↪ AUTO_UPDATE_STATISTICS_ASYNC OFF
37  ALTER DATABASE [WebTesting] SET ↵
         ↪ DATE_CORRELATION_OPTIMIZATION OFF
38  ALTER DATABASE [WebTesting] SET TRUSTWORTHY OFF
39  ALTER DATABASE [WebTesting] SET ALLOW_SNAPSHOT_ISOLATION OFF
40  ALTER DATABASE [WebTesting] SET PARAMETERIZATION SIMPLE
41  ALTER DATABASE [WebTesting] SET READ_COMMITTED_SNAPSHOT OFF
```

```
42  ALTER DATABASE [WebTesting] SET HONOR_BROKER_PRIORITY OFF
43  ALTER DATABASE [WebTesting] SET READ_WRITE
44  ALTER DATABASE [WebTesting] SET RECOVERY SIMPLE
45  ALTER DATABASE [WebTesting] SET MULTI_USER
46  ALTER DATABASE [WebTesting] SET PAGE_VERIFY ↵
        ↳ TORN_PAGE_DETECTION
47  ALTER DATABASE [WebTesting] SET DB_CHAINING OFF
48  GO
```

4.1.2 Creating Employees Table

Our database will have a single table which stores details of all the employees. Use Listing 4.2 SQL to create the 'Employees' table.

Listing 4.2: Creating the Employees Table

```
1  /***************************************************************
2   * All rights reserved. Copyright 2016 Arkenstone-ltd.com       *
3   ***************************************************************/
4  USE [WebTesting]
5  GO
6
7  SET ANSI_NULLS ON
8  SET QUOTED_IDENTIFIER ON
9  CREATE TABLE [dbo].[Employees](
10     [EmployeeID] [nvarchar](10) NOT NULL,
11     [Title] [nvarchar](20) NOT NULL,
12     [Name] [nvarchar](40) NOT NULL,
13     [Gender] [nvarchar](1) NULL,
14     [DateOfBirth] [datetime] NULL,
15     [Email] [nvarchar](75) NULL,
16     [ContractJob] [nvarchar](3) NULL,
17     [Postcode] [nvarchar](10) NULL,
18   CONSTRAINT [PK_Employees] PRIMARY KEY CLUSTERED
19  (
20     [EmployeeID] ASC
21  )WITH (PAD_INDEX = OFF, STATISTICS_NORECOMPUTE = OFF, ↵
        ↳ IGNORE_DUP_KEY = OFF, ALLOW_ROW_LOCKS = ON, ↵
        ↳ ALLOW_PAGE_LOCKS = ON) ON [PRIMARY]
22  ) ON [PRIMARY]
23  GO
```

4.1.3 Creating The Test Data

Now using Notepad, Excel or any other suitable editor, create an 'Employees.csv' file in the 'C:\WebTesting\WebTestingDB' folder with the data as shown below:

```
EmployeeID,Title,Name,Gender,DateOfBirth,Email,ContractJob,PostalCode
10001,Mrs,Carla Brown,2,02/05/1965,carla.brown@arkenstone-ltd.com,Yes,SN1 5GS
10002,Mr,James Jones,1,03/12/1978,James.Jones@arkenstone-ltd.com,Yes,MK17 5TY
10003,Miss,D Mellons,2,10/10/1970,D.Mellons@arkenstone-ltd.com,No,HP11 8YZ
10004,Miss,Sarah Smith,2,25/12/1982,sarah.smith@arkenstone-ltd.com,No,SN1 5GS
10005,Mrs,Nicola,2,31/12/1978,Nicola@arkenstone-ltd.com,Yes,BR7 4TY
```

This is the same data as used by our demo website.

4.1.4 Loading The Test Data

Use Listing 4.3 SQL Query to load 'Employees.csv' test data into the 'Employees' table.

Listing 4.3: Loading the 'Employees.csv' Test Data

```sql
/*****************************************************************
 * All rights reserved. Copyright 2016 Arkenstone-ltd.com         *
 *****************************************************************/
USE [WebTesting]
GO

SET DATEFORMAT dmy;
GO

Truncate table dbo.[Employees]
BULK INSERT dbo.[Employees] FROM
    'C:\WebTesting\WebTestingDB\Employees.csv' WITH
    (FIRSTROW = 2, FIELDTERMINATOR = ',', ROWTERMINATOR
    = '\n')
GO
```

Now we are ready with a local database which we will use to compare the data displayed in our demo website.

4.2 Table Handling - Summary Reports

A tabular report is the most common type of report displayed on a web page. The report's output is organized in a row-column format, with each column usually corresponding to a field in the database table. A summary report is similar to a tabular report, but displays rows of data in a grouped form with subtotals and totals. In this section, we will learn how to automate a typical summary report *Employee Report by Gender* as shown in Figure A.11. In doing so, we will also learn how to perform automated verification tasks on a Table element. We will perform the following Test Scenario for a demonstration purpose:

- Launch the demo website.
- Click on the *Login* link.
- Login with the user 'Admin'.
- Click on the *Reports* link.
- Verify the summary report displayed on web page with the counts in database.

4.2.1 Object Repository

The Admin user's *Home* page as shown in Figure A.10 has the following screen elements:

\multicolumn{4}{c	}{**Admin's Home Page Elements**}
Element	*Type*	*Attribute*	*Value*
Home	Link	text	Home
Reports	Link	text	Reports
Employee List	Link	text	Employee List
Logout	Link	text	Logout

When you click the *Reports* link, the *Employee Report by Gender* page is displayed as shown in Figure A.11 with the following elements:

\multicolumn{4}{c	}{**Admin's Reports Page Elements**}
Element	*Type*	*Attribute*	*Value*
GenderCounts	Table	id	tblCounts
Total Employees	Span	id	TotalEmployees

Now double click the 'Repository.cs' file in the 'Solution Explorer' and add the code for 'HomeAdmin' and 'ReportsAdmin' as shown in Listing 4.4.

Listing 4.4: 'Repository.cs' - Code for Admin's Home and Reports page

```
1  public static class HomeAdmin
2  {
3      public static string lnkHome_ByLinkText { get { ↵
           ↪ return "Home"; } }
```

```
4         public static string lnkReports_ByLinkText { get {
              ↪ return "Reports"; } }
5         public static string lnkEmployeeList_ByLinkText { get
              ↪ { return "Employee List"; } }
6         public static string lnkLogout_ByLinkText { get {
              ↪ return "Logout"; } }
7   }
8
9   public static class ReportsAdmin
10  {
11        public static string tblReportByGender_ById { get {
              ↪ return "tblCounts"; } }
12        public static string lblTotal_ById { get { return
              ↪ "TotalEmployees"; } }
13  }
```

Line 1: Admin user's *Home* page elements.
Line 9: *Employee Report by Gender* page elements.

4.2.2 Configuration Parameters

Let's add some configuration parameters which we will need later on. Double click on the 'Config.cs' file in the 'Solution Explorer' and add Listing 4.5 code to it.

Listing 4.5: 'Config.cs' - Parameters to support summary reports

```
1   public const string MALE_TEXT = "Male";
2   public const string FEMALE_TEXT = "Female";
3
4   public const string connectionString =
        ↪ "Server=localhost;Database=WebTesting;Uid=sa;
        ↪ Pwd=sa;Connect Timeout=180;";
```

Line 1: Defines a string constant for the "Male" text.
Line 2: Defines a string constant for the "Female" text.
Line 4: Defines a string constant for the database connection.

The connection string's parameters are:

- Server - identifies the server. This could be a local machine (localhost), a machine domain name or an IP Address. In our case, we have specified a localhost.

- Database - identifies the database to connect to on the server. In our case, we are connecting to the 'WebTesting' database. If you gave a different name while creating the database, please change this parameter to the name you used.

- Uid - name of the user configured in the SQL Server. I've used the 'sa' user, change it if you are connecting to the database with a different user id.

- Pwd - password matching the SQL Server Uid.

- Connect Timeout - the length of time (in seconds) to wait for a connection to the server before terminating the attempt and generating an error.

4.2.3 Utility Functions

Let's now define some new functions in the Utility file as follows:

GetCountOfRecs - Gets count of records via the provided SQL Query		
Input Parameters	*stringSQL*	SQL Query to be used to get count of records.
Return Value	*count*	Returns count of records.

CompareDetails - Compares the count of expected and actual value of gender type and reports the outcome		
Input Parameters	*driver*	Object driver to control the browser
	stgGenderType	Gender type either Config.MALE or Config.FEMALE
	actValue	Actual value of count to compare with
Return Value	*void*	Returns nothing.

Add Listing 4.6 code to the 'Utility.cs' file.

Listing 4.6: 'Utility.cs' - Code for GetCountOfRecs and CompareDetails

```
1  using System.Data.SqlClient;
2
3  public static Int32 GetCountOfRecs(string stringSQL)
4  {
5      Utility.Log.Info("SQL is: " + stringSQL);
6      using (SqlConnection con = new ↵
             SqlConnection(Config.connectionString))
7      {
8          con.Open();
9
10         using (SqlCommand command = new ↵
                SqlCommand(stringSQL, con))
11         using (SqlDataReader reader = ↵
                command.ExecuteReader())
```

```
12          {
13              while (reader.Read())
14              {
15                  Int32 cnt = reader.GetInt32(0);
16                  Utility.Log.Info("Record count: " + ↵
                        ↪ cnt);
17                  return cnt;
18              }
19
20              return -1;
21          }
22      }
23  }
24
25  public static void CompareDetails(this IWebDriver driver, ↵
        ↪ string stgGenderType, string actValue)
26  {
27      String stringSQL = "Select Count(*) from ↵
            ↪ [dbo].[Employees] where [Gender] = '" + ↵
            ↪ stgGenderType +"'";
28      ReportExpectedVsActual(driver, ↵
            ↪ GetCountOfRecs(stringSQL).ToString(), actValue);
29  }
```

Line 1: Import needed to support database connectivity.
Line 6: Initialises a new instance of the `SqlConnection` class with a given connection string.
Line 8: Opens the database connection.
Line 10: Initialises a new instance of the `SqlCommand` class.
Line 11: Sends the command text to the connection and builds the `SqlDataReader`.
Line 13: While there is data, advances the `SqlDataReader`.
Line 15: Gets the value of first column as a 32-bit signed integer.
Line 16: It is always a good practice to log the count.
Line 17: Returns the count.
Line 20: Returns -1 if there was nothing in the `SqlDataReader`.
Line 27: Constructs the SQL string with the gender type.
Line 28: Compares the expected and the actual value and reports the outcome.

4.2.4 Page Logic

4.2.4.1 Home Page - Admin

The Admin's *Home* page of our demo website will have the following actions:

Action	Description
ClickHome()	This action will navigate to Admin user's *Home* page.
ClickReports()	This action will navigate to the *Employee Report by Gender* page.
ClickEmployeeList()	This action will navigate to the *Employee List* page.
ClickLogout()	This action will log the Admin user out and navigate to the generic *Home* page.

Let's now add the page logic for the Admin user's *Home* page. In the 'Solution Explorer', right click on the 'Pages' folder, click Add ⇒ Class. Type name as 'pageAdminHome.cs' and click the Add button. Add Listing 4.7 code to it.

Listing 4.7: 'pageAdminHome.cs' - Code for Admin's Home page

```
1  /******************************************************************
2   * All rights reserved. Copyright 2016 Arkenstone-ltd.com *
3   ******************************************************************/
4  using System;
5  using OpenQA.Selenium;
6
7  namespace WebTesting.Pages
8  {
9      class pageAdminHome : pageBase
10     {
11         private static readonly String Url = Config.URL;
12
13         public pageAdminHome(IWebDriver driver) :
                base(driver, Url)
14         {
15         }
16
17         public void ClickHome()
18         {
19             Utility.FindElementAndClick(driver,
                    By.LinkText(Repository.HomeAdmin.
                    lnkHome_ByLinkText));
20         }
21
22         public void ClickReports()
```

```
23              {
24                  Utility.FindElementAndClick(driver, ↵
                    ↪ By.LinkText(Repository.HomeAdmin. ↵
                    ↪ lnkReports_ByLinkText));
25              }
26
27          public void ClickEmployeeList()
28              {
29                  Utility.FindElementAndClick(driver, ↵
                    ↪ By.LinkText(Repository.HomeAdmin. ↵
                    ↪ lnkEmployeeList_ByLinkText));
30              }
31
32          public void ClickLogout()
33              {
34                  Utility.FindElementAndClick(driver, ↵
                    ↪ By.LinkText(Repository.HomeAdmin. ↵
                    ↪ lnkLogout_ByLinkText));
35              }
36      }
37  }
```

Ensure that you are using the right repository elements i.e. 'Repository.HomeAdmin' in all the function calls.

4.2.4.2 Reports Page - Admin

The Admin's *Reports* page of our demo website will have the following actions:

Action	Description
VerifyReportDetails()	This action will verify the details of the *Employee Report by Gender* with the values in the database.

Let's now add the page logic for *Reports* page. In the 'Solution Explorer', right click on the 'Pages' folder, click Add ⇒ Class. Type the name as 'pageAdminReports.cs' and click the Add button. Add Listing 4.8 code to it.

Listing 4.8: 'pageAdminReports.cs' - Code for Admin's Reports page

```
1  /*************************************************************
2   * All rights reserved. Copyright 2016 Arkenstone-ltd.com     *
3   *************************************************************/
```

```csharp
using System;
using OpenQA.Selenium;
using System.Collections.ObjectModel;

namespace WebTesting.Pages
{
    class pageAdminReports : pageBase
    {
        private static readonly String Url = Config.URL;

        public pageAdminReports(IWebDriver driver) :
            base(driver, Url)
        {
        }

        public void VerifyReportDetails()
        {
            ReadOnlyCollection<IWebElement> rowCollection
                = Utility.FindElementsAndReturn(driver,
                By.XPath("//*[@id='" +
                Repository.ReportsAdmin.
                tblReportByGender_ById +
                "']/tbody/tr"));

            Utility.Log.Info("Number of rows in this
                table: " + rowCollection.Count);

            int i_RowNum = 0;

            string[,] a = new string[rowCollection.Count,
                2];

            foreach (IWebElement rowElement in
                rowCollection)
            {
                ReadOnlyCollection<IWebElement>
                    colCollection = rowElement.
                    FindElements(By.XPath("td"));
                int i_ColNum = 0;

                Utility.Log.Info("Checking row: " +
                    (i_RowNum));

                foreach (IWebElement colElement in
                    colCollection)
```

```
36                    {
37                        a[i_RowNum, i_ColNum] = ↵
                         ↪ colElement.Text;
38                        Utility.Log.Info("Row: " + (i_RowNum) ↵
                         ↪ + " Column: " + i_ColNum + " ↵
                         ↪ Text: " + a[i_RowNum, ↵
                         ↪ i_ColNum]);
39
40                        i_ColNum = i_ColNum + 1;
41                    }
42                    i_RowNum = i_RowNum + 1;
43                }
44
45                for (int i = 1; i < rowCollection.Count; ↵
                     ↪ i++)
46                {
47                    switch (a[i, 0])
48                    {
49                        case Config.FEMALE_TEXT:
50                            Utility.CompareDetails(driver, ↵
                                 ↪ Config.FEMALE, a[i, 1]);
51                            break;
52
53                        case Config.MALE_TEXT:
54                            Utility.CompareDetails(driver, ↵
                                 ↪ Config.MALE, a[i, 1]);
55                            break;
56                    }
57                }
58
59                Utility.ReportExpectedVsActual(driver, ↵
                     ↪ Utility.FindElementAndReturn(driver, ↵
                     ↪ By.Id(Repository. ↵
                     ↪ ReportsAdmin.lblTotal_ById)).Text, ↵
                     ↪ Utility.GetCountOfRecs("Select Count(*) ↵
                     ↪ from [dbo].[Employees]").ToString());
60            }
61        }
62 }
```

Line 4 - 6: Imports needed to support the new functionality.

Line 18: Function to verify the report *Employee Report by Gender*.

Line 20: Using XPath, gets all the table row data into a row collection. Note how we are passing the `id` of the table.

Line 22: Logs total row count of the table.

Line 24: Initialises the row counter.
Line 26: Initialises a two dimensional array with the number of rows in the table and two columns (number of columns same as in the web page table).
Line 28: Iterates through the row collection.
Line 30: Using XPath, gets all the table column data into a column collection.
Line 31: Initialises the column counter.
Line 33: Logs the current row number.
Line 35: Iterates through the column collection.
Line 37: Stores the column text into the two dimensional array at row and column position. Our goal is to store all the table data into the two dimensional array which we will use later on.
Line 38: Logs the two dimensional array's value at the current row and column position.
Line 40: Increments the column counter.
Line 42: Increments the row counter.
Line 45: Iterates through the two dimensional array from row 1. Row 0 is the header row of the table. Note that C# arrays are zero indexed i.e. the array indexes start at zero.
Line 47: Array items a[i, 0] denote the first column of the table which store employee's gender.
Line 49 - 50: If it is a "Female" then calls function `CompareDetails` with expected value as "Female" and actual value as `a[i, 1]`.
Line 53 - 54: If it is a "Male" then calls function `CompareDetails` with expected value as "Male" and actual value as `a[i, 1]`.
Line 59: Compares the expected value of the total displayed on the web page with the actual count received via SQL Query and reports the outcome.

4.2.5 Creating Tests

Let's now add a new test which will test the Admin user's functionality. In the 'Solution Explorer', right click on the 'Tests' folder, click Add ⇒ Class. Type the name as 'TestAdminUser.cs' and click the Add button. Add Listing 4.9 code to it.

Listing 4.9: 'TestAdminUser.cs' - Tests for Admin user

```
1  /***************************************************************
2   * All rights reserved. Copyright 2016 Arkenstone-ltd.com       *
3   ***************************************************************/
4  using System;
5  using OpenQA.Selenium;
6  using NUnit.Framework;
7  using WebTesting.Pages;
8
9  namespace WebTesting.Tests
10 {
```

```csharp
11      public class TestAdminUser
12      {
13          IWebDriver driver;
14
15          [SetUp]
16          public void Setup()
17          {
18              driver = Utility.SetupDriver(driver);
19              Utility.TestResult = Config.PASS;
20          }
21
22          [TearDown]
23          public void Teardown()
24          {
25              if (TestContext.CurrentContext.Result.Status 
                    == TestStatus.Failed)
26              {
27                  Utility.Log.Error("***** Teardown ==> 
                        Test FAILED ***** =>" + 
                        TestContext.CurrentContext.Test.FullName);
28                  Utility.SaveScreenShot(driver, 
                        TestContext.CurrentContext.Test.Name 
                        + "(" + 
                        TestContext.CurrentContext.Result.Status 
                        + ")");
29              }
30              else if 
                    (TestContext.CurrentContext.Result.Status 
                    == TestStatus.Passed)
31              {
32                  Utility.Log.Info("PASS => " + 
                        TestContext.CurrentContext.Test.FullName);
33              }
34
35              driver.Quit();
36
37              Utility.SaveLogFile(TestContext.CurrentContext.
                    Test.FullName.Substring(17) + " (" + 
                    TestContext.CurrentContext.Result.Status 
                    + ") ");
38          }
39
40          [Test]
41          public void VerifyReportByGender()
42          {
```

```
43              try
44              {
45                  Utility.Log.Info("Starting test: " + ↵
                        ↪ TestContext.CurrentContext ↵
                        ↪ .Test.FullName);
46
47                  var home = new pageHome(driver);
48                  home.Visit();
49                  home.ClickLogin();
50
51                  var login = new pageLogin(driver);
52                  login.Login("Admin", "Admin123");
53
54                  var homeAdmin = new pageAdminHome(driver);
55                  homeAdmin.ClickReports();
56
57                  var rep = new pageAdminReports(driver);
58                  rep.VerifyReportDetails();
59
60                  Utility.ReportResult();
61              }
62              catch (Exception exception)
63              {
64                  Utility.Log.Error("exception" + ↵
                        ↪ exception.ToString());
65                  throw exception;
66              }
67          }
68      }
69 }
```

Line 55: Clicks the *Reports* link in the Admin user's *Home* Page.
Line 58: Calls the `VerifyReportDetails` function in the page logic.

4.2.6 Executing Tests

Execute the test and you will see an output as shown in Figure 4.1.

Automated Web Testing

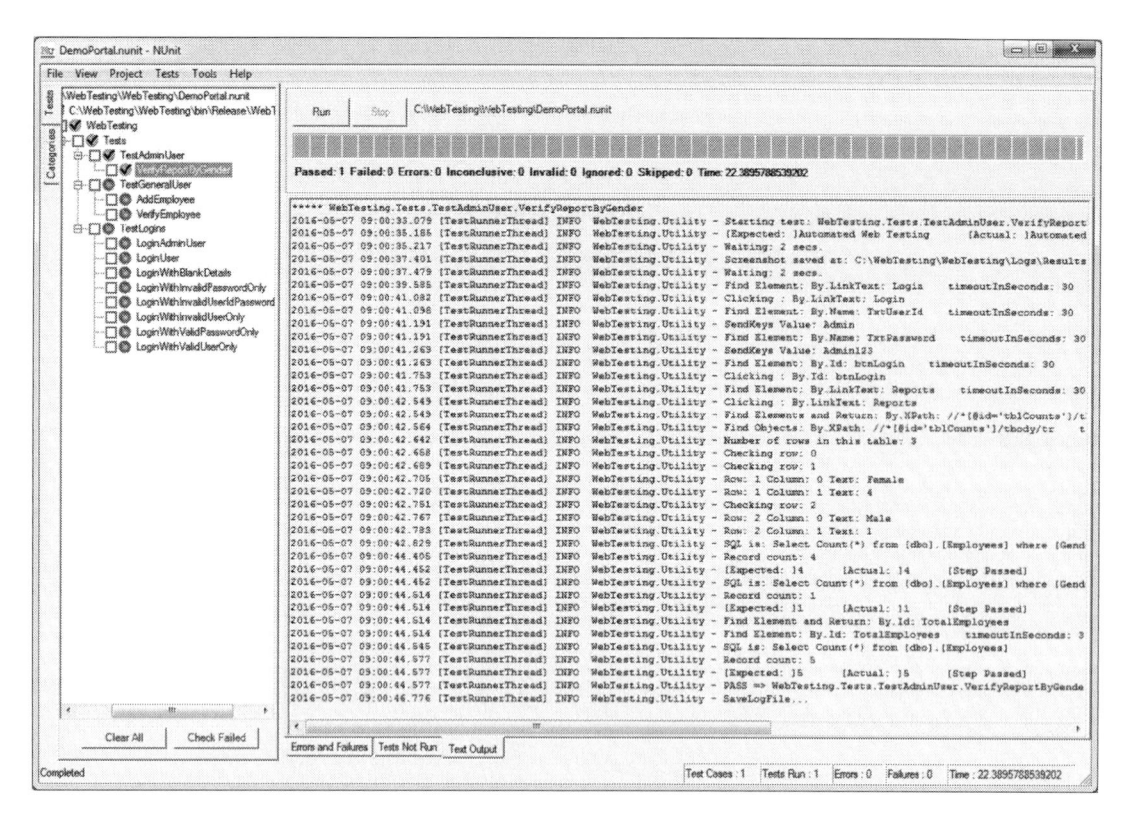

Figure 4.1: Console Output - Admin Report By Gender

4.3 Table Handling - Tabular Reports

In this section we will learn how to automate a typical tabular report *Employee List* as shown in Figure A.12. In doing so, we will also learn how to perform automated verification tasks on a Table element which has CheckBoxes displayed in its columns.

We will cover three scenarios in this section:

Test Scenario 1

- Launch the demo website.

- Click on the *Login* link.

- Login with the user 'Admin'.

- Click on the *Employee List* link.

- Verify the employees' list displayed on web page with the values in our database.

Test Scenario 2

- Launch the demo website.

140 Chapter 4

- Click on the *Login* link.
- Login with the user 'Admin'.
- Click on the *Employee List* link.
- Click on the Employee Id "10002" in the employee list table.
- Verify the employee's details displayed on web page with the corresponding values in the database.

Test Scenario 3

- Launch the demo website.
- Click on the *Login* link.
- Login with the user 'Admin'.
- Click on the *Employee List* link.
- Randomly select a row from the Employees table in our database.
- Click on the corresponding Employee Id in the web page.
- Verify the employee's details displayed on web page with the random row fetched from the database.

4.3.1 Object Repository

Admin user's *Employee List* page as shown in Figure A.12 has the following screen elements:

Employee List Admin Elements			
Element	**Type**	**Attribute**	**Value**
Employees	Table	id	TblEmployees
Total	Label	id	TotalEmployees

Now double click the 'Repository.cs' file in the 'Solution Explorer' and add the code for 'EmployeeListAdmin' as shown in Listing 4.10.

Listing 4.10: 'Repository.cs' - Repository for Admin's Employee List page

```
1  public static class EmployeeListAdmin
2  {
3      public static string tblEmployeesTable_ById { get { ↵
           ↪ return "TblEmployees"; } }
```

```
4       public static string lblTotal_ById { get { return ↵
        ↪ "TotalEmployees"; } }
5   }
```

Line 1 Elements of the Employee List page.

4.3.2 Configuration Parameters

Let's add some configuration parameters which we will need later on. Double click on the 'Config.cs' file in the 'Solution Explorer' and add the Listing 4.11 code to it.

Listing 4.11: 'Config.cs' - Codes to support tabular reports

```
1  public const string UNKNOWN_TEXT = "Unknown";
2
3  public const string YES = "Yes";
4  public const string NO = "No";
```

Line 1: Defines a string constant for the "Unknown" text.
Line 3: Defines a string constant for the "Yes" text.
Line 4: Defines a string constant for the "No" text.

4.3.3 Utility Functions

Let's now define some new functions in the Utility file as follows:

DecodeGender - Decodes the gender code and returns its text value		
Input Parameters	*genderCode*	Gender code to be decoded
Return Value	*genderText*	Returns gender text.

DecodeContract - Decodes the contract type from a Yes/No value		
Input Parameters	*contCode*	Contract code to be decoded.
Return Value	*string*	Returns True, False or Unknown.

Add Listing 4.12 code to the 'Utility.cs' file.

Listing 4.12: 'Utility.cs' - Code for DecodeGender and DecodeContract

```
1  public static String DecodeGender(string genderCode)
2  {
3      if (genderCode.Trim().Equals(Config.MALE))
4          return Config.MALE_TEXT;
```

```
5      else if (genderCode.Trim().Equals(Config.FEMALE))
6          return Config.FEMALE_TEXT;
7      else
8          return Config.UNKNOWN_TEXT;
9  }
10
11 public static String DecodeContract(string contCode)
12 {
13     if (contCode.Trim().Equals(Config.YES))
14         return Config.TRUE;
15     else if (contCode.Trim().Equals(Config.NO))
16         return Config.FALSE;
17     else
18         return Config.UNKNOWN_TEXT;
19 }
```

Line 3: If the gender code is a male then returns its text's equivalent.
Line 5: If the gender code is a female then returns its text's equivalent.
Line 7: Otherwise returns an unknown text.
Line 13: If the contract code is a yes then returns a true value.
Line 15: If the contract code is a no then returns a false value.
Line 17: Otherwise returns an unknown text.

4.3.4 Page Logic

The *Employee List* page of our demo website will have the following actions:

Action	Description
VerifyEmployeeList()	This action will verify the details of the complete employees list with the values in the database.
VerifyEmployeeWithDB()	This action will verify the details of an individual employee with the values in the database.
VerifyEmployeeWithDBRandom()	This action will verify a randomly selected employee from the database with its corresponding details in the web page.

Let's now add the page logic for the *Employee List* page. In the 'Solution Explorer', right click on the 'Pages' folder, click Add ⇒ Class. Type the name as 'pageAdminEmpList.cs' and click the Add button. Add Listing 4.13 code to it.

Listing 4.13: 'pageAdminEmpList.cs' - Code for Admin's Employee List page

```
1  /**************************************************************
2   * All rights reserved. Copyright 2016 Arkenstone-ltd.com *
3   **************************************************************/
4  using System;
5  using OpenQA.Selenium;
6  using System.Collections.ObjectModel;
7  using System.Data.SqlClient;
8
9  namespace WebTesting.Pages
10 {
11     class pageAdminEmpList : pageBase
12     {
13         private static readonly String Url = Config.URL;
14
15         public pageAdminEmpList(IWebDriver driver) : ←
               ↪ base(driver, Url)
16         {
17         }
18
19         public void VerifyEmployeeList()
20         {
21             ReadOnlyCollection<IWebElement> rowCollection ←
                   ↪ = Utility.FindElementsAndReturn(driver, ←
                   ↪ By.XPath("//*[@id='" + ←
                   ↪ Repository.EmployeeListAdmin. ←
                   ↪ tblEmployeesTable_ById + ←
                   ↪ "']/tbody/tr"));
22
23             Utility.Log.Info("Number of rows in this ←
                   ↪ table: " + rowCollection.Count);
24
25             int i_RowNum = 0;
26
27             string[,] a = new string[rowCollection.Count, ←
                   ↪ 6];
28
29             foreach (IWebElement rowElement in ←
                   ↪ rowCollection)
30             {
31                 ReadOnlyCollection<IWebElement> ←
```

```csharp
                        colCollection = rowElement.
                            FindElements(By.XPath("td"));
32                      int i_ColNum = 0;
33
34                      Utility.Log.Info("Checking row: " +
                            (i_RowNum));
35
36                      foreach (IWebElement colElement in
                            colCollection)
37                      {
38                          String stg;
39                          if (i_ColNum == 5)
40                              stg =
                                    Utility.FindElementAndReturn(
                                    driver, By.XPath("//tr[" +
                                    (i_RowNum + 1) +
                                    "]/td[6]/input[@type='checkbox']"
                                    )).Selected.ToString();
41                          else
42                              stg = colElement.Text;
43
44                          a[i_RowNum, i_ColNum] = stg;
45                          Utility.Log.Info("Row: " + (i_RowNum)
                                + " Column: " + i_ColNum + "
                                Text: " + a[i_RowNum,
                                i_ColNum]);
46
47                          i_ColNum = i_ColNum + 1;
48                      }
49                      i_RowNum = i_RowNum + 1;
50                  }
51
52                  for (int i = 1; i < rowCollection.Count;
                        i++)
53                  {
54                      string stringSQL = "SELECT [EmployeeID],
                            [Title], [Name], [Gender],
                            [DateOfBirth], [ContractJob]" +
                            "\r\n";
55                      stringSQL = stringSQL + "FROM
                            [dbo].[Employees] where EmployeeID =
                            '" + a[i, 0] + "'";
56
57                      Utility.Log.Info("SQL is: " +
                            stringSQL);
```

```
58
59                      String actEmpId = "", actTitle = "", ↵
                           ↪ actName = "", actGender = "", actDob ↵
                           ↪ = "", actContract = "";
60
61                      using (SqlConnection con = new ↵
                           ↪ SqlConnection(Config.connectionString))
62                      {
63                          con.Open();
64
65                          using (SqlCommand command = new ↵
                               ↪ SqlCommand(stringSQL, con))
66                          using (SqlDataReader reader = ↵
                               ↪ command.ExecuteReader())
67                          {
68                              while (reader.Read())
69                              {
70                                  actEmpId = ↵
                                       ↪ reader.GetString(0);        ↵
                                       ↪
71                                  actTitle = reader.GetString(1);
72                                  actName = reader.GetString(2);
73                                  actGender = reader.GetString(3);
74                                  actDob = ↵
                                       ↪ reader.GetDateTime(4) ↵
                                       ↪ .ToString();
75                                  actContract = ↵
                                       ↪ reader.GetString(5);
76                              }
77                          }
78                      }
79
80                      Utility.ReportExpectedVsActual(driver, ↵
                           ↪ a[i, 0], actEmpId);
81                      Utility.ReportExpectedVsActual(driver, ↵
                           ↪ a[i, 1], actTitle);
82                      Utility.ReportExpectedVsActual(driver, ↵
                           ↪ a[i, 2], actName);
83                      Utility.ReportExpectedVsActual(driver, ↵
                           ↪ a[i, 3], ↵
                           ↪ Utility.DecodeGender(actGender));
84                      Utility.ReportExpectedVsActual(driver, ↵
                           ↪ a[i, 4], actDob.Substring(0, 10));
85                      Utility.ReportExpectedVsActual(driver, ↵
                           ↪ a[i, 5], ↵
```

```
                         ↪ Utility.DecodeContract(actContract)); ←
                         ↪
86              }
87
88              Utility.ReportExpectedVsActual(driver, ←
                    ↪ Utility.FindElementAndReturn(driver, ←
                    ↪ By.Id(Repository.EmployeeListAdmin ←
                    ↪ .lblTotal_ById)).Text, ←
                    ↪ Utility.GetCountOfRecs("Select Count(*) ←
                    ↪ from [dbo].[Employees]").ToString());
89          }
90      }
91 }
```

Line 21: Using XPath, gets all the table row data into a row collection. Note how we are passing the `id` of the table.

Line 23: Logs total row count of the table.

Line 25: Initialises the row counter.

Line 27: Initialises a two dimensional array with the number of rows in the table and six columns (number of columns same as in the web page table).

Line 29: Iterates through the row collection.

Line 31: Using XPath, gets all the table column data into a column collection.

Line 32: Initialises the column counter.

Line 34: Logs the current row number.

Line 36: Iterates through the column collection.

Line 39: For the last table column i.e. Contract, if the CheckBox is selected then stores its value in the temporary variable.

Line 42: Otherwise just stores the column's text value in the temporary variable.

Line 44: Stores the temporary variable value into the two dimensional array at row and column position. Remember our goal is to store all the table data into the two dimensional array which we will use later on.

Line 45: Logs the two dimensional array's value at the current row and column position.

Line 47: Increments the column counter.

Line 49: Increments the row counter.

Line 52: Iterates through the two dimensional array from row 1. Row 0 is the header row of the table. Note that C# arrays are zero indexed i.e. the array indexes start at zero.

Line 54 - Line 55: Construct the SQL Query to fetch data from the database table for the given employee id. Note that `a[i, 0]` denotes first column of the table which stores the employee id.

Line 57: Logs the SQL Query.

Line 59: Initialises variables to store data fetched from the SQL Query.

Line 70 - 75: Store data fetched from the SQL Query into variables. Note the use of `ToString()` function to convert datetime into a string value.

Line 80 - 85: Compare the expected values in the array with the actual values fetched

from the database table and report the outcome.
Line 83: Uses the Utility function `DecodeGender` to decode the gender.
Line 85: Uses the Utility function `DecodeContract` to decode the contract.
Line 88: Compares the expected value of the total displayed on the web page with the actual count received via the SQL Query and reports the outcome.

Now let's add logic to verify the details of an individual employee in the 'pageAdminEmpList.cs' file as shown in Listing 4.14.

Listing 4.14: 'pageAdminEmpList.cs' - Code for VerifyEmployeeWithDB

```
1  public void VerifyEmployeeWithDB(String empId)
2  {
3      Utility.FindElementAndClick(driver, By.XPath("id('" +
           Repository.EmployeeListAdmin.tblEmployeesTable_ById
           + "')//td[1][contains(text(),'" + empId +
           "')]"));
4
5      string stringSQL = "SELECT [EmployeeID], [Title],
           [Name], [Gender], [DateOfBirth], [Email],
           [ContractJob], [Postcode]" + "\r\n";
6      stringSQL = stringSQL + "FROM [dbo].[Employees] where
           EmployeeID = '" + empId + "'";
7
8      Utility.Log.Info("SQL is: " + stringSQL);
9
10     String expEmpId = "", expTitle = "", expName = "",
           expGender = "", expDob = "", expEmail = "",
           expContract = "", expPostcode = "";
11
12     using (SqlConnection con = new
           SqlConnection(Config.connectionString))
13     {
14         con.Open();
15
16         using (SqlCommand command = new
               SqlCommand(stringSQL, con))
17         using (SqlDataReader reader =
               command.ExecuteReader())
18         {
19             while (reader.Read())
20             {
21                 expEmpId = reader.GetString(0);
22                 expTitle = reader.GetString(1);
```

```
23                  expName = reader.GetString(2);
24                  expGender = reader.GetString(3);
25                  expDob = reader.GetDateTime(4).ToString();
26                  expEmail = reader.GetString(5);
27                  expContract = reader.GetString(6);
28                  expPostcode = reader.GetString(7);
29              }
30          }
31      }
32
33      Utility.ReportExpectedVsActual(driver, expEmpId, ↵
            ↪ Utility.FindElementAndReturn(driver, ↵
            ↪ By.Name(Repository.EmployeeDetail. ↵
            ↪ txtEmployeeId_ByName)).GetAttribute("Value"));
34      Utility.ReportExpectedVsActual(driver, expTitle, ↵
            ↪ Utility.FindElementAndReturn(driver, ↵
            ↪ By.Name(Repository.EmployeeDetail. ↵
            ↪ lbTitle_ByName)).Text);
35      Utility.ReportExpectedVsActual(driver, expName, ↵
            ↪ Utility.FindElementAndReturn(driver, ↵
            ↪ By.Id(Repository.EmployeeDetail. ↵
            ↪ txtName_ById)).GetAttribute("Value"));
36      Utility.ReportExpectedVsActual(driver, expGender, ↵
            ↪ Utility.GetSelectedRadioButton(driver, ↵
            ↪ Repository.EmployeeDetail. ↵
            ↪ rbGender_ById).ToString());
37      Utility.ReportExpectedVsActual(driver, ↵
            ↪ expDob.Substring(0, 10), ↵
            ↪ Utility.FindElementAndReturn(driver, ↵
            ↪ By.Name(Repository.EmployeeDetail. ↵
            ↪ txtDateOfBirth_ByName)).GetAttribute("Value"));
38      Utility.ReportExpectedVsActual(driver, expEmail, ↵
            ↪ Utility.FindElementAndReturn(driver, ↵
            ↪ By.Name(Repository.EmployeeDetail. ↵
            ↪ txtEmail_ByName)).GetAttribute("Value"));
39      Utility.ReportExpectedVsActual(driver, ↵
            ↪ Utility.DecodeContract(expContract), ↵
            ↪ Utility.FindElementAndReturn(driver, ↵
            ↪ By.Name(Repository.EmployeeDetail. ↵
            ↪ cbContractJob_ByName)).Selected.ToString());
40      Utility.ReportExpectedVsActual(driver, expPostcode, ↵
            ↪ Utility.FindElementAndReturn(driver, ↵
            ↪ By.Id(Repository.EmployeeDetail. ↵
            ↪ txtPostcode_ById)).GetAttribute("Value"));
41  }
```

Line 1: Verifies an employee with the values stored in the database for a given employee id 'empId'.
Line 3: Clicks the table row containing the employee id. XPath query is used to identify the table column containing the employee id.
Line 5 - 6: Constructs the SQL Query to fetch data for the 'empId'.
Line 21 - 28: Store data fetched from the SQL Query into variables. Note the use of ToString() function to convert datetime into a string value.
Line 33, 35, 37, 38 and 40: Compare the expected database values with the actual values on the web page. Note the use of GetAttribute("Value") function to retrieve element's value.
Line 34: Note the use of .Text to retrieve element's value.
Line 36: Note the use of GetSelectedRadioButton function.
Line 39: Note the use of Selected.ToString() function to retrieve element's value.

Now let's add logic to verify a randomly selected employee in the 'pageAdminEmpList.cs' file as shown in Listing 4.15.

Listing 4.15: 'pageAdminEmpList.cs' - Code for VerifyEmployeeWithDBRandom

```
1   public void VerifyEmployeeWithDBRandom()
2   {
3       string stringSQL = "SELECT TOP 1 [EmployeeID], ↵
            ↪ [Title], [Name], [Gender], [DateOfBirth], ↵
            ↪ [Email], [ContractJob], [Postcode]" + "\r\n";
4       stringSQL = stringSQL + "FROM [dbo].[Employees] Order ↵
            ↪ by NEWID()";
5
6       Utility.Log.Info("SQL is: " + stringSQL);
7
8       String expEmpId = "", expTitle = "", expName = "", ↵
            ↪ expGender = "", expDob = "", expEmail = "", ↵
            ↪ expContract = "", expPostcode = "";
9
10      using (SqlConnection con = new ↵
            ↪ SqlConnection(Config.connectionString))
11      {
12          con.Open();
13
14          using (SqlCommand command = new ↵
                ↪ SqlCommand(stringSQL, con))
15          using (SqlDataReader reader = ↵
                ↪ command.ExecuteReader())
```

```csharp
16          {
17              while (reader.Read())
18              {
19                  expEmpId = reader.GetString(0);
20                  expTitle = reader.GetString(1);
21                  expName = reader.GetString(2);
22                  expGender = reader.GetString(3);
23                  expDob = reader.GetDateTime(4).ToString();
24                  expEmail = reader.GetString(5);
25                  expContract = reader.GetString(6);
26                  expPostcode = reader.GetString(7);
27              }
28          }
29      }
30
31      Utility.Log.Info("Going for random EmpId: " + expEmpId);
32      Utility.FindElementAndClick(driver, By.XPath("id('" +
            Repository.EmployeeListAdmin.tblEmployeesTable_ById
            + "')//td[1][contains(text(),'" + expEmpId +
            "')]"));
33
34      Utility.ReportExpectedVsActual(driver, expEmpId,
            Utility.FindElementAndReturn(driver,
            By.Name(Repository.EmployeeDetail.
            txtEmployeeId_ByName)).GetAttribute("Value"));
35      Utility.ReportExpectedVsActual(driver, expTitle,
            Utility.FindElementAndReturn(driver,
            By.Name(Repository.EmployeeDetail.
            lbTitle_ByName)).Text);
36      Utility.ReportExpectedVsActual(driver, expName,
            Utility.FindElementAndReturn(driver,
            By.Id(Repository.EmployeeDetail.
            txtName_ById)).GetAttribute("Value"));
37      Utility.ReportExpectedVsActual(driver, expGender,
            Utility.GetSelectedRadioButton(driver,
            Repository.EmployeeDetail.rbGender_ById).ToString());
38      Utility.ReportExpectedVsActual(driver,
            expDob.Substring(0, 10),
            Utility.FindElementAndReturn(driver,
            By.Name(Repository.EmployeeDetail.
            txtDateOfBirth_ByName)).GetAttribute("Value"));
39      Utility.ReportExpectedVsActual(driver, expEmail,
            Utility.FindElementAndReturn(driver,
            By.Name(Repository.EmployeeDetail.
            txtEmail_ByName)).GetAttribute("Value"));
```

```
40          Utility.ReportExpectedVsActual(driver, ↵
              ↪ Utility.DecodeContract(expContract), ↵
              ↪ Utility.FindElementAndReturn(driver, ↵
              ↪ By.Name(Repository.EmployeeDetail. ↵
              ↪ cbContractJob_ByName)).Selected.ToString());
41          Utility.ReportExpectedVsActual(driver, expPostcode, ↵
              ↪ Utility.FindElementAndReturn(driver, ↵
              ↪ By.Id(Repository.EmployeeDetail. ↵
              ↪ txtPostcode_ById)).GetAttribute("Value"));
42      }
```

Line 1: Verifies randomly selected employee from the database with the corresponding values in the web page.

Line 3: Uses 'SELECT TOP' clause to specify the number of records to return which is one in our case.

Line 4: The 'Order by NEWID()' statement selects different record each time the SQL Query is executed.

Line 32: Clicks the corresponding Employee Id in the web page table as fetched from the database table.

4.3.5 Creating Tests

Let's now add new tests in 'TestAdminUser.cs' as shown in Listing 4.16.

Listing 4.16: 'TestAdminUser.cs' - Additional tests

```
1   [Test]
2   public void VerifyEmployeeList()
3   {
4       try
5       {
6           Utility.Log.Info("Starting test: " + ↵
                ↪ TestContext.CurrentContext.Test.FullName);
7
8           var home = new pageHome(driver);
9           home.Visit();
10          home.ClickLogin();
11
12          var login = new pageLogin(driver);
13          login.Login("Admin", "Admin123");
14
15          var homeAdmin = new pageAdminHome(driver);
16          homeAdmin.ClickEmployeeList();
17
```

```csharp
18            var empList = new pageAdminEmpList(driver);
19            empList.VerifyEmployeeList();
20
21            Utility.ReportResult();
22        }
23        catch (Exception exception)
24        {
25            Utility.Log.Error("exception" +
                  ↪ exception.ToString());
26            throw exception;
27        }
28 }
29
30 [Test]
31 public void VerifyEmployeeById()
32 {
33      try
34      {
35            Utility.Log.Info("Starting test: " +
                  ↪ TestContext.CurrentContext.Test.FullName);
36
37            var home = new pageHome(driver);
38            home.Visit();
39            home.ClickLogin();
40
41            var login = new pageLogin(driver);
42            login.Login("Admin", "Admin123");
43
44            var homeAdmin = new pageAdminHome(driver);
45            homeAdmin.ClickEmployeeList();
46
47            var empList = new pageAdminEmpList(driver);
48            empList.VerifyEmployeeWithDB("10002");
49
50            Utility.ReportResult();
51       }
52       catch (Exception exception)
53       {
54            Utility.Log.Error("exception" +
                  ↪ exception.ToString());
55            throw exception;
56       }
57 }
58
59 [Test]
```

```
60  public void VerifyEmployeeByIdRandom()
61  {
62      try
63      {
64          Utility.Log.Info("Starting test: " + ↩
                ↪ TestContext.CurrentContext.Test.FullName);
65
66          var home = new pageHome(driver);
67          home.Visit();
68          home.ClickLogin();
69
70          var login = new pageLogin(driver);
71          login.Login("Admin", "Admin123");
72
73          var homeAdmin = new pageAdminHome(driver);
74          homeAdmin.ClickEmployeeList();
75
76          var empList = new pageAdminEmpList(driver);
77          empList.VerifyEmployeeWithDBRandom();
78
79          Utility.ReportResult();
80      }
81      catch (Exception exception)
82      {
83          Utility.Log.Error("exception" + ↩
                ↪ exception.ToString());
84          throw exception;
85      }
86  }
```

Line 1: New test `VerifyEmployeeList`.
Line 16: Clicks the *View Employee List* link in Admin user's *Home* Page.
Line 19: Calls the `VerifyEmployeeList` function in the page logic.
Line 30: New test `VerifyEmployeeById`.
Line 45: Clicks the *View Employee List* link in Admin user's *Home* Page.
Line 48: Calls the `VerifyEmployeeWithDB` function with employee id "10002".
Line 59: New test `VerifyEmployeeByIdRandom`.
Line 74: Clicks the *View Employee List* link in Admin user's *Home* Page.
Line 77: Calls the `VerifyEmployeeWithDBRandom` function to randomly select a record from the database and verifies corresponding values in the web page.

4.3.6 Executing Tests

Execute the test and you will see an output as shown in Figure 4.2.

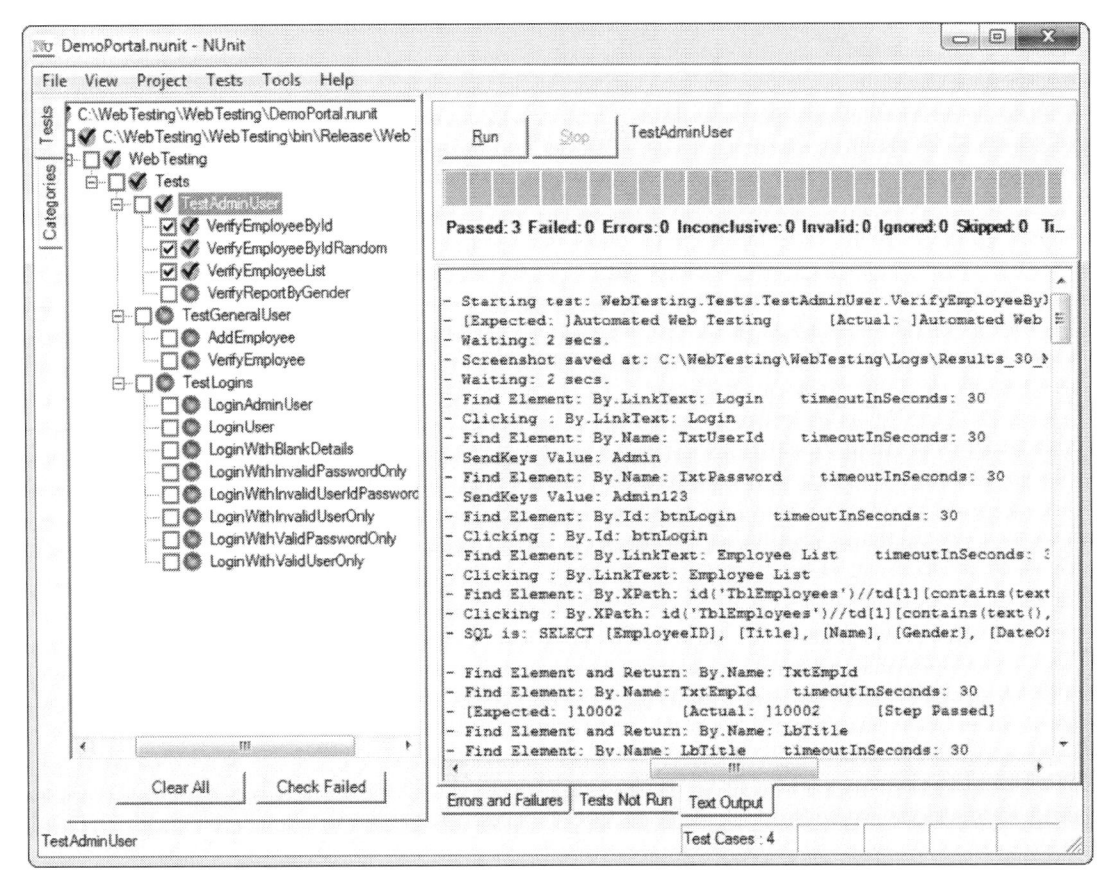

Figure 4.2: Console Output - Admin Employee List

4.4 Creating Test Result Summary

For each test we include the overall test result outcome in the test result file name which tells us whether the final result was a Pass or Fail. When we look at the result folder at a later stage, we will need to go through the entire folder to identify the test(s) that failed. This may be quite cumbersome task if there are a lot of results to scroll through. However, it would be really helpful if the test execution could also provide a summary of the outcome of each test. So let's enhance our Automation Framework to generate a test result summary file.

4.4.1 Configuration Parameters

First of all, add a configuration variable which we will need later on. Double click on the 'Config.cs' file in the 'Solution Explorer' and add the Listing 4.17 code to it.

Listing 4.17: 'Config.cs' - Parameters for test result summary file

```
1  public static string SUMMARY_FILENAME = ↵
        Config.ResultFolder + @"\Summary" + ↵
```

```
↪ DateTime.Now.ToString("_dd_MMM_yyyy HH_mm_ss", ←
↪ System.Globalization.CultureInfo. ←
↪ GetCultureInfo("en-GB")) + ".csv";
```

Line 1: Defines a configuration variable to hold the summary file name with the current date and timestamp.

4.4.2 Utility Functions

We will now define two new generic functions as follows:

SetupSummaryFile - Sets up the test summary file		
Input Parameters	*none*	No parameters
Return Value	*void*	Returns nothing

CreateSummaryFileEntry - Creates an entry into the test summary file		
Input Parameters	*strData*	Data to be written to the test summary file
Return Value	*void*	Returns nothing

Add Listing 4.18 code to the 'Utility.cs' file.

Listing 4.18: 'Utility.cs' - Code for SetupSummaryFile and CreateSummaryFileEntry

```
1  public static void SetupSummaryFile()
2  {
3      Log.Info("SetupSummaryFile");
4      var targetPath = Config.ResultFolder;
5      if (!Directory.Exists(targetPath))
6      {
7          Directory.CreateDirectory(targetPath);
8  
9          FileStream fs1 = new ←
               ↪ FileStream(Config.SUMMARY_FILENAME, ←
               ↪ FileMode.Create, FileAccess.Write);
10         StreamWriter writer = new StreamWriter(fs1);
11         writer.Write("Date Time, Test Name, Test Result, ←
               ↪ Log File" + Environment.NewLine);
12         writer.Close();
13     }
14 }
15
```

```
16  public static void CreateSummaryFileEntry(String strData)
17  {
18      Log.Info("CreateSummaryFileEntry");
19      FileStream fs1 = new ↵
            ↪ FileStream(Config.SUMMARY_FILENAME, ↵
            ↪ FileMode.Append, FileAccess.Write);
20      StreamWriter writer = new StreamWriter(fs1);
21      writer.Write(strData + Environment.NewLine);
22      writer.Close();
23  }
```

Line 5: Sets up the summary file if the result folder doesn't exist. Please note that the setup is required for the first time only.
Line 7: Creates the result folder.
Line 9: Initialises a new instance of the `FileStream` class with the specified pathname, creation mode and access permission.

- FileName - the summary file is created with the name as is stored in the `Config.SUMMARY_FILENAME`.

- FileMode `Create` - operating system should create a new file. If the file already exists, it will be overwritten.

- FileAccess `Write` - write access to the file. Data can be written to the file.

Line 10: Initialises a new instance of the `StreamWriter` class for the specified stream.
Line 11: Writes the header record followed by a new line character.
Line 12: Closes the stream.
Line 19: Opens the summary file in Append mode i.e. open the file and seek to the end of the file.
Line 20: Initialises the `StreamWriter` class.
Line 21: Writes the string of data followed by a new line character.
Line 22: Closes the stream.

4.4.3 Updating Page Logic

Update the `Visit` logic in 'pageHome.cs' as shown in Listing 4.19.

Listing 4.19: 'pageHome.cs' - Setup test summary file

```
1  public void Visit()
2  {
3      GoToSite();
4      Utility.SetupSummaryFile();
5      Utility.ReportExpectedVsActual(driver, "Automated Web ↵
            ↪ Testing", driver.Title);
```

```
6        Utility.SaveScreenShot(driver, ↵
            ↪ TestContext.CurrentContext.Test.Name);
7    }
```

Line 4: Calls the generic function to setup the test summary file.

4.4.4 Updating Tests

Update the 'TestLogins.cs' file as shown in Listing 4.20.

Listing 4.20: 'TestLogins.cs' - Updates to generate a test result summary file

```
1  [TearDown]
2  public void Teardown()
3  {
4      if (TestContext.CurrentContext.Result.Status == ↵
            ↪ TestStatus.Failed)
5      {
6          Utility.Log.Error("***** Teardown ==> Test FAILED ↵
            ↪ ***** =>" + ↵
            ↪ TestContext.CurrentContext.Test.FullName);
7          Utility.SaveScreenShot(driver, ↵
            ↪ TestContext.CurrentContext.Test.Name + "(" + ↵
            ↪ TestContext.CurrentContext.Result.Status + ↵
            ↪ ")");
8      }
9      else if (TestContext.CurrentContext.Result.Status == ↵
            ↪ TestStatus.Passed)
10     {
11         Utility.Log.Info("PASS => " + ↵
            ↪ TestContext.CurrentContext.Test.FullName);
12     }
13
14     driver.Quit();
15
16     Utility.SaveLogFile(TestContext.CurrentContext.Test. ↵
            ↪ FullName.Substring(17) + " (" + ↵
            ↪ TestContext.CurrentContext.Result.Status + ") ");
17
18     if (Utility.TestResult == Config.FAIL)
19         Utility.CreateSummaryFileEntry(DateTime.Now. ↵
            ↪ ToString() + "," + ↵
            ↪ TestContext.CurrentContext.Test.FullName. ↵
            ↪ Substring(17) + ",FAIL" + "," + ↵
```

```
                  ↪ Config.CURRENT_LOGFILE);
20     else
21         Utility.CreateSummaryFileEntry(DateTime.Now. ↩
              ↪ ToString() + "," + ↩
              ↪ TestContext.CurrentContext.Test.FullName. ↩
              ↪ Substring(17) + ",PASS" + "," + ↩
              ↪ Config.CURRENT_LOGFILE);
22 }
```

Line 18: If the test has failed then creates a *Fail* entry in the test summary file. Note the way the entry string is being constructed with comma separated values in line with the header row.

Line 20: If the test has passed then creates a *Pass* entry in the test summary file.

4.4.5 Executing Tests

Execute the test and you will see a Test Summary File as shown in Figures 4.3. Figure 4.4 shows the contents of the Test Summary File.

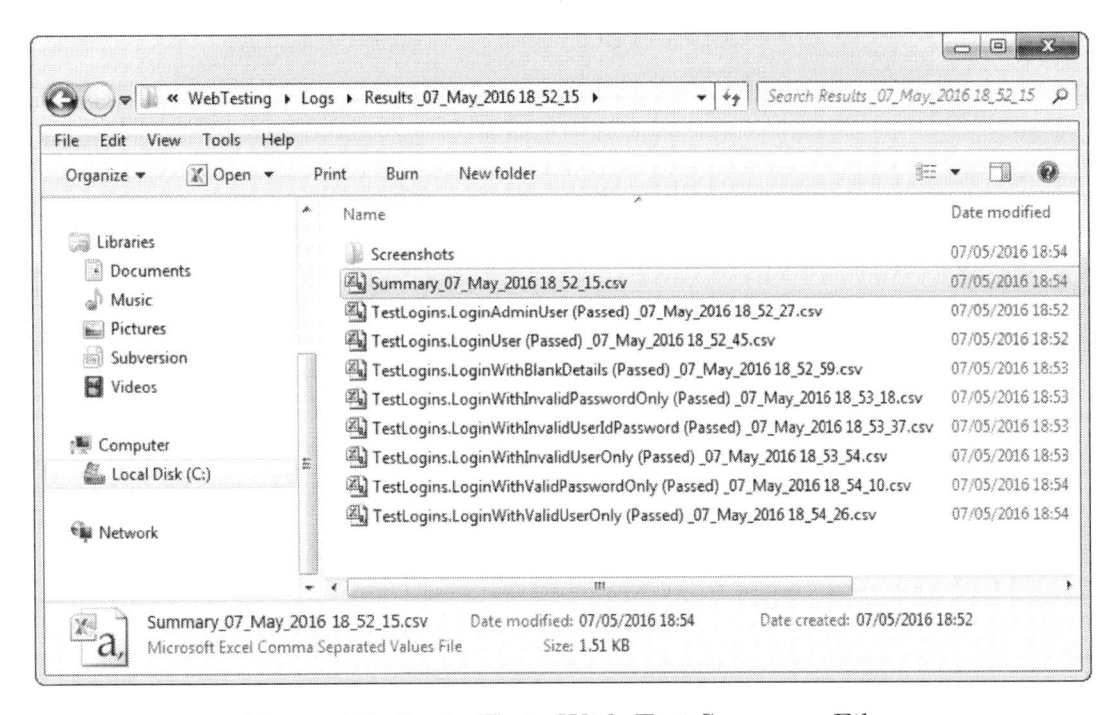

Figure 4.3: Login Tests With Test Summary File

Automated Web Testing

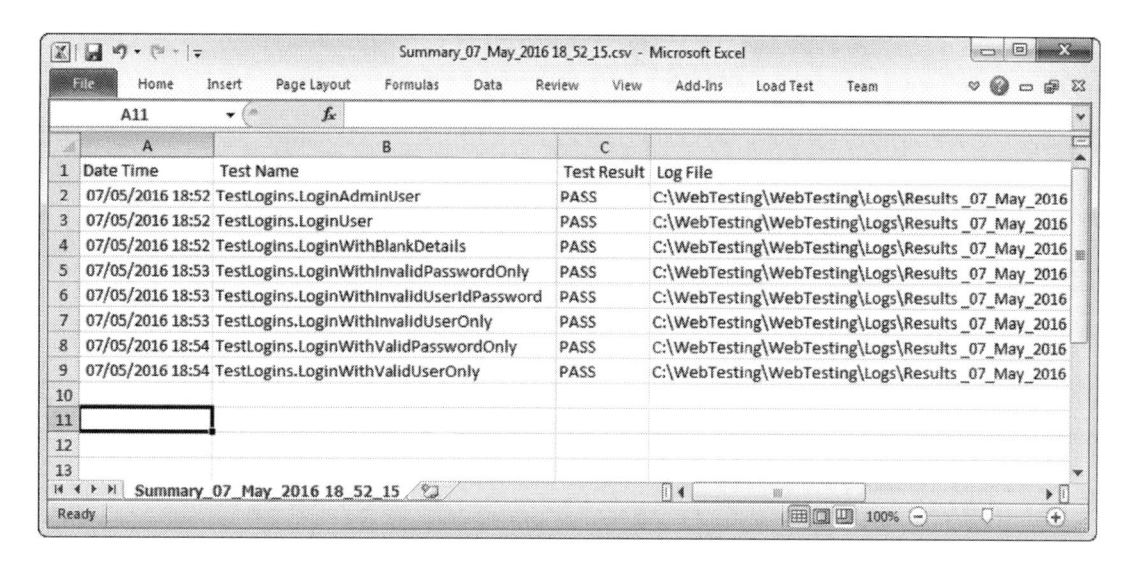

Figure 4.4: Test Summary File Contents

Similarly, update 'TestGeneralUser.cs' and 'TestAdminUser.cs' files to support the test summary file creation.

Chapter 5

Data Driven Testing

Data Driven Testing

In this chapter, we will learn:

- *About Data Driven Testing*
- *How to use Excel XLS and XLSX files as a data source for the automated testing*
- *About adding some important features to our Automation Framework*

So let's get on with it...

DATA Driven Testing (DDT) is the creation of automated test scripts where test data is read from a data file instead of using the same hard-coded values, each time the test runs. By using the data driven testing approach, we can test how the web application handles various inputs effectively. To get a larger test coverage, you should perform automated tests with different input data. Consider the scenario where we add an employee or view an employee via automated test. The automated test contains only those values that you entered during the coding and (most likely) these values do not cause any errors in the web application, but other data may cause them. So, we should run our automated tests with different set of input data to ensure that the web application works as expected for various input values. This approach is called Data Driven Testing.

A data driven test will read data from a storage, an Excel file in our case, rather than use hard-coded values. Such a separation of data makes a test simpler and easy to maintain. On the other hand, a test containing several sets of hard-coded values can be rather difficult to maintain. If you need more input data, you will have to modify the test itself e.g. in order to verify an employee whose id is "10004" instead of "10002", you have to either update the existing test or write a new test. However, if the test is written with the data driven testing approach, you can have all the employee data in an Excel file and randomly pick an employee id during the test execution, hence giving you more data coverage at runtime. There is no need to modify the existing test or write a new test with this approach. We will cover two Excel formats – XLSX and XLS (Excel 97 – 2003) for the data sources.

In order to use Excel as data source, we will use NPOI which is the .NET version of POI Java project (http://poi.apache.org/). POI is an open source project which helps you read and write Excel files.

5.1 Adding Necessary References

First of all, let's add the necessary references to support Excel files.

- In the 'Solution Explorer' window, right click on 'References' and select Add Reference.

- Click the 'Browse...' button and navigate to 'C:\NPOI\dotnet4' folder. Your location may differ depending on where you extracted NPOI files.

- Select files 'NPOI.dll', 'NPOI.OOXML.dll' and 'NPOI.OpenXml4Net.dll' as shown in Figure 5.1. Use the Ctrl key to select multiple files.

- Click the Add button and then press OK.

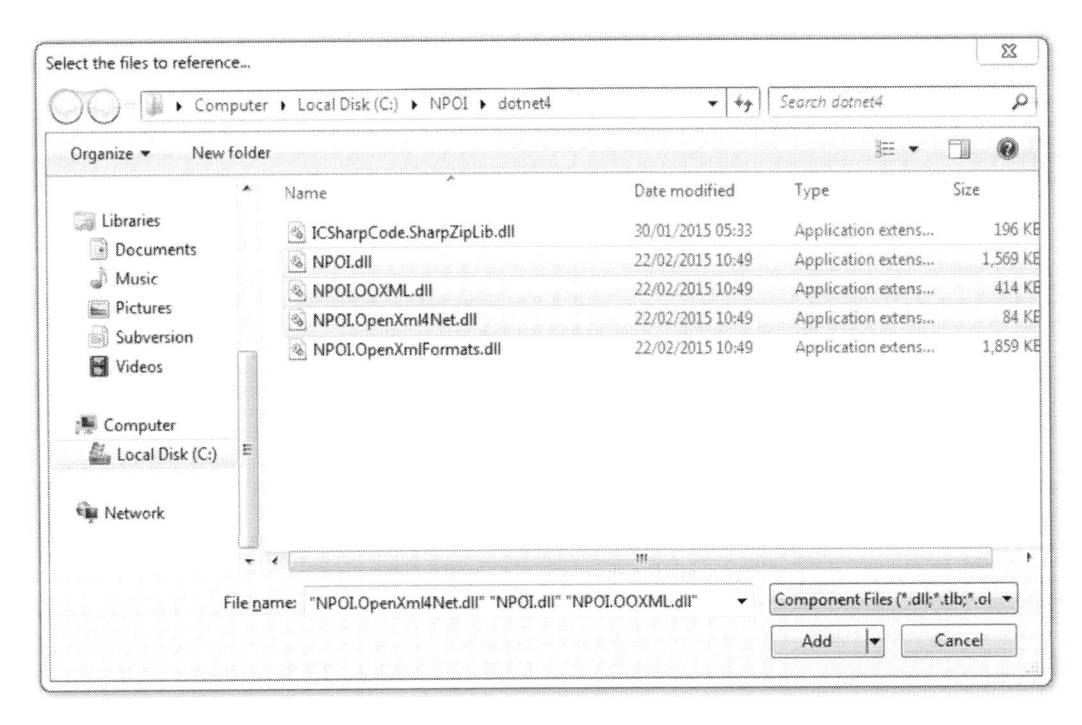

Figure 5.1: Adding References to Support Excel Files

5.2 Configuration Parameters

Let's add a configuration variable which we will need throughout our Automation Framework. Double click on the 'Config.cs' file in the 'Solution Explorer' and add the Listing 5.1 code to it.

Listing 5.1: 'Config.cs' - Parameters to support Excel data source

```
1  public const string UNKNOWN_CODE = "-99";
```

Line 1: Defines a string constant to hold the value of an Unknown Code.

5.3 Excel XLS Format

5.3.1 Utility Functions

EncodeGender - Encodes a gender text to its configured code		
Input Parameters	*genderText*	Gender text to be encoded
Return Value	*genderCode*	Returns the gender code

GetSpreadSheetXLS - Gets the Spreadsheet data in XLS format into a two dimensional array		
Input Parameters	*pathName*	Path and name of the XLS file to read
	sheetNumber	Sheet number of the XLS file to read
Return Value	*Spreadsheet Data*	Returns the spreadsheet data in a two dimensional array

ExcelDateParse - Converts Excel date format to a defined date format		
Input Parameters	*ExcelDate*	Date in Excel format
Return Value	*date*	Returns the date in yyyy-MM-dd format

Add Listing 5.2 code to the 'Utility.cs' file.

Listing 5.2: 'Utility.cs' - Changes to support XLS file format

```
1  using NPOI.HSSF.UserModel;
2
3  public static String EncodeGender(string genderText)
4  {
5      if (genderText.Trim().Equals(Config.MALE_TEXT))
6          return Config.MALE;
```

```
7       else if ↵
            ↪ (genderText.Trim().Equals(Config.FEMALE_TEXT))
8           return Config.FEMALE;
9       else
10          return Config.UNKNOWN_CODE;
11  }
12
13  public static String[][] GetSpreadSheetXLS(String ↵
        ↪ pathName, int sheetNumber)
14  {
15      Utility.Log.Info("GetSpreadSheetXLS....... File: " + ↵
            ↪ pathName + "         Sheet: " + sheetNumber);
16      String[][] ssData = { };
17
18      try {
19
20          FileStream ExcelFileToRead = new ↵
                ↪ FileStream(pathName, FileMode.Open, ↵
                ↪ FileAccess.Read);
21          HSSFWorkbook workbk = new ↵
                ↪ HSSFWorkbook(ExcelFileToRead);
22
23          HSSFSheet sheet = (HSSFSheet) ↵
                ↪ workbk.GetSheetAt(sheetNumber);
24
25          Utility.Log.Info("SHEET Name: " + ↵
                ↪ sheet.SheetName);
26
27          Utility.Log.Info("SHEET LastRowNum: " + ↵
                ↪ sheet.LastRowNum);
28          Utility.Log.Info("SHEET ColumnCount: " + ↵
                ↪ sheet.GetRow(0).Cells.Count);
29
30          int rowCount = sheet.LastRowNum + 1;
31          int colCount = sheet.GetRow(0).Cells.Count;
32
33          Array.Resize(ref ssData, rowCount);
34
35          int i = 0;
36
37          while (sheet.GetRow(i) != null)
38          {
39              Array.Resize(ref ssData[i], colCount);
40
41              for (int j = 0; j < ↵
```

```
                         ↪ sheet.GetRow(i).Cells.Count; j++)
42              {
43                  var cell = sheet.GetRow(i).GetCell(j);
44
45                  if (cell != null)
46                  {
47                      Utility.Log.Info("CellType: " + ↵
                         ↪ cell.CellType);
48
49                      switch (cell.CellType)
50                      {
51                          case ↵
                             ↪ NPOI.SS.UserModel.CellType.Numeric:
52                              ssData[i][j] = ↵
                                 ↪ sheet.GetRow(i).GetCell(j). ↵
                                 ↪ NumericCellValue.ToString();
53                              break;
54                          case ↵
                             ↪ NPOI.SS.UserModel.CellType.String:
55                              ssData[i][j] = ↵
                                 ↪ sheet.GetRow(i).GetCell(j). ↵
                                 ↪ StringCellValue.ToString();
56                              break;
57                      }
58
59                      Utility.Log.Info("Row: " + (i) + "    ↵
                         ↪ Col: " + (j) + "   " + ↵
                         ↪ ssData[i][j] + " ");
60                  }
61              }
62
63              i++;
64          }
65
66          return ssData;
67      }
68      catch (Exception exception)
69      {
70          Utility.Log.Error("GetSpreadSheetXLS Exception: " ↵
             ↪ + exception.ToString());
71          throw exception;
72      }
73 }
74
75 public static String ExcelDateParse(String ExcelDate)
```

```
76  {
77      double dt = Double.Parse(ExcelDate);
78
79      DateTime dt1 = ↵
          ↪ NPOI.SS.UserModel.DateUtil.GetJavaDate(dt);
80
81      return dt1.ToString();
82  }
```

Line 1: Additional import required to support the functionality.
Line 5: If the gender text is a "Male" then returns the male's code.
Line 7: If the gender text is a "female" then returns the female's code.
Line 10: Otherwise returns an unknown code.
Line 15: Logs the received parameters.
Line 16: Initialises the two dimensional array.
Line 20: Initialises a new instance of the `FileStream` class with the specified pathname, creation mode and access permission:

- PathName - path and name of the XLS file.

- FileMode `Open` - the operating system should open an existing file.

- FileAccess `Read` - read access to the file. Data can be read from the file.

Line 21: Initialises a new instance of the `HSSFWorkbook` class - high level representation of a workbook.
Line 23: Gets the worksheet specified by the sheet number.
Line 25: Logs the sheet name.
Line 27: Logs the last row number in the sheet.
Line 28: Logs the column count of the first row.
Line 30: Initialises a variable for the row count.
Line 31: Initialises a variable for the column count
Line 33: Resizes the data array to the row count - to accommodate all the rows.
Line 35: Initialises a row variable.
Line 37: Loops while there are rows in the worksheet.
Line 39: Resizes current row of the data array to the column count - to accommodate all the columns.
Line 41: Loops while there are columns in the current row.
Line 43: Gets the cell at the current row and column position.
Line 45: Ensures that the cell is not null.
Line 51: If the cell type is numeric, gets its numeric value and stores it in the two dimensional array at the current row and column position.
Line 54: If the cell type is string, gets its string value and stores it in the two dimensional array at the current row and column position.
Line 59: Logs the array data at the current row and column position.
Line 63: Increments the row variable.
Line 66: Returns the spreadsheet data.

5.3.2 Data Driven - Login

Let's write a data driven login test that will read data from an Excel file in the XLS format, rather than hard-coded values. We will perform the following Test Scenario to demonstrate data driven login:

- Launch the demo website.
- Click on the *Login* link.
- Read the user credentials from the test data file in XLS format.
- Login the general user with the credentials read above.

5.3.2.1 Test Data File

As you know, the demo website has two users - 'Tester' and 'Admin'. We will create the login credentials for both of these users in the data source. Here are the steps to create the test data file in XLS format.

- Open Excel and create test data as shown in Figure 5.2.
- Row 1 is the header row.
- Column A contains the User id and Column B contains the Password.
- Rename the worksheet as 'Login'.

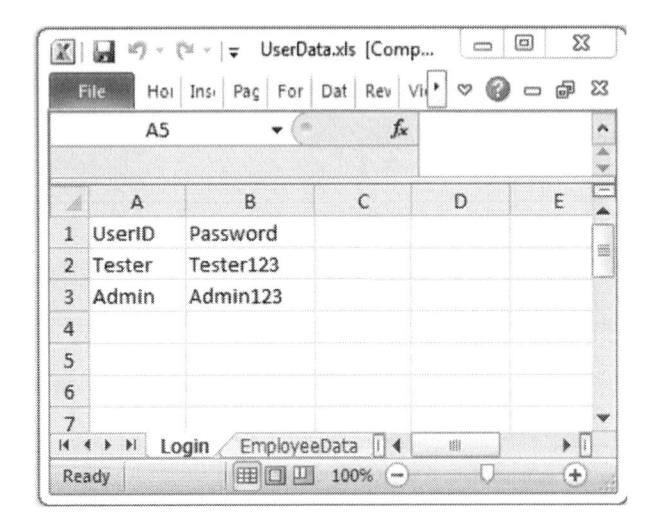

Figure 5.2: XLS Format- Creating Login Test Data

- Save data file as 'UserData.xls' in 'C:\WebTesting\WebTesting\TestData' folder. Ensure that the "Save as type" is 'Excel 97-2003 Workbook (*.xls)'.
- Close Excel.

5.3.2.2 Creating Test

Add Listing 5.3 code to the 'TestLogins.cs' file.

Listing 5.3: 'TestLogins.cs' - Code for test LoginUserXLSData

```
1  [Test]
2  public void LoginUserXLSData()
3  {
4      try
5      {
6          Utility.Log.Info("Starting test: " + ↵
                 TestContext.CurrentContext.Test.FullName);
7
8          var home = new pageHome(driver);
9          home.Visit();
10         home.ClickLogin();
11
12         var login = new pageLogin(driver);
13
14         String[][] data = Utility.GetSpreadSheetXLS( ↵
                 @"C:\WebTesting\WebTesting\TestData\UserData.xls", ↵
                 0);
15
16         login.Login(data[1][0], data[1][1]);
17         Utility.ReportResult();
18     }
19     catch (Exception exception)
20     {
21         Utility.Log.Error("exception" + ↵
                 exception.ToString());
22         throw exception;
23     }
24 }
```

Line 1: New login test to use Excel XLS file as a data source.
Line 14: Gets the spreadsheet data in a two dimensional array. Note that second parameter 0 corresponds to the first worksheet.
Line 16: Calls the Login function with the data read from the XLS file. Parameter 'data[1][0]' is the user id 'Tester' and 'data[1][1]' is its password 'Tester123'. Note that C# arrays are zero indexed i.e. the array indexes start at zero.

Automated Web Testing

5.3.2.3 Executing Test

Execute the test and you will see an output as shown in Figure 5.3. The login credentials are read from the XLS file and the user is logged in successfully.

> ☞ If the Test Data file in Excel is not closed, you will get an error "System.IO.IOException: The process cannot access the file 'C:\WebTesting\WebTesting\TestData\UserData.xls' because it is being used by another process." Ensure that the Test Data file in Excel is closed before executing the test.

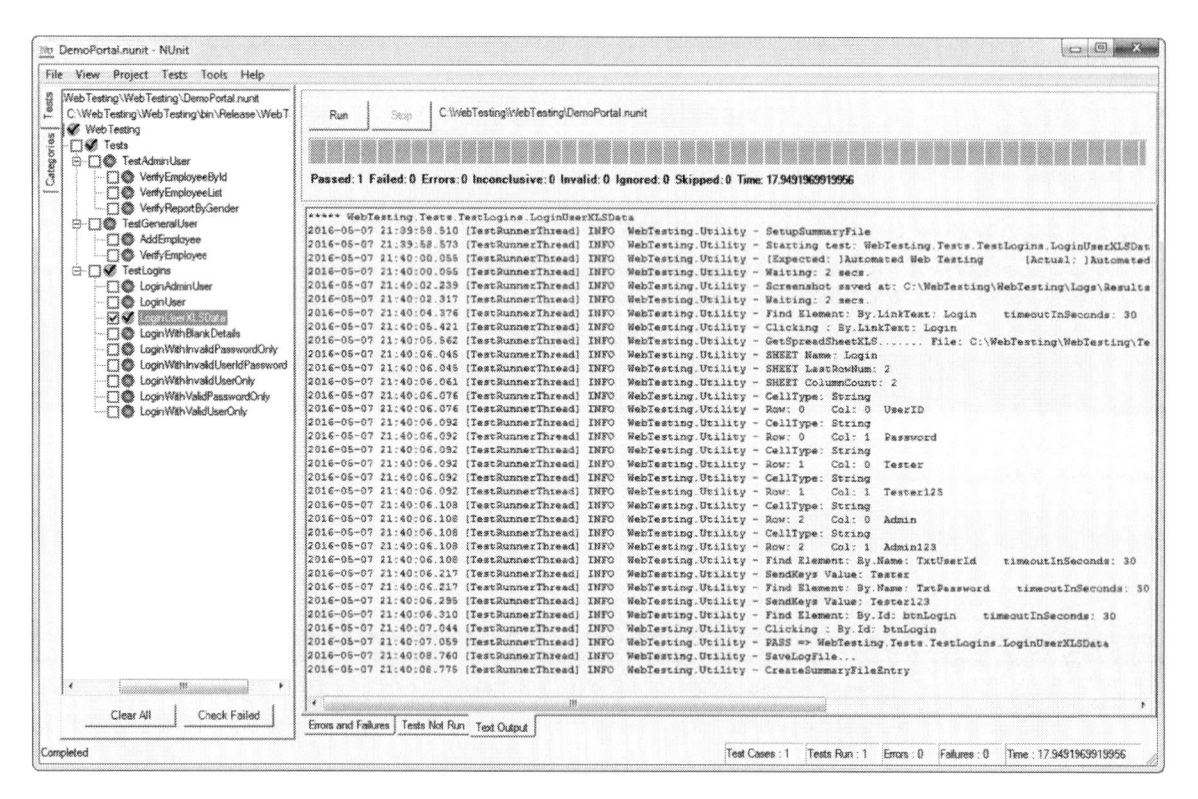

Figure 5.3: Data Driven Login Output

5.3.3 Data Driven - Add Employee

Let's write a data driven test to add an employee as per the following Test Scenario:

- Launch the demo website.

- Click on the *Login* link.

- Read user credentials from the test data file in XLS format.

- Login the general user with the credentials read above.

- Click on the *Add Employee* link.

- Read the employee data to be added from the test data file in XLS format.

- Add the employee using the data read above

5.3.3.1 Test Data File

- Open 'UserData.xls' file, add a new worksheet and create the test data as shown in Figure 5.4.

- Row 1 is the header row.

- Rename the worksheet as 'EmployeeData'.

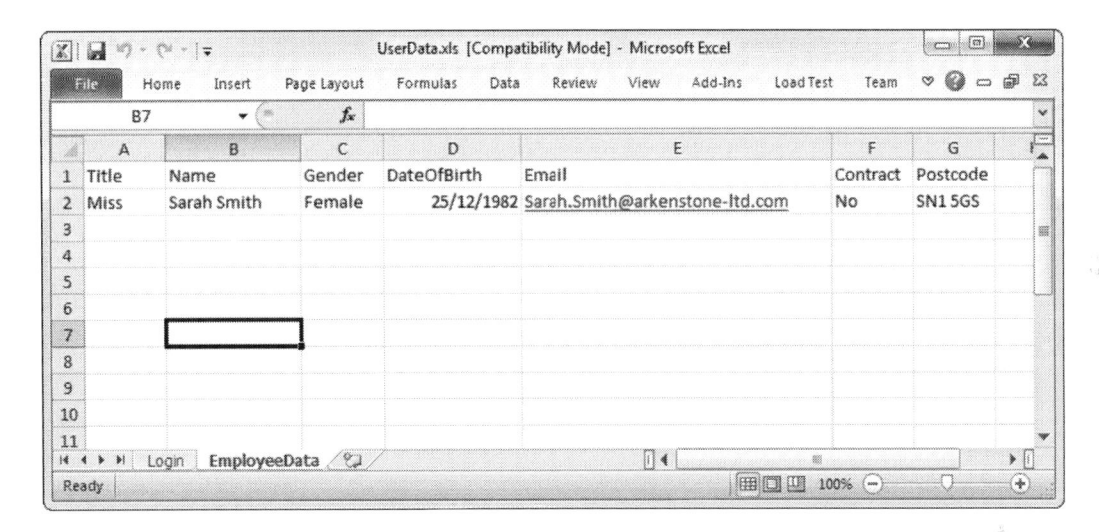

Figure 5.4: XLS Format - Creating Employee Data

- Save the data file. Ensure that the "Save as type" is 'Excel 97-2003 Workbook (*.xls)'.

- Close Excel.

5.3.3.2 Page Logic

We will add a new action to the *Add Employee* page's logic as follows:

Action	Description
AddEmployeeXLSData()	This action will add an employee using data read from an XLS file.

Let's now add the page logic as shown in Listing 5.4 to the 'pageTesterAddEmployee.cs' file.

Listing 5.4: 'pageTesterAddEmployee.cs' - New function AddEmployeeXLSData

```
1  public void AddEmployeeXLSData()
2  {
3      String[][] data = Utility.GetSpreadSheetXLS(
            @"C:\WebTesting\WebTesting\TestData\UserData.xls",
            1);
4
5      Utility.SelectOptionInList(driver,
            By.Name(Repository.EmployeeDetail.lbTitle_ByName),
            data[1][0]);
6      Utility.FindElementAndSendKeys(driver,
            By.Id(Repository.EmployeeDetail.txtName_ById),
            data[1][1]);
7      Utility.SelectRadioButton(driver,
            Repository.EmployeeDetail.rbGender_ById,
            Utility.EncodeGender(data[1][2]));
8      Utility.FindElementAndSendKeys(driver,
            By.Name(Repository.EmployeeDetail.
            txtDateOfBirth_ByName),
            Utility.ExcelDateParse(data[1][3]));
9      Utility.FindElementAndSendKeys(driver,
            By.Name(Repository.EmployeeDetail.txtEmail_ByName),
            data[1][4]);
10
11     if (data[1][5].Equals(Config.YES))
12         Utility.FindElementAndClick(driver,
                By.Name(Repository.EmployeeDetail.
                cbContractJob_ByName));
13
14     Utility.FindElementAndSendKeys(driver,
            By.Id(Repository.EmployeeDetail.txtPostcode_ById),
            data[1][6]);
15
16     Utility.FindElementAndClick(driver,
            By.Id(Repository.EmployeeDetail.btnAdd_ById));
17
18     Utility.HandleAlert(driver,
            Config.RECORD_ADDED_SUCCESSFULLY);
19 }
```

Line 1: New test to add an employee using Excel XLS file as a data source.
Line 3: Gets the spreadsheet data in a two dimensional array. Note that the second parameter 1 corresponds to the second worksheet.

Line 5: Parameter 'data[1][0]' is the Title 'Miss'. Note that C# arrays are zero indexed i.e. the array indexes start at zero.
Line 6: Parameter 'data[1][1]' is the Name 'Sarah Smith'.
Line 7: Parameter 'data[1][2]' is the Gender 'Female'.
Line 8: Parameter 'data[1][3]' is the DateOfBirth '25/12/1982'.
Line 9: Parameter 'data[1][4]' is the Email 'Sarah.Smith@arkenstone-ltd.com'.
Line 11: Parameter 'data[1][5]' is the Contract 'No'.
Line 14: Parameter 'data[1][6]' is the Postcode 'SN1 5GS'.
Line 16: Clicks the Add button.
Line 18: Verifies the success message.

5.3.3.3 Creating Test

Add Listing 5.5 code to the 'TestGeneralUser.cs' file.

Listing 5.5: 'TestGeneralUser.cs' - New test AddEmployeeXLSData

```
1  [Test]
2  public void AddEmployeeXLSData()
3  {
4      try
5      {
6          Utility.Log.Info("Starting test: " +
                TestContext.CurrentContext.Test.FullName);
7
8          var home = new pageHome(driver);
9          home.Visit();
10         home.ClickLogin();
11
12         var login = new pageLogin(driver);
13         String[][] data = Utility.GetSpreadSheetXLS(
                @"C:\WebTesting\WebTesting\TestData\UserData.xls",
                0);
14
15         login.Login(data[1][0], data[1][1]);
16
17         var homeTester = new pageTesterHome(driver);
18         homeTester.ClickAddEmployee();
19
20         var emp = new pageTesterAddEmployee(driver);
21         emp.AddEmployeeXLSData();
22
23         Utility.ReportResult();
24     }
```

```
25      catch (Exception exception)
26      {
27          Utility.Log.Error("exception" + ↵
              ↪ exception.ToString());
28          throw exception;
29      }
30  }
```

Line 1: New test to add an employee using Excel XLS file as a data source.
Line 13: Gets the spreadsheet data in a two dimensional array. Note that the second parameter 0 corresponds to the first worksheet.
Line 15: Logins with the data read from the first worksheet.
Line 21: Adds employee using data read from the second worksheet.

5.3.3.4 Executing Test

Execute the test and you will see an output as shown in Figure 5.5. The employee was added using data read from the XLS file.

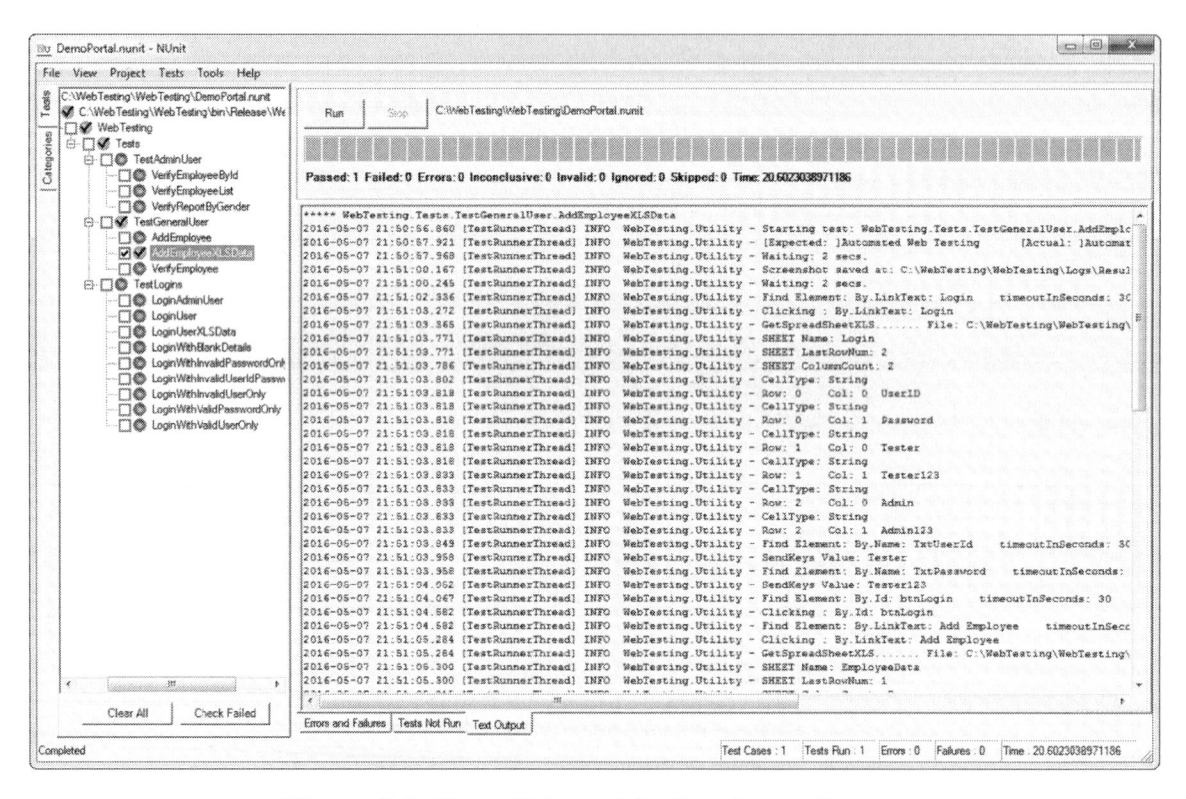

Figure 5.5: Data Driven Add Employee Output

5.3.4 Data Driven - View Employee Verification

Let's write a data driven test to verify an employee with the data read from the Excel file as per the following Test Scenario:

- Launch the demo website.
- Click on the *Login* link.
- Read the user credentials from the test data file in XLS format.
- Login the general user with the credentials read above.
- Click on the *View Employee* link.
- Read the employee data to be verified from the test data file in XLS format.
- Verify the employee using data read above

5.3.4.1 Page Logic

We will now add a new action to the *View Employee* page's logic as follows:

Action	Description
VerifyEmployeeXLSData()	This action will verify the employee details displayed on the web page with data read from the XLS file.

Let's now add the page logic as shown in Listing 5.6 to the 'pageTesterViewEmployee.cs' file.

Listing 5.6: 'pageTesterViewEmployee.cs' - Code for VerifyEmployeeXLSData

```
1  public void VerifyEmployeeXLSData()
2  {
3      String[][] data = Utility.GetSpreadSheetXLS(
           @"C:\WebTesting\WebTesting\TestData\UserData.xls",
           1);
4
5      Utility.ReportExpectedVsActual(driver, "10004",
           Utility.FindElementAndReturn(driver,
           By.Name(Repository.EmployeeDetail.
           txtEmployeeId_ByName)).GetAttribute("Value"));
6      Utility.ReportExpectedVsActual(driver, data[1][0],
           Utility.FindElementAndReturn(driver,
           By.Name(Repository.EmployeeDetail.lbTitle_ByName)).
           Text);
7      Utility.ReportExpectedVsActual(driver, data[1][1],
           Utility.FindElementAndReturn(driver,
           By.Id(Repository.EmployeeDetail.txtName_ById)).
           GetAttribute("Value"));
```

```
8       Utility.ReportExpectedVsActual(driver, ↵
          ↪ Utility.EncodeGender(data[1][2]), ↵
          ↪ Utility.GetSelectedRadioButton(driver, ↵
          ↪ Repository.EmployeeDetail.rbGender_ById).ToString());
9       Utility.ReportExpectedVsActual(driver, ↵
          ↪ Utility.ExcelDateParse(data[1][3]).Substring(0, ↵
          ↪ 10), Utility.FindElementAndReturn(driver, ↵
          ↪ By.Name(Repository.EmployeeDetail. ↵
          ↪ txtDateOfBirth_ByName)).GetAttribute("Value"));
10      Utility.ReportExpectedVsActual(driver, ↵
          ↪ data[1][4].ToLower(), ↵
          ↪ Utility.FindElementAndReturn(driver, ↵
          ↪ By.Name(Repository.EmployeeDetail.txtEmail_ByName)). ↵
          ↪ GetAttribute("Value").ToLower());
11      Utility.ReportExpectedVsActual(driver, ↵
          ↪ Utility.DecodeContract(data[1][5]), ↵
          ↪ Utility.FindElementAndReturn(driver, ↵
          ↪ By.Name(Repository.EmployeeDetail. ↵
          ↪ cbContractJob_ByName)).Selected.ToString());
12      Utility.ReportExpectedVsActual(driver, data[1][6], ↵
          ↪ Utility.FindElementAndReturn(driver, ↵
          ↪ By.Id(Repository.EmployeeDetail.txtPostcode_ById)). ↵
          ↪ GetAttribute("Value"));
13
14      Utility.FindElementAndClick(driver, ↵
          ↪ By.CssSelector(Repository. ↵
          ↪ EmployeeDetail.btnClose_ByCSS));
15  }
```

Line 3: Gets the spreadsheet data in a two dimensional array from the second worksheet.
Line 6 - 12: Verify values with the data read from the worksheet.

5.3.4.2 Creating Test

Add Listing 5.7 code to the 'TestGeneralUser.cs' file.

Listing 5.7: 'TestGeneralUser.cs' - Code for VerifyEmployeeXLSData

```
1  [Test]
2  public void VerifyEmployeeXLSData()
3  {
4      try
5      {
```

```
 6              Utility.Log.Info("Starting test: " + ↵
                ↪ TestContext.CurrentContext.Test.FullName);
 7
 8              var home = new pageHome(driver);
 9              home.Visit();
10              home.ClickLogin();
11
12              var login = new pageLogin(driver);
13              String[][] data = Utility.GetSpreadSheetXLS( ↵
                ↪ @"C:\WebTesting\WebTesting\TestData\UserData.xls", ↵
                ↪ 0);
14
15              login.Login(data[1][0], data[1][1]);
16
17              var homeTester = new pageTesterHome(driver);
18              homeTester.ClickViewEmployee();
19
20              var emp = new pageTesterViewEmployee(driver);
21              emp.VerifyEmployeeXLSData();
22
23              Utility.ReportResult();
24          }
25          catch (Exception exception)
26          {
27              Utility.Log.Error("exception" + ↵
                ↪ exception.ToString());
28              throw exception;
29          }
30 }
```

Line 1: New test to verify an employee using Excel XLS file as a data source.

Line 13: Gets the spreadsheet data in a two dimensional array. Note that the second parameter 0 corresponds to the first worksheet.

Line 15: Logins with the data read from the first worksheet.

Line 21: Verifies the employee using data read from the second worksheet.

5.3.4.3 Executing Test

Execute the test and you will see an output as shown in Figure 5.6. The employee is verified with the data read from the data file in XLS format.

Automated Web Testing

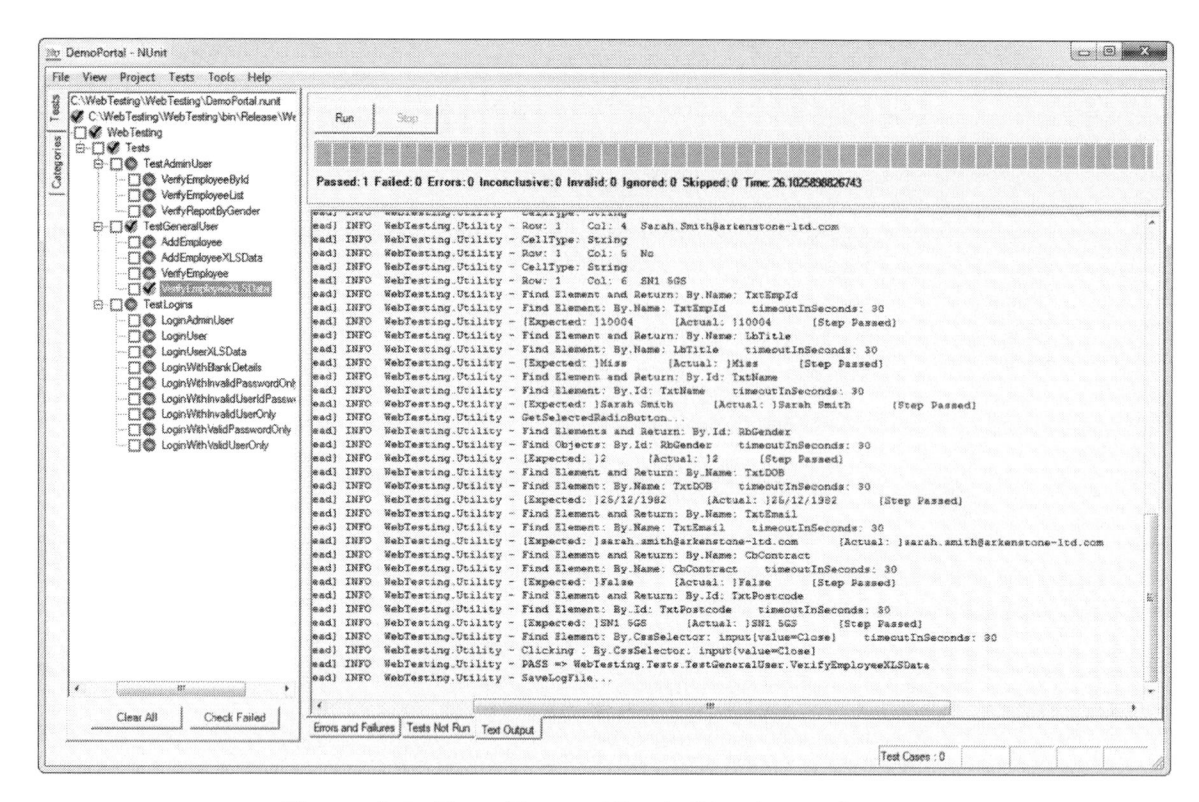

Figure 5.6: Data Driven Verify Employee Output

5.4 Excel XLSX Format

5.4.1 Utility Functions

GetSpreadSheetXLSX - Gets the Spreadsheet data in XLSX format into a two dimensional array		
Input Parameters	*pathName*	Path and name of the XLSX file to read
	sheetNumber	Sheet number of the XLSX file to read
Return Value	*Spreadsheet Data*	Returns the spreadsheet data in a two dimensional array

Add Listing 5.8 to the 'Utility.cs' file.

Listing 5.8: 'Utility.cs' - Code for GetSpreadSheetXLSX

```
1  using NPOI.XSSF.UserModel;
2
3  public static String[][] GetSpreadSheetXLSX(String ↵
      ↪ pathName, int sheetNumber)
4  {
```

```csharp
 5      Utility.Log.Info("GetSpreadSheetXLSX....... File: " +
            pathName + "      Sheet: " + sheetNumber);
 6      String[][] ssData = { };
 7
 8      try
 9      {
10          FileStream ExcelFileToRead = new
                FileStream(pathName, FileMode.Open,
                FileAccess.Read);
11          XSSFWorkbook workbk = new
                XSSFWorkbook(ExcelFileToRead);
12
13          XSSFSheet sheet =
                (XSSFSheet)workbk.GetSheetAt(sheetNumber);
14
15          Utility.Log.Info("SHEET Name: " +
                sheet.SheetName);
16
17          Utility.Log.Info("SHEET LastRowNum: " +
                sheet.LastRowNum);
18          Utility.Log.Info("SHEET ColumnCount: " +
                sheet.GetRow(0).Cells.Count);
19
20          int rowCount = sheet.LastRowNum + 1;
21          int colCount = sheet.GetRow(0).Cells.Count;
22
23          Array.Resize(ref ssData, rowCount);
24
25          int i = 0;
26
27          while (sheet.GetRow(i) != null)
28          {
29              Array.Resize(ref ssData[i], colCount);
30
31              for (int j = 0; j <
                    sheet.GetRow(i).Cells.Count; j++)
32              {
33                  var cell = sheet.GetRow(i).GetCell(j);
34
35                  if (cell != null)
36                  {
37                      Utility.Log.Info("CellType: " +
                            cell.CellType);
38
39                      switch (cell.CellType)
```

```
40                              {
41                                      case ↵
                                         ↪ NPOI.SS.UserModel.CellType.Numeric:
42                                          ssData[i][j] = ↵
                                             ↪ sheet.GetRow(i).GetCell(j). ↵
                                             ↪ NumericCellValue.ToString();
43                                          break;
44                                      case ↵
                                         ↪ NPOI.SS.UserModel.CellType.String:
45                                          ssData[i][j] = ↵
                                             ↪ sheet.GetRow(i).GetCell(j). ↵
                                             ↪ StringCellValue.ToString();
46                                          break;
47                              }
48
49                              Utility.Log.Info("Row: " + (i) + "          ↵
                                  ↪ Col: " + (j) + "        " + ↵
                                  ↪ ssData[i][j] + " ");
50                          }
51                      }
52
53                      i++;
54                  }
55
56              return ssData;
57          }
58          catch (Exception exception)
59          {
60              Utility.Log.Error("GetSpreadSheetXLS Exception: " ↵
                  ↪ + exception.ToString());
61              throw exception;
62          }
63 }
```

Line 1: Additional import required to support the functionality.
Line 5: Logs the received parameters.
Line 6: Initialises the two dimensional array.
Line 10: Initialises a new instance of the `FileStream` class with the specified pathname, creation mode and access permission:

- PathName - path and name of the XLS file.

- FileMode `Open` - the operating system should open an existing file.

- FileAccess `Read` - read access to the file. Data can be read from the file.

Line 11: Initialises a new instance of the `XSSFWorkbook` class - high level representation of a workbook.
Line 13: Gets the worksheet specified by the sheet number.
Line 15: Logs the sheet name.
Line 17: Logs the last row number in the sheet.
Line 18: Logs the column count of the first row.
Line 20: Initialises a variable for the row count.
Line 21: Initialises a variable for the column count
Line 23: Resizes the data array to the row count - to accommodate all the rows.
Line 25: Initialises a row variable.
Line 27: Loops while there are rows in the worksheet.
Line 29: Resizes current row of the data array to the column count - to accommodate all the columns.
Line 31: Loops while there are columns in the current row.
Line 33: Gets the cell at the current row and column position.
Line 35: Ensures that the cell is not null.
Line 41: If the cell type is numeric, gets its numeric value and stores it in the two dimensional array at the current row and column position.
Line 44: If the cell type is string, gets its string value and stores it in the two dimensional array at the current row and column position.
Line 49: Logs the array data at the current row and column position.
Line 53: Increments the row variable.
Line 56: Returns the spreadsheet data.

5.4.2 Data Driven - Employee List Verification

Let's write a test to verify the *Employee List* for the Admin user that will read data from the Excel file in the XLSX format as per the following Test Scenario:

- Launch the demo website.

- Click on the *Login* link.

- Read the user credentials from the test data file in XLSX format.

- Login the admin user with the credentials read above.

- Click on the *Employee List* link.

- Read the 'employee list' data to be verified from the test data file in XLSX format.

- Verify the employee list using the data read above

5.4.2.1 Test Data File

Here are the steps to create the test data in XLSX format.

- Open Excel and create the test data as shown in Figure 5.7.

Automated Web Testing

- Row 1 is the header row.
- Column A contains the User id and Column B contains the Password.
- Rename the worksheet as 'Login'.

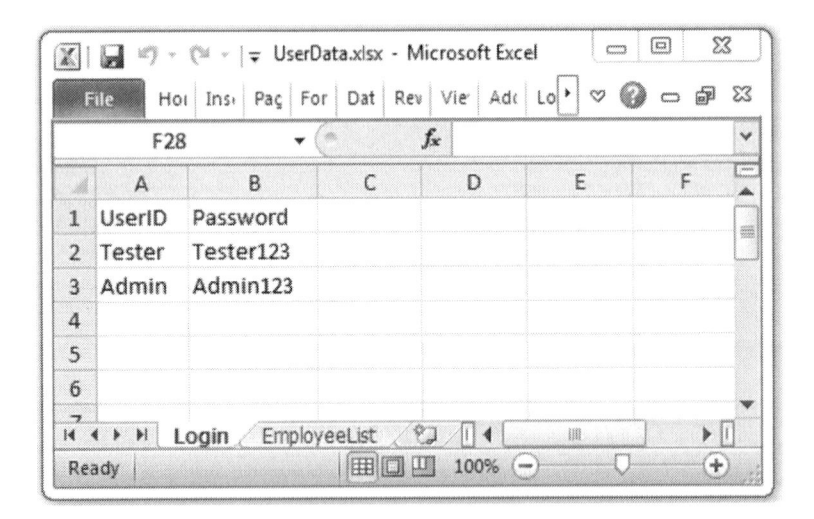

Figure 5.7: XLSX Format - Creating Login Test Data

- Add a new worksheet and create the test data as shown in Figure 5.8.
- Row 1 is the header row.
- Rename the worksheet as 'EmployeeList'.
- Save the data file as 'UserData.xlsx' in 'C:\WebTesting\WebTesting\TestData' folder. Ensure that the "Save as type" is 'Excel Workbook (*.xlsx)'.

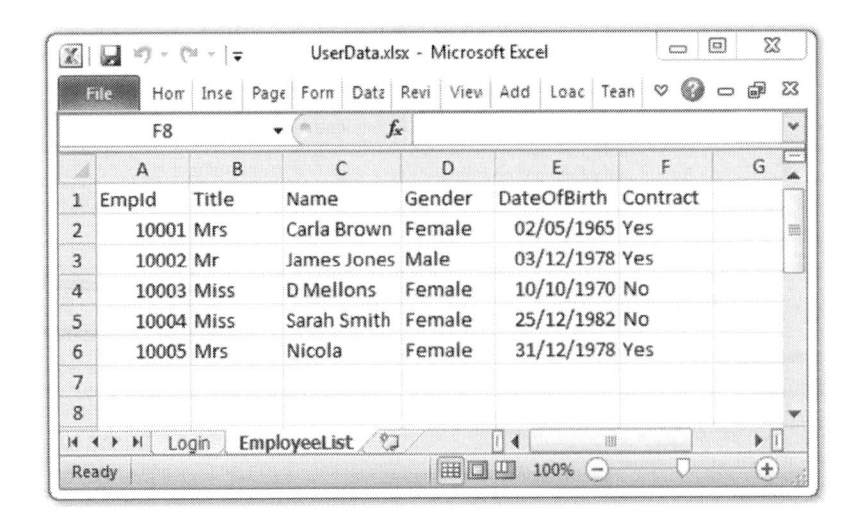

Figure 5.8: XLSX Format - Creating Employee List Test Data

5.4.2.2 Page Logic

We will add a new action to the *Employee List* page's logic as follows:

Action	Description
VerifyEmployeeListXLSXData()	This action will verify the employees' details displayed in the web page with the data fetched from the XLSX file.

Let's now add the page logic, as shown in Listing 5.9, to the 'pageAdminEmpList.cs' file.

Listing 5.9: 'pageAdminEmpList.cs' - Code for VerifyEmployeeListXLSXData

```
 1  public void VerifyEmployeeListXLSXData()
 2  {
 3      ReadOnlyCollection<IWebElement> rowCollection =
            Utility.FindElementsAndReturn(driver,
            By.XPath("//*[@id='" +
            Repository.EmployeeListAdmin.tblEmployeesTable_ById
            + "']/tbody/tr"));
 4
 5      Utility.Log.Info("Number of rows in this table: " +
            rowCollection.Count);
 6
 7      int i_RowNum = 0;
 8
 9      string[,] a = new string[rowCollection.Count, 6];
10
11      foreach (IWebElement rowElement in rowCollection)
12      {
13          ReadOnlyCollection<IWebElement> colCollection =
                rowElement.FindElements(By.XPath("td"));
14          int i_ColNum = 0;
15
16          Utility.Log.Info("Checking row: " + (i_RowNum));
17
18          foreach (IWebElement colElement in colCollection)
19          {
20              String stg;
21              if (i_ColNum == 5)
22                  stg =
                        Utility.FindElementAndReturn(driver,
```

```csharp
                            By.XPath("//tr[" + (i_RowNum + 1) +
                                "]/td[6]/input[@type='checkbox']")).
                                Selected.ToString();
23                  else
24                      stg = colElement.Text;
25
26                  a[i_RowNum, i_ColNum] = stg;
27                  Utility.Log.Info("Row: " + (i_RowNum) + "
                        Column: " + i_ColNum + " Text: " +
                        a[i_RowNum, i_ColNum]);
28
29                  i_ColNum = i_ColNum + 1;
30              }
31              i_RowNum = i_RowNum + 1;
32          }
33
34          String[][] data = Utility.GetSpreadSheetXLSX(
                @"C:\WebTesting\WebTesting\TestData\UserData.xlsx",
                1);
35
36          for (int i = 1; i < rowCollection.Count; i++)
37          {
38              Utility.ReportExpectedVsActual(driver, a[i, 0],
                    data[i][0]);
39              Utility.ReportExpectedVsActual(driver, a[i, 1],
                    data[i][1]);
40              Utility.ReportExpectedVsActual(driver, a[i, 2],
                    data[i][2]);
41              Utility.ReportExpectedVsActual(driver, a[i, 3],
                    data[i][3]);
42              Utility.ReportExpectedVsActual(driver, a[i, 4],
                    Utility.ExcelDateParse(data[i][4]).Substring(0,
                    10));
43              Utility.ReportExpectedVsActual(driver, a[i, 5],
                    Utility.DecodeContract(data[i][5]));
44          }
45
46      Utility.ReportExpectedVsActual(driver,
                Utility.FindElementAndReturn(driver,
                By.Id(Repository.EmployeeListAdmin.lblTotal_ById)).
                Text, Utility.GetCountOfRecs("Select Count(*)
                from [dbo].[Employees]").ToString());
47      }
```

Line 26: Gets the web page table data in a two dimensional array.
Line 34: Gets the spreadsheet data in a two dimensional array from the second worksheet.
Line 36: Verifies the values read from the web page table with the data read from the worksheet.

5.4.2.3 Creating Test

Add Listing 5.7 code to the 'TestAdminUser.cs' file.

Listing 5.10: 'TestAdminUser.cs' - Code for VerifyEmployeeListXLSXData

```
1  [Test]
2  public void VerifyEmployeeListXLSXData()
3  {
4      try
5      {
6          Utility.Log.Info("Starting test: " + 
                TestContext.CurrentContext.Test.FullName);
7
8          var home = new pageHome(driver);
9          home.Visit();
10         home.ClickLogin();
11
12         var login = new pageLogin(driver);
13         String[][] data = Utility.GetSpreadSheetXLSX( 
                @"C:\WebTesting\WebTesting\TestData\UserData.xlsx", 
                0);
14
15         login.Login(data[2][0], data[2][1]);
16
17         var homeAdmin = new pageAdminHome(driver);
18         homeAdmin.ClickEmployeeList();
19
20         var empList = new pageAdminEmpList(driver);
21         empList.VerifyEmployeeListXLSXData();
22
23         Utility.ReportResult();
24     }
25     catch (Exception exception)
26     {
27         Utility.Log.Error("exception" + 
                exception.ToString());
28         throw exception;
29     }
```

```
30  }
```

Line 1: New test to verify employee list using Excel XLSX file as a data source.
Line 13: Gets the spreadsheet data in a two dimensional array. Note that the second parameter 0 corresponds to the first worksheet.
Line 15: Logins with the data read from the first worksheet. Note that 'data[2][0]' is user id 'Admin' and 'data[2][1]' is its password.
Line 21: Verifies the employee list using data read from the second worksheet.

5.4.2.4 Executing Test

Execute the test and you will see an output as shown in Figure 5.9. The *Employee List* table data is verified with the data read from the Excel file in XLSX format.

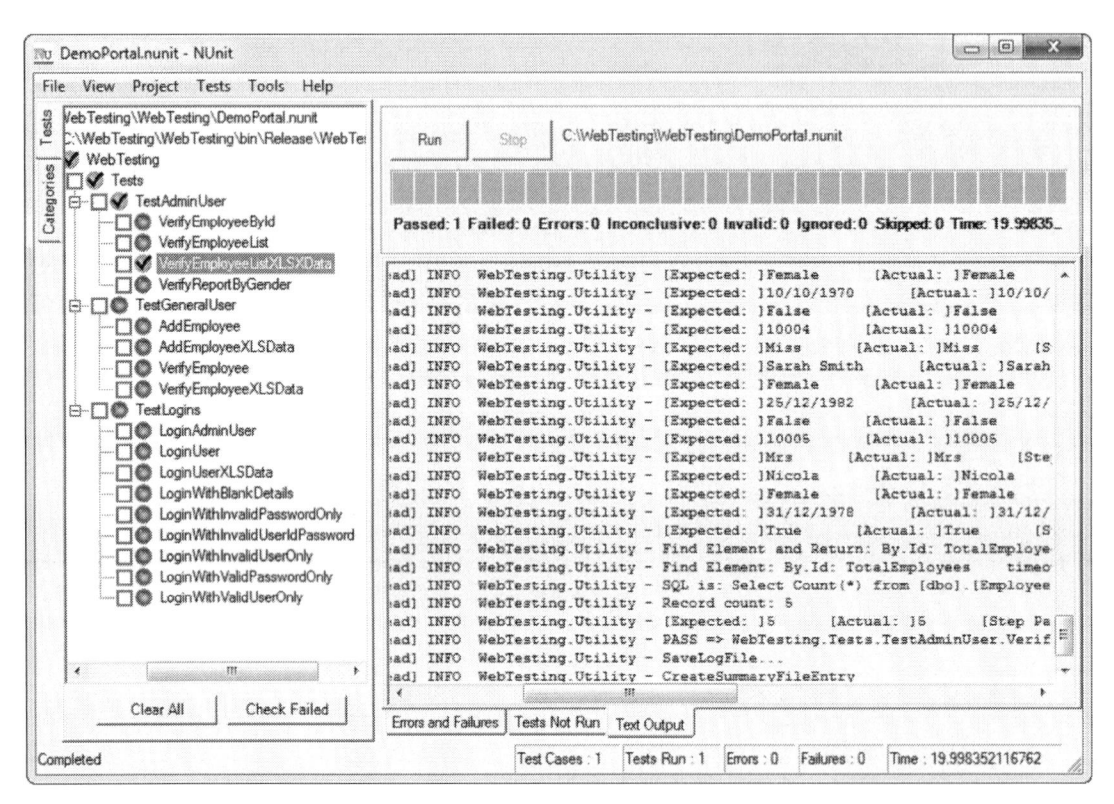

Figure 5.9: Data Driven Verify Employee List Output

5.5 Automation Framework - Adding More Features

5.5.1 Test Step Failure Threshold

Let us consider a scenario where you are executing a long test with many test steps. The current Automation Framework will execute all of the steps and only report any failures at the end. Sometimes you may want to fail the test as soon as the first failure occurs. On the other hand, you may want to continue the test execution until you reach a predefined threshold of test step failures. So let's see how we can achieve this.

We will perform the following Test Scenario to demonstrate the test step failure threshold:

- Launch the demo website.
- Login with the user 'Tester'.
- Click on the *View Employee* link.
- Verify the employee with a test step failure threshold of 3 i.e. make the test fail once three test steps have failed.

5.5.1.1 Configuration Parameters

Let's add some configuration variables which we will need throughout our Automation Framework. Double click on the 'Config.cs' file in the 'Solution Explorer' and add the Listing 5.11 code to it.

Listing 5.11: 'Config.cs' - Parameters for Test Step Failure Threshold

```
1  public static int STEP_PASS = 0;
2  public static int STEP_FAIL = 1;
3  public static int STEP_FAIL_THRESHOLD = 3;
```

Line 1: Defines an integer value of a *Passed* step.
Line 2: Defines an integer value of a *Failed* step.
Line 3: Defines the test step failure threshold. A value of 3 means when the Automation Framework encounters 3 failures then it will stop executing further steps in the test.

5.5.1.2 Utility Functions

Let's define a new Utility function.

CheckFailureThreshold - Checks for the failure threshold; if reached then fails the test		
Input Parameters	*count*	Current count of failures
Return Value	*void*	Returns nothing

Add Listing 5.12 code to the 'Utility.cs' file.

Listing 5.12: 'Utility.cs' - Code for CheckFailureThreshold

```
1  public static void CheckFailureThreshold(int count)
```

```
2  {
3      if (count >= Config.STEP_FAIL_THRESHOLD)
4      {
5          Log.Error("Test Step Failure Threshold reached... ↵
                ↪ Failing Test.");
6          ReportResult();
7      }
8  }
```

Line 3: If current failure count reaches the configured threshold, reports the result and fails the test.

We need to update the existing function `ReportExpectedVsActual` as defined below:

ReportExpectedVsActual - Reports the outcome of expected verses actual result comparison		
Input Parameters	*driver*	Object driver to control the browser
	expected	Expected result
	actual	Actual result
Return Value	*int*	Returns integer value of Pass or Fail configured parameters

Update 'Utility.cs' file as shown in Listing 5.13.

Listing 5.13: 'Utility.cs' - Updated code for ReportExpectedVsActual

```
1  public static int ReportExpectedVsActual(this IWebDriver ↵
       ↪ driver, string expected, string actual)
2  {
3      if (expected.Trim() == actual.Trim())
4      {
5          Log.Info("[Expected: ]" + expected + "          ↵
                ↪ [Actual: ]" + actual + "          [Step Passed]");
6          return Config.STEP_PASS;
7      }
8      else
9      {
10         Log.Error("[Expected: ]" + expected + "          ↵
                ↪ [Actual: ]" + actual + "          [Step Failed]");
11         TestResult = Config.FAIL;
12         SaveScreenShot(driver, ↵
                ↪ TestContext.CurrentContext.Test.FullName + " ↵
                ↪ (Step Failure) ");
```

```
13            return Config.STEP_FAIL;
14      }
15 }
```

Line 1: Returns an int instead of void.
Line 6: Returns Config.STEP_PASS if the test step passes.
Line 13: Returns Config.STEP_FAIL if the test step fails.

5.5.1.3 Page Logic

We will add a new action to the *View Employee* page's logic as follows:

Action	Description
VerifyEmployeeWithFailureThreshold()	This action will verify the employee's details with checks for the failure threshold.

Add the additional function in the page logic 'pageTesterViewEmployee.cs' file as shown in Listing 5.14.

Listing 5.14: 'pageTesterViewEmployee.cs' - Code to Verify Employee With Failure Threshold

```
1  public void VerifyEmployeeWithFailureThreshold()
2  {
3      int failedTimes = 0;
4
5      failedTimes += Utility.ReportExpectedVsActual(driver, ↵
          ↪ "10009", Utility.FindElementAndReturn(driver, ↵
          ↪ By.Name(Repository.EmployeeDetail. ↵
          ↪ txtEmployeeId_ByName)).GetAttribute("Value"));
6      Utility.CheckFailureThreshold(failedTimes);
7
8      failedTimes += Utility.ReportExpectedVsActual(driver, ↵
          ↪ "Mr", Utility.FindElementAndReturn(driver, ↵
          ↪ By.Name(Repository.EmployeeDetail. ↵
          ↪ lbTitle_ByName)).Text);
9      Utility.CheckFailureThreshold(failedTimes);
10
11     failedTimes += Utility.ReportExpectedVsActual(driver, ↵
          ↪ "Joe Blog", Utility.FindElementAndReturn(driver, ↵
          ↪ By.Id(Repository.EmployeeDetail.txtName_ById)). ↵
          ↪ GetAttribute("Value"));
```

```
12      Utility.CheckFailureThreshold(failedTimes);
13
14      failedTimes += Utility.ReportExpectedVsActual(driver,
            ↪ "6", Utility.GetSelectedRadioButton(driver,
            ↪ Repository.EmployeeDetail.rbGender_ById).ToString());
15      Utility.CheckFailureThreshold(failedTimes);
16
17      failedTimes += Utility.ReportExpectedVsActual(driver,
            ↪ "28/12/1982",
            ↪ Utility.FindElementAndReturn(driver,
            ↪ By.Name(Repository.EmployeeDetail.
            ↪ txtDateOfBirth_ByName)).GetAttribute("Value"));
18      Utility.CheckFailureThreshold(failedTimes);
19
20      failedTimes += Utility.ReportExpectedVsActual(driver,
            ↪ "joe.blog@arkenstone-ltd.com",
            ↪ Utility.FindElementAndReturn(driver,
            ↪ By.Name(Repository.EmployeeDetail.txtEmail_ByName)).
            ↪ GetAttribute("Value"));
21      Utility.CheckFailureThreshold(failedTimes);
22
23      failedTimes += Utility.ReportExpectedVsActual(driver,
            ↪ Config.FALSE,
            ↪ Utility.FindElementAndReturn(driver,
            ↪ By.Name(Repository.EmployeeDetail.
            ↪ cbContractJob_ByName)).Selected.ToString());
24      Utility.CheckFailureThreshold(failedTimes);
25
26      failedTimes += Utility.ReportExpectedVsActual(driver,
            ↪ "SN1 9GS", Utility.FindElementAndReturn(driver,
            ↪ By.Id(Repository.EmployeeDetail.txtPostcode_ById)).
            ↪ GetAttribute("Value"));
27      Utility.CheckFailureThreshold(failedTimes);
28
29      Utility.FindElementAndClick(driver,
            ↪ By.CssSelector(Repository.EmployeeDetail.
            ↪ btnClose_ByCSS));
30 }
```

Line 3: Initialises variable 'failedTimes' to hold the value of *the number of times* the test step has failed.

Line 5: Increments the value of variable 'failedTimes' for each failed test step. Remember that the function 'ReportExpectedVsActual' returns a zero value for a passed test step.

Line 6: Checks if the failure count has reached the threshold value by passing its current value to the 'CheckFailureThreshold' function.

5.5.1.4 Creating Test

Add Listing 5.15 code to 'TestGeneralUser.cs' file.

Listing 5.15: 'TestGeneralUser.cs' - Code for VerifyEmployeeWithFailureThreshold

```
[Test]
public void VerifyEmployeeWithFailureThreshold()
{
    try
    {
        Utility.Log.Info("Starting test: " + 
            TestContext.CurrentContext.Test.FullName);

        var home = new pageHome(driver);
        home.Visit();
        home.ClickLogin();

        var login = new pageLogin(driver);
        login.Login("Tester", "Tester123");

        var homeTester = new pageTesterHome(driver);
        homeTester.ClickViewEmployee();

        var emp = new pageTesterViewEmployee(driver);
        emp.VerifyEmployeeWithFailureThreshold();

        Utility.ReportResult();
    }
    catch (Exception exception)
    {
        Utility.Log.Error("exception" + 
            exception.ToString());
        throw exception;
    }
}
```

Line 1: New test to verify an employee with failure threshold.
Line 19: Calls the page logic function `VerifyEmployeeWithFailureThreshold`.

5.5.1.5 Executing Test

Execute the test and you will see the test failing after 3 test step failures as shown in Figure 5.10.

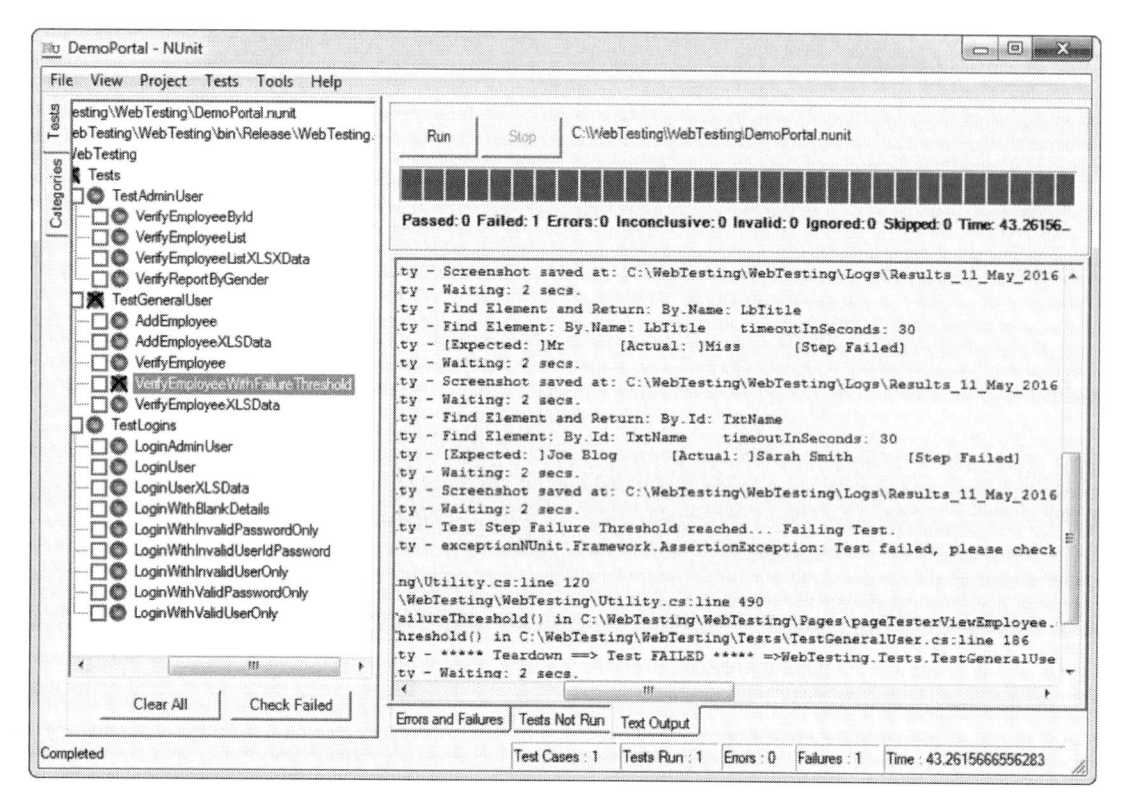

Figure 5.10: Step Failure Threshold Output

5.5.2 Log Failed Test Steps Only

The Automation Framework uses the generic function 'ReportExpectedVsActual' to compare the expected and actual values and then reports the outcome. If your test script is performing a lot of comparisons, your log file may become very large. In that case you may want to log expected vs. actual comparisons only if there is a failure. In other words, we don't want to log the passed steps, only the failed test steps. We need to add a feature to our Automation Framework which determines whether the framework should log all comparisons or only failures.

We will perform the following Test Scenario to demonstrate the logging of failed test steps only.

- Launch the demo website.
- Login with the user 'Tester'.
- Click on the *View Employee* link.

- Verify the employee but log failed test steps only.

5.5.2.1 Configuration Parameters

Let's add another configuration variable which we will need throughout our Automation Framework. Double click on the 'Config.cs' file in the 'Solution Explorer' and add the Listing 5.16 code to it.

Listing 5.16: 'Config.cs' - Parameters to log all compares

```
public static bool LOG_ALL_COMPARE = false;
```

Line 1: Defines a boolean configuration parameter to instruct whether to log all compares or not. A false value will log failures only.

5.5.2.2 Utility Functions

Update the ReportExpectedVsActual function in 'Utility.cs' file as shown in Listing 5.17.

Listing 5.17: 'Utility.cs' - Updates to ReportExpectedVsActual

```
public static int ReportExpectedVsActual(this IWebDriver 
    driver, string expected, string actual)
{
    if (expected.Trim() == actual.Trim())
    {
        if (Config.LOG_ALL_COMPARE)
        {
            Log.Info("Expected: " + expected + "         
                Actual: " + actual + "        Step Passed:");
        }
        return Config.STEP_PASS;
    }
    else
    {
        Log.Error("[Expected: ]" + expected + "         
            [Actual: ]" + actual + "        [Step Failed]");
        TestResult = Config.FAIL;
        SaveScreenShot(driver, 
            TestContext.CurrentContext.Test.FullName + " 
            (Step Failure) ");
        return Config.STEP_FAIL;
    }
```

```
18    }
```

Line 1: Logs a passed test step if `Config.LOG_ALL_COMPARE` is true.

5.5.2.3   Executing Test

Let's now execute the test 'VerifyEmployeeWithFailureThreshold' and this time it will only log the failed comparisons as shown in Figure 5.11.

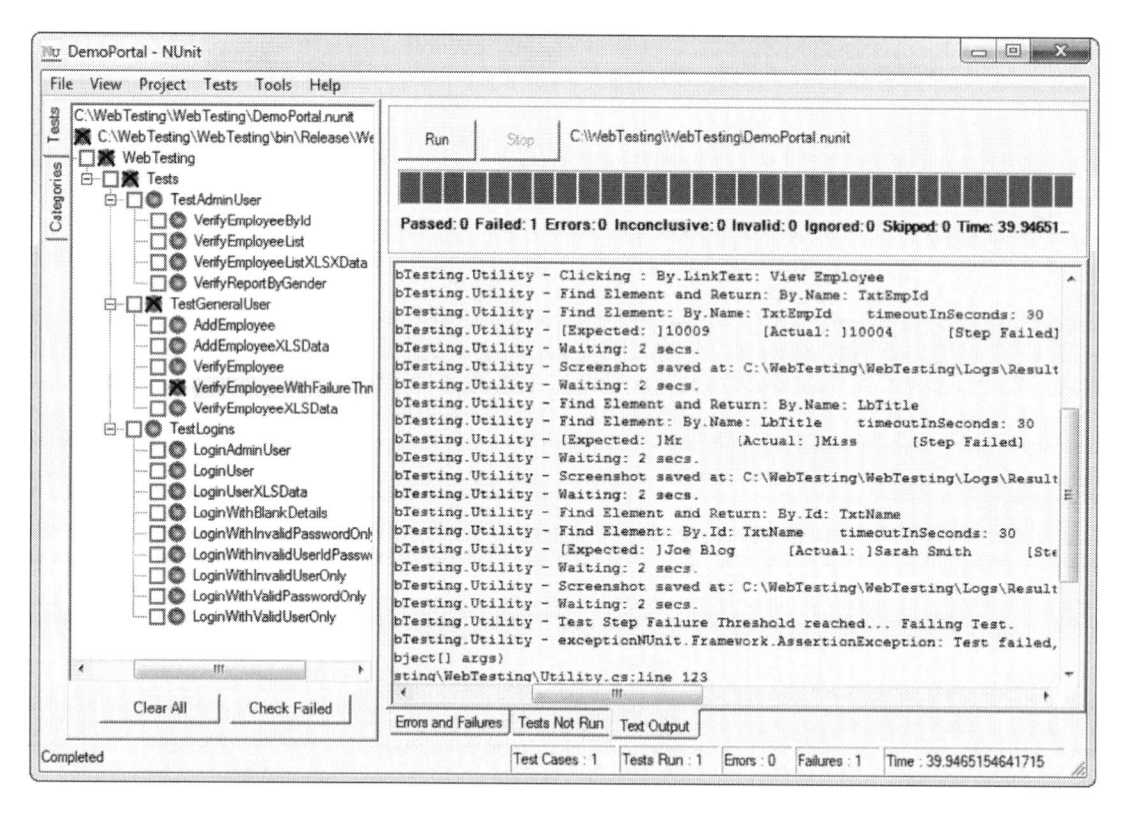

Figure 5.11: Log Failed Test Steps Only Output

At this point you may want to set the configuration parameter `Config.LOG_ALL_COMPARE` to 'true' so that it logs all the compares.

5.5.3   Comparing Decimals With Tolerance

As a general rule, we can confidently use the 'ReportExpectedVsActual' function to report the outcome of test steps where the parameters are passed on as strings. However, when we are comparing two decimal numbers (passed as strings) the function may report unnecessary failures. For example, if the values being compared are held in a different number of decimal places or if the difference between them is 'insignificant', the function will still report them as failures because it does an exact comparison. Also, the decimal values of the expected result may differ from the actual result because of the way the calculations are performed in the programming language being used. In this situation you may want to ignore any minor difference between the expected and the actual result e.g. if the expected result is 123.055556 and the actual result calculated by the application is 123.0555. You may want to ignore the difference of 0.000056 when reporting the result and pass the test step. So here is how we do it.

We will perform the following Test Scenario to demonstrate the comparison of decimal numbers with tolerance:

- Configure the difference threshold to '0.0001'

- Compare '123.055556' and '123.0555' and show that the difference of '0.000056' is ignored because it is below the threshold.

- Compare '123.0555' and '123.055556' and show that the difference of '-0.000056' is ignored because its absolute value is below the threshold.

5.5.3.1 Configuration Parameters

Let's add a new configuration variable. Double click on the 'Config.cs' file in the 'Solution Explorer' and add the Listing 5.11 code to it.

Listing 5.18: 'Config.cs' - Parameter for difference tolerance

```
1 public static double DIFFERENCE_TOLERANCE = 0.0001;
```

Line 1: Ignores difference of 0.0001 between the expected and the actual result.

5.5.3.2 Utility Functions

Let's define a new utility function.

ReportExpectedVsActualWithTolerance - Reports the outcome of expected verses actual result comparison with tolerance		
Input Parameters	*expected*	Expected result
	actual	Actual result
Return Value	*int*	Returns integer value of Pass or Fail configured parameters

Add Listing 5.19 to the 'Utility.cs' file.

Listing 5.19: 'Utility.cs' - Code for ReportExpectedVsActualWithTolerance

```
1 public static int ↵
    ↪ ReportExpectedVsActualWithTolerance(String exp, ↵
    ↪ String act)
```

```csharp
2  {
3      exp = exp.Trim();
4      act = act.Trim();
5      double expDbl, actDbl, diff;
6
7      String expFormatted = String.Format("{0:#,0.0000}", ↵
          ↪ double.Parse(exp));
8      String actFormatted = String.Format("{0:#,0.0000}", ↵
          ↪ double.Parse(act));
9
10     expDbl = double.Parse(expFormatted);
11     actDbl = double.Parse(actFormatted);
12     diff = Math.Abs(expDbl * Config.DIFFERENCE_TOLERANCE);
13
14     if (expFormatted.Equals(actFormatted))
15     {
16         Log.Info("[Expected:] " + exp + "    [Actual:] " ↵
              ↪ + act + "    [Step Passed]");
17         return Config.STEP_PASS;
18     }
19     else if (Math.Abs(actDbl - expDbl) <= diff)
20     {
21         Log.Info("Ignored minor difference of " + ↵
              ↪ String.Format("{0:#,0.0000}", (actDbl - ↵
              ↪ expDbl)) + " between expDbl = " + expDbl + " ↵
              ↪ and actDbl = " + actDbl);
22         Log.Info("Original [Expected:] " + exp + "   ↵
              ↪ Original [Actual:] " + act + "    [Step ↵
              ↪ Passed]");
23         return Config.STEP_PASS;
24     }
25     else
26     {
27         Log.Error("[Expected:] " + exp + "    [Actual:] " ↵
              ↪ + act + "    [Step FAILED]");
28         Log.Info("Difference of " + ↵
              ↪ String.Format("{0:#,0.0000}", (actDbl - ↵
              ↪ expDbl)) + " between expDbl = " + expDbl + " ↵
              ↪ and actDbl = " + actDbl);
29         TestResult = Config.FAIL;
30         return Config.STEP_FAIL;
31     }
32 }
```

Line 7 and 8: Format the expected and the actual values to the same precision.

Line 10 and 11: Convert the expected and the actual values to the 'double' format.
Line 14: First of all, checks if the formatted values are equal.
Line 19: Now checks if the 'double' values are equal after ignoring the tolerance difference. Also logs additional information.
Line 25: Otherwise reports a failure and logs additional information.

5.5.3.3 Creating Test

Add Listing 5.20 code to 'TestGeneralUser.cs' file.

Listing 5.20: 'TestGeneralUser.cs' - Code for CompareDecimalNumbers

```
[Test]
public void CompareDecimalNumbers()
{
    try
    {
        Utility.Log.Info("Starting test: " +
            TestContext.CurrentContext.Test.FullName);

        Utility.ReportExpectedVsActualWithTolerance(
            "123.055556", "123.0555");

        Utility.ReportExpectedVsActualWithTolerance(
            "123.0555", "123.055556");

        Utility.ReportResult();
    }
    catch (Exception exception)
    {
        Utility.Log.Error("exception" +
            exception.ToString());
        throw exception;
    }
}
```

Line 8 - 10: Call the 'ReportExpectedVsActualWithThreshold' function. The test should pass after ignoring the difference.

5.5.3.4 Executing Test

Execute the test and you will see an output as shown in Figure 5.12. The test passes after ignoring the difference.

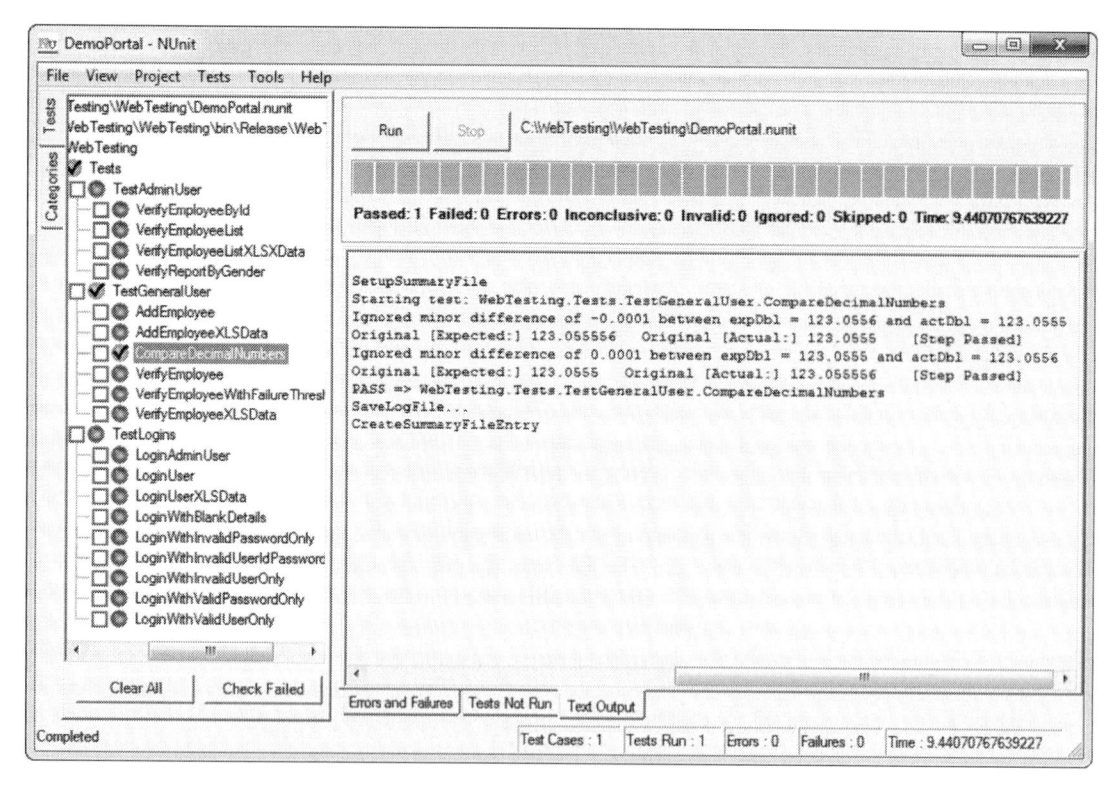

Figure 5.12: Compare Decimals With Tolerance

Chapter 6

Cross Browser Testing

Cross Browser Testing

In this chapter, we will learn:

- *About automating tests using commonly used browsers*
- *How to use various load options with these browsers*
- *How to use workarounds for commonly occurring problems*
- *About adding some important features to our Automation Framework*

So let's get on with it...

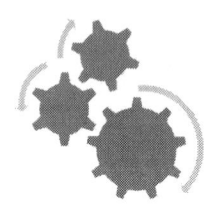

CROSS Browser Testing is simply what its name suggests: to test the website in multiple browsers and ensuring that it works in a consistent and intended way. There are lots of web browsers these days and they have been developed in different ways. Some are exclusively compatible with certain operating systems, while some provide features that other browsers lack. Some browsers provide the means to restrict certain features to a specific operating system. As a tester, you may view the web application under test using Internet Explorer and it looks pretty cool. But when you view it in Firefox, it may not only look awful but some of the vital features may not work at all. To make things even more challenging, these variations don't just exist between different browsers (e.g. Internet Explorer, Firefox, Safari etc.) but even between different versions of the same browser! These variations make it essential to perform Cross Browser Testing to ensure that each browser renders pages as intended and allows the user to complete business transactions.

In this book, we will cover the following mostly used browsers for cross browser testing purpose:

- Mozilla Firefox
- Google Chrome

- Internet Explorer
- Microsoft Edge
- Safari
- Opera

Before starting the tests, please ensure that you have installed the relevant browsers.

6.1 Mozilla Firefox

6.1.1 Firefox WebDriver

WebDriver is the core tool for automating web application testing. The WebDriver makes direct calls to the browser using each browser's native support for automation. How these direct calls are made and the features they support depends on the browser we are using. In order to use the Firefox browser, we don't need any WebDriver as it is already built-into the Selenium.

6.1.2 Configuration Parameters

Let's add some configuration parameters which we will need later on. Double click on the 'Config.cs' file in 'Solution Explorer' and add the Listing 6.1 code to it.

Listing 6.1: 'Config.cs' - Parameters for Firefox

```
1 public const string FIREFOX = "Firefox";
2 public static string BROWSER = FIREFOX;
```

Line 1: Defines a constant string to hold the value "Firefox".
Line 2: Defines a static string to hold the value of current browser which is set to configuration parameter `FIREFOX`. We will change the value of this parameter if we need to use a different browser as we will see later.

6.1.3 Utility Functions

Update the `SetupDriver` function in the 'Utility.cs' file as shown in Listing 6.2.

Listing 6.2: 'Utility.cs' - Updated code for SetupDriver

```
1 public static IWebDriver SetupDriver(this IWebDriver driver)
2 {
3     try
```

```
 4    {
 5        switch (Config.BROWSER)
 6        {
 7            case Config.FIREFOX:
 8                driver = new FirefoxDriver();
 9                break;
10
11            default:
12                ReportExpectedVsActual(driver, "Invalid ↵
                    ↪ value of BROWSER Parameter.", ↵
                    ↪ Config.BROWSER);
13                break;
14        }
15
16        return driver;
17    }
18    catch (Exception ex)
19    {
20        Log.Error("SetupDriver Exception: " + ↵
            ↪ ex.ToString());
21        throw ex;
22    }
23 }
```

Line 5: Checks the value of currently configured browser.
Line 7: If FIREFOX then initialises the Firefox WebDriver.
Line 12: If SetupDriver function is called with an unknown browser name then reports an error and fails the test.

6.1.4 Executing Tests

As we have been doing, recompile the 'WebTesting.dll' and run the 'LoginUser' test. Firefox browser is launched and the test is executed as shown in Figure 6.1

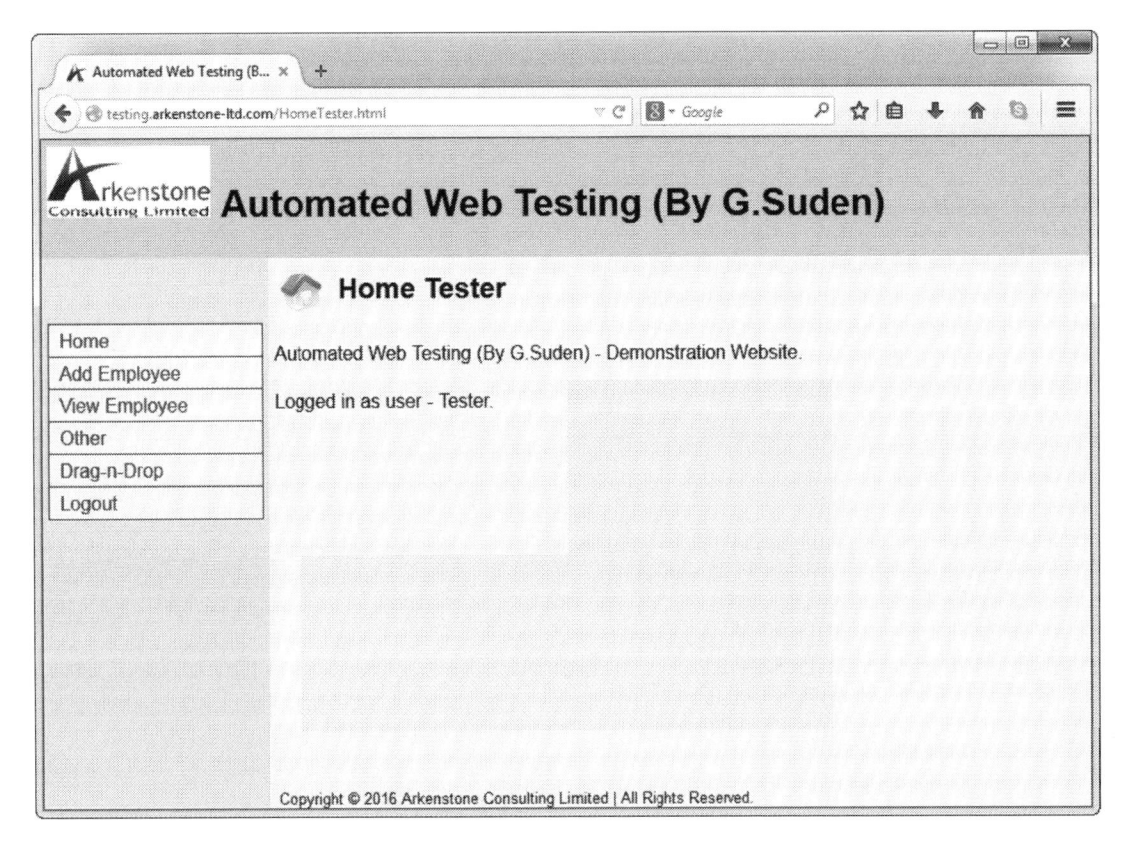

Figure 6.1: Firefox Browser

6.1.5 Loading Firefox Add-ons

You might have noticed that when we executed our test above using Firefox, the Firebug Add-on icon was not present in the browser. By default, no Add-on is loaded when we launch our test in this manner. However, sometimes you may want the Firebug to be loaded as you may want to use it after your test has finished or failed.

> Our `Teardown()` function closes the browser window after the test has finished. If you don't want to close the browser after test finishes then just comment that line i.e. `//driver.Quit();`

Let's learn how to activate the Firebug Add-on in Firefox when executing tests. We will dynamically add the required Add-on in the profile when launching Firefox. First of all perform the following steps to download the required 'xpi' file.

1. Go to `https://addons.mozilla.org/en-US/firefox/addon/firebug/`

2. Right-click on the "Add To Firefox" and save as 'C:\Selenium\Firebug\firebug-2.0.13-fx.xpi'. The version of 'xpi' file may differ in your case.

We will perform the following Test Scenario to demonstrate the activation of the Firebug Add-on:

- Launch the demo website.
- Login with the user 'Tester'.
- Ensure that the Firebug Add-on is available in the Firefox browser.

6.1.5.1 Creating Test

In the 'Solution Explorer', right click on the 'Tests' folder, click Add ⇒ Class. Type the name as 'TestFirefox.cs' and click the Add button. Add the Listing 6.3 code to it.

Listing 6.3: 'TestFirefox.cs' - Code for LoadFirefoxWithFirebug

```
/****************************************************************
 * All rights reserved. Copyright 2016 Arkenstone-ltd.com *
 ****************************************************************/
using System;
using OpenQA.Selenium;
using NUnit.Framework;
using WebTesting.Pages;
using OpenQA.Selenium.Firefox;

namespace WebTesting.Tests
{
    public class TestFirefox
    {
        IWebDriver driver;

        [SetUp]
        public void Setup()
        {
            Utility.TestResult = Config.PASS;
        }


        [TearDown]
        public void Teardown()
        {
            if (TestContext.CurrentContext.Result.Status ←
                ↪ == TestStatus.Failed)
            {
```

```csharp
28                        Utility.Log.Error("***** Teardown ==>
                              Test FAILED ***** =>" +
                              TestContext.CurrentContext.Test.
                              FullName);
29                        Utility.SaveScreenShot(driver,
                              TestContext.CurrentContext.Test.Name
                              + "(" +
                              TestContext.CurrentContext.Result.
                              Status + ")");
30                    }
31                    else if
                          (TestContext.CurrentContext.Result.Status
                          == TestStatus.Passed)
32                    {
33                        Utility.Log.Info("PASS => " +
                              TestContext.CurrentContext.Test.
                              FullName);
34                    }
35
36                    //driver.Quit();
37
38                    Utility.SaveLogFile(TestContext.CurrentContext
                          .Test.FullName.Substring(17) + " (" +
                          TestContext.CurrentContext.Result.
                          Status + ") ");
39
40                    if (Utility.TestResult == Config.FAIL)
41                    {
42                        Utility.CreateSummaryFileEntry(DateTime.
                              Now.ToString() + "," +
                              TestContext.CurrentContext.Test.
                              FullName.Substring(17) + ",FAIL" +
                              "," + Config.CURRENT_LOGFILE);
43                    }
44                    else
45                        Utility.CreateSummaryFileEntry(DateTime.
                              Now.ToString() + "," +
                              TestContext.CurrentContext.Test.
                              FullName.Substring(17) + ",PASS" +
                              "," + Config.CURRENT_LOGFILE);
46
47            }
48
49            [Test]
50            public void LoadFirefoxWithFirebug()
```

Automated Web Testing

```
51              {
52                  try
53                  {
54                      Utility.Log.Info("Starting test: " + ↵
                            TestContext.CurrentContext.Test.FullName);
55
56                      String pathFirebug = ↵
                            @"C:\Selenium\Firebug\firebug ↵
                            -2.0.13-fx.xpi";
57                      FirefoxProfile myProfile = new ↵
                            FirefoxProfile();
58                      myProfile.AddExtension(pathFirebug);
59                      myProfile.SetPreference( ↵
                            "extensions.firebug.currentVersion", ↵
                            "100.0");
60
61                      driver = new FirefoxDriver(myProfile);
62
63                      var home = new pageHome(driver);
64                      home.Visit();
65                      home.ClickLogin();
66
67                      var login = new pageLogin(driver);
68                      login.Login("Tester", "Tester123");
69
70                      Utility.ReportResult();
71                  }
72                  catch (Exception exception)
73                  {
74                      Utility.Log.Error("exception" + ↵
                            exception.ToString());
75                      throw exception;
76                  }
77              }
78          }
79      }
```

Line 16: Note that the Setup() function doesn't initialise the driver. We will initialise it in the test. It has been done so for our demo purpose, so that we don't disturb our Automation Framework code we have written so far because we will be making changes to it to demonstrate different aspects of using Firefox.

Line 36: Comment this line so that the browser doesn't close after the test execution.

Line 56: The path where we downloaded the 'xpi' file.

Line 58: Adds Firefox Extension (specified with the path filename) to this profile.

Line 59: Sets the current version very high so that we don't get the Firebug window launched when the browser starts.

> Note that we are not loading the default Firefox profile because it already has Firebug added to it.

6.1.5.2 Executing Test

This time when we execute the test, Firefox is launched along with Firebug as shown in Figure 6.2.

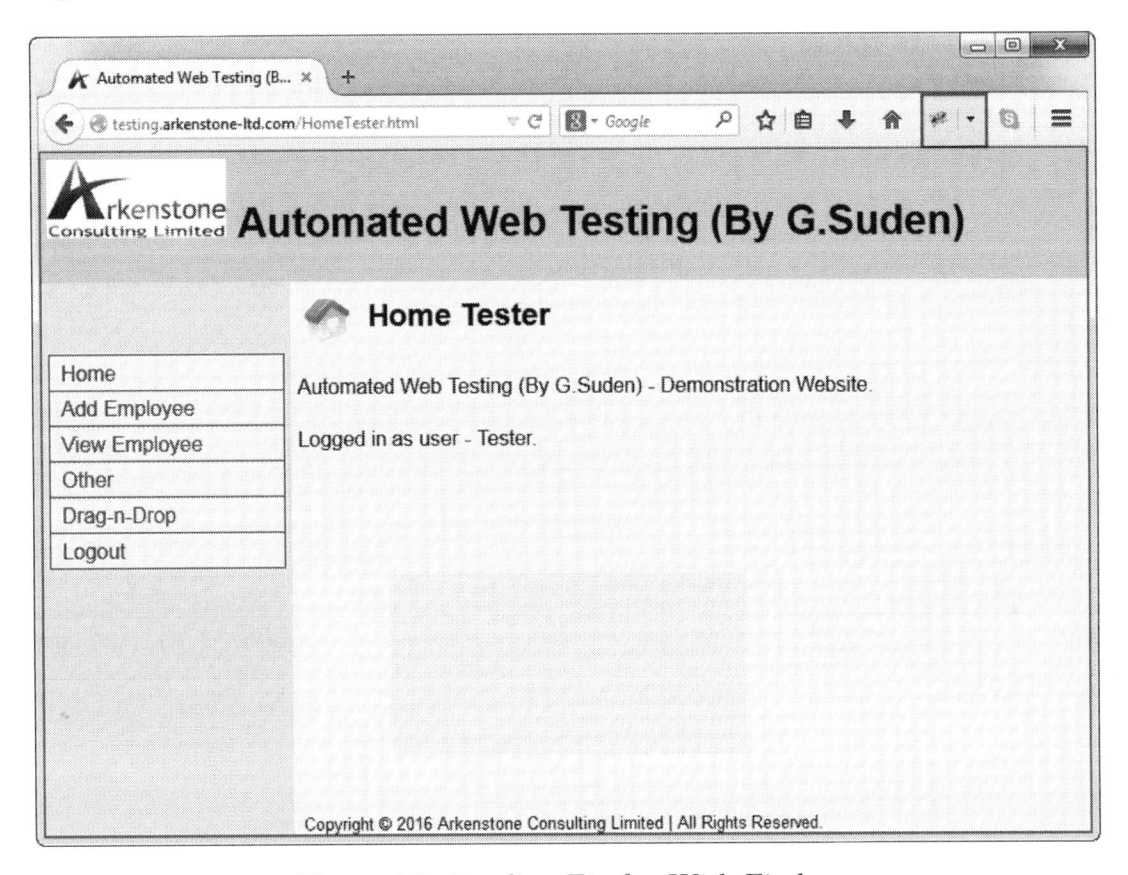

Figure 6.2: Loading Firefox With Firebug

6.1.6 Loading Default Firefox Profile

Firefox saves personal information such as bookmarks, passwords and user preferences in a set of files called profile. You can have multiple Firefox profiles, each containing a separate set of user information. Let's first of all see how to load Default profile when Firefox is launched.

We will perform the following Test Scenario to demonstrate the loading of a Default profile:

- Launch the demo website.

- Login with the user 'Tester'.

- Ensure that the Default profile is loaded which already has Firebug available in it.

6.1.6.1 Creating Test

Add a new test to 'TestFirefox.cs' file as shown in Listing 6.4.

Listing 6.4: 'TestFirefox.cs' - Code for LoadDefaultProfile

```
/****************************************************************
 * All rights reserved. Copyright 2016 Arkenstone-ltd.com        *
 ****************************************************************/
using System.IO;

[Test]
public void LoadDefaultProfile()
{
    try
    {
        Utility.Log.Info("Starting test: " + ↵
            TestContext.CurrentContext.Test.FullName);

        string pathToCurrentUserProfiles = ↵
            Environment.ExpandEnvironmentVariables ↵
            ("%APPDATA%") + ↵
            @"\Mozilla\Firefox\Profiles";
        string[] pathsToProfiles = ↵
            Directory.GetDirectories( ↵
            pathToCurrentUserProfiles, "*.default", ↵
            SearchOption.TopDirectoryOnly);

        Utility.Log.Info("APPDATA: " + ↵
            Environment.ExpandEnvironmentVariables ↵
            ("%APPDATA%"));
        Utility.Log.Info("pathsToProfiles[0]: " + ↵
            pathsToProfiles[0]);

        if (pathsToProfiles.Length != 0)
        {
            FirefoxProfile myProfile = new ↵
                FirefoxProfile(pathsToProfiles[0]);
            driver = new FirefoxDriver(myProfile);
        }
```

```
24
25              var home = new pageHome(driver);
26              home.Visit();
27              home.ClickLogin();
28
29              var login = new pageLogin(driver);
30              login.Login("Tester", "Tester123");
31
32              Utility.ReportResult();
33          }
34          catch (Exception exception)
35          {
36              Utility.Log.Error("exception" + ↵
                    ↪ exception.ToString());
37              throw exception;
38          }
39      }
```

Line 4: Additional import required to support the functionality.

Line 13: Gets the path to the current user profiles.

Line 14: Gets the path to the profiles. Search option to include only the current directory in the search operation.

Line 19: Ensures that it is not empty.

Line 21: Initialises a new instance of the `FirefoxProfile` class using the specific profile directory.

Line 22: Initialises a new instance of the `FirefoxDriver` class for the given profile.

6.1.6.2 Executing Test

Execute the test and you will see an output window as shown in Figure 6.3. The log shows the path of the Default profile loaded. The browser window will show the Firebug Add-on.

Automated Web Testing

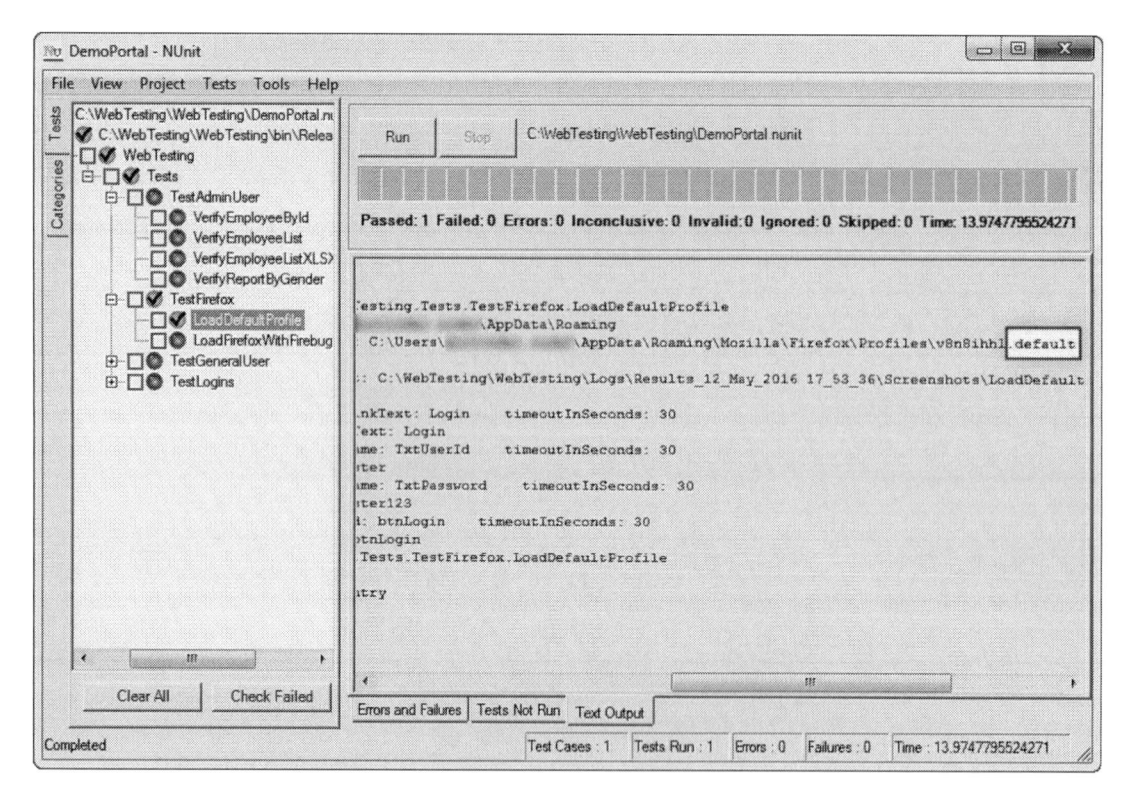

Figure 6.3: Loading Firefox Default Profile

6.1.7 Loading Specific Firefox Profile

As mentioned before, you can have multiple Firefox profiles, each containing a separate set of user information. Let's see how we can create a new Firefox profile using the Profile Manager.

☞ Please ensure that Firefox is completely closed before you start the Profile Manager.

- Press the Windows Key+R to open the Run dialog as shown in Figure 6.4.
- Type 'Firefox -P' in the entry box.
- Click the OK button.

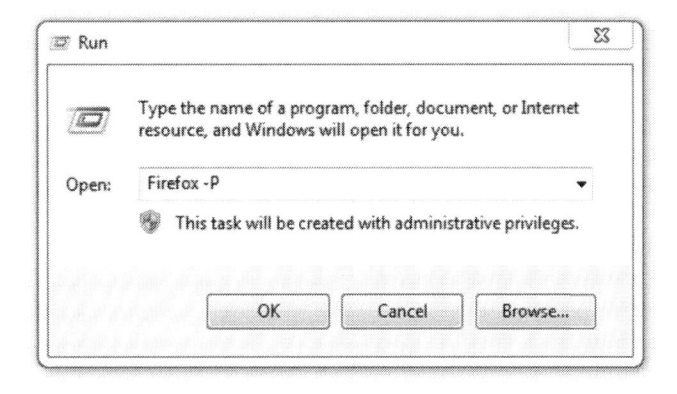

Figure 6.4: Open Run Dialog

- The Firefox Profile Manager (Choose User Profile) window should open as shown in Figure 6.5.

- Click the Create Profile... button to start the Create Profile Wizard.

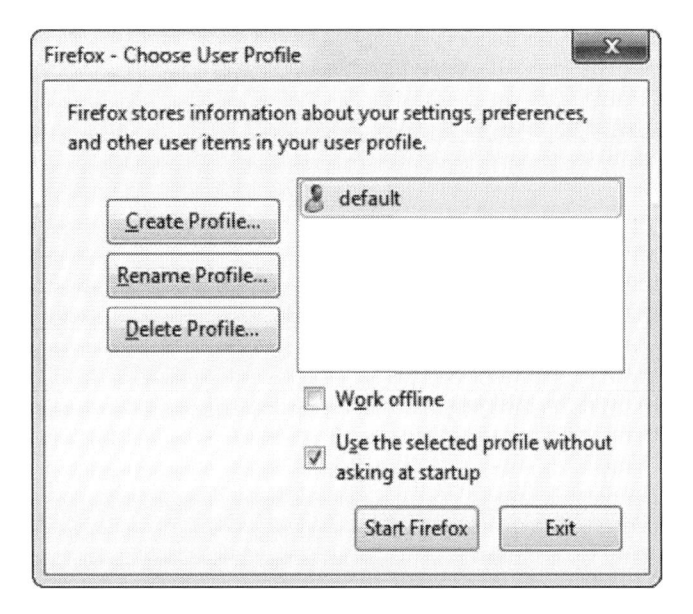

Figure 6.5: Choose User Profile

- Click the Next button to begin creating a new profile.

- Enter 'Automation' as the new profile name as shown in Figure 6.6.

- Click the Finish button to create this new profile.

Automated Web Testing

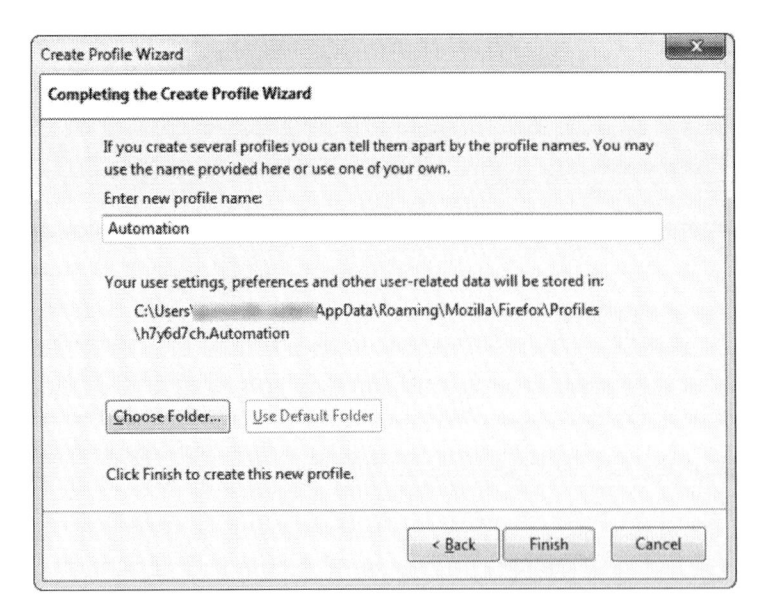

Figure 6.6: Create User Profile

- Ensure that the 'default' profile is selected for 'Use the selected profile without asking at start-up' option as shown in Figure 6.7.

- Click the Exit button.

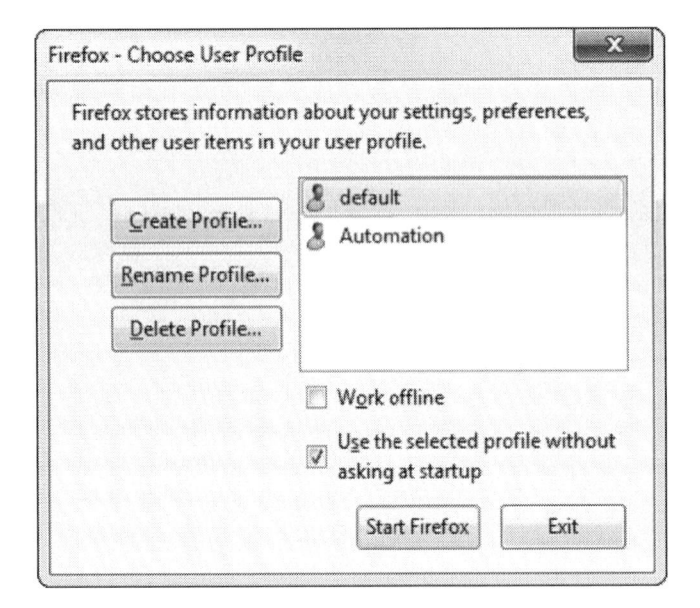

Figure 6.7: Start-up User Profile

We will perform the following Test Scenario to demonstrate the loading of our 'Automaton' profile:

- Launch the demo website.

- Login with the user 'Tester'.

- Ensure that the 'Automaton' profile is loaded.
- Ensure that Firebug Add-on is not loaded.

6.1.7.1 Creating Test

Add a new test to 'TestFirefox.cs' file as shown in Listing 6.5.

Listing 6.5: 'TestFirefox.cs' - Code to load specific profile

```
[Test]
public void LoadSpecificProfile()
{
    try
    {
        Utility.Log.Info("Starting test: " +
            TestContext.CurrentContext.Test.FullName);

        string pathToCurrentUserProfiles =
            Environment.ExpandEnvironmentVariables
            ("%APPDATA%") + @"\Mozilla\Firefox\Profiles";
        string[] pathsToProfiles =
            Directory.GetDirectories(
            pathToCurrentUserProfiles, "*.Automation",
            SearchOption.TopDirectoryOnly);

        Utility.Log.Info("APPDATA: " +
            Environment.ExpandEnvironmentVariables
            ("%APPDATA%"));
        Utility.Log.Info("pathsToProfiles[0]: " +
            pathsToProfiles[0]);

        if (pathsToProfiles.Length != 0)
        {
            FirefoxProfile myProfile = new
                FirefoxProfile(pathsToProfiles[0]);
            driver = new FirefoxDriver(myProfile);
        }

        var home = new pageHome(driver);
        home.Visit();
        home.ClickLogin();

        var login = new pageLogin(driver);
        login.Login("Tester", "Tester123");
```

```
26
27          Utility.ReportResult();
28      }
29      catch (Exception exception)
30      {
31          Utility.Log.Error("exception" + exception.ToString());
32          throw exception;
33      }
34 }
```

Line 8: Gets the path to the current user profiles.
Line 9: Gets the path to the profiles. Search option to include only the current directory in the search operation.
Line 14: Ensures that it is not empty.
Line 16: Initialises a new instance of the `FirefoxProfile` class using the specific profile directory.
Line 17: Initialises a new instance of the `FirefoxDriver` class for the given profile.

6.1.7.2 Executing Test

Execute the test and you will see an output window as shown in Figure 6.8. The log shows the path of the 'Automation' profile loaded. The browser window will also show no Firebug Add-on.

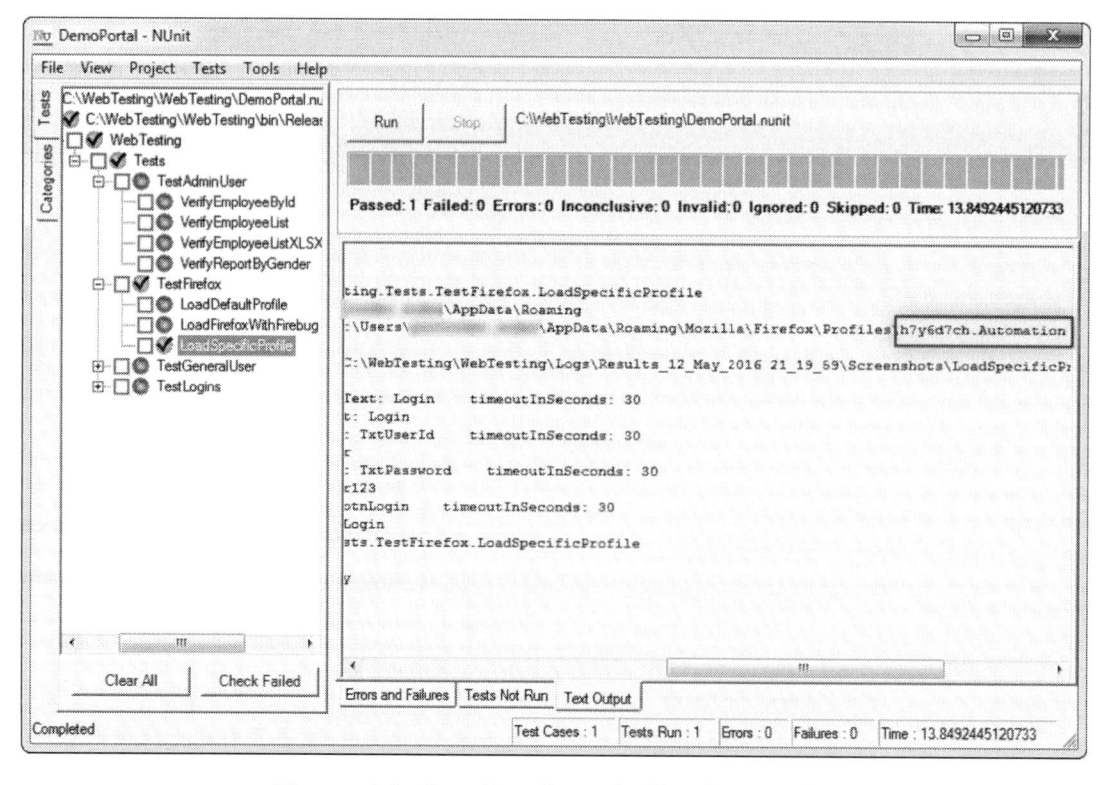

Figure 6.8: Loading Specific Firefox Profile

6.1.8 Setting Firefox Preferences

Sometimes when you launch a test for execution, you may want to set some preferences in the profile .e.g. disable the "search suggestions". The setting of such preferences may be necessary to mimic the actual user environment. You can see a list of preferences by typing "about:config" in the URL window of Firefox browser.

For a demo Test Scenario purpose, we will launch Firefox with our 'Automation' profile having the following preferences on start-up:

- Launch the demo website.

- Login with the user 'Tester'.

- Ensure that "search suggestions" is disabled. Search plugins can offer "search suggestions" of similar search queries as the user enters a query in the search bar. This preference controls whether or not search suggestions are enabled.

> Note that depending upon the settings of the **'default'** profile on my workstation I see "search suggestions" as shown in Figure 6.9 when I search for the word 'testing'. You may get a different result on your workstation depending on how the 'default' profile is setup.

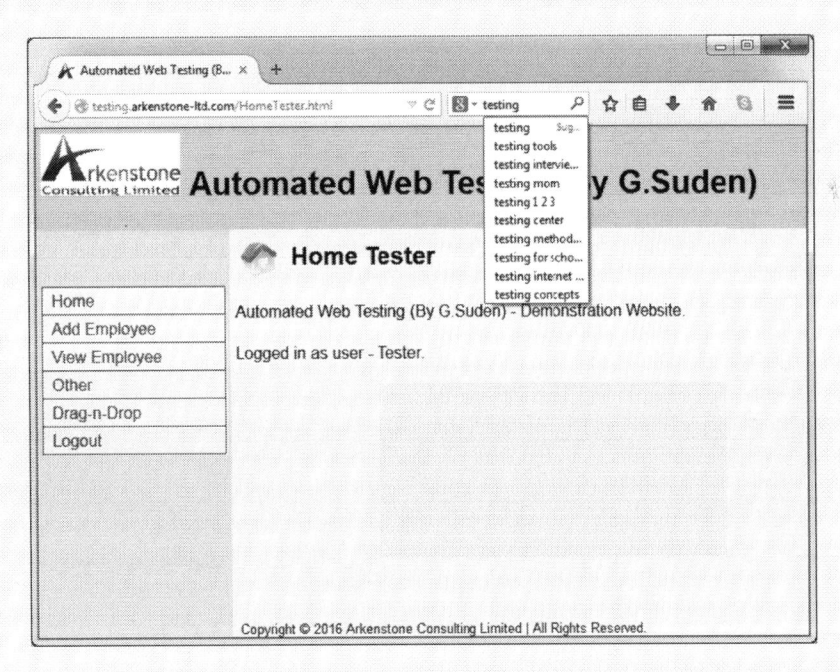

Figure 6.9: With Search Suggest - Default Profile

- Ensure that the warning page is displayed on using "about:config". The "about:config" configuration screen in Mozilla Firefox provides access to many preferences. Some of these can be harmful to change without knowing the ramifications. A warning page is displayed before the user can use "about:config" to change settings.

☞ Note that depending upon the settings of the **'default'** profile on my workstation I see no warning page as shown in Figure 6.10 when I go to 'about:config'. You may get a different result on your workstation depending on how the 'default' profile is setup.

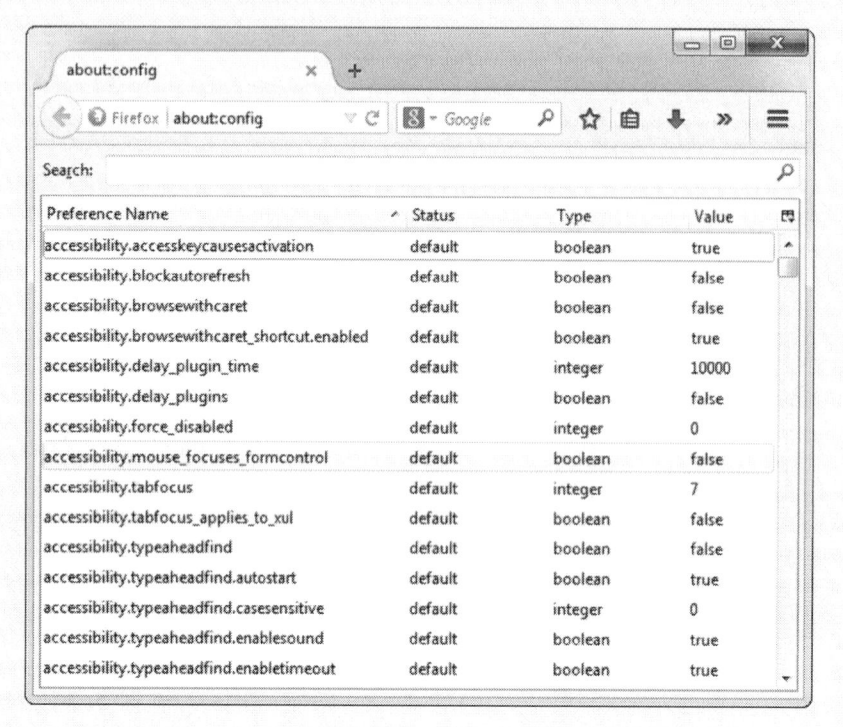

Figure 6.10: About:Config - Default Profile

- Ensure that when we open a New Tab Page on the Firefox browser, it defaults to a blank page. Please note that this only works for Firefox version 40 and bellow.

☞ Note that depending upon the settings of the **'default'** profile on my workstation I see a Google search page as shown in Figure 6.11 when I click on the new tab plus sign. You may get a different result on your workstation depending on how the 'default' profile is setup.

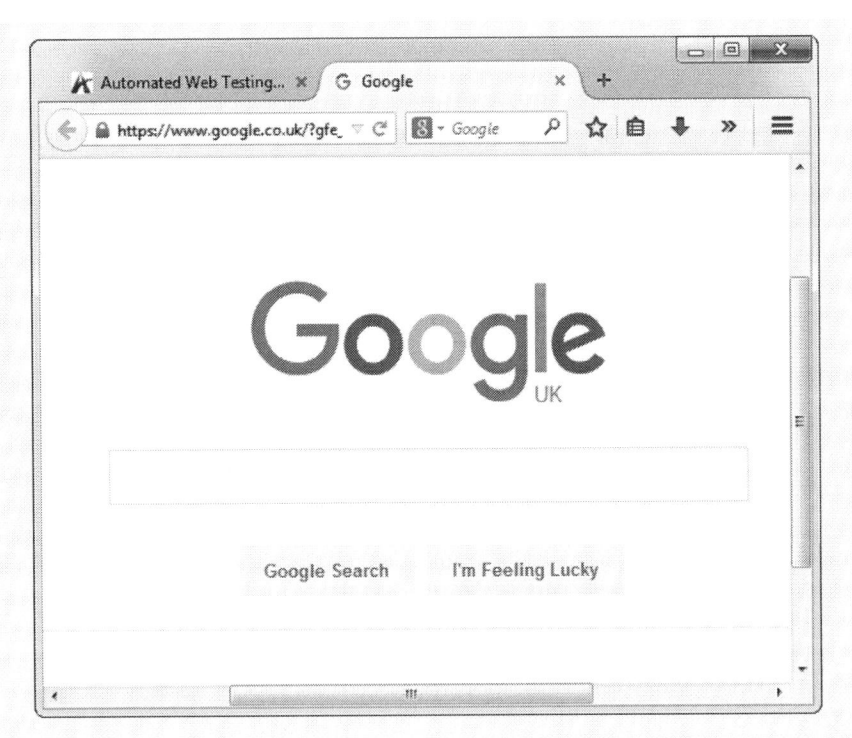

Figure 6.11: New Tab - Default Profile

- Ensure that the backspace key is disabled in the browser. Note that the backspace key is mapped to the browser 'Back' function in Mozilla Firefox.

> ☞ In order to see the 'Back' button in action using Firefox's 'default' profile, perform the following actions:
> - Launch Firefox with **'default'** profile
> - Search for 'testing' in Google
> - Click on any link from the search results
> - Press the 'Back' button on your keyboard and it will take you back to the search results

6.1.8.1 Creating Test

Let's learn how to set these preferences in the profile. Add a new test to the 'TestFirefox.cs' file as shown in Listing 6.6.

Listing 6.6: 'TestFirefox.cs' - Code for LoadProfileWithPreferences

```
1  [Test]
2  public void LoadProfileWithPreferences()
```

```csharp
{
    try
    {
        Utility.Log.Info("Starting test: " +
            TestContext.CurrentContext.Test.FullName);

        string pathToCurrentUserProfiles =
            Environment.ExpandEnvironmentVariables
            ("%APPDATA%") + @"\Mozilla\Firefox\Profiles";
        string[] pathsToProfiles =
            Directory.GetDirectories(
            pathToCurrentUserProfiles, "*.Automation",
            SearchOption.TopDirectoryOnly);

        Console.WriteLine("APPDATA: " +
            Environment.ExpandEnvironmentVariables
            ("%APPDATA%"));
        Console.WriteLine("pathsToProfiles[0]: " +
            pathsToProfiles[0]);

        if (pathsToProfiles.Length != 0)
        {
            FirefoxProfile myProfile = new
                FirefoxProfile(pathsToProfiles[0]);
            myProfile.SetPreference(
                "browser.search.suggest.enabled",
                false);
            myProfile.SetPreference(
                "general.warnOnAboutConfig", true);
            myProfile.SetPreference("browser.newtab.url",
                "about:blank");
            myProfile.SetPreference(
                "browser.backspace_action", 2);
            driver = new FirefoxDriver(myProfile);
        }

        var home = new pageHome(driver);
        home.Visit();
        home.ClickLogin();

        var login = new pageLogin(driver);
        login.Login("Tester", "Tester123");

        Utility.ReportResult();
    }
```

```
33      catch (Exception exception)
34      {
35          Utility.Log.Error("exception" + ↵
            ↪ exception.ToString());
36          throw exception;
37      }
38  }
```

Line 17: A false value of `"browser.search.suggest.enabled"` preference will disable the search suggestions.

Line 18: A true value of `"general.warnOnAboutConfig"` preference will display a warning page.

Line 19: An `"about:blank"` value of `"browser.newtab.url"` preference will display a blank page on clicking the 'Open a new tab' icon (the plus sign) in the browser.

Line 20: A value of 2 for the `"browser.backspace_action"` preference will disable the backspace key action. Note that keyboard backspace key action can have values: 0=go back, 1=page up, 2=disable

6.1.8.2 Executing Test

Execute the test and you will see the results as follows:

- With Search suggestions turned off when I search for the word 'testing' the output is as shown in Figure 6.12 where no suggestions dropdown appears.

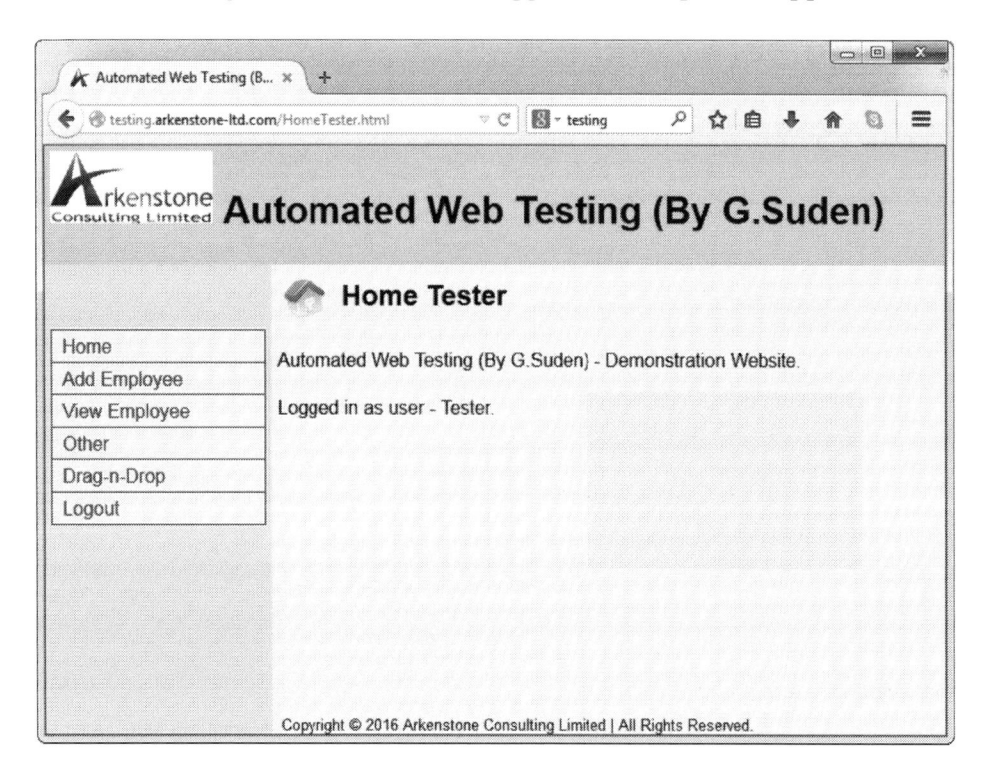

Figure 6.12: Without Search Suggest - Automation Profile

- The warning page displayed before the user can use the "about:config" to change settings as shown in Figure 6.13. .

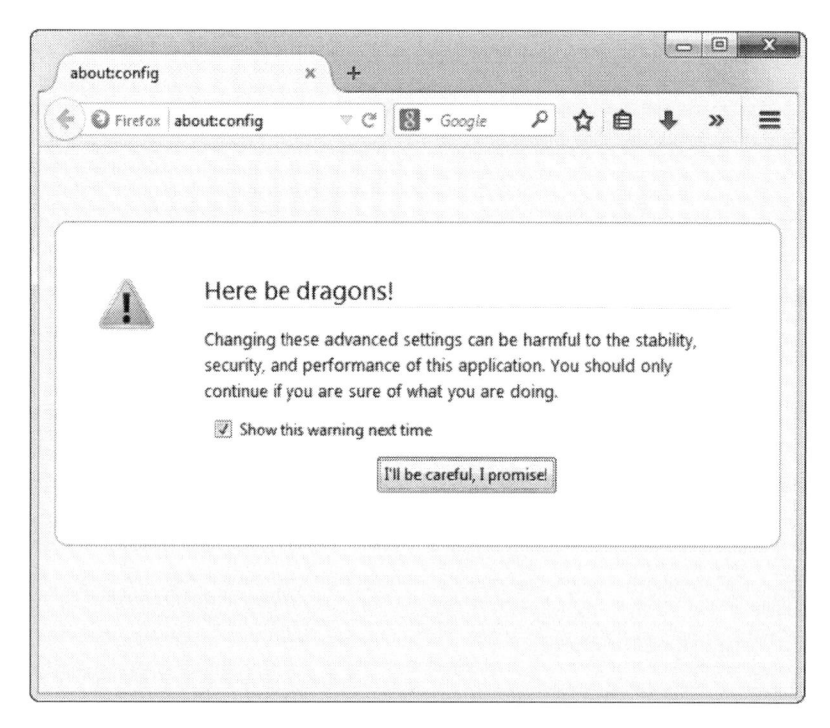

Figure 6.13: About:Config - Automation Profile

- Displays a blank page when the New Tab Page is clicked as shown in Figure 6.14.

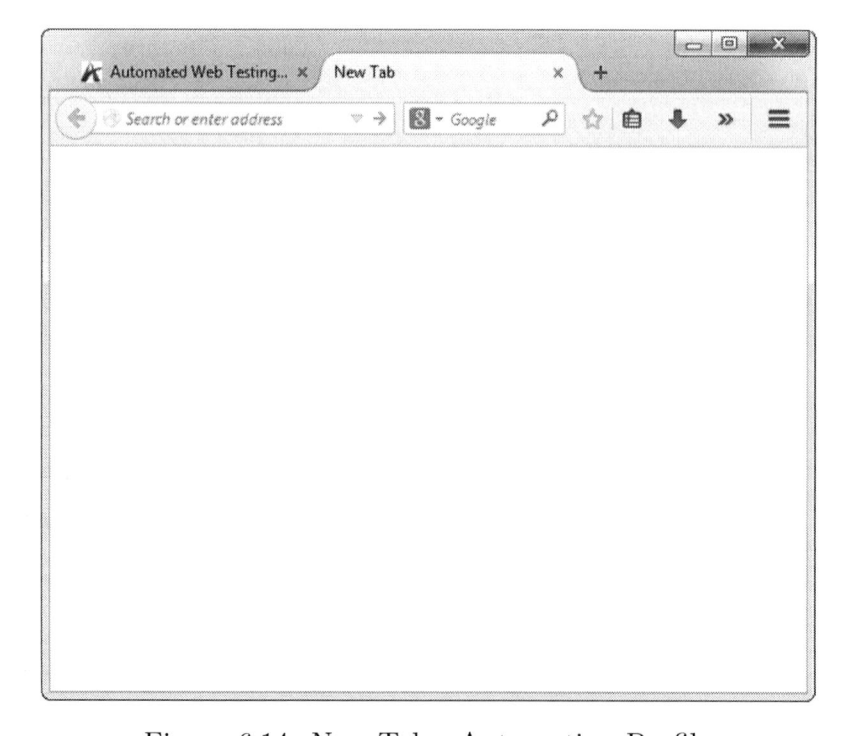

Figure 6.14: New Tab - Automation Profile

- The backspace key is no longer mapped to the browser 'Back' function. Perform the following actions:
    - Search for 'testing' in Google
    - Click on any link from the search results
    - Press the 'Back' button on your keyboard and this time it will *not* take you back to the search results.

6.2 Google Chrome

6.2.1 Chrome Driver

Chrome Driver is a separate executable that WebDriver uses to control the Chrome browser. Download Chrome Driver from:

http://www.seleniumhq.org/download/

http://chromedriver.storage.googleapis.com/index.html?path=2.20/

Extract 'chromedriver.exe' to 'C:\Selenium\chromedriver_win32'

6.2.2 Configuration Parameters

Let's add some configuration parameters which we will need. Double click on the 'Config.cs' file in 'Solution Explorer' and add the Listing 6.7 code to it.

Listing 6.7: 'Config.cs' - Parameters for Chrome

```
1  public const string CHROME = "Chrome";
2  public const string CHROME_DRIVER_PATH = ↵
       ↪ @"C:\Selenium\chromedriver_win32";
3  public static string BROWSER = CHROME;
```

Line 1: Defines a constant string to hold the value "Chrome".
Line 2: Defines location of the extracted Chrome Driver.
Line 3: Sets the current browser to `CHROME`. Please note that this line is not a new statement, it is just a code update where its previous value was `FIREFOX`.

6.2.3 Utility Functions

Update the `SetupDriver` function in the 'Utility.cs' file to add a new case statement as shown in Listing 6.8.

Automated Web Testing

Listing 6.8: 'Utility.cs' - Support for Chrome

```
1  using OpenQA.Selenium.Chrome;
2
3  case Config.CHROME:
4      driver = new ChromeDriver(Config.CHROME_DRIVER_PATH);
5      break;
```

Line 1: Additional import required to support the Chrome browser.
Line 3: If the configured browser is CHROME then initialises the Chrome driver by providing location of the extracted Chrome Driver.

6.2.4 Executing Tests

Execute the 'LoginUser' test and you should see a window as shown in Figure 6.15. The test will be executed via the Chrome browser.

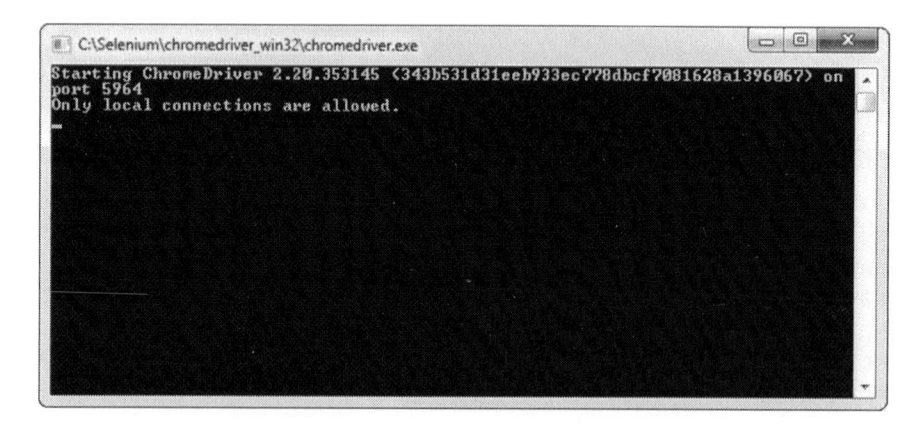

Figure 6.15: ChromeDriver Window

6.2.5 Adding Chrome Options - Disable Extensions

Selenium requires a helper extension to function. If an enterprise policy lockdown is in effect for security reasons, you may see an error during test execution as shown in Figure 6.16.

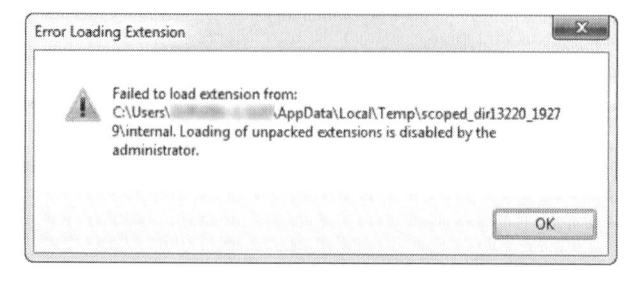

Figure 6.16: Load Extension Failure

222   Chapter 6

Automated Web Testing

A workaround that you can use in such instance is to load the Chrome browser with "disable-extensions" option. ChromeOptions has convenient methods for setting the Chrome driver specific capabilities. Let's perform the following Test Scenario to demonstrate the disable extension option:

- Launch the demo website.
- Login with the user 'Admin'.
- Ensure that Chrome is loaded with the extensions disabled i.e. we shouldn't see the error message as shown in Figure 6.16 and the test should execute successfully.

6.2.5.1 Creating Tests

In the 'Solution Explorer', right click on the 'Tests' folder, click Add ⇒ Class. Type the name as 'TestChrome.cs' and click the Add button. Add the Listing 6.9 code to it.

Listing 6.9: 'TestChrome.cs' - Code for LoadWithDisableExtensionsOption

```
/*****************************************************************
 * All rights reserved. Copyright 2016 Arkenstone-ltd.com *
 *****************************************************************/
using System;
using OpenQA.Selenium;
using NUnit.Framework;
using WebTesting.Pages;
using OpenQA.Selenium.Chrome;

namespace WebTesting.Tests
{
    public class TestChrome
    {
        IWebDriver driver;

        [SetUp]
        public void Setup()
        {
            Utility.TestResult = Config.PASS;
        }


        [TearDown]
        public void Teardown()
        {
            if (TestContext.CurrentContext.Result.Status ↩
                ↪ == TestStatus.Failed)
```

Chapter 6   223

```
27              {
28                  Utility.Log.Error("***** Teardown ==> ↵
                        Test FAILED ***** =>" + ↵
                        TestContext.CurrentContext.Test. ↵
                        FullName);
29                  Utility.SaveScreenShot(driver, ↵
                        TestContext.CurrentContext.Test.Name ↵
                        + "(" + ↵
                        TestContext.CurrentContext.Result. ↵
                        Status + ")");
30              }
31              else if ↵
                    (TestContext.CurrentContext.Result.Status ↵
                    == TestStatus.Passed)
32              {
33                  Utility.Log.Info("PASS => " + ↵
                        TestContext.CurrentContext.Test. ↵
                        FullName);
34              }
35
36              //driver.Quit();
37
38              Utility.SaveLogFile(TestContext.CurrentContext. ↵
                    Test.FullName.Substring(17) + " (" + ↵
                    TestContext.CurrentContext.Result.Status ↵
                    + ") ");
39
40              if (Utility.TestResult == Config.FAIL)
41              {
42                  Utility.CreateSummaryFileEntry(DateTime. ↵
                        Now.ToString() + "," + ↵
                        TestContext.CurrentContext.Test.FullName ↵
                        .Substring(17) + ",FAIL" + "," + ↵
                        Config.CURRENT_LOGFILE);
43              }
44              else
45                  Utility.CreateSummaryFileEntry(DateTime. ↵
                        Now.ToString() + "," + ↵
                        TestContext.CurrentContext.Test.FullName ↵
                        .Substring(17) + ",PASS" + "," + ↵
                        Config.CURRENT_LOGFILE);
46          }
47
48          [Test]
49          public void LoadWithDisableExtensionsOption()
```

```
50                    {
51                        try
52                        {
53                            Utility.Log.Info("Starting test: " + ↵
                             ↪ TestContext.CurrentContext.Test. ↵
                             ↪ FullName);
54
55                            ChromeOptions myOptions = new ↵
                             ↪ ChromeOptions();
56                            myOptions.AddArgument("disable-extensions");
57
58                            driver = new ↵
                             ↪ ChromeDriver(Config.CHROME_DRIVER_PATH, ↵
                             ↪ myOptions);
59
60                            var home = new pageHome(driver);
61                            home.Visit();
62                            home.ClickLogin();
63
64                            var login = new pageLogin(driver);
65                            login.Login("Admin", "Admin123");
66
67                            Utility.ReportResult();
68                        }
69                        catch (Exception exception)
70                        {
71                            Utility.Log.Error("exception" + ↵
                             ↪ exception.ToString());
72                            throw exception;
73                        }
74                    }
75                }
76 }
```

Line 16: Note that the Setup() function doesn't initialise the driver. We will initialise it in the test. It has been done so for our demo purpose, so that we don't disturb our Automation Framework code we have written so far because we will be making changes to it to demonstrate different aspects of using Chrome.

Line 55: Initialises a new instance of the ChromeOptions class.

Line 56: Adds argument "disable-extensions" to the Chrome.exe command line.

Line 58: Initialises a new instance of the ChromeDriver class with Chrome Driver path and the option.

6.2.5.2 Executing Tests

Execute the test and you should see the Chrome browser launching as shown in Figure 6.17 without any errors. The test executes successfully this time.

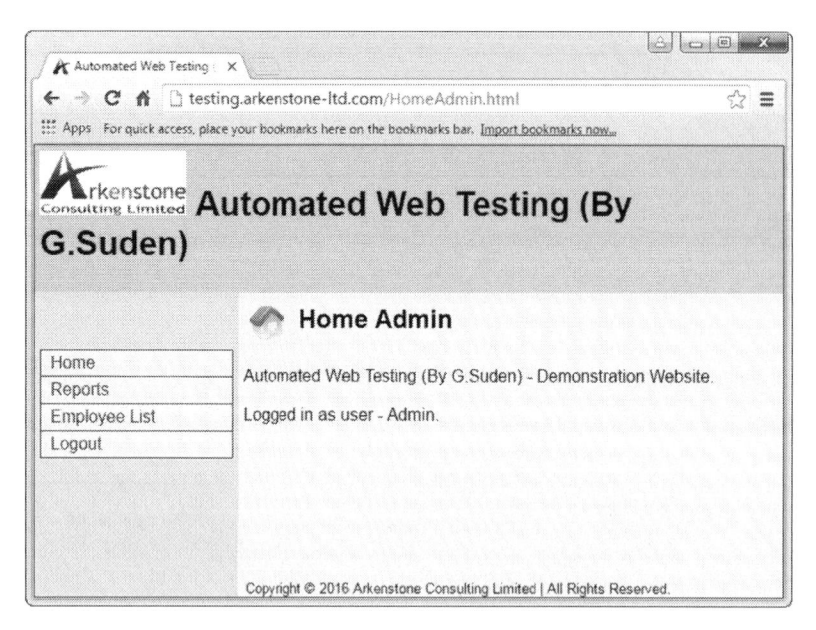

Figure 6.17: Chrome Loaded With Disable Extensions

6.2.6 Adding Chrome Options - Allow File Access

Before I deployed the demo website on the web server (`testing.arkenstone-ltd.com`), it was residing on my local workstation. Using the Chrome browser, when I logged in as the Admin user and clicked the *Employee List* link, I was thrown an error on the page as shown in Figure 6.18. Since the data being loaded in the Employee List table resided on my local workstation, the Google Chrome browser would not load local file by default (due to security reason) and hence resulting in an error.

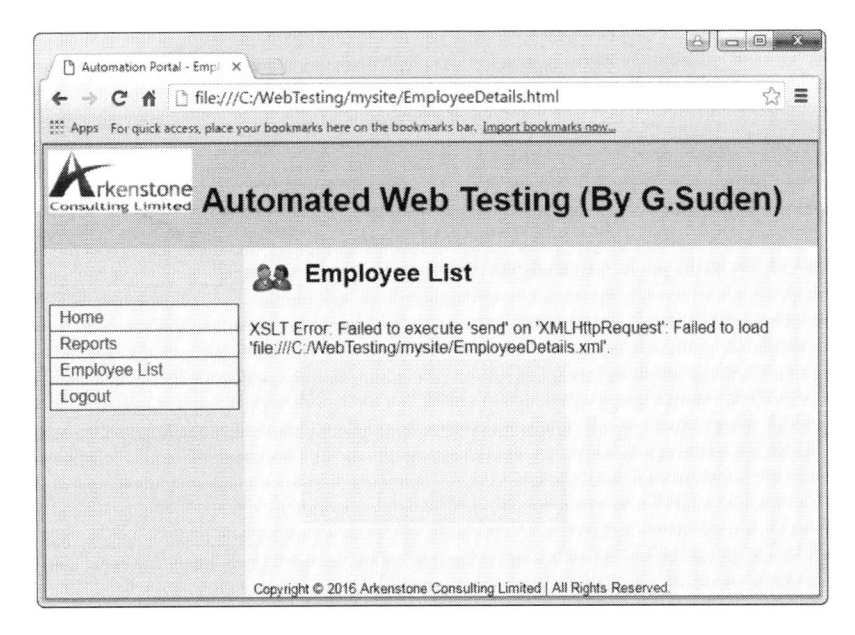

Figure 6.18: Chrome Without File Access Option

A workaround to this problem is to load the Chrome browser with the "--allow-file-access-from-files" option. Let's perform the following Test Scenario to demonstrate the allow file access option:

- Launch the demo website.

- Login with the user 'Admin'.

- Click on the *Employee List* link.

- Ensure that Chrome is loaded with the allow file access option i.e. we shouldn't see the error message as shown in Figure 6.18 and the test should execute successfully.

- Verify the employees' list.

6.2.6.1 Creating Tests

Add the Listing 6.10 code to the 'TestChrome.cs' file.

Listing 6.10: 'TestChrome.cs' - Code for LoadWithAllowFileAccessOptions

```
/***************************************************************
 * All rights reserved. Copyright 2016 Arkenstone-ltd.com       *
 ***************************************************************/
[Test]
public void LoadWithAllowFileAccessOption()
{
    try
```

```
 8      {
 9          Utility.Log.Info("Starting test: " + ↵
                ↪ TestContext.CurrentContext.Test.FullName);
10
11          ChromeOptions myOptions = new ChromeOptions();
12          myOptions.AddArgument("--allow-file-access-from-files");
13
14          driver = new ↵
                ↪ ChromeDriver(Config.CHROME_DRIVER_PATH, ↵
                ↪ myOptions);
15
16          var home = new pageHome(driver);
17          home.Visit();
18          home.ClickLogin();
19
20          var login = new pageLogin(driver);
21          login.Login("Admin", "Admin123");
22
23          var homeAdmin = new pageAdminHome(driver);
24          homeAdmin.ClickEmployeeList();
25
26          var empList = new pageAdminEmpList(driver);
27          empList.VerifyEmployeeList();
28
29          Utility.ReportResult();
30      }
31      catch (Exception exception)
32      {
33          Utility.Log.Error("exception" + ↵
                ↪ exception.ToString());
34          throw exception;
35      }
36 }
```

Line 11: Initialises a new instance of the `ChromeOptions` class.
Line 12: Adds argument "`--allow-file-access-from-files`" to the Chrome.exe command line.
Line 14: Initialises a new instance of the `ChromeDriver` class with Chrome Driver path and the option.

6.2.6.2 Executing Tests

Execute the test and you should see it executing successfully as shown in Figure 6.19.

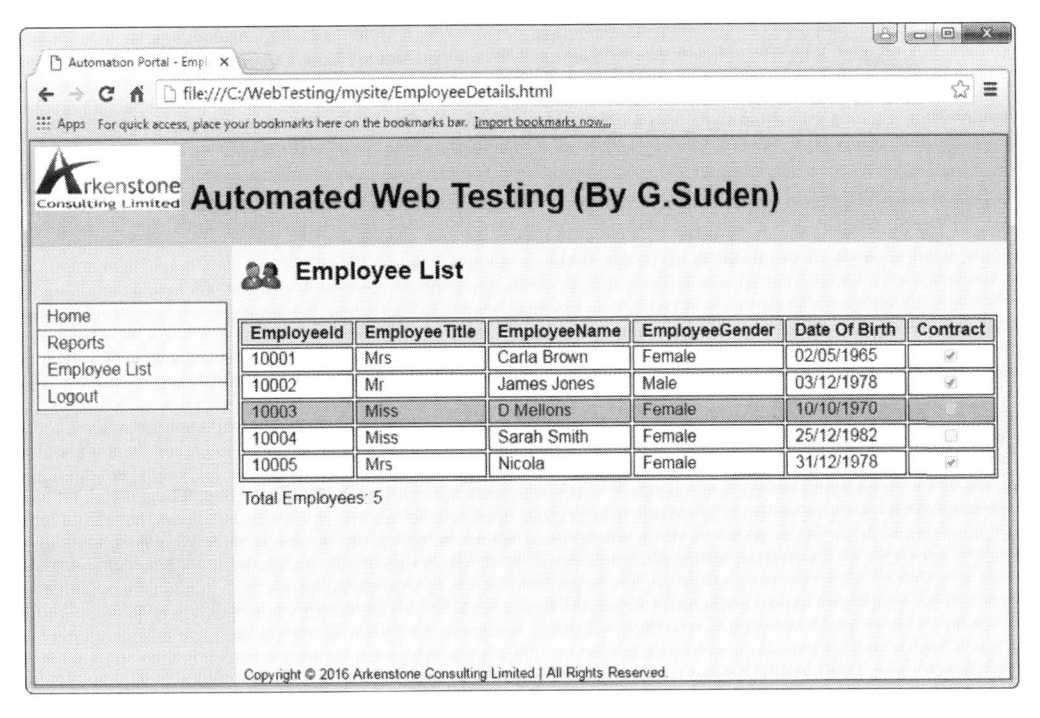

Figure 6.19: Chrome With File Access Option

6.2.7 Adding Chrome Extensions

Extensions are small software programs that can modify and enhance the functionality of the Chrome browser. Sometimes you may want to add an extension when the Chrome browser starts up. Let's see how we can achieve this by adding the 'ColorPick Eyedropper' extension when Chrome starts up. Perform the following steps to download the extension:

1. Go to `http://chrome-extension-downloader.com/`

2. Download Extension with ID **'ohcpnigalekghcmgcdcenkpelffpdolg'**.

3. Save to 'C:\Selenium\ColorPick\ColorPick-Eyedropper_v0.0.2.9.crx'. The version of 'crx' file may differ in your case.

We will perform the following Test Scenario to demonstrate the addition of Chrome extensions:

- Launch the demo website.

- Ensure that the Chrome extension 'ColorPick Eyedropper' is loaded.

- Login with the user 'Admin'.

- Click on the *Employee List* link.

- Verify the employees' list.

Automated Web Testing

6.2.7.1 Creating Test

Add a new test to the 'TestChrome.cs' file as shown in Listing 6.11.

Listing 6.11: 'TestChrome.cs' - Code for test LoadWithExtension

```
1  [Test]
2  public void LoadWithExtension()
3  {
4      try
5      {
6          Utility.Log.Info("Starting test: " + ↵
               TestContext.CurrentContext.Test.FullName);
7
8          ChromeOptions myOptions = new ChromeOptions();
9          myOptions.AddExtension( ↵
               @"C:\Selenium\ColorPick\ColorPick- ↵
               Eyedropper_v0.0.2.9.crx");
10
11         driver = new ↵
               ChromeDriver(Config.CHROME_DRIVER_PATH, ↵
               myOptions);
12
13         var home = new pageHome(driver);
14         home.Visit();
15         home.ClickLogin();
16
17         var login = new pageLogin(driver);
18         login.Login("Admin", "Admin123");
19
20         var homeAdmin = new pageAdminHome(driver);
21         homeAdmin.ClickEmployeeList();
22
23         var empList = new pageAdminEmpList(driver);
24         empList.VerifyEmployeeList();
25
26
27         Utility.ReportResult();
28     }
29     catch (Exception exception)
30     {
31         Utility.Log.Error("exception" + ↵
               exception.ToString());
32         throw exception;
```

33   }
34 }

Line 8: Initialises a new instance of the `ChromeOptions` class.
Line 9: Adds the colour picker extension by specifying the path to the 'crx' file.

6.2.7.2 Executing Test

Execute the test and you will see the Chrome browser loaded with the 'ColorPick Eyedropper' extension as shown in Figure 6.20.

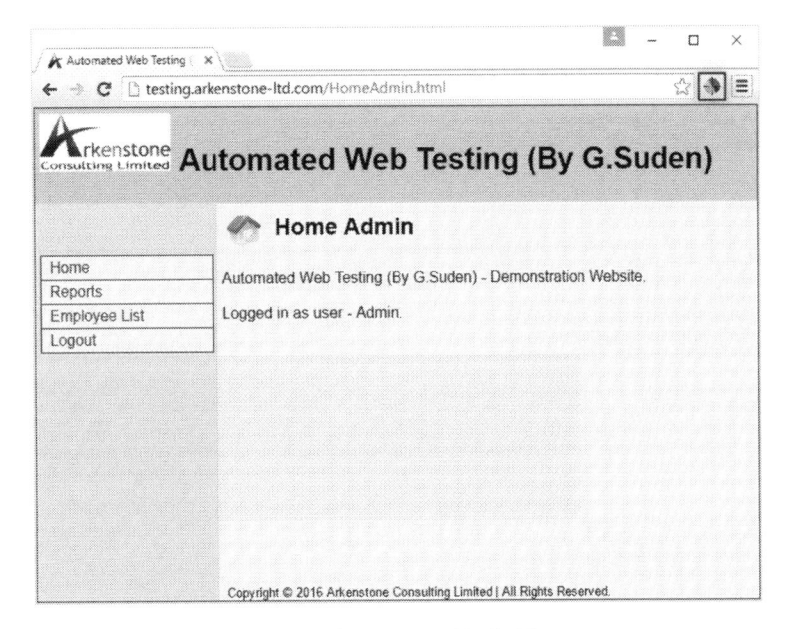

Figure 6.20: Chrome With Extension

6.3 Internet Explorer

6.3.1 Internet Explorer Driver

Internet Explorer Driver is a separate executable that WebDriver uses to control the IE browser. Download Internet Explorer Driver from:

http://www.seleniumhq.org/download/

Extract 'IEDriverServer.exe' to 'C:\Selenium\IEDriverServer_x64_2.48.0'

6.3.2 Configuration Parameters

Let's add some configuration parameters which we will need. Double click on the Config.cs file in Solution Explorer and add the Listing 6.12 code to it.

Listing 6.12: 'Config.cs' - Parameters for Internet Explorer

```
1  public const string INTERNETEXPLORER = ↵
        ↪ "InternetExplorer";
2  public const string INTERNETEXPLORER_DRIVER_PATH = ↵
        ↪ @"C:\Selenium\IEDriverServer_x64_2.48.0";
3  public static string BROWSER = INTERNETEXPLORER;
```

Line 1: Defines a constant string to hold the value "InternetExplorer".
Line 2: Defines location of the extracted Internet Explorer Driver.
Line 3: Sets the current browser to INTERNETEXPLORER.

6.3.3 Utility Functions

Update the `SetupDriver` function in the 'Utility.cs' file to add a new case statement as shown in Listing 6.13.

Listing 6.13: 'Utility.cs' - Support for Internet Explorer

```
1  using OpenQA.Selenium.IE;
2
3  case Config.INTERNETEXPLORER:
4      InternetExplorerOptions options = new ↵
            ↪ InternetExplorerOptions();
5      options. ↵
            ↪ IntroduceInstabilityByIgnoringProtectedModeSettings ↵
            ↪ = true;
6      driver = new InternetExplorerDriver( ↵
            ↪ Config.INTERNETEXPLORER_DRIVER_PATH, options);
7      break;
```

Line 1: Additional import required to support the Internet Explorer browser.
Line 3: If the configured browser is INTERNETEXPLORER then initialises the Internet Explorer driver by providing location of the extracted IE Driver. Note that we are ignoring the settings of the Internet Explorer Protected Mode.

6.3.4 Executing Tests

Execute the test 'LoginUser' and you should see a window as shown in Figure 6.21. The test is executed using the Internet Explorer browser.

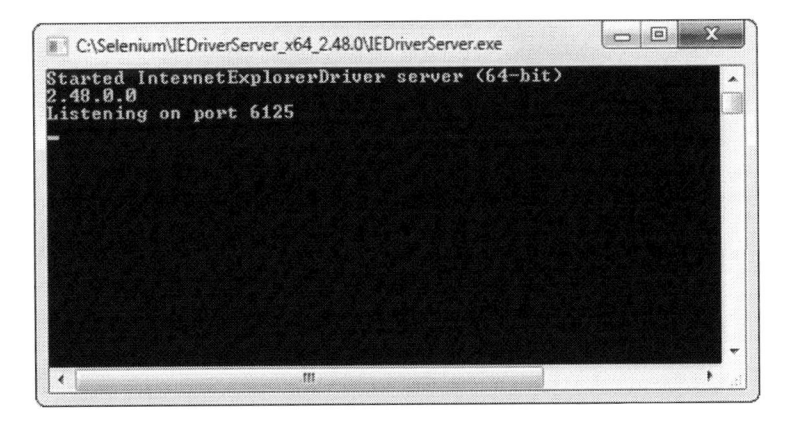

Figure 6.21: Internet Explorer WebDriver Window

6.3.5 Internet Explorer Options

How many times you have started an automated test using Internet Explorer only for it to crash straight away because the zoom was not set to 100%. Here is a way to ignore the zoom level in Internet Explorer while running your tests. We will use the option "IgnoreZoomLevel" when the Internet Explorer Driver starts up.

> Note that if you are identifying an element via its *relative position* in your website under test, the test may fail with a zoom level of 125%.

Let's perform the following Test Scenario to demonstrate the ignore zoom level option:

- Launch the demo website.
- Ensure that Internet Explorer's zoom level is ignored during test execution.
- Login with the user 'Admin'.
- Click on the *Employee List* link.
- Verify the employees' list.

6.3.5.1 Creating Tests

In the 'Solution Explorer', right click on the 'Tests' folder, click Add ⇒ Class. Type the name as 'TestIE.cs' and click the Add button. Add the Listing 6.14 code to it.

Listing 6.14: 'TestIE.cs' - Code for LoadWithOptions

```
1  /***************************************************************
2   * All rights reserved. Copyright 2016 Arkenstone-ltd.com       *
3   ***************************************************************/
4  using System;
```

```csharp
 5  using OpenQA.Selenium;
 6  using NUnit.Framework;
 7  using WebTesting.Pages;
 8  using OpenQA.Selenium.IE;
 9
10  namespace WebTesting.Tests
11  {
12      public class TestIE
13      {
14          IWebDriver driver;
15
16          [SetUp]
17          public void Setup()
18          {
19              Utility.TestResult = Config.PASS;
20          }
21
22
23          [TearDown]
24          public void Teardown()
25          {
26              if (TestContext.CurrentContext.Result.Status ↵
                    ↪ == TestStatus.Failed)
27              {
28                  Utility.Log.Error("***** Teardown ==> ↵
                        ↪ Test FAILED ***** =>" + ↵
                        ↪ TestContext.CurrentContext.Test. ↵
                        ↪ FullName);
29                  Utility.SaveScreenShot(driver, ↵
                        ↪ TestContext.CurrentContext.Test.Name ↵
                        ↪ + "(" + ↵
                        ↪ TestContext.CurrentContext.Result. ↵
                        ↪ Status + ")");
30              }
31              else if ↵
                    ↪ (TestContext.CurrentContext.Result.Status ↵
                    ↪ == TestStatus.Passed)
32              {
33                  Utility.Log.Info("PASS => " + ↵
                        ↪ TestContext.CurrentContext.Test. ↵
                        ↪ FullName);
34              }
35
36              //driver.Quit();
37
```

```csharp
38                    Utility.SaveLogFile(TestContext.
                          CurrentContext.
                          Test.FullName.Substring(17) + " (" +
                          TestContext.CurrentContext.Result.Status
                          + ") ");
39
40              if (Utility.TestResult == Config.FAIL)
41              {
42                  Utility.CreateSummaryFileEntry(DateTime.
                          Now.ToString() + "," +
                          TestContext.CurrentContext.Test.
                          FullName.Substring(17) + ",FAIL" +
                          "," + Config.CURRENT_LOGFILE);
43              }
44              else
45                  Utility.CreateSummaryFileEntry(DateTime.
                          Now.ToString() + "," +
                          TestContext.CurrentContext.Test.
                          FullName.Substring(17) + ",PASS" +
                          "," + Config.CURRENT_LOGFILE);
46          }
47
48          [Test]
49          public void LoadWithOptions()
50          {
51              try
52              {
53                  Utility.Log.Info("Starting test: " +
                          TestContext.CurrentContext.
                          Test.FullName);
54
55                  InternetExplorerOptions options = new
                          InternetExplorerOptions();
56                  options.IntroduceInstabilityByIgnoring
                          ProtectedModeSettings = true;
57                  options.IgnoreZoomLevel = true;
58                  options.EnableNativeEvents = false;
59
60                  driver = new InternetExplorerDriver(
                          Config.INTERNETEXPLORER_DRIVER_PATH,
                          options);
61
62                  var home = new pageHome(driver);
63                  home.Visit();
64                  home.ClickLogin();
```

```
65
66                    var login = new pageLogin(driver);
67                    login.Login("Admin", "Admin123");
68
69                    var homeAdmin = new pageAdminHome(driver);
70                    homeAdmin.ClickEmployeeList();
71
72                    var empList = new pageAdminEmpList(driver);
73                    empList.VerifyEmployeeList();
74
75                    Utility.ReportResult();
76                }
77                catch (Exception exception)
78                {
79                    Utility.Log.Error("exception" + ↵
                     ↪ exception.ToString());
80                    throw exception;
81                }
82            }
83        }
84 }
```

Line 16: Note that the **Setup()** function doesn't initialise the driver. We will initialise it in the test. It has been done so for our demo purpose, so that we don't disturb our Automation Framework code we have written so far because we will be making changes to it to demonstrate different aspects of using Internet Explorer.

Line 55: Initialises a new instance of the **InternetExplorerOptions** class.

Line 56: Please note that "**IntroduceInstabilityByIgnoringProtectedModeSettings**" is one word although it has been shown in two lines so that it remains within the textual width of the book.

Line 57: Adds option to ignore the zoom level.

Line 58: Don't use native events while interacting with the elements.

6.3.5.2 Executing Test

☞ Before you execute the test, please ensure to set Internet Explorer browser's zoom level to 125% and close it.

Execute the test and you should see a window as shown in Figure 6.22. The test is executed successfully with the browser's zoom level 125%.

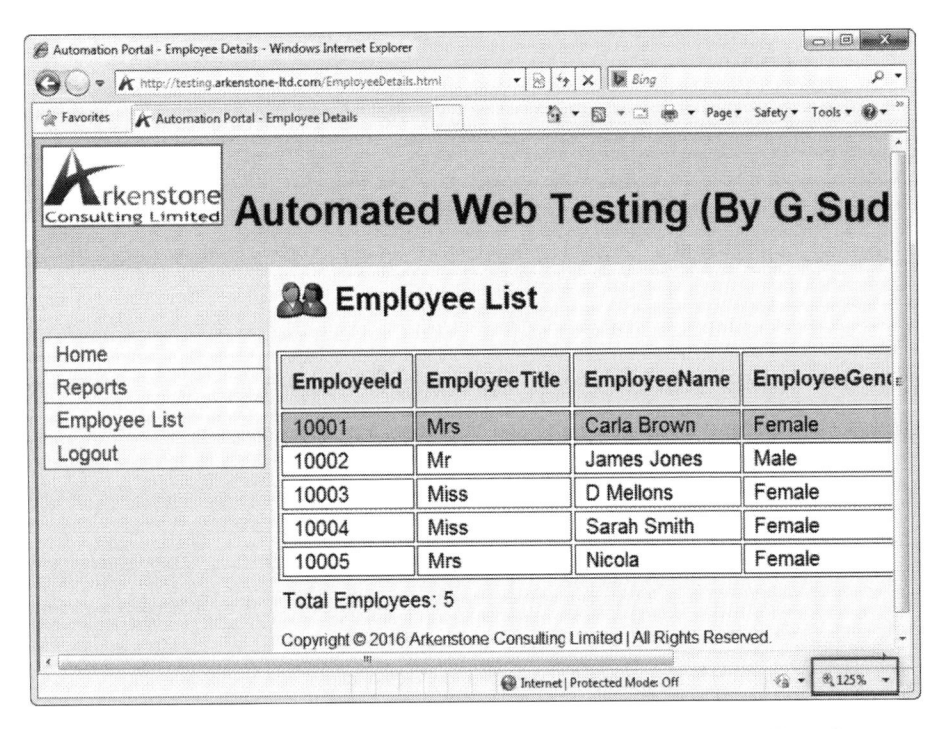

Figure 6.22: Internet Explorer With Ignore Zoom Level

6.4 Microsoft Edge

6.4.1 Microsoft Edge WebDriver

For Windows 10, you will need to install the MicrosoftWebDriver.exe to use Microsoft Edge browser. Download Microsoft WebDriver as follows:

For Windows 10 *Build 10240*
https://www.microsoft.com/en-us/download/details.aspx?id=48212

For Windows 10 *Fall 2015 Update Build 10586*
https://www.microsoft.com/en-us/download/details.aspx?id=49962

Download and install using the 'msi' file.

6.4.2 Configuration Parameters

Let's add some configuration parameters which we will need. Double click on the 'Config.cs' file in 'Solution Explorer' and add the Listing 6.15 code to it.

Listing 6.15: 'Config.cs' - Parameters for Microsoft Edge

```
1 public const string EDGE = "Edge";
```

```
2  public const string EDGE_DRIVER_PATH = @"C:\Program Files ↵
    ↪ (x86)\Microsoft Web Driver";
3  public static string BROWSER = EDGE;
```

Line 1: Defines a constant string to hold the value "Edge".
Line 2: Defines location of the installed Microsoft Edge WebDriver.
Line 3: Sets the current browser to EDGE.

6.4.3 Utility Functions

Update the `SetupDriver` function in the 'Utility.cs' file to add a new case statement as shown in Listing 6.16.

Listing 6.16: 'Utility.cs' - Support for Microsoft Edge

```
1  using OpenQA.Selenium.Edge;
2
3  case Config.EDGE:
4      driver = new EdgeDriver(Config.EDGE_DRIVER_PATH);
5      break;
```

Line 1: Additional import required to support the Microsoft Edge browser.
Line 3: If the configured browser is EDGE then initialises the Edge driver by providing location of the installed Edge WebDriver.

6.4.4 Executing Tests

Execute the 'LoginUser' test and you should see a WebDriver window as shown in Figure 6.23. The test is executed using Microsoft Edge browser.

Figure 6.23: Microsoft Edge WebDriver Window

6.4.5 Edge Options

As we have done with the other browsers, let's learn how to use Edge Options by specifying the behaviour 'waiting for page loads' in the Edge driver. You can use any of the page load strategies as defined below:

1. Default i.e. indicates the behaviour is not set.

2. Normal i.e. waits for pages to load and ready state to be 'complete'.

3. Eager i.e. waits for pages to load and for ready state to be 'interactive' or 'complete'.

4. None i.e. does not wait for pages to load, returning immediately.

Let's perform the following Test Scenario to demonstrate the use of page load strategies:

- Launch the demo website.

- Ensure that the Edge is loaded with the 'Eager' page load strategy and the test should execute successfully.

- Login with the user 'Admin'.

- Click on the *Employee List* link.

- Verify the employees' list.

6.4.5.1 Creating Tests

In the 'Solution Explorer', right click on the 'Tests' folder, click Add ⇒ Class. Type the name as 'TestEdge.cs' and click the Add button. Add the Listing 6.17 code to it.

Listing 6.17: 'TestEdge.cs' - Code for LoadWithOptions

```
/****************************************************************
 * All rights reserved. Copyright 2016 Arkenstone-ltd.com        *
 ****************************************************************/
using System;
using OpenQA.Selenium;
using NUnit.Framework;
using WebTesting.Pages;
using OpenQA.Selenium.Edge;

namespace WebTesting.Tests
{
    public class TestEdge
    {
```

```csharp
14          IWebDriver driver;
15
16          [SetUp]
17          public void Setup()
18          {
19              Utility.TestResult = Config.PASS;
20          }
21
22
23          [TearDown]
24          public void Teardown()
25          {
26              if (TestContext.CurrentContext.Result.Status
                    == TestStatus.Failed)
27              {
28                  Utility.Log.Error("***** Teardown ==>
                        Test FAILED ***** =>" +
                        TestContext.CurrentContext.Test.
                        FullName);
29                  Utility.SaveScreenShot(driver,
                        TestContext.CurrentContext.Test.Name
                        + "(" +
                        TestContext.CurrentContext.Result.
                        Status + ")");
30              }
31              else if
                    (TestContext.CurrentContext.Result.Status
                    == TestStatus.Passed)
32              {
33                  Utility.Log.Info("PASS => " +
                        TestContext.CurrentContext.Test.
                        FullName);
34              }
35
36              //driver.Quit();
37
38              Utility.SaveLogFile(TestContext.CurrentContext.
                    Test.FullName.Substring(17) + " (" +
                    TestContext.CurrentContext.Result.Status
                    + ") ");
39
40              if (Utility.TestResult == Config.FAIL)
41              {
42                  Utility.CreateSummaryFileEntry(DateTime.
                        Now.ToString() + "," +
```

```
                            ↪ TestContext.CurrentContext.Test.  ↵
                            ↪ FullName.Substring(17) + ",FAIL" + ↵
                            ↪ "," + Config.CURRENT_LOGFILE);
43              }
44              else
45                  Utility.CreateSummaryFileEntry(DateTime.  ↵
                            ↪ Now.ToString() + "," +  ↵
                            ↪ TestContext.CurrentContext.Test.  ↵
                            ↪ FullName.Substring(17) + ",PASS" + ↵
                            ↪ "," + Config.CURRENT_LOGFILE);
46          }
47
48          [Test]
49          public void LoadWithOptions()
50          {
51              try
52              {
53                  Utility.Log.Info("Starting test: " + ↵
                            ↪ TestContext.CurrentContext.Test.  ↵
                            ↪ FullName);
54
55                  EdgeOptions myOptions = new ↵
                            ↪ EdgeOptions();
56                  myOptions.PageLoadStrategy = ↵
                            ↪ EdgePageLoadStrategy.Eager;
57
58                  driver = new ↵
                            ↪ EdgeDriver(Config.EDGE_DRIVER_PATH, ↵
                            ↪ myOptions);
59
60                  var home = new pageHome(driver);
61                  home.Visit();
62                  home.ClickLogin();
63
64                  var login = new pageLogin(driver);
65                  login.Login("Admin", "Admin123");
66
67                  var homeAdmin = new pageAdminHome(driver);
68                  homeAdmin.ClickEmployeeList();
69
70                  var empList = new pageAdminEmpList(driver);
71                  empList.VerifyEmployeeList();
72
73                  Utility.ReportResult();
74              }
```

```
75              catch (Exception exception)
76              {
77                  Utility.Log.Error("exception" + ↵
                    ↪ exception.ToString());
78                  throw exception;
79              }
80          }
81      }
82  }
```

Line 16: Note that the `Setup()` function doesn't initialise the driver. We will initialise it in the test. It has been done so for our demo purpose, so that we don't disturb our Automation Framework code we have written so far because we will be making changes to it to demonstrate different aspects of using Windows Edge browser.

Line 55: Initialises a new instance of the `EdgeOptions` class.

Line 56: Adds option Eager i.e. wait for pages to load and for ready state to be 'interactive' or 'complete'.

6.4.5.2 Executing Test

Execute the test and you should see a window as shown in Figure 6.24. The test is executed using Microsoft Edge browser with the 'Eager' page load strategy.

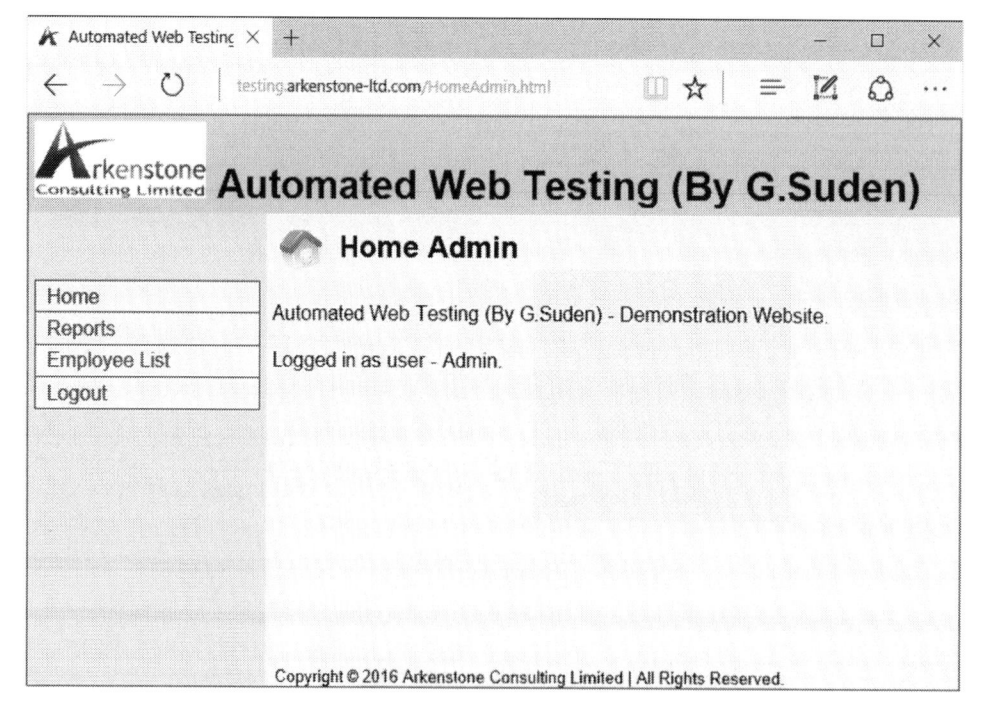

Figure 6.24: Microsoft Edge Load With Options

6.5 Safari

6.5.1 SafariDriver

The SafariDriver is implemented as a Safari browser extension. Download SafariDriver from: `http://www.seleniumhq.org/download/`

Simply drag and drop the latest copy of 'SafariDriver.safariextz' to the Safari browser and click the "install" button.

> ☞ Note that sometimes the install window is hidden behind the browser so you may have to minimise Safari browser window to view the installation window.

6.5.2 Configuration Parameters

Let's add some configuration parameters which we will need. Double click on the 'Config.cs' file in 'Solution Explorer' and add the Listing 6.18 code to it.

Listing 6.18: 'Config.cs' - Parameters for Safari

```
1  public const string SAFARI = "Safari";
2  public static string BROWSER = SAFARI;
```

Line 1: Defines a constant string to hold the value "Safari".
Line 2: Sets the current browser to SAFARI.

6.5.3 Utility Functions

Update the `SetupDriver` function in the 'Utility.cs' file to add a new case statement as shown in Listing 6.19.

Listing 6.19: 'Utility.cs' - Support for Safari

```
1  using OpenQA.Selenium.Safari;
2
3  case Config.SAFARI:
4      driver = driver = new SafariDriver();
5      break;
```

Line 1: Additional import required to support the Safari browser.
Line 3: If the configured browser is SAFARI then initialises the Safari driver.

6.5.4 Executing Tests

There seems to be a compatibility issue between Safari WebDriver 2.48 (installed in Safari browser v5.1.7) and Selenium 2.53.0. Download Selenium 'selenium-dotnet-2.47.0' and it works fine! Note that no WebDriver window is shown for Safari.

6.5.5 Safari Options

Let's learn how to use Safari Options to instruct the SafariDriver to delete all the existing session data when starting a new session. This includes browser history, cache, cookies, HTML5 local storage, and HTML5 databases.

We will perform the following Test Scenario to demonstrate this capability:

- Launch the demo website.

- Ensure that a clean session is loaded when Safari starts and the test should execute successfully.

- Login with the user 'Admin'.

- Click on the *Employee List* link.

- Verify the employees' list.

6.5.5.1 Creating Tests

In the 'Solution Explorer', right click on the 'Tests' folder, click Add ⇒ Class. Type the name as 'TestSafari.cs' and click the Add button. Add the Listing 6.20 code to it.

Listing 6.20: 'TestSafari.cs' - Code for LoadWithOptions

```
/***************************************************************
 * All rights reserved. Copyright 2016 Arkenstone-ltd.com       *
 ***************************************************************/
using System;
using OpenQA.Selenium;
using NUnit.Framework;
using WebTesting.Pages;
using OpenQA.Selenium.Safari;

namespace WebTesting.Tests
{
    public class TestSafari
    {
        IWebDriver driver;
```

```
15
16          [SetUp]
17          public void Setup()
18          {
19              Utility.TestResult = Config.PASS;
20          }
21
22          [TearDown]
23          public void Teardown()
24          {
25              if (TestContext.CurrentContext.Result.Status ↵
                    == TestStatus.Failed)
26              {
27                  Utility.Log.Error("***** Teardown ==> ↵
                        Test FAILED ***** =>" + ↵
                        TestContext.CurrentContext.Test. ↵
                        FullName);
28                  Utility.SaveScreenShot(driver, ↵
                        TestContext.CurrentContext.Test.Name ↵
                        + "(" + ↵
                        TestContext.CurrentContext.Result. ↵
                        Status + ")");
29              }
30              else if ↵
                    (TestContext.CurrentContext.Result.Status ↵
                    == TestStatus.Passed)
31              {
32                  Utility.Log.Info("PASS => " + ↵
                        TestContext.CurrentContext.Test. ↵
                        FullName);
33              }
34
35              //driver.Quit();
36
37              Utility.SaveLogFile(TestContext.CurrentContext. ↵
                    Test.FullName.Substring(17) + " (" + ↵
                    TestContext.CurrentContext.Result.Status ↵
                    + ") ");
38
39              if (Utility.TestResult == Config.FAIL)
40              {
41                  Utility.CreateSummaryFileEntry(DateTime. ↵
                        Now.ToString() + "," + ↵
                        TestContext.CurrentContext.Test. ↵
                        FullName.Substring(17) + ",FAIL" + ↵
```

```csharp
                        "," + Config.CURRENT_LOGFILE);
42              }
43              else
44                  Utility.CreateSummaryFileEntry(DateTime.
                        Now.ToString() + "," +
                        TestContext.CurrentContext.Test.
                        FullName.Substring(17) + ",PASS" +
                        "," + Config.CURRENT_LOGFILE);
45          }
46
47          [Test]
48          public void LoadWithOptions()
49          {
50              try
51              {
52                  Utility.Log.Info("Starting test: " +
                        TestContext.CurrentContext.Test.FullName);
53
54                  SafariOptions myOptions = new
                        SafariOptions();
55                  myOptions.AddAdditionalCapability(
                        "cleanSession", true);
56
57                  driver = new SafariDriver(myOptions);
58
59                  var home = new pageHome(driver);
60                  home.Visit();
61                  home.ClickLogin();
62
63                  var login = new pageLogin(driver);
64                  login.Login("Admin", "Admin123");
65
66                  var homeAdmin = new pageAdminHome(driver);
67                  homeAdmin.ClickEmployeeList();
68
69                  var empList = new pageAdminEmpList(driver);
70                  empList.VerifyEmployeeList();
71
72                  Utility.ReportResult();
73              }
74              catch (Exception exception)
75              {
76                  Utility.Log.Error("exception" +
                        exception.ToString());
77                  throw exception;
```

```
78              }
79          }
80      }
81 }
```

Line 16: Note that the `Setup()` function doesn't initialise the driver. We will initialise it in the test. It has been done so for our demo purpose, so that we don't disturb our Automation Framework code we have written so far because we will be making changes to it to demonstrate different aspects of using Safari.

Line 54: Initialises a new instance of the `SafariOptions` class.

Line 55: Adds the additional capability "`cleanSession`".

Line 57: Initialises a new instance of the `SafariDriver` class with the additional capability.

6.5.5.2 Executing Test

Execute the test and you should see a window as shown in Figure 6.25 where Safari is launched with a clean session.

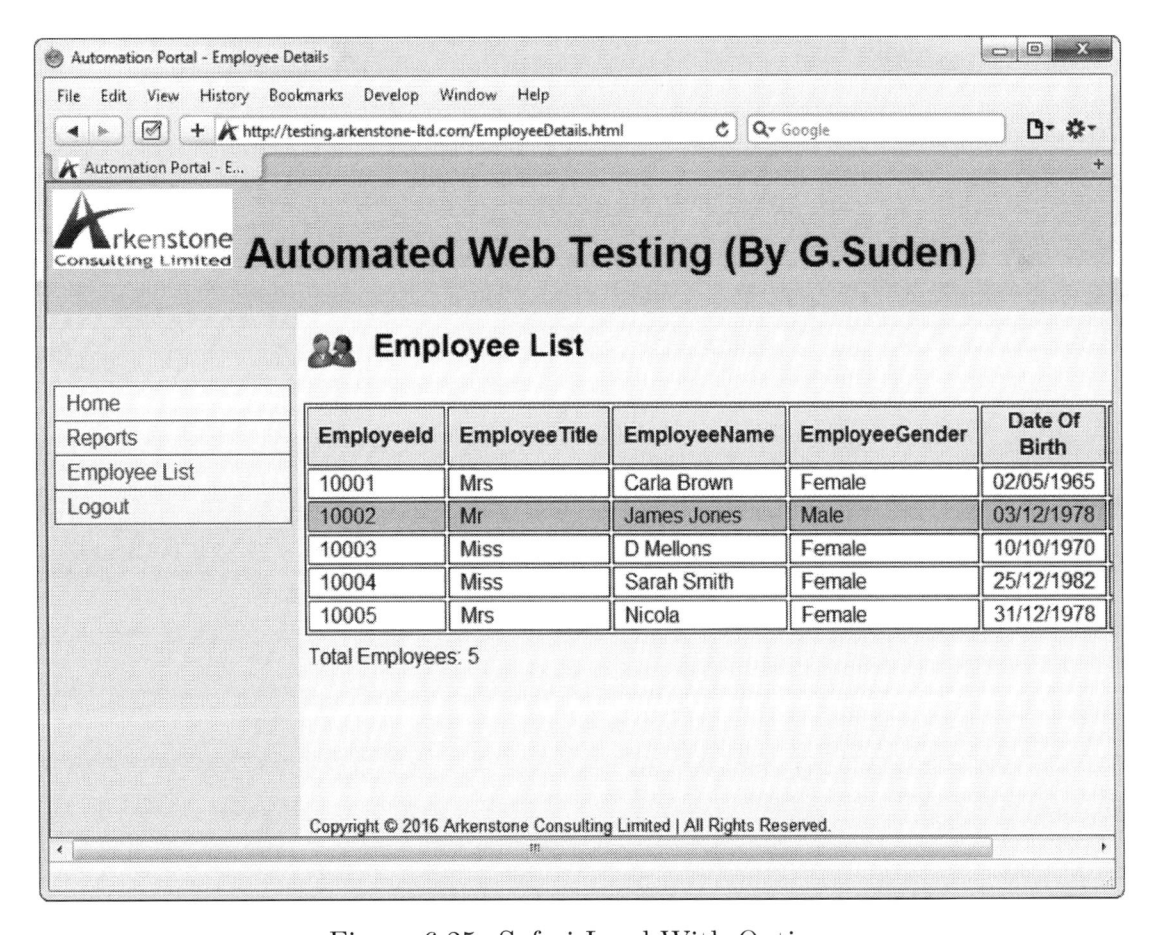

Figure 6.25: Safari Load With Options

6.6 Opera

6.6.1 Opera WebDriver

In order to execute tests with the Opera browser, you will need to download the Opera WebDriver from:

https://github.com/operasoftware/operachromiumdriver/releases

Extract 'operadriver.exe' to 'C:\Selenium\operadriver_win64'

6.6.2 Configuration Parameters

Let's add some configuration parameters which we will need. Double click on the 'Config.cs' file in 'Solution Explorer' and add the Listing 6.21 code to it.

Listing 6.21: 'Config.cs' - Parameters for Opera

```
1  public const string OPERA = "Opera";
2  public const string OPERA_DRIVER_PATH = ↵
       ↪ @"C:\Selenium\operadriver_win64";
3  public static string BROWSER = OPERA;
```

Line 1: Defines a constant string to hold the value "Opera".
Line 2: Defines location of the extracted Opera Driver.
Line 3: Sets the current browser to OPERA.

6.6.3 Utility Functions

Update the SetupDriver function in the 'Utility.cs' file to add a new case statement as shown in Listing 6.22.

Listing 6.22: 'Utility.cs' - Support for Opera

```
1  using OpenQA.Selenium.Opera;
2
3  case Config.OPERA:
4      driver = new OperaDriver(Config.OPERA_DRIVER_PATH);
5      break;
```

Line 1: Additional import required to support the Opera browser.
Line 3: If the configured browser is OPERA then initialises the Opera driver by providing location of the extracted Opera Driver.

6.6.4 Executing Tests

Execute the 'LoginUser' test and you should see an OperaDriver window as shown in Figure 6.26.

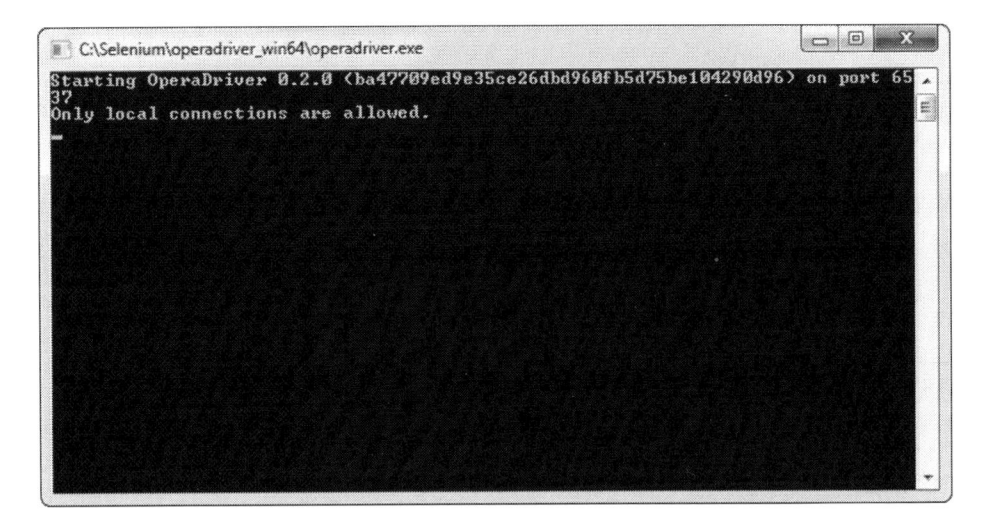

Figure 6.26: Opera WebDriver Window

6.6.5 Opera Options

The Opera browser throws a similar error message when loading a local file as we saw for Chrome (see Figure 6.18 for the error message). Let's apply the same workaround as we did for Chrome i.e. load the Opera browser with the "--allow-file-access-from-files" option. We will also set the location of the Opera browser's binary executable file.

We'll perform the following Test Scenario to demonstrate these features:

- Launch the demo website.

- Ensure that Opera browser's binary executable is successfully launched.

- Ensure that Opera is loaded with the allow file access option and the test should execute successfully.

- Login with the user 'Admin'.

- Click on the *Employee List* link.

- Verify the employees' list.

6.6.5.1 Creating Tests

In the 'Solution Explorer', right click on the 'Tests' folder, click Add ⇒ Class. Type the name as 'TestOpera.cs' and click the Add button. Add the Listing 6.23 code to it.

Listing 6.23: 'TestOpera.cs' - Support for Opera Options

```csharp
/***************************************************************
 * All rights reserved. Copyright 2016 Arkenstone-ltd.com       *
 ***************************************************************/
using System;
using OpenQA.Selenium;
using NUnit.Framework;
using WebTesting.Pages;
using OpenQA.Selenium.Opera;

namespace WebTesting.Tests
{
    public class TestOpera
    {
        IWebDriver driver;

        [SetUp]
        public void Setup()
        {
            Utility.TestResult = Config.PASS;
        }

        [TearDown]
        public void Teardown()
        {
            if (TestContext.CurrentContext.Result.Status
                 == TestStatus.Failed)
            {
                Utility.Log.Error("***** Teardown ==>
                     Test FAILED ***** =>" +
                     TestContext.CurrentContext.Test.
                     FullName);
                Utility.SaveScreenShot(driver,
                     TestContext.CurrentContext.Test.Name
                     + "(" +
                     TestContext.CurrentContext.Result.
                     Status + ")");
            }
            else if
                 (TestContext.CurrentContext.Result.Status
                 == TestStatus.Passed)
            {
                Utility.Log.Info("PASS => " +
```

```
33                    }
34
35            //driver.Quit();
36
37            Utility.SaveLogFile(TestContext.CurrentContext.
                  Test.FullName.Substring(17) + " (" +
                  TestContext.CurrentContext.Result.Status
                  + ") ");
38
39         if (Utility.TestResult == Config.FAIL)
40            {
41                    Utility.CreateSummaryFileEntry(DateTime.
                          Now.ToString() + "," +
                          TestContext.CurrentContext.Test.
                          FullName.Substring(17) + ",FAIL" +
                          "," + Config.CURRENT_LOGFILE);
42            }
43            else
44                    Utility.CreateSummaryFileEntry(DateTime.
                          Now.ToString() + "," +
                          TestContext.CurrentContext.Test.
                          FullName.Substring(17) + ",PASS" +
                          "," + Config.CURRENT_LOGFILE);
45         }
46
47         [Test]
48         public void LoadWithOptions()
49         {
50            try
51            {
52                    Utility.Log.Info("Starting test: " +
                          TestContext.CurrentContext.Test.
                          FullName);
53
54                    OperaOptions myOptions = new
                          OperaOptions();
55                    myOptions.BinaryLocation = @"C:\Program
                          Files (x86)\Opera\launcher.exe";
56                    myOptions.AddArgument(
                          "--allow-file-access-from-files");
57
58                    driver = new
                          OperaDriver(Config.OPERA_DRIVER_PATH,
```

```
59                          ↪ myOptions);
60                  var home = new pageHome(driver);
61                  home.Visit();
62                  home.ClickLogin();
63
64                  var login = new pageLogin(driver);
65                  login.Login("Admin", "Admin123");
66
67                  var homeAdmin = new pageAdminHome(driver);
68                  homeAdmin.ClickEmployeeList();
69
70                  var empList = new pageAdminEmpList(driver);
71                  empList.VerifyEmployeeList();
72
73                  Utility.ReportResult();
74              }
75              catch (Exception exception)
76              {
77                  Utility.Log.Error("exception" + ↵
                        ↪ exception.ToString());
78                  throw exception;
79              }
80          }
81      }
82 }
```

Line 16: Note that the Setup() function doesn't initialise the driver. We will initialise it in the test. It has been done so for our demo purpose, so that we don't disturb our Automation Framework code we have written so far because we will be making changes to it to demonstrate different aspects of using Opera.

Line 54: Initialises a new instance of the OperaOptions class.

Line 55: Sets the location of the Opera browser's binary executable file. You may have to change the location depending on where you installed Opera browser on your workstation.

Line 56: Adds argument "--allow-file-access-from-files" to the command line.

Line 58: Initialises a new instance of the OperaDriver class with the Opera Driver path and the option.

6.6.5.2 Executing Test

Execute the test and you should see a window as shown in Figure 6.27, and the test is executed successfully.

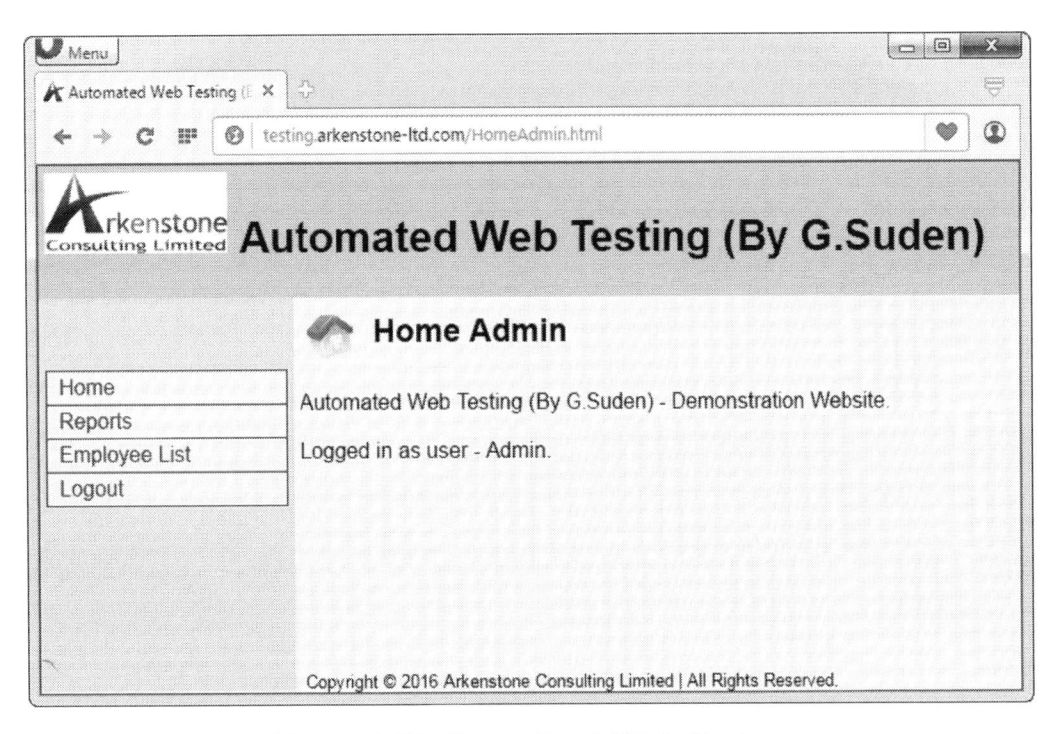

Figure 6.27: Opera Load With Options

6.7 Automation Framework - Adding More Features

Before we end this chapter, let's add some more features to our Automation Framework. So here we go...

6.7.1 Testing On Different Environments

When we are testing, generally, we have to test on a number of different environments, for example:

- Development Environment - to have an early view of the website under test
- Functional Test Environment
- System Test Environment
- User Acceptance Test Environment
- And others...

For all these different environments, you will have to set different values of the configuration variables in the 'Config.cs' file e.g. the website URL, location of folders containing test results, web drivers etc. What we would like is to define a separate set of the parameter values for different environments. Let's see how to do it.

Listing 6.24 shows the complete code of the 'Config.cs' file written so far. We have also used the `#define` directive to define three environments as follows:

- FT_ENV - Functional Test Environment
- ST_ENV - System Test Environment
- UAT_ENV - User Acceptance Test Environment

Depending upon the environment we are using for the test, we will comment the other two environments e.g. in our case, the System and the User Acceptance Test Environment define directives have been commented out. Ensure that at a time, only one directive is uncommented and all other such directives are commented.

Listing 6.24: 'Config.cs' - Complete code so far

```
/*****************************************************************
 * All rights reserved. Copyright 2016 Arkenstone-ltd.com *
 *****************************************************************/

#define FT_ENV
//#define ST_ENV
//#define UAT_ENV

using System;

namespace WebTesting
{
    public static class Config
    {
        public const string FIREFOX = "Firefox";
        public const string CHROME = "Chrome";
        public const string INTERNETEXPLORER = 
            "InternetExplorer";
        public const string EDGE = "Edge";
        public const string SAFARI = "Safari";
        public const string OPERA = "Opera";

        public static string BROWSER = FIREFOX;

#if FT_ENV
        public const string ENVIRONMENT = "FT";
        public const string URL = 
            @"http://testing.arkenstone-ltd.com/";
        public const string connectionString = 
            "Server=localhost;Database=WebTesting;
            Uid=sa;Pwd=sa;connect timeout=180;";
```

```
28          public static string ResultFolder = ↵
              Environment.CurrentDirectory.Replace( ↵
              @"bin\Release", @"Logs\") + "Results_" + ↵
              DateTime.Now.ToString("dd_MMM_yyyy ↵
              HH_mm_ss", System.Globalization.CultureInfo. ↵
              GetCultureInfo("en-GB"));
29          public static string ScreenShotFolder = ↵
              ResultFolder + @"\Screenshots\";
30          public const string CHROME_DRIVER_PATH = ↵
              @"C:\Selenium\chromedriver_win32";
31          public const string INTERNETEXPLORER_DRIVER_PATH ↵
              = @"C:\Selenium\IEDriverServer_x64_2.48.0";
32          public const string EDGE_DRIVER_PATH = ↵
              @"C:\Program Files (x86)\Microsoft Web Driver";
33          public const string OPERA_DRIVER_PATH = ↵
              @"C:\Selenium\operadriver_win64";
34
35  #elif ST_ENV
36          public const string ENVIRONMENT = "ST";
37          public const string URL = ↵
              @"http://testing.arkenstone-ltd.com/";
38          public const string connectionString = ↵
              "Server=localhost;Database=WebTesting; ↵
              Uid=sa;Pwd=sa;connect timeout=180;";
39          public static string ResultFolder = ↵
              System.Environment.CurrentDirectory.Replace( ↵
              @"bin\Release", @"Logs\") + "Results_" + ↵
              DateTime.Now.ToString("dd_MMM_yyyy ↵
              HH_mm_ss", System.Globalization.CultureInfo. ↵
              GetCultureInfo("en-GB"));
40          public static string ScreenShotFolder = ↵
              ResultFolder + @"\Screenshots\";
41          public const string CHROME_DRIVER_PATH = ↵
              @"C:\Selenium\chromedriver_win32";
42          public const string INTERNETEXPLORER_DRIVER_PATH ↵
              = @"C:\Selenium\IEDriverServer_x64_2.48.0";
43          public const string EDGE_DRIVER_PATH = ↵
              @"C:\Program Files (x86)\Microsoft Web Driver";
44          public const string OPERA_DRIVER_PATH = ↵
              @"C:\Selenium\operadriver_win64";
45
46  #elif UAT_ENV
47          public const string ENVIRONMENT = "UAT";
48          public const string URL = ↵
              @"http://testing.arkenstone-ltd.com/";
```

```csharp
        public const string connectionString =
            "Server=localhost;Database=WebTesting;
            Uid=sa;Pwd=sa;connect timeout=180;";
        public static string ResultFolder =
            System.Environment.CurrentDirectory.Replace(
            @"bin\Release", @"Logs\") + "Results_" +
            DateTime.Now.ToString("dd_MMM_yyyy
            HH_mm_ss", System.Globalization.CultureInfo.
            GetCultureInfo("en-GB"));
        public static string ScreenShotFolder =
            ResultFolder + @"\Screenshots\";
        public const string CHROME_DRIVER_PATH =
            @"C:\Selenium\chromedriver_win32";
        public const string INTERNETEXPLORER_DRIVER_PATH
            = @"C:\Selenium\IEDriverServer_x64_2.48.0";
        public const string EDGE_DRIVER_PATH =
            @"C:\Program Files (x86)\Microsoft Web Driver";
        public const string OPERA_DRIVER_PATH =
            @"C:\Selenium\operadriver_win64";

#endif

        public const string PASS = "Pass";
        public const string FAIL = "Fail";

        public static int OBJECT_TIMEOUT_SECS = 30;

        public static string CURRENT_LOGFILE = "";

        public const string USERID_MANDATORY_ERROR =
            "Error: User ID is mandatory";
        public const string PASSWORD_MANDATORY_ERROR =
            "Error: Password is mandatory";
        public const string INVALID_USERID_PASSWORD_ERROR
            = "Error: Invalid User ID or Password";

        public const string RECORD_ADDED_SUCCESSFULLY =
            "Record added successfully.";

        public const string MALE = "1";
        public const string FEMALE = "2";
        public const string UNKNOWN_CODE = "-99";

        public const string MALE_TEXT = "Male";
        public const string FEMALE_TEXT = "Female";
```

```
78          public const string UNKNOWN_TEXT = "Unknown";
79
80          public const string TRUE = "True";
81          public const string FALSE = "False";
82
83          public const string YES = "Yes";
84          public const string NO = "No";
85
86          public static string SUMMARY_FILENAME = ↵
              ↪ Config.ResultFolder + @"\Summary" + ↵
              ↪ DateTime.Now.ToString("_dd_MMM_yyyy ↵
              ↪ HH_mm_ss", System.Globalization.CultureInfo. ↵
              ↪ GetCultureInfo("en-GB")) + ".csv";
87
88          public static int STEP_PASS = 0;
89          public static int STEP_FAIL = 1;
90          public static int STEP_FAIL_THRESHOLD = 3;
91
92          public static bool LOG_ALL_COMPARE = false;
93
94          public static double DIFFERENCE_TOLERANCE = 0.0001;
95      }
96 }
```

Line 5: Defines the Functional Test Environment directive, where we want to perform the automated testing.

Line 6: Defines the System Test Environment directive, which has been commented as we are not using this environment.

Line 7: Defines the User Acceptance Test Environment directive, which has been commented as we are not using this environment.

Line 24: The #if directive will compile the code between the directives only if the specified symbol is defined. Since we have defined the FT_ENV directive, statements from Line 25 to 33 will be compiled.

Line 25: Defines the environment string "FT"

Line 35: Since ST_ENV directive is not defined (as it is commented), statements from Line 36 to 44 will not be compiled.

Line 36: Defines the environment string "ST"

Line 46: Since UAT_ENV directive is not defined (as it is commented), statements from Line 47 to 55 will not be compiled.

Line 47: Defines the environment string "UAT"

Line 57: The #endif directive specifies the end of a conditional directive, which began with the #if directive.

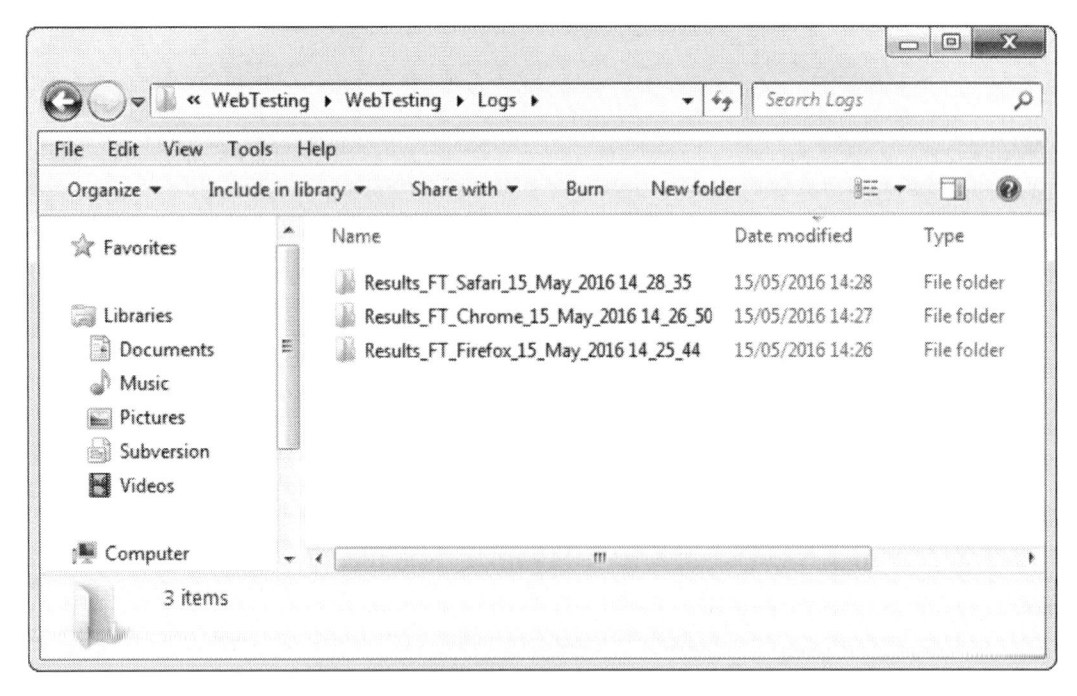

6.7.2 Logging Environment and Browser Name

As we are now using multiple environments with different browsers, it will be very useful to log the environment and browser name as part of the result folder so that we can easily identify the test results. Change the declaration of the 'ResultFolder' in 'Config.cs' file as shown in the Listing 6.25.

Listing 6.25: 'Config.cs' - Parameters for logging the environment and browser names

```
1  public static string ResultFolder = ↵
       Environment.CurrentDirectory.Replace(@"bin\Release", ↵
       @"Logs\") + "Results_" + ENVIRONMENT + "_" + BROWSER ↵
       + "_"+ DateTime.Now.ToString("dd_MMM_yyyy HH_mm_ss", ↵
       System.Globalization.CultureInfo. ↵
       GetCultureInfo("en-GB"));
```

Line 1: Adds the environment and the browser name to the result folder using the configuration parameters `ENVIRONMENT` and `BROWSER` respectively.

You will see the output folder created with the environment and browser names used during the test execution as shown in Figure 6.28.

Figure 6.28: Logging Environment And Browser Name

6.7.3 Logging System Info.

It is always helpful to log the values of useful configuration parameters so that we can have a look at them when we go through the log files at a later stage e.g. what was the value of "Difference Tolerance" when the test was executed. I usually log these values at the start of each test. Let's perform the following Test Scenario for demonstration:

- Launch the demo website.

- Login with the user 'Tester'.

- Ensure that at the beginning of each test the following information is displayed:
    - Environment used during testing.
    - Browser used during testing.
    - URL of the Application Under Test.
    - Website Version Number.
    - Result folder name.
    - Screenshot folder name.
    - Step fail threshold used.
    - Difference tolerance used.
    - Whether to log all compares or not.
    - Database connection string used.

- The result folder name should also have website version number in it to easily locate the results of a particular version.

6.7.3.1 Configuration Parameters

Let's add some configuration parameters which we will need. Double click on the 'Config.cs' file in 'Solution Explorer' and add the Listing 6.26 code to it.

Listing 6.26: 'Config.cs' - Parameters for Website Version Number

```
1  public static string VersionNo = "";
```

Line 1: Defines a static string to hold the value of website version number.

6.7.3.2 Utility Functions

Let's define three new functions in the Utility file as follows:

AddVersionToPath - Adds website version number to a path		
Input Parameters	str	Path to add the version number to
Return Value	str	Returns the updated path with version number added to it

AddVersionInfo - Adds version number info to the result and screenshot folders		
Input Parameters	driver	Object driver to control the browser
Return Value	void	Returns nothing

LogSysInfo - Logs useful system information		
Input Parameters	none	No parameters
Return Value	void	Returns nothing

Add the new functions in the 'Utility.cs' file as shown in Listing 6.27.

Listing 6.27: 'Utility.cs' - Code to log system information

```csharp
public static string AddVersionToPath(string str)
{
    if (!Config.VersionNo.Equals(""))
        if (!str.Contains(Config.VersionNo))
            return str.Replace("Results_", "Results_" + ↵
                Config.VersionNo + "_");
        else
            return str;
    else
        return str;
}

public static void AddVersionInfo(this IWebDriver driver)
{
    IWebElement element = ↵
        Utility.FindElementAndReturn(driver, ↵
        By.Id(Repository.Home.lblSysVersion_ById));
    Config.VersionNo = element.Text.Trim();

    Config.ResultFolder = ↵
        AddVersionToPath(Config.ResultFolder);
    Config.ScreenShotFolder = ↵
        AddVersionToPath(Config.ScreenShotFolder);
    Config.SUMMARY_FILENAME = ↵
        AddVersionToPath(Config.SUMMARY_FILENAME);
```

```
20  }
21
22  public static void LogSysInfo()
23  {
24      Log.Info("********** Logging Sys Info **********");
25      Log.Info("Environment: " + Config.ENVIRONMENT);
26      Log.Info("Browser: " + Config.BROWSER);
27      Log.Info("URL: " + Config.URL);
28      Log.Info("Website Version is: " + Config.VersionNo);
29      Log.Info("Result Folder: " + Config.ResultFolder);
30      Log.Info("ScreenShot Folder: " + ↵
              ↪ Config.ScreenShotFolder);
31      Log.Info("Summary File: " + Config.SUMMARY_FILENAME);
32      Log.Info("Step Fail Threshold: " + ↵
              ↪ Config.STEP_FAIL_THRESHOLD);
33      Log.Info("Difference Tolerance: " + ↵
              ↪ Config.DIFFERENCE_TOLERANCE);
34      Log.Info("Log All Compare: " + Config.LOG_ALL_COMPARE);
35      Log.Info("Database Connection: " + ↵
              ↪ Config.connectionString);
36      Log.Info("*****************************************");
37  }
```

Line 3: Ensures that version number has a value.
Line 4: Ensures that version number is not already inserted.
Line 5: Inserts version number in the path string.
Line 9: Otherwise returns the path string back as it is.
Line 14: Finds the version number element on the web page.
Line 15: Removes leading and trailing blanks.
Line 17: Adds the version number to the result folder name.
Line 18: Adds the version number to the screenshot folder name.
Line 19: Adds the version number to the summary file name.
Line 22: Logs values of the useful configuration parameters.

6.7.3.3 Updating Page Logic

Update the Visit function of 'pageHome.cs' file as shown in Listing 6.28.

Listing 6.28: 'pageHome.cs' - updated code for Visit()

```
1  public void Visit()
2  {
3      GoToSite();
4      Utility.AddVersionInfo(driver);
```

```
5        Utility.LogSysInfo();
6        Utility.SetupSummaryFile();
7        Utility.ReportExpectedVsActual(driver, "Automated Web ↵
         ↪ Testing", driver.Title);
8        Utility.SaveScreenShot(driver, ↵
         ↪ TestContext.CurrentContext.Test.Name);
9  }
```

Line 4: Adds version info to the folder names.
Line 5: Calls the Utility function `LogSysInfo` to log useful configuration parameters values.

6.7.3.4 Executing Tests

Now whenever you execute any test, useful configuration parameter values will be logged in the test result file. The output is as shown in Figure 6.29.

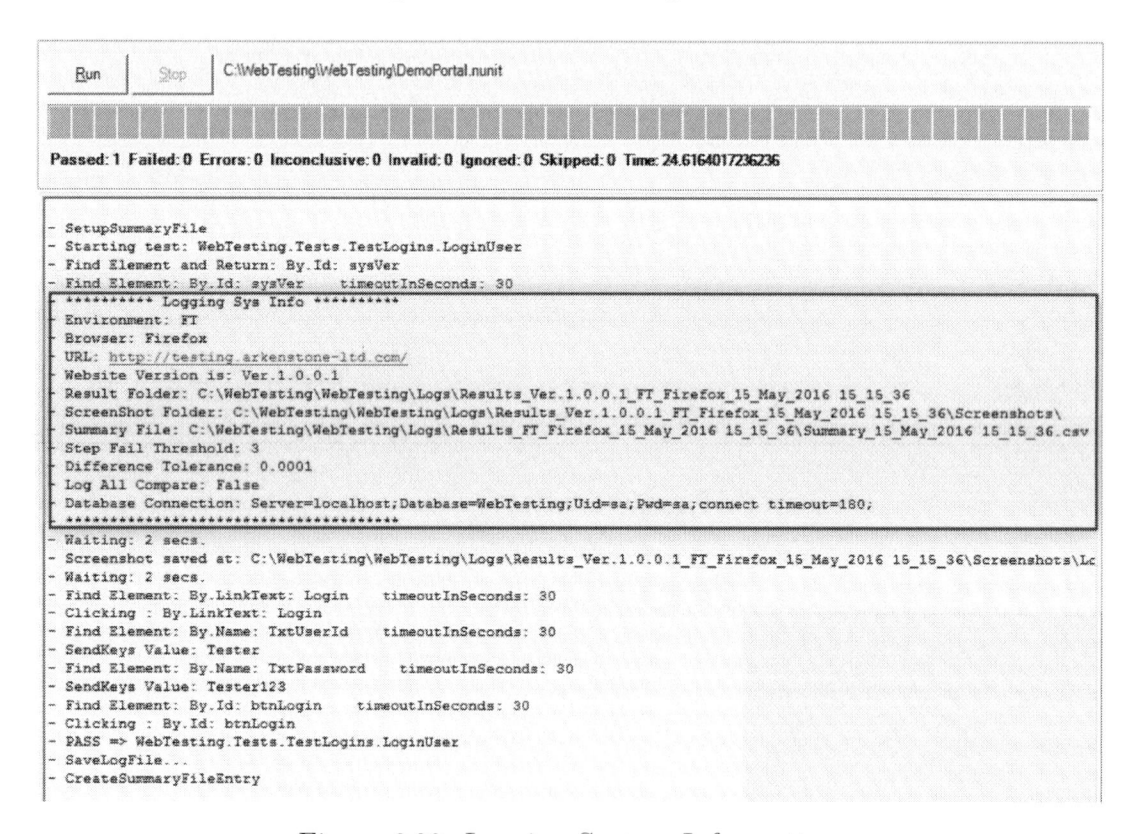

Figure 6.29: Logging System Information

You will see the output folder created with the version number of the website as shown in Figure 6.30.

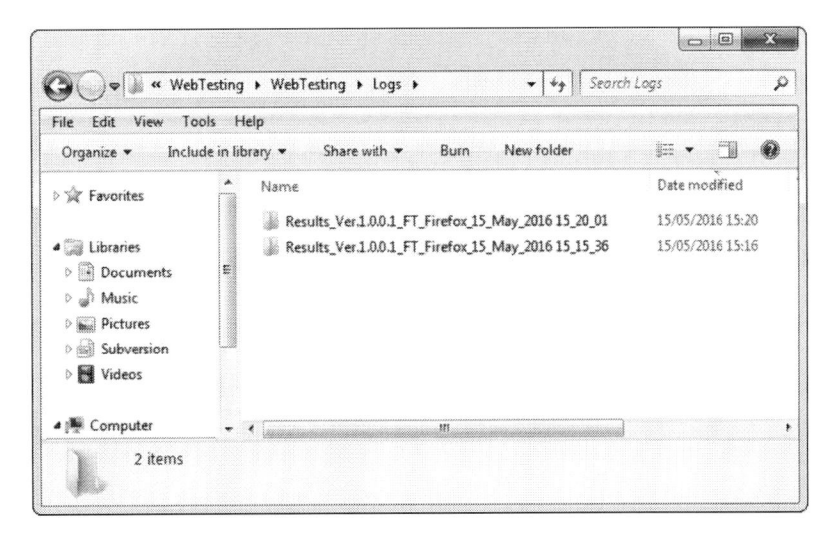

Figure 6.30: Logging Version No

Chapter 7

Web Services Testing

Web Services Testing

In this chapter, we will learn:

- *About Web Services*
- *How to write a demo web service for our automated testing perspective*
- *How to automate Web Services testing via WebRequest method*
- *How to automate Web Services testing via HttpWebRequest SOAP method*
- *How to automate Web Services testing via Service Reference method*

So let's get on with it...

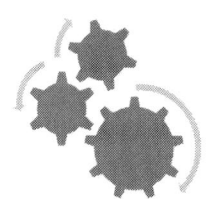

W<span></span>HAT is a Web Service? A web service is a piece of software that makes itself available over the internet and uses a standardised XML messaging system to code and decode data. By using web services, an application can publish its functions to the rest of the world. For example, we invoke a web service by sending the Employee ID in an XML Request Message and then wait for the Employee Details in an XML Response Message, as shown in Figure 7.1.

Interoperability is one of the most important features of web services. Interoperability is the ability for two different implementations of web services to communicate with one another. Interoperability is perhaps the most critical feature of web services, for without it, communication is not possible. Web services can exchange data between different applications and different platforms and hence solve the interoperability problem by giving different applications a way to link their data. We can build a web service in C# on a Windows platform that can be invoked from JavaServer pages running on a Linux platform.

A typical web service has the following features:

- Uses a standardised XML messaging system
- Is available over the internet
- Interoperable
- Platform independent
- Operating system independent
- Language independent
- Easily discoverable

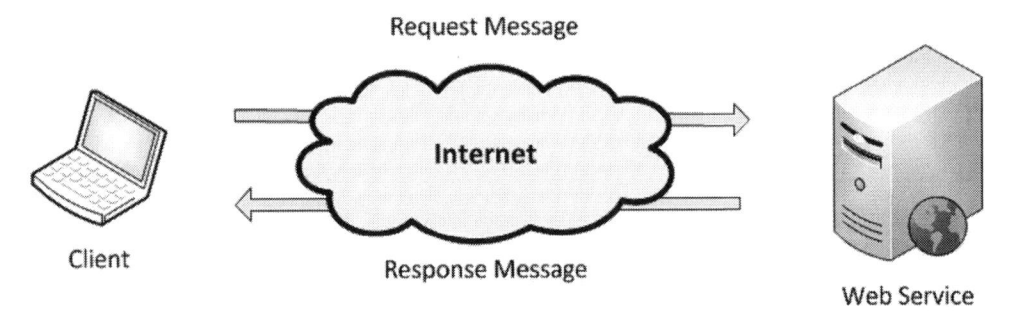

Figure 7.1: Web Services Overview

In this chapter we will learn how to perform an automated web services testing. Since we would need a web service to test against, we will write our own simple demo web service as we already have the necessary tools for it, namely Microsoft® Visual Studio Express 2015 for Web. Our demo web service will accept an Employee ID and will return the corresponding Employee Details. Don't worry if you are not familiar with web services, this chapter will provide step-by-step instructions on how to write the web service and subsequently test it using automation. So let's get on with it.

7.1 Demo Web Service

Please follow these steps to create the demo web service:

- Launch 'Visual Studio Express for Web' from its installed location or from the desktop shortcut.
- Open the WebTesting solution.
- Right click on 'Solution' in the 'Solution Explorer'.

Automated Web Testing

- Click Add ⇒ New Project... as shown in Figure7.2

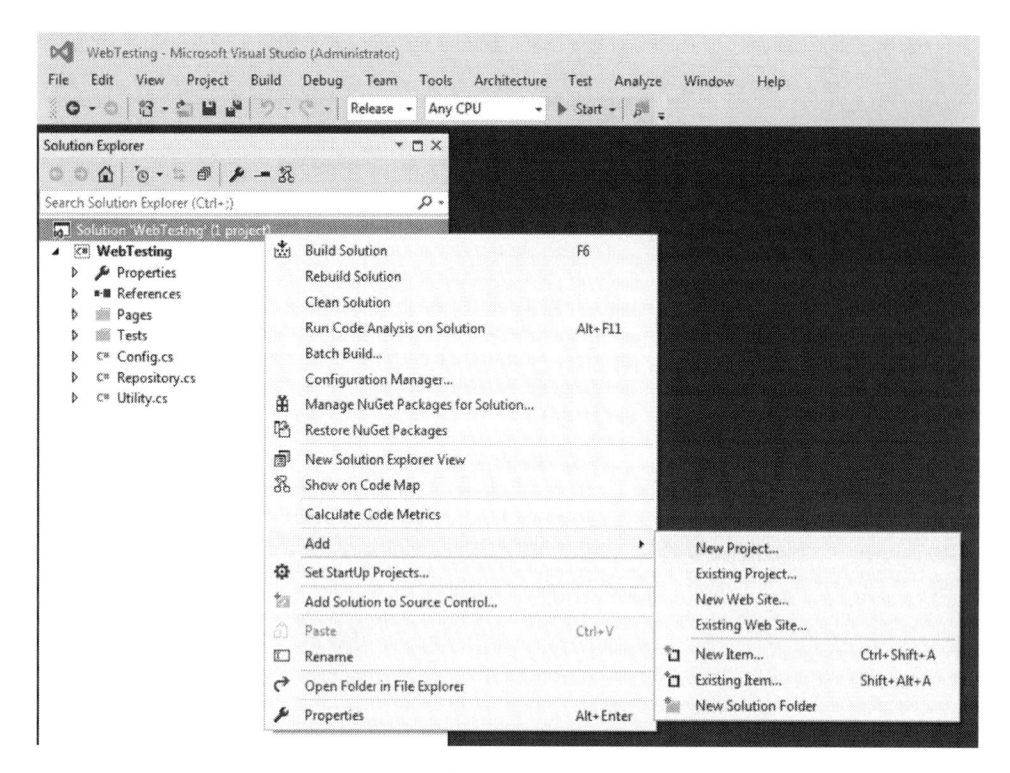

Figure 7.2: Add Web Service Project

- Select 'ASP .NET Web Application' under Web.
- Type the 'Name' as MyWebService as shown in Figure7.3 and click the OK button.

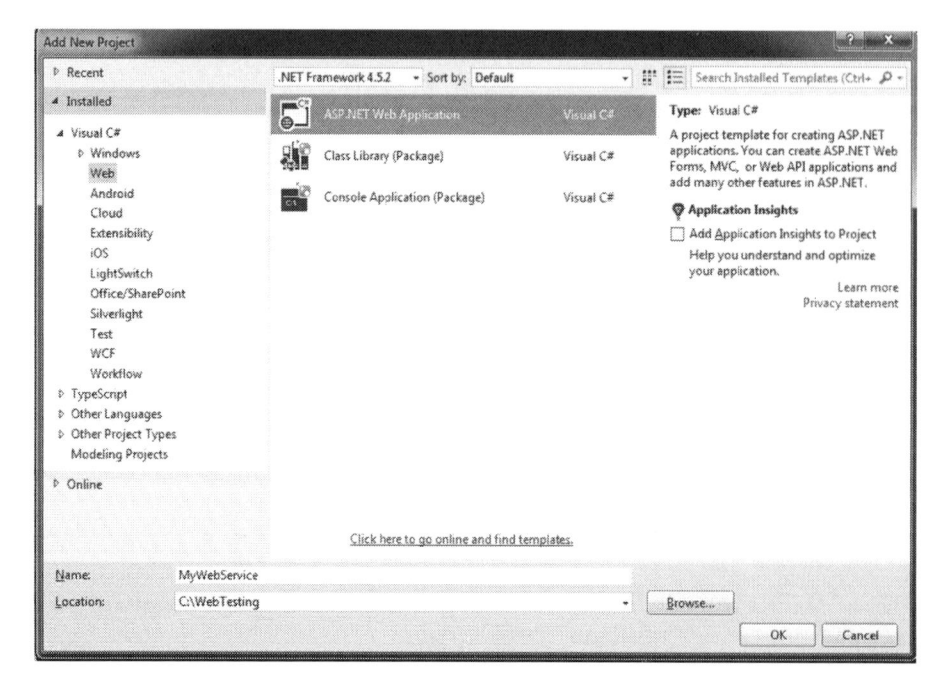

Figure 7.3: My Web Service

- Select the 'Empty' Template

- Ensure that 'Host in the cloud' is not checked and leave everything else as default as shown in Figure7.4

- Click the OK button

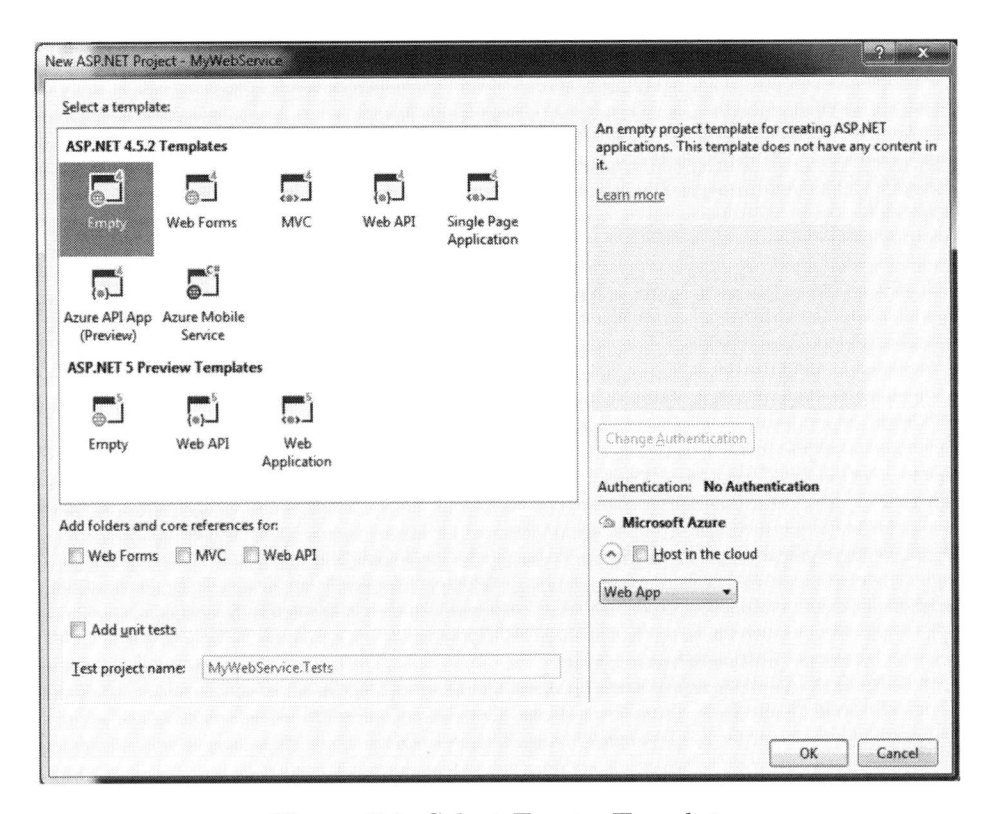

Figure 7.4: Select Empty Template

☞ If you are using any other version of Visual Studio than Express for Web and the 'ASP .NET Web Application' under Web is not listed, you might have to perform the following steps:

- Close all instances of Visual Studio.

- Go to the Control Panel on your workstation and select 'Programs and Features'.

- Find Microsoft Visual Studio 2015, right click on it and select Change.

- Follow the on-screen instructions and then select Modify.

- Ensure that 'Microsoft Web Developer Tools' is selected as shown in Figure 7.5 and follow the on-screen instructions to update Visual Studio.

Figure 7.5: Web Tools

7.1.1 Creating The Web Service

Let's now write the necessary code to create our demo web service.

- In the 'Solution Explorer', right click on MyWebService and select Add → New Item...

- Select 'Web Service (ASMX)'.

- Type the 'Name' as EmployeeWebService.asmx as shown in Figure 7.6.

- Click the Add button.

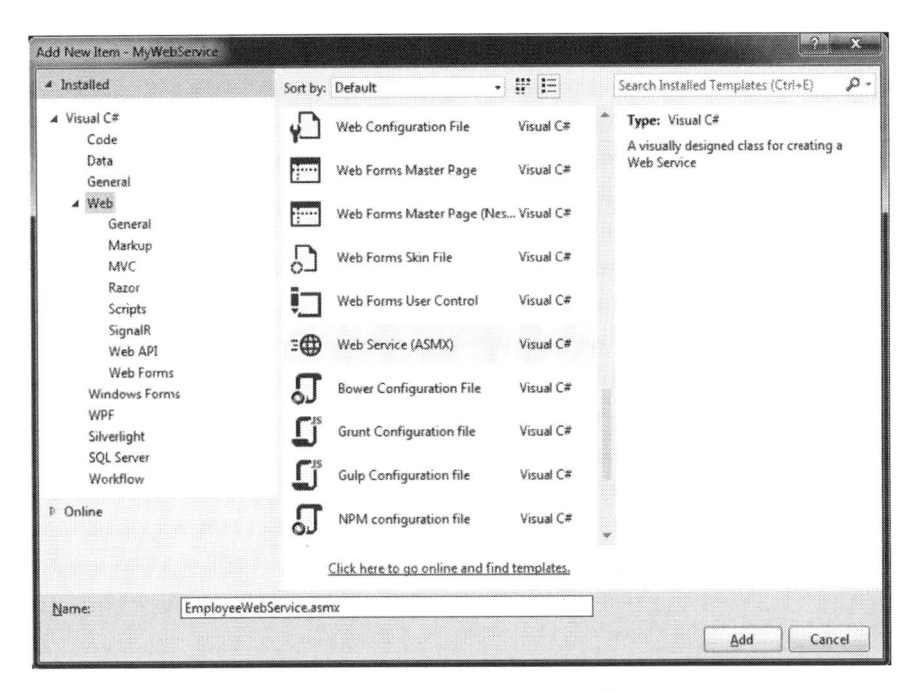

Figure 7.6: Employee Web Service

Add Listing 7.1 code to the 'EmployeeWebService.asmx' file.

☞ This is probably not the best way a developer would code a web service but will give us something to test against!

Listing 7.1: 'EmployeeWebService.asmx' - Code for Employee Web Service

```
1  using System;
2  using System.Web.Services;
3
4  namespace MyWebService
5  {
6      [WebService(Namespace = "http://tempuri.org/")]
7      [WebServiceBinding(ConformsTo = ↵
           WsiProfiles.BasicProfile1_1)]
8      [System.ComponentModel.ToolboxItem(false)]
9
10     public class EmployeeWebService : ↵
           System.Web.Services.WebService
11     {
12
13         public class Employee
14         {
15             public string EmpID { get; set; }
16             public string Title { get; set; }
```

```csharp
17              public string Name { get; set; }
18              public string Gender { get; set; }
19              public string BirthDate { get; set; }
20              public string Contract { get; set; }
21          }
22
23          [WebMethod]
24          public Employee GetEmployee(String employeeID)
25          {
26              Employee emp = new Employee();
27
28              switch (employeeID)
29              {
30                  case "10001":
31                      emp.EmpID = "10001";
32                      emp.Title = "Mrs";
33                      emp.Name = "Carla Brown";
34                      emp.Gender = "Female";
35                      emp.BirthDate = "02/05/1965";
36                      emp.Contract = "Yes";
37                      break;
38
39                  case "10002":
40                      emp.EmpID = "10002";
41                      emp.Title = "Mr";
42                      emp.Name = "James Jones";
43                      emp.Gender = "Male";
44                      emp.BirthDate = "03/12/1978";
45                      emp.Contract = "Yes";
46                      break;
47
48                  case "10003":
49                      emp.EmpID = "10003";
50                      emp.Title = "Miss";
51                      emp.Name = "D Mellons";
52                      emp.Gender = "Female";
53                      emp.BirthDate = "10/10/1970";
54                      emp.Contract = "No";
55                      break;
56
57                  case "10004":
58                      emp.EmpID = "10004";
59                      emp.Title = "Miss";
60                      emp.Name = "Sarah Smith";
61                      emp.Gender = "Female";
```

```
62                emp.BirthDate = "25/12/1982";
63                emp.Contract = "No";
64                break;
65
66            case "10005":
67                emp.EmpID = "10005";
68                emp.Title = "Mrs";
69                emp.Name = "Nicola";
70                emp.Gender = "Female";
71                emp.BirthDate = "31/12/1978";
72                emp.Contract = "Yes";
73                break;
74
75            default:
76                emp.EmpID = "Invalid EmployeeID";
77                emp.Title = "Invalid EmployeeID";
78                emp.Name = "Invalid EmployeeID";
79                emp.Gender = "Invalid EmployeeID";
80                emp.BirthDate = "Invalid EmployeeID";
81                emp.Contract = "Invalid EmployeeID";
82                break;
83         }
84
85         return emp;
86      }
87   }
88 }
```

Line 13: Defines the `Employee` record.

Line 23: Attaching the `WebMethod` attribute to a public method exposes the method as part of the XML web service and hence callable from the remote web clients.

Line 28: Assigns values to the employee record based on the value of 'employeeID'.

Line 75: For any other value of the 'employeeID', just returns the value "Invalid EmployeeID".

Line 85: Returns the employee record.

7.1.2 Running The Web Service

Let's now run our demo web service so that it is ready to take any requests.

- In the 'Solution Explorer', right click on MyWebService and select 'Set as StartUp Project' as shown in Figure 7.7

Automated Web Testing

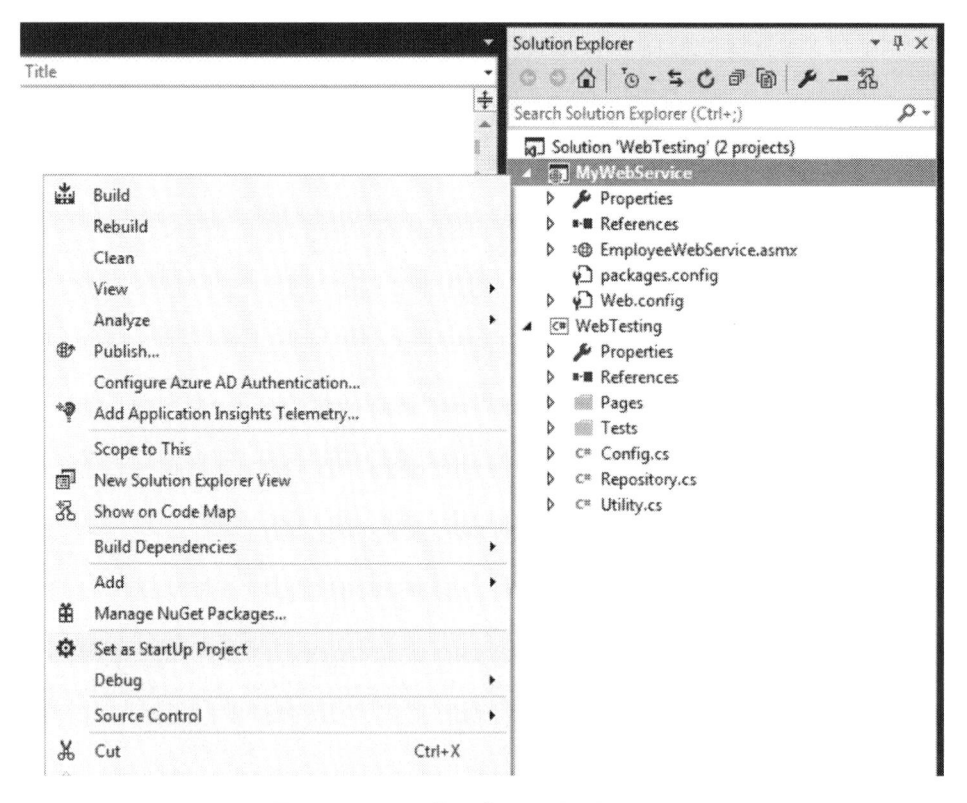

Figure 7.7: Set StartUp Project

Select 'EmployeeWebService.asmx' in the 'Solution Explorer' and press `Ctrl` + `F5` and you should see a browser window launching as shown in Figure 7.8.

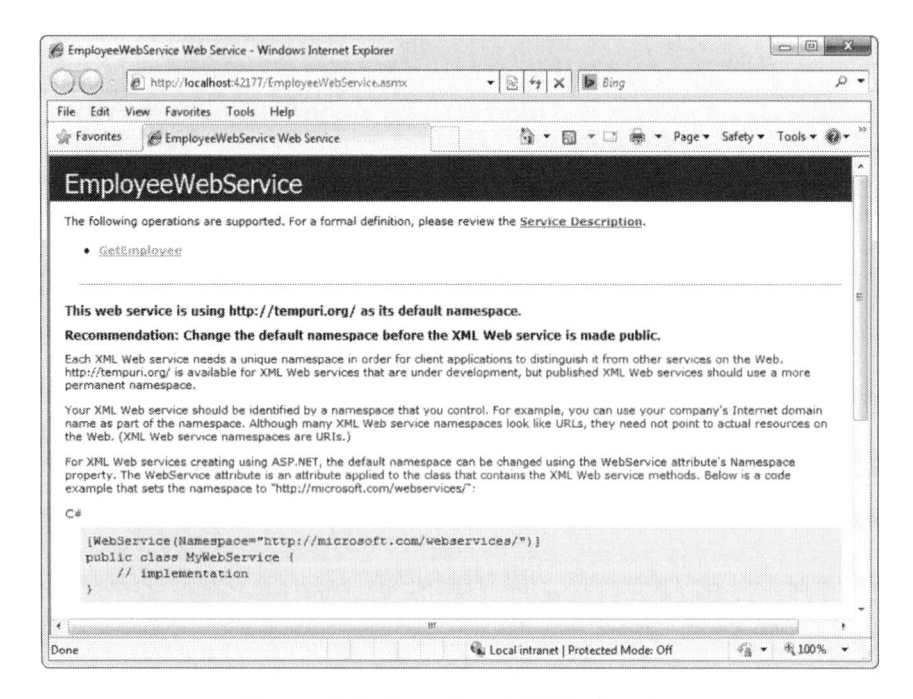

Figure 7.8: Localhost Web Service

☞ If 'Internet Information Services' (IIS) is turned off on your workstation, you may see a window as shown in Figure 7.9.

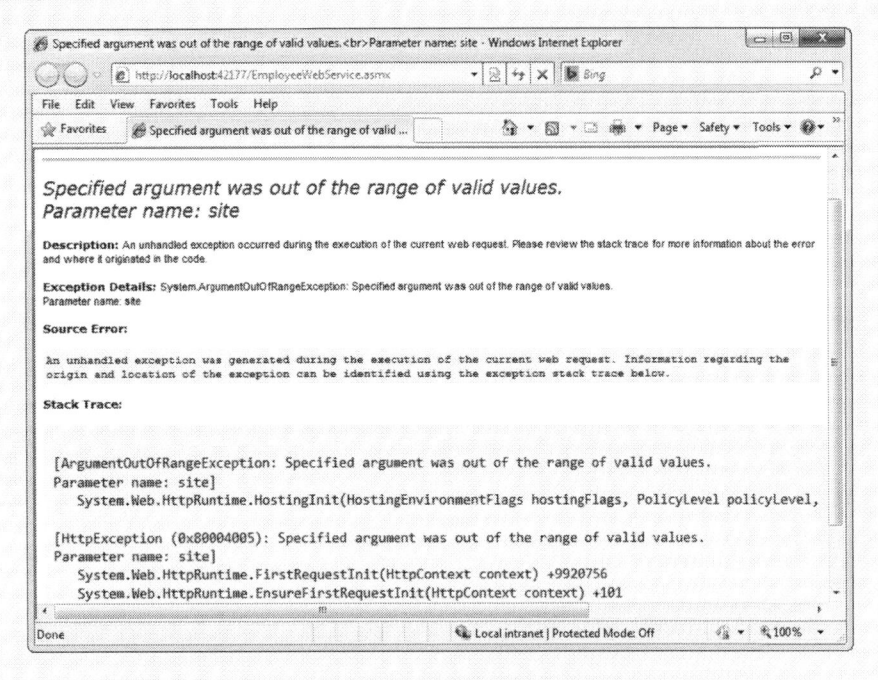

Figure 7.9: Internet Information Services Error

In order to resolve this issue, follow these steps:

- Go to the Control Panel

- Select 'Turn Windows features on or off'

- Select 'Internet Information Services' as shown in Figure 7.10 and click the OK button.

Figure 7.10: Internet Information Service Turned On

Now when you select 'EmployeeWebService.asmx' in the 'Solution Explorer' and press ⌈Ctrl⌉+⌈F5⌉, you should see a browser window launching as shown in Figure 7.8. You can ensure that IIS Express is running from the Windows System Tray as shown in Figure 7.11.

☞ The Windows System Tray is located in the Windows Taskbar (usually at the bottom right corner next to the clock). You may have to click the arrow (facing upward) to see all the icons.

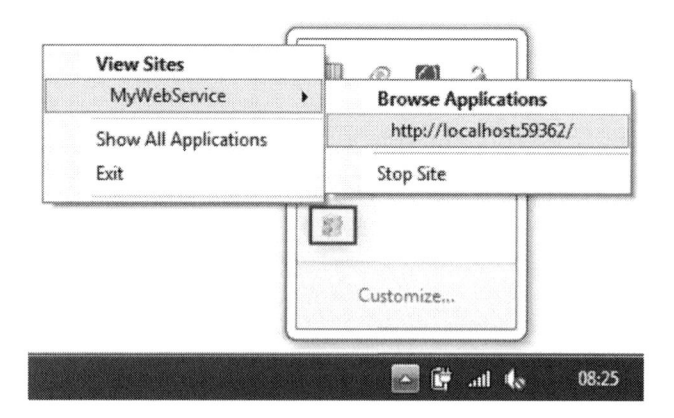

Figure 7.11: IIS Express Running

7.1.3 Invoking The Web Service

Let's now invoke our web service. Click on the GetEmployee link (see Figure 7.8), and you will see a window as shown in Figure 7.12.

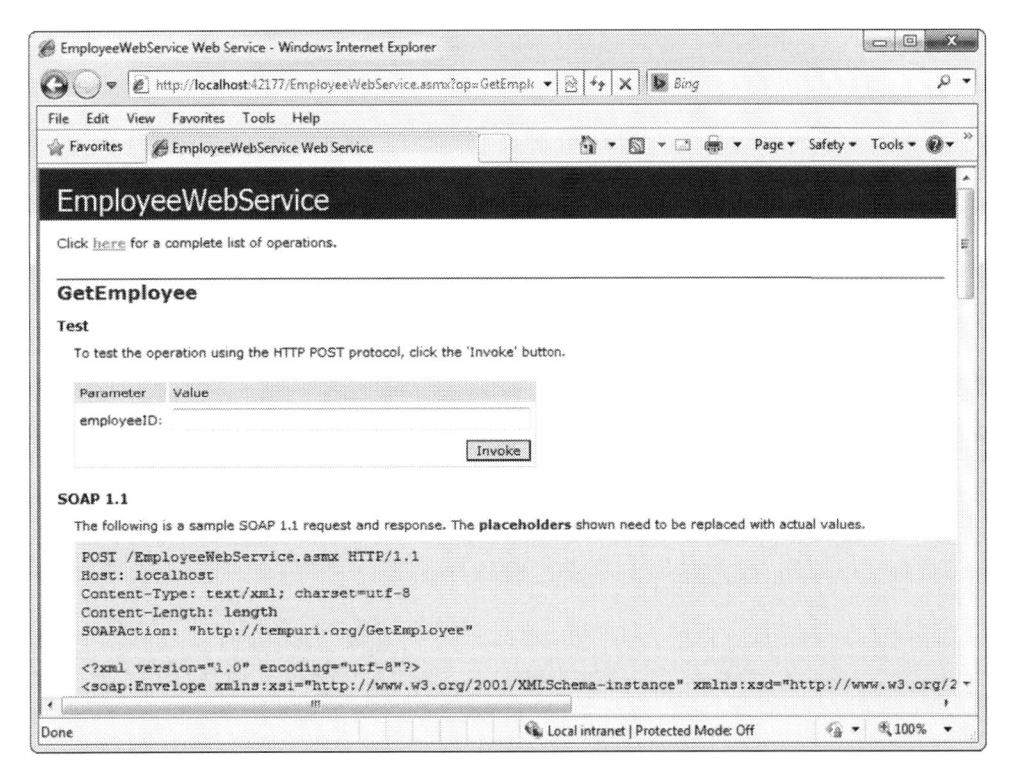

Figure 7.12: Get Employee Web Service

Enter '10004' in the employeeID field and press the Invoke button. You will see a window as shown in Figure 7.13.

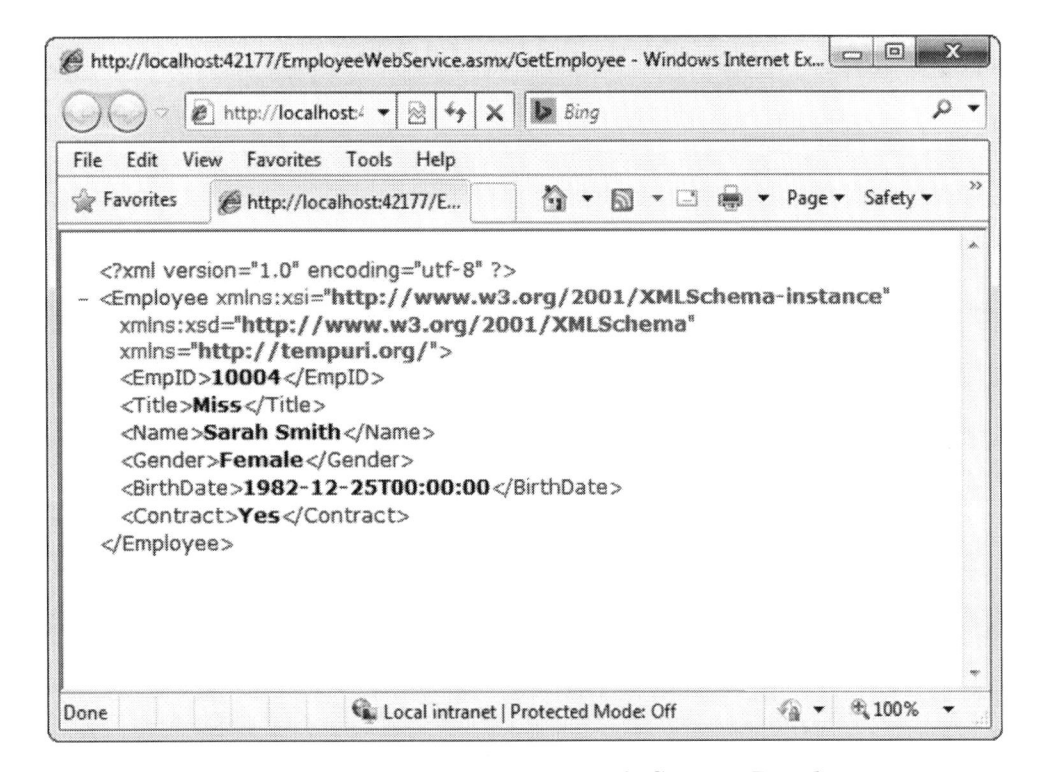

Figure 7.13: Get Employee Web Service Result

We have now successfully invoked the web service by calling it with an Employee ID "10004" and the result is displayed in the web browser. Try different values of an Employee Id and see if you get the right results. Let's now learn how to automate the testing of this web service.

7.2 Testing The Web Service via WebRequest

Let's perform the following Test Scenario to demonstrate accessing our web service via the WebRequest method:

- Setup an Employee record with the *expected result* values for the Employee ID = 10004.

- Call the demo web service via the WebRequest method with the Employee ID = 10004 to get the *actual result* values.

- Compare both the *expected and actual result* values and report the outcome.

7.2.1 Utility Functions

First of all, let's define three new utility functions as follows:

ReportExpectedVsActualEx - Reports the outcome of expected verses actual result comparison without the browser driver		
Input Parameters	*expResult*	Expected result
	actResult	Actual result
Return Value	*int*	Returns the integer value of Pass or Fail configured parameters

GetEmployeeByWebRequest - Gets an employee's details by the WebRequest method		
Input Parameters	*empId*	Employee Id
Return Value	*XmlDocument*	Returns the XmlDocument containing the employee record

VerifyEmployee - Compares an employee's record with the XML message and reports the outcome		
Input Parameters	*employeeRecord*	Expected values in the EmployeeRecord format
	xmlDocument	Actual values in the XML format
Return Value	*void*	Returns nothing

Add Listing 7.2 code to the 'Utilty.cs' file.

Listing 7.2: 'Utilty.cs' - Code for ReportExpectedVsActualEx , VerifyEmployee and GetEmployeeByWebRequest

```
using System.Net;
using System.Xml;

public static int ReportExpectedVsActualEx(string ↵
    expected, string actual)
{
    if (expected.Trim() == actual.Trim())
    {
        if (Config.LOG_ALL_COMPARE)
        {
            Log.Info("Expected: " + expected + "     ↵
                Actual: " + actual + "      Step Passed:");
        }
        return Config.STEP_PASS;
    }
    else
    {
        Log.Error("[Expected: ]" + expected + "      ↵
            [Actual: ]" + actual + "      [Step Failed]");
        TestResult = Config.FAIL;
        return Config.STEP_FAIL;
    }
}

public struct EmployeeRecord
{
    public string EmpID;
    public string Title;
    public string Name;
    public string Gender;
    public string BirthDate;
    public string Contract;
}

public static XmlDocument GetEmployeeByWebRequest(String ↵
    empId)
{
    try
    {
        WebRequest request = WebRequest.Create( ↵
            "http://localhost:59362/EmployeeWebService.asmx ↵
```

```csharp
                    /GetEmployee");

        request.Method = "POST";

        string postData = "employeeID=" + empId;
        byte[] byteArray =
            Encoding.UTF8.GetBytes(postData);

        request.ContentType =
            "application/x-www-form-urlencoded";

        request.ContentLength = byteArray.Length;

        Stream dataStream = request.GetRequestStream();

        dataStream.Write(byteArray, 0, byteArray.Length);

        dataStream.Close();

        WebResponse response = request.GetResponse();

        Log.Info(((HttpWebResponse)response).StatusDescription);

        dataStream = response.GetResponseStream();

        StreamReader reader = new StreamReader(dataStream);

        string responseFromServer = reader.ReadToEnd();

        Log.Info(responseFromServer);

        reader.Close();
        dataStream.Close();
        response.Close();

        XmlDocument xml = new XmlDocument();
        xml.LoadXml(responseFromServer);

        return xml;
    }
    catch (Exception exception)
    {
        Utility.Log.Error("exception" + exception.ToString());
        throw exception;
    }
```

```
79  }
80
81  public static void VerifyEmployee(EmployeeRecord emp, ↵
        ↪ XmlDocument xml)
82  {
83      ReportExpectedVsActualEx(emp.EmpID, ↵
            ↪ (xml.GetElementsByTagName("EmpID"))[0].InnerXml);
84      ReportExpectedVsActualEx(emp.Title, ↵
            ↪ xml.GetElementsByTagName("Title").Item(0).InnerXml);
85      ReportExpectedVsActualEx(emp.Name, ↵
            ↪ xml.GetElementsByTagName("Name").Item(0).InnerXml);
86      ReportExpectedVsActualEx(emp.Gender, ↵
            ↪ xml.GetElementsByTagName("Gender").Item(0).InnerXml);
87      ReportExpectedVsActualEx(emp.BirthDate, ↵
            ↪ (xml.GetElementsByTagName("BirthDate").Item(0). ↵
            ↪ InnerXml).Substring(0, 10));
88      ReportExpectedVsActualEx(emp.Contract, ↵
            ↪ xml.GetElementsByTagName("Contract").Item(0). ↵
            ↪ InnerXml);
89  }
```

Line 1 and 2: Additional imports required to support the new functionality.

Line 22: Creates a structure for the employee record.

Line 36: Creates the `WebRequest`. Please change the port number (59362) to the value you see in your workstation's browser window

Line 38: Sets the 'Method' property of the request to "POST".

Line 40: Creates the `POST` data.

Line 41: Converts it to a byte array.

Line 43: Sets the 'ContentType' property of the `WebRequest`.

Line 45: Sets the 'ContentLength' property of the `WebRequest`.

Line 47: Gets the request stream.

Line 49: Writes the data to the request stream.

Line 51: Closes the Stream object.

Line 53: Gets the response.

Line 55: Logs the status.

Line 57: Gets the stream containing content returned by the server.

Line 59: Opens the stream using a `StreamReader` for easy access.

Line 61: Reads the content.

Line 63: Logs the content.

Line 65 - 67: Clean up the streams.

Line 69: Initialises a new instance of the `XmlDocument` class.

Line 70: Loads the XML document with response from the server.

Line 72: Returns the XML document.

Line 81: A new function that compares employee record with the XML message and reports the outcome.

Line 83: Uses notation ("EmpID"))[0].InnerXml to read a tag value.
Line 84: Uses notation ("Title").Item(0).InnerXml to read a tag value.
Line 87: Uses the Substring function to compare first 10 characters.

7.2.2 Creating Test

In the 'Solution Explorer', right click on the 'Tests' folder and click Add ⇒ Class. Type the name as 'TestWebServices.cs' and click Add. Add the Listing 7.3 code to it.

Listing 7.3: 'TestWebServices.cs' - Code for WebServicesWebRequest

```
/***************************************************************
 * All rights reserved. Copyright 2016 Arkenstone-ltd.com       *
 ***************************************************************/
using System;
using NUnit.Framework;
using System.Xml;

namespace WebTesting.Tests
{
    public class TestWebServices
    {
        [SetUp]
        public void Setup()
        {
            Utility.TestResult = Config.PASS;
            Utility.SetupSummaryFile();
        }

        [TearDown]
        public void Teardown()
        {
            if (TestContext.CurrentContext.Result.Status ↵
                ↪ == TestStatus.Failed)
            {
                Utility.Log.Error("***** Teardown ==> ↵
                    ↪ Test FAILED ***** =>" + ↵
                    ↪ TestContext.CurrentContext.Test. ↵
                    ↪ FullName);
            }
            else if ↵
                ↪ (TestContext.CurrentContext.Result.Status ↵
                ↪ == TestStatus.Passed)
            {
```

```csharp
28                    Utility.Log.Info("PASS => " +
                          TestContext.CurrentContext.Test.
                          FullName);
29                }
30
31            Utility.SaveLogFile(TestContext.CurrentContext.
                  Test.FullName.Substring(17) + " (" +
                  TestContext.CurrentContext.Result.Status
                  + ") ");
32
33            if (Utility.TestResult == Config.FAIL)
34            {
35                Utility.CreateSummaryFileEntry(DateTime.
                      Now.ToString() + "," +
                      TestContext.CurrentContext.Test.
                      FullName.Substring(17) + ",FAIL" +
                      "," + Config.CURRENT_LOGFILE);
36            }
37            else
38                Utility.CreateSummaryFileEntry(DateTime.
                      Now.ToString() + "," +
                      TestContext.CurrentContext.Test.
                      FullName.Substring(17) + ",PASS" +
                      "," + Config.CURRENT_LOGFILE);
39        }
40
41        [Test]
42        public void WebServicesWebRequest()
43        {
44            try
45            {
46                Utility.Log.Info("Starting test: " +
                      TestContext.CurrentContext.Test.
                      FullName);
47
48                Utility.EmployeeRecord empRec;
49
50                empRec.EmpID = "10004";
51                empRec.Title = "Miss";
52                empRec.Name = "Sarah Smith";
53                empRec.Gender = "Female";
54                empRec.BirthDate = "25/12/1982";
55                empRec.Contract = "No";
56
57                XmlDocument xmlRec =
```

Automated Web Testing

```
58                        ↪ Utility.GetEmployeeByWebRequest ↩
                          ↪ ("10004");
59
60                        Utility.VerifyEmployee(empRec, xmlRec);
61
62                        Utility.ReportResult();
63                  }
                    catch (Exception exception)
64                  {
65                        Utility.Log.Error("exception" + ↩
                          ↪ exception.ToString());
66                        throw exception;
67                  }
68              }
69          }
70  }
```

Line 12: No need to setup the browser driver as we don't need it for the web services testing.
Line 16: Setup the test summary file.
Line 48: Declares a record of type `EmployeeRecord`.
Line 50 - 55: Assign expected result values.
Line 57: Gets the actual result values of employee data from the web service.
Line 59: Verifies both records by calling the Utility function '`VerifyEmployee`' we created earlier.

7.2.3 Executing Tests

Ensure that 'IIS Express' is running as shown in Figure 7.11. The output is shown in Figure 7.14 for a successful execution.

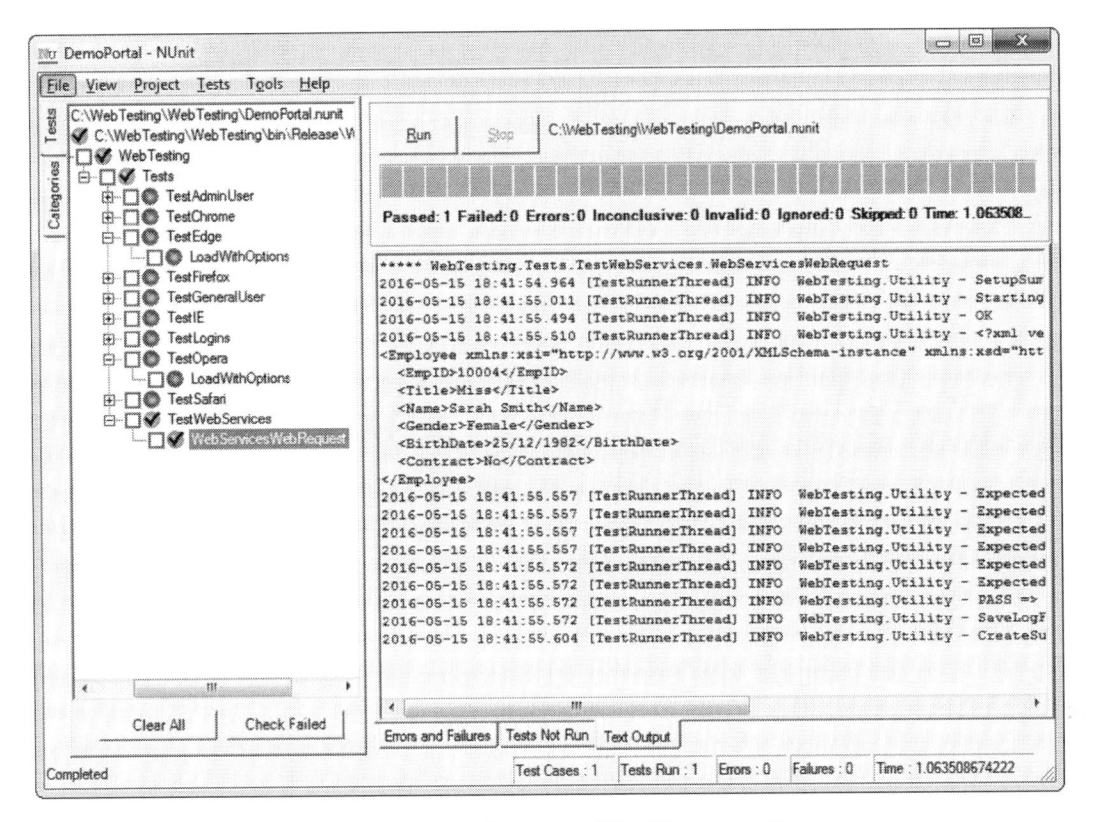

Figure 7.14: Web Services WebRequest Output

7.3 Testing The Web Service via HttpWebRequest SOAP

Let's perform the following Test Scenario to demonstrate accessing our web service via the HttpWebRequest SOAP method:

- Call the demo web service via HttpWebRequest SOAP method with the Employee ID = 10004 to get the *actual result* values.

- Read the *expected result* values from the database for Employee ID = 10004.

- Compare both the *expected and actual result* values and report the outcome.

7.3.1 Utility Functions

First of all, let's define two new utility functions as follows:

GetEmployeeByHttpWebRequest - Gets an employee's details by the HttpWebRequest method		
Input Parameters	*empId*	Employee Id
Return Value	*XmlDocument*	Returns the XmlDocument containing the employee record

Chapter 7   285

VerifyEmployeeWithDB - Compares the XML message with the database values and reports the outcome		
Input Parameters	*empId*	Expected result Employee Id (for data retrieval from the database)
	xmlDocument	Actual values in the XML format
Return Value	*void*	Returns nothing

Add the Listing 7.4 code to the 'Utilty.cs' file

Listing 7.4: 'Utilty.cs' - Additional code

```
1  public static XmlDocument
       GetEmployeeByHttpWebRequest(String empId)
2  {
3      try
4      {
5          HttpWebRequest webRequest =
               (HttpWebRequest)WebRequest.Create(
               @"http://localhost:59362/
               EmployeeWebService.asmx?op=GetEmployee");
6          webRequest.Headers.Add(@"SOAP:Action");
7          webRequest.ContentType =
               "text/xml;charset=\"utf-8\"";
8          webRequest.Accept = "text/xml";
9          webRequest.Method = "POST";
10
11         XmlDocument soapEnvelopeXml = new XmlDocument();
12         String stg = "<?xml version=\"1.0\"
               encoding=\"utf-8\"?>" + Environment.NewLine
               +
13             "<soap:Envelope
                   xmlns:soap=\"http://schemas.xmlsoap.org/
                   soap/envelope/\"
                   xmlns:xsi=\"http://www.w3.org/
                   2001/XMLSchema-instance\"
                   xmlns:xsd=\"http://www.w3.org/
                   2001/XMLSchema\">" + Environment.NewLine +
14             "<soap:Body>" + Environment.NewLine +
15             "   <GetEmployee
                   xmlns=\"http://tempuri.org/\">" +
                   Environment.NewLine +
16             "      <employeeID>" + empId +
                   "</employeeID>" + Environment.NewLine +
```

```csharp
17                "    </GetEmployee>" + Environment.NewLine +
18                "</soap:Body>" + Environment.NewLine +
19                "</soap:Envelope>";
20
21            Log.Info("stg: " + stg);
22
23            soapEnvelopeXml.LoadXml(stg);
24
25            using (Stream stream = ↵
                    webRequest.GetRequestStream())
26            {
27                soapEnvelopeXml.Save(stream);
28            }
29
30            string soapResult;
31
32            using (WebResponse response = ↵
                    webRequest.GetResponse())
33            {
34                using (StreamReader rd = new ↵
                        StreamReader(response.GetResponseStream()))
35                {
36                    soapResult = rd.ReadToEnd();
37                    Log.Info(soapResult);
38                }
39            }
40
41            XmlDocument xml = new XmlDocument();
42            xml.LoadXml(soapResult);
43
44            return xml;
45        }
46        catch (Exception exception)
47        {
48            Utility.Log.Error("exception" + ↵
                    exception.ToString());
49            throw exception;
50        }
51    }
52
53    public static void VerifyEmployeeWithDB(String empId, ↵
            XmlDocument xml)
54    {
55        string stringSQL = "SELECT [EmployeeID], [Title], ↵
                [Name], [Gender], [DateOfBirth], [ContractJob]" ↵
```

```
56          stringSQL = stringSQL + "FROM [dbo].[Employees] where
               EmployeeID = '" + empId + "'";
57
58          Utility.Log.Info("SQL is: " + stringSQL);
59
60          String actEmpId = "", actTitle = "", actName = "",
               actGender = "", actDob = "", actContract = "";
61
62          using (SqlConnection con = new
               SqlConnection(Config.connectionString))
63          {
64              con.Open();
65
66              using (SqlCommand command = new
                   SqlCommand(stringSQL, con))
67              using (SqlDataReader reader =
                   command.ExecuteReader())
68              {
69                  while (reader.Read())
70                  {
71                      actEmpId = reader.GetString(0);
72                      actTitle = reader.GetString(1);
73                      actName = reader.GetString(2);
74                      actGender = reader.GetString(3);
75                      actDob = reader.GetDateTime(4).ToString();
76                      actContract = reader.GetString(5);
77                  }
78              }
79          }
80
81          ReportExpectedVsActualEx(actEmpId,
               (xml.GetElementsByTagName("EmpID"))[0].InnerXml);

82          ReportExpectedVsActualEx(actTitle,
               xml.GetElementsByTagName("Title").Item(0).InnerXml);
83          ReportExpectedVsActualEx(actName,
               xml.GetElementsByTagName("Name").Item(0).InnerXml);
84          ReportExpectedVsActualEx(DecodeGender(actGender),
               xml.GetElementsByTagName("Gender").Item(0).InnerXml);
85          ReportExpectedVsActualEx(actDob.Substring(0, 10),
               (xml.GetElementsByTagName("BirthDate").Item(0).
               InnerXml).Substring(0, 10));
86          ReportExpectedVsActualEx(actContract,
               xml.GetElementsByTagName("Contract").Item(0).
```

```
             ↪ InnerXml);
87 }
```

Line 5: Initialises a new `WebRequest` instance for the specified URI. Please change the port number (59362) to the value you see in your workstation's browser window.
Line 6: Adds a header - with the name and value separated by a colon i.e. "SOAP:Action".
Line 7: Sets the 'ContentType' property of the `WebRequest`.
Line 8: Sets the 'Accept' property to accept "text/xml".
Line 9: Sets the 'Method' property to "POST" to post data to the URI.
Line 11: Initialises a new instance of the `XmlDocument`.
Line 12: Constructs the SOAP Envelop.
Line 16: Inserts the Employee ID in the SOAP Envelop.
Line 23: Loads the XML document from the specified string.
Line 25: Gets the stream to use to write request data.
Line 27: Saves the XML document to the specified stream.
Line 32: Gets the response from the web service.
Line 34: Initialises a new instance of the `StreamReader` class for the specified stream.
Line 36: Reads all characters from the current position to the end of the stream.
Line 42: Loads the SOAP result into XML document.
Line 44: Returns the XML document.
Line 55 - 56: Construct the SQL Query to fetch data.
Line 71 - 76: Store data from the database into temporary variables.
Line 81 - 86: Compare data fetched from the database with values from the web service and report the outcome.

7.3.2 Creating Test

Add the Listing 7.5 code to the 'TestWebServices.cs' file.

Listing 7.5: 'TestWebServices.cs' - Code for WebServicesHttpWebRequest

```
1  [Test]
2  public void WebServicesHttpWebRequest()
3  {
4      try
5      {
6          Utility.Log.Info("Starting test: " +
               ↪ TestContext.CurrentContext.Test.FullName);
7
8          XmlDocument xmlRec =
               ↪ Utility.GetEmployeeByHttpWebRequest
               ↪ ("10004");
9
10         Utility.VerifyEmployeeWithDB("10004", xmlRec);
```

```
11
12              Utility.ReportResult();
13      }
14      catch (Exception exception)
15      {
16              Utility.Log.Error("exception" +
                   ↪ exception.ToString());
17              throw exception;
18      }
19 }
```

Line 8: Gets the employee details by the `HttpWebRequest` method for employee id "10004".

Line 10: Verifies the employee details with database values for employee id "10004".

7.3.3 Executing Tests

Ensure that 'IIS Express' is running as shown in Figure 7.11. The output is shown in Figure 7.15 for a successful execution.

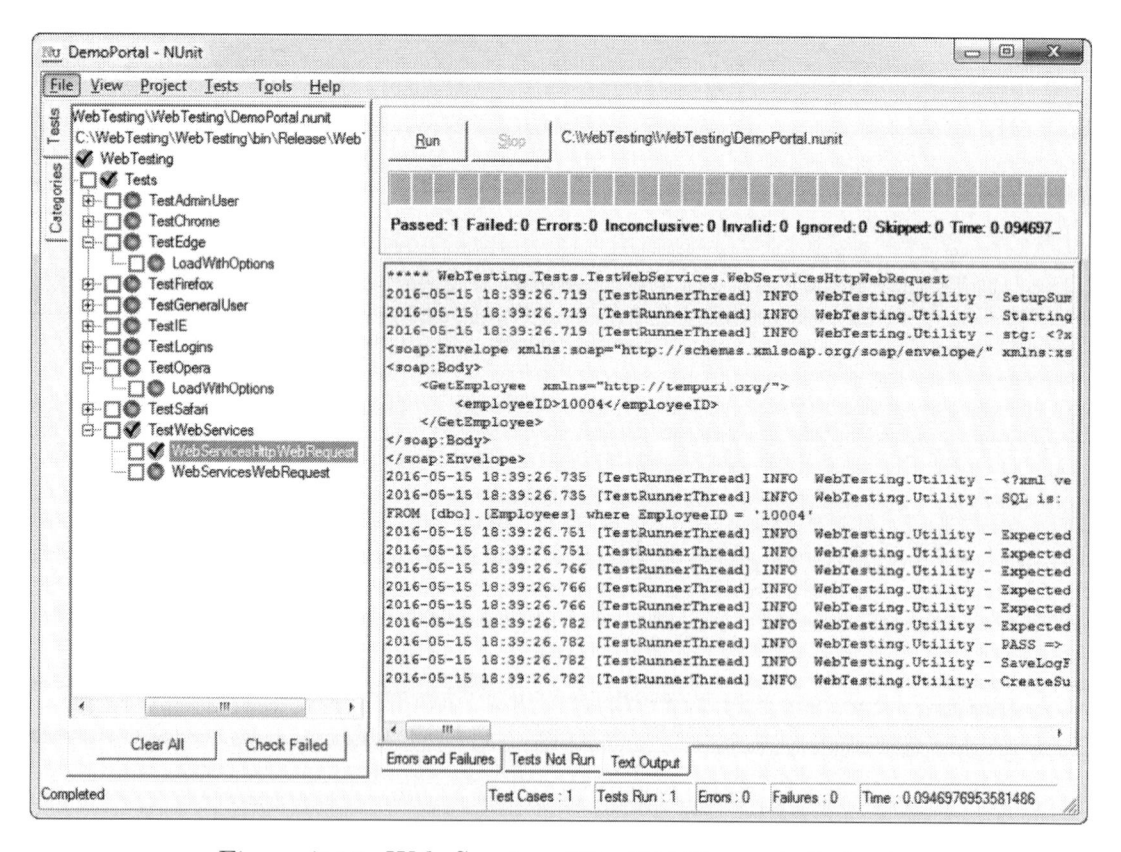

Figure 7.15: Web Services HttpWebRequest Output

7.4 Testing The Web Service via Service Reference

Let's perform the following Test Scenario to demonstrate the process of accessing our web service via the Service Reference method:

- Call the demo web service via the Service Reference method with the Employee ID = 10004 to get the *actual result* values.

- Read the *expected result* values from the Excel Worksheet.

- Compare both the *expected and actual result* values and report the outcome.

7.4.1 Adding Service Reference

Add the web service reference as follows:

- In the 'Solution Explorer', right click on the 'Services' in WebTesting project and select 'Add Service Reference...' as shown in Figure 7.16. Please change the port number (59362) to the value you see in your workstation's browser window.

- Click on the Go button. After a successful connection, you should be able to see EmployeeWebService in the Services box.

- Type the 'Namespace' as EmployeeWebService.

- Press the OK button.

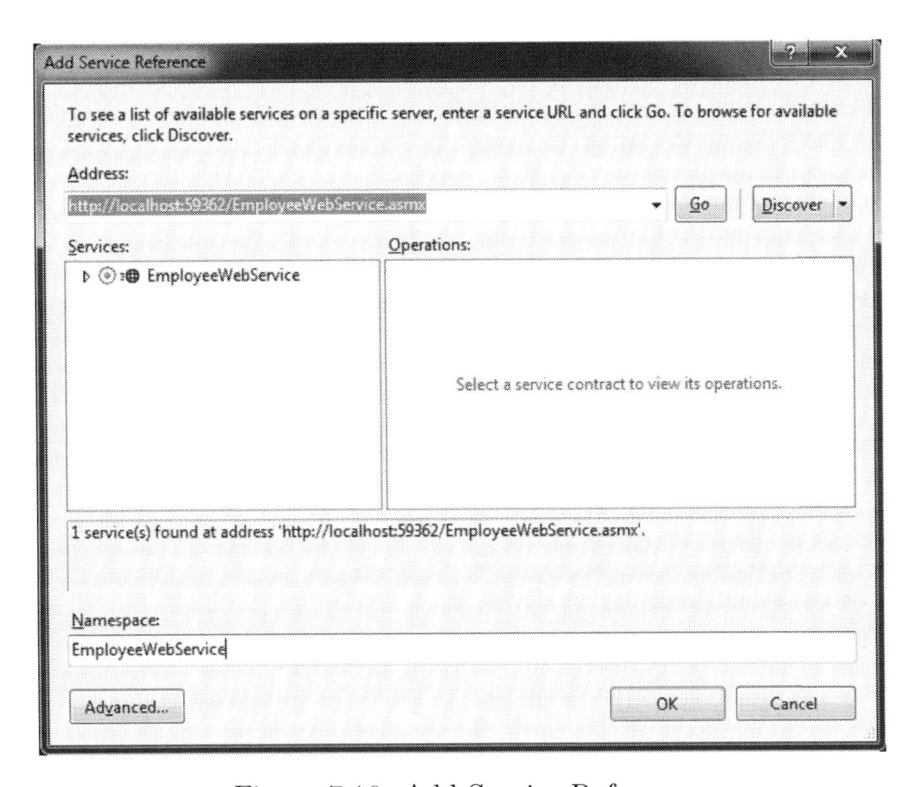

Figure 7.16: Add Service Reference

Automated Web Testing

- Right click on the 'app.cofig' file in the WebTesting project and select Properties.
- Ensure that the settings are as shown in Figure 7.17

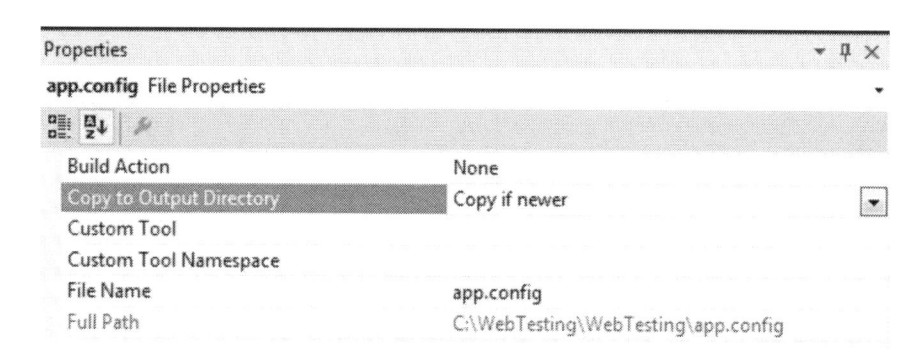

Figure 7.17: App Config File Properties

7.4.2 Utility Functions

Let's define two new Utility functions as follows:

GetEmployeeByServiceReference - Gets an employee's details by the Service Reference method		
Input Parameters	empId	Employee ID
Return Value	empRec	Returns the employee record

VerifyEmployeeWithXLSData - Compares an employee's record with the data from an XLS source and reports the outcome		
Input Parameters	empID	Employee Id
	empRec	Employee record
Return Value	void	Returns nothing

Add Listing 7.6 code to the 'Utility.cs' file.

Listing 7.6: 'Utility.cs' - Additional code

```
1  public static EmployeeWebService.Employee ←
       ↪ GetEmployeeByServiceReference(String empId)
2  {
3      try
4      {
5          EmployeeWebService.EmployeeWebServiceSoapClient ←
               ↪ ser1 = new EmployeeWebService. ←
               ↪ EmployeeWebServiceSoapClient();
```

```csharp
6            EmployeeWebService.Employee empRec = ↵
                ↪ ser1.GetEmployee(empId);
7            return empRec;
8        }
9        catch (Exception exception)
10       {
11           Utility.Log.Error("exception" + ↵
                ↪ exception.ToString());
12           throw exception;
13       }
14   }
15
16   public static void VerifyEmployeeWithXLSData(String ↵
        ↪ empID, EmployeeWebService.Employee empRec)
17   {
18       String[][] data = Utility.GetSpreadSheetXLS( ↵
            ↪ @"C:\WebTesting\WebTesting\TestData\UserData.xls", ↵
            ↪ 1);
19
20       ReportExpectedVsActualEx(empID, empRec.EmpID);
21       ReportExpectedVsActualEx(data[1][0], empRec.Title);
22       ReportExpectedVsActualEx(data[1][1], empRec.Name);
23       ReportExpectedVsActualEx(data[1][2], empRec.Gender);
24       ReportExpectedVsActualEx(ExcelDateParse(data[1][3]). ↵
            ↪ Substring(0, 10), empRec.BirthDate);
25       ReportExpectedVsActualEx(data[1][5], empRec.Contract); ↵
            ↪
26   }
```

Line 5: Initialises a new instance of the `EmployeeWebServiceSoapClient` class.

Line 6: Gets the employee record for the specified employee id.

Line 7: Returns the `Employee` record.

Line 18: Reads data in the XLS file into a two dimensional array.

Line 20: Note that we are comparing the employee id with the supplied id as the XLS file doesn't store the Employee ID.

Line 21 - 25: Compare the XLS data with the data fetched via the web service.

7.4.3 Creating Test

Add Listing 7.7 code to the 'TestWebServices.cs' file.

Listing 7.7: 'TestWebServices.cs' - Code for WebServicesServiceReference

```csharp
1    [Test]
```

```
 2  public void WebServicesServiceReference()
 3  {
 4      try
 5      {
 6          String empId = "10004";
 7
 8          EmployeeWebService.Employee empRec =
                 Utility.GetEmployeeByServiceReference(empId);
 9
10          Utility.VerifyEmployeeWithXLSData(empId,
                 empRec);
11
12          Utility.ReportResult();
13      }
14      catch (Exception exception)
15      {
16          Utility.Log.Error("exception" +
                 exception.ToString());
17          throw exception;
18      }
19  }
```

Line 8: Calls the Utility function `GetEmployeeByServiceReference` with Employee ID "10004".

Line 10: Verifies the employee details with the data in the XLS file.

7.4.4 Executing Tests

Before we can execute the test, we need to make some changes to the NUnit Project as follows:

1. Within NUnit, go to Project → Edit...

2. Specify the Configuration File Name as 'app.config' as shown in Figure 7.18

3. In the Project Editor window, select File → Save.

4. Close the Project Editor window (click 'Yes' to project reload if asked).

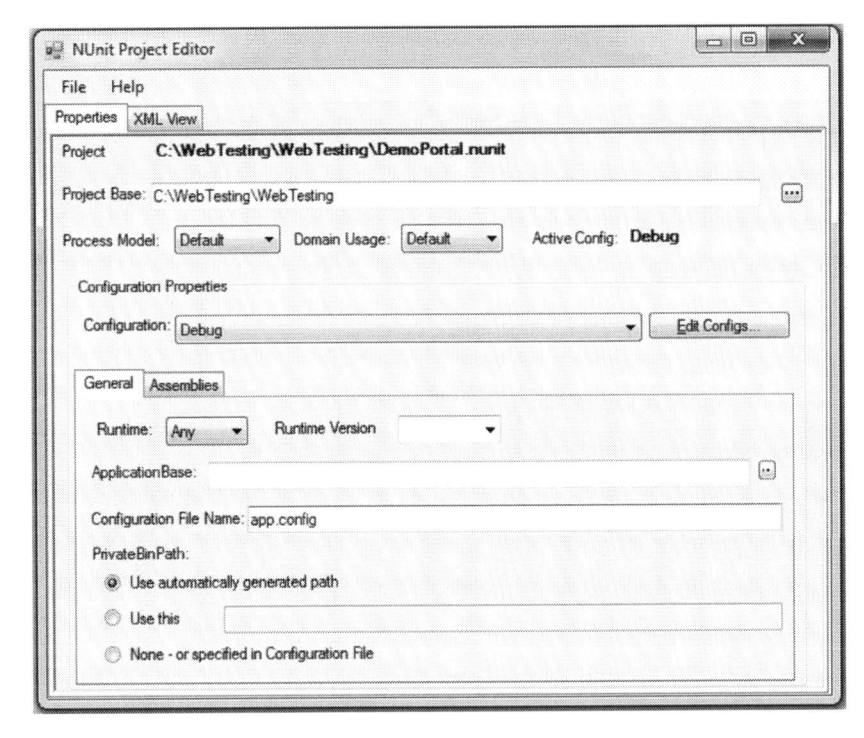

Figure 7.18: Specify Configuration File Name

Ensure that 'IIS Express' is running as shown in Figure 7.11. The output is shown in Figure 7.19 for a successful execution.

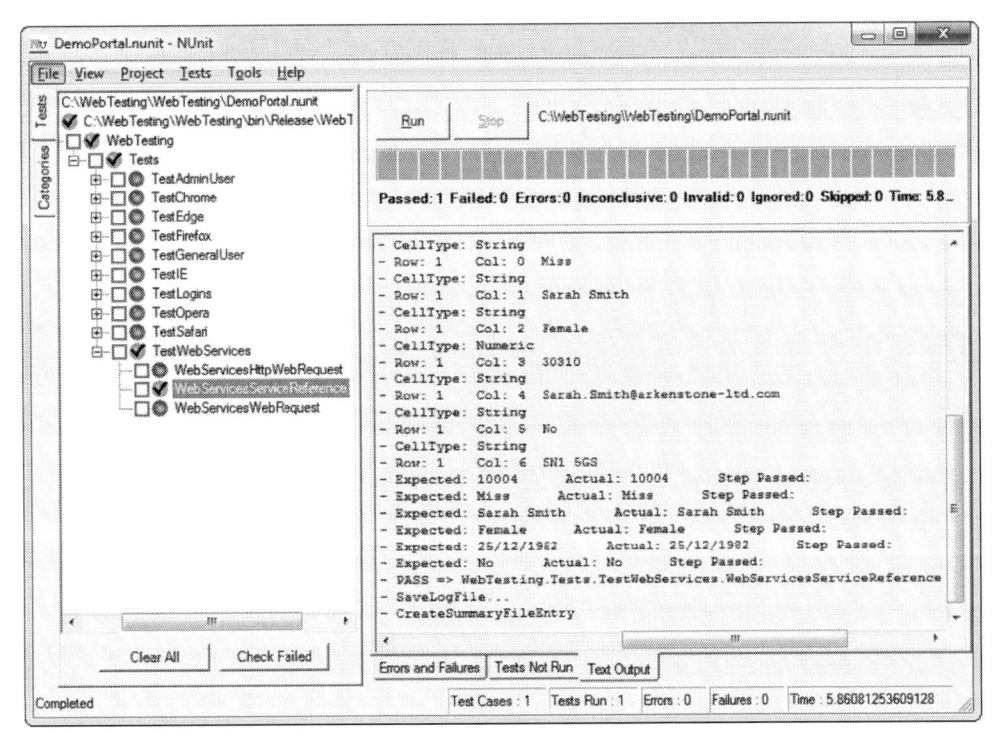

Figure 7.19: Web Services Service Reference Output

Chapter 8

Miscellaneous

Miscellaneous

In this chapter, we will learn:

- *How to find missing images on a web page*
- *How to find broken links on a web page*
- *How to find Tooltips displayed on elements*
- *How to perform the 'Drag-and-Drop' operation on elements*
- *How to perform a 'Context Click' on elements*
- *How to execute a JavaScript in the browser*

So let's get on with it...

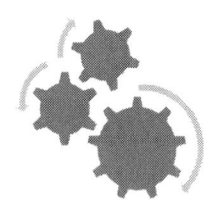

EACH website has its own unique functionality to serve its own purpose. However, there are certain aspects which are common among all websites to make it both user friendly and intuitive e.g. having lots of images, links, Drag-and-Drop features, Tooltips etc. Apart from testing the main functionality provided by the website, as an automation tester, you would also need to check that these additional features of the website are working correctly. In this section I have shown how to automate such functionality which has proved very useful in my automation career.

The default browser used in automating tests in this section is Firefox unless specified explicitly.

8.1 Finding Missing Images

There is a famous saying, *"A picture is worth a thousand words."* because an image conveys its meaning more effectively than a description. Most websites use a lot of images to convey their message. However, there are times, when a website goes live, that some of the images go missing and there could be a number of reasons for that e.g. all images not deployed, a copy-paste error, wrong folder/file names etc. A website may contain thousands of images and it may not be possible to check the presence of all the images manually every time a build is deployed, so it becomes more prudent to find such missing images via automation. Let's see how we can automate the following Test Scenario to find out missing images on a page in our demo website:

- Launch the demo website.
- Login with the user 'Tester'.
- Click on the *Other* link.
- Verify if there are any missing images in this page.

☞ The demo website has one missing image in this page as shown in Figure A.8 so that the test should purposely fail.

8.1.1 Utility Functions

VerifyImagesOnPage - Verifies images on a web page; reports and returns the missing ones		
Input Parameters	*driver*	Object driver to control the browser
Return Value	*list*	Returns a list of missing images

Add Listing 8.1 code to the 'Utility.cs' file.

Listing 8.1: 'Utility.cs' - Code to verify and return missing images on a web page

```
1  using System.Collections.Generic;
2
3  public static string[] VerifyImagesOnPage(this IWebDriver ↵
       ↪ driver)
4  {
5      Log.Info("VerifyImagesOnPage... ");
6      Wait(3);
7
8      List<string> invalidSrc = new List<string>();
9
```

```csharp
10      ReadOnlyCollection<IWebElement> elements = ↵
          ↪ driver.FindElements(By.TagName("img"));
11      List<string> list = new List<string>();
12
13      foreach (IWebElement item in elements)
14      {
15          list.Add(item.GetAttribute("src"));
16      }
17      foreach (string item in list)
18      {
19          HttpWebRequest lxRequest = ↵
              ↪ (HttpWebRequest)WebRequest.Create(item);
20
21          try
22          {
23              HttpWebResponse lxResponse = ↵
                  ↪ (HttpWebResponse)lxRequest.GetResponse();
24
25              using (BinaryReader reader = new ↵
                  ↪ BinaryReader(lxResponse. ↵
                  ↪ GetResponseStream()))
26              {
27                  Byte[] lnByte = reader.ReadBytes(1 * 1024 ↵
                      ↪ * 1024 * 10);
28                  if (lnByte.Length > 0)
29                  {
30                      Log.Info("Valid Image Link: " + item);
31                  }
32              }
33          }
34
35          catch (Exception exception)
36          {
37              if (!invalidSrc.Contains(item))
38              {
39                  Log.Error("Error in image link ↵
                      ↪ validation: " + item + " Exception: ↵
                      ↪ " + exception.ToString());
40                  invalidSrc.Add(item);
41              }
42          }
43      }
44
45      ReportExpectedVsActual(driver, "0", ↵
          ↪ invalidSrc.Count.ToString());
```

```
46          return invalidSrc.ToArray();
47 }
```

Line 1: Additional import required to support the functionality.
Line 8: Defines an empty list to store invalid image sources.
Line 10: Reads all the image elements on a page into a collection.
Line 11: Defines an empty list.
Line 13: Loops through the collection of image elements read above.
Line 15: Adds the image source into the list.
Line 17: Loops through the image source list.
Line 19: Makes an `HttpWebRequest` on the image source.
Line 23: Gets the `HttpWebResponse` from the request we just made above.
Line 25: Initialises a new instance of the `BinaryReader` class with the response stream.
Line 27: Reads the specified number of bytes from the current stream into a byte array.
Line 28: If the number of bytes read is greater than zero then it is taken to be a valid image file.
Line 37: Catches any exceptions like 404 Error. Also ensures that the list is not already reported in the invalid source list.
Line 39: Logs an error for the invalid image source.
Line 40: Adds the item to the invalid source list.
Line 45: At the end of loop, compares the invalid source list count with "0" (zero). If it is not equal to "0" it will result into a failed test step.
Line 46: Returns the invalid source list.

8.1.2 Creating Tests

Add Listing 8.2 code to the 'TestGeneralUser.cs' file.

Listing 8.2: 'TestGeneralUser.cs' - Test to find missing images

```
1  [Test]
2  public void FindMissingImages()
3  {
4      try
5      {
6          Utility.Log.Info("Starting test: " + ↵
                 ↪ TestContext.CurrentContext.Test.FullName);
7
8          var home = new pageHome(driver);
9          home.Visit();
10         home.ClickLogin();
11
12         var login = new pageLogin(driver);
13         login.Login("Tester", "Tester123");
```

Automated Web Testing

```
14
15            var homeTester = new pageTesterHome(driver);
16            homeTester.ClickOther();
17
18            Utility.VerifyImagesOnPage(driver);
19
20            Utility.ReportResult();
21        }
22        catch (Exception exception)
23        {
24            Utility.Log.Error("exception" + ↵
                 ↪ exception.ToString());
25            throw exception;
26        }
27 }
```

Line 18: Calls the Utility function to verify and return missing images.

8.1.3 Executing Tests

Execute the test and you will see an output as shown in Figure 8.1. The test fails due to a missing image on the page.

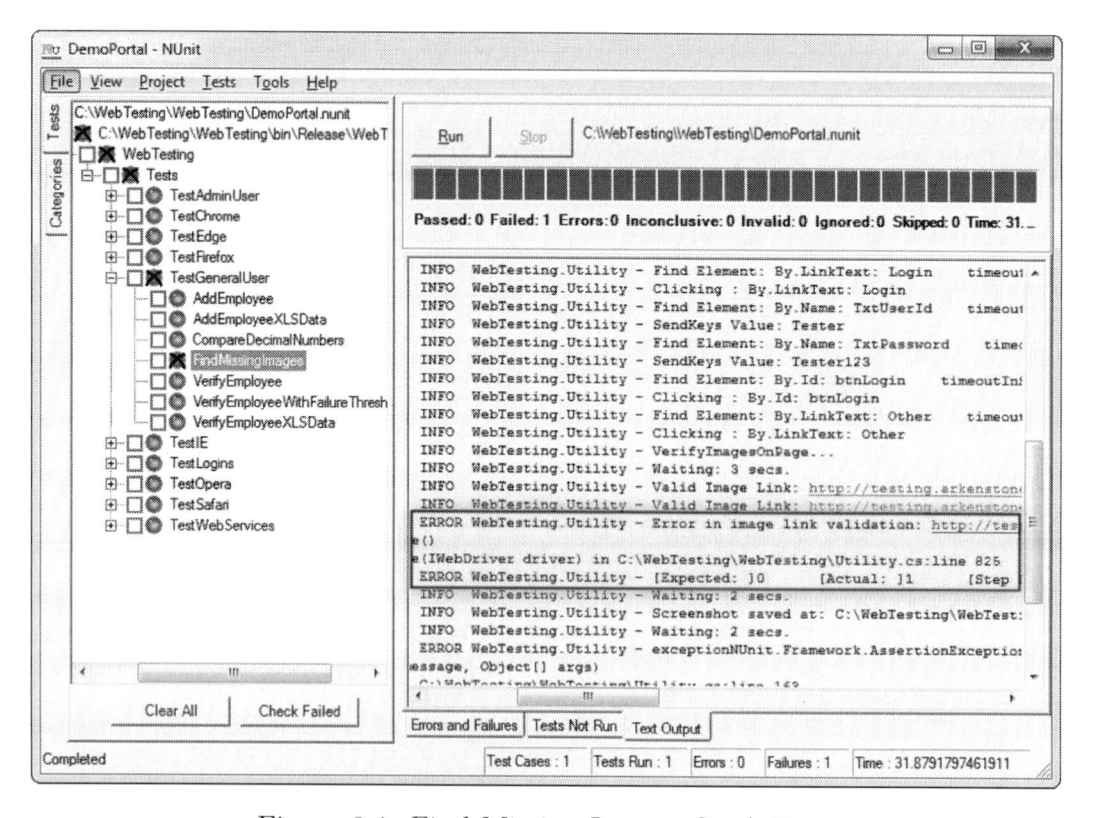

Figure 8.1: Find Missing Images On A Page

302 Chapter 8

8.2 Finding Broken Links

Links are found in almost all websites. Links allow users to navigate from one page to another. This navigation may be to another page in your website or to an external website. As with images, our automation should also allow broken links to be identified automatically. Here is a Test Scenario that we are going to verify:

- Launch the demo website.
- Go to the *Help* page.
- Verify that the links on the *Help* page are working.
- Go to the *Login* page.
- Login with the user 'Tester'.
- Go to the *Other* page.
- Verify that the links on the *Other* page are working.
- Ignore email addresses from the verification.

☞ The *Help* page has an email address as shown in Figure A.3, which should be ignored from the verification. The *Other* page has a missing link as shown in Figure A.8, so our test should purposely fail.

8.2.1 Utility Functions

Let's define two new Utility functions as follows:

VerifyLinksOnPage - Verifies links on a web page; reports and returns the broken ones		
Input Parameters	*driver*	Object driver to control the browser
Return Value	*list*	Returns list of broken links

IsElementPresent - Checks if the element is enabled and displayed on the web page		
Input Parameters	*driver*	Object driver to control the browser
	by	Mechanism by which to find the element within the browser
Return Value	*bool*	Returns 'true' if the element is enabled and displayed

Add Listing 8.3 code to the 'Utility.cs' file.

Listing 8.3: 'Utility.cs' - Code to verify and return broken links

```
using System.Linq;

public static string[] VerifyLinksOnPage(this IWebDriver ←
    ↪ driver)
{
    Log.Info("VerifyLinksOnPage... ");
    Wait(3);
    List<string> invalidLink = new List<string>();

    List<IWebElement> links = new List<IWebElement>();
    links = driver.FindElements(By.TagName("a")).ToList();

    string[] ignoreList = new string[] { ←
        ↪ "http://www.ignore1.com/", ←
        ↪ "http://www.ignore2.com" };

    string[] gs = new string[100];
    int i = 0;

    foreach (var link in links)
    {
        if ((link.GetAttribute("href") != null) &
            (!link.Text.Contains("@")))
        {
            gs[i] = link.GetAttribute("href");
            i = i + 1;
        }
    }

    Log.Info("Total links on page: " + i);

    for (int ii = 0; ii <= i - 1; ii++)
    {
        if (!(ignoreList.Contains(gs[ii], ←
            ↪ StringComparer.OrdinalIgnoreCase)))
        {
            Log.Info("href is: " + gs[ii]);

            driver.Url = gs[ii];

            if (IsElementPresent(driver, ←
                ↪ By.TagName("body")))
```

```csharp
38              if (driver.FindElement(By.TagName("body"))
                    .Text.Contains("Page not found") |
39                  driver.FindElement(By.TagName("body"))
                        .Text.Contains("could not be resolved
                        by DNS") |
40                  driver.FindElement(By.TagName("body"))
                        .Text.Contains("Server not found")
                        |
41                  driver.FindElement(By.TagName("body"))
                        .Text.Contains("Something has gone
                        wrong") |
42                  driver.FindElement(By.TagName("body"))
                        .Text.Contains("Internal Server
                        Error"))
43              {
44                  ReportExpectedVsActual(driver, "Issue with
                        Page: ", gs[ii]);
45                  invalidLink.Add(gs[ii]);
46              }
47          else
48              Log.Info("Page OK.");
49      }
50      else
51      Log.Info("Ignored Link: " + gs[ii]);
52  }
53
54  ReportExpectedVsActual(driver, "0",
        invalidLink.Count.ToString());
55  return invalidLink.ToArray();
56 }
57
58 public static bool IsElementPresent(this IWebDriver
        driver, By by)
59 {
60      bool a = false;
61
62      try
63      {
64          a = driver.FindElement(by).Enabled &
                driver.FindElement(by).Displayed;
65          return a;
66      }
67      catch (NoSuchElementException ex)
68      {
69          Log.Error("IsElementPresent exception: " +
```

```
             ↪ ex.ToString());
70       return a;
71    }
72 }
```

Line 1: Additional import required to support the functionality.
Line 7: Defines an empty list to store invalid links.
Line 9: Defines an empty list to store all links.
Line 10: Gets all the links on the page into this list.
Line 12: An ignore list where you can specify links to be ignored for the test as they may not be accessible from your QA environment or are under development and hence not available. The book has added two dummy links to be ignored for the demo purpose.
Line 14: Defines an array of strings.
Line 15: Initialises a counter.
Line 17: Loops through all the links.
Line 20: Ensures that "href" is not null and ignores links that are email ids.
Line 22: Adds the link to the array of strings.
Line 23: Increments the counter.
Line 29: Loops through the array of strings.
Line 31: Ensures that the link is not in the 'ignore list'.
Line 35: Navigates to the link.
Line 37: Calls the Utility function `IsElementPresent` to check for the "body" element.
Line 38 - 44: Check that the "body" doesn't contain any of the messages. You will have to add/modify the messages in your test to match what is displayed by the website in such scenarios.
Line 47: Otherwise logs an OK message.
Line 55: Returns the invalid link list.
Line 60: Initialises the default return value.
Line 64 and 65: Return true if the element is enabled and displayed.
Line 70: Returns false in case of an error.

8.2.2 Creating Tests

Add Listing 8.2 code to the 'TestGeneralUser.cs' file.

Listing 8.4: 'TestGeneralUser.cs' - Test to find broken links

```
1 [Test]
2 public void FindBrokenLinks()
3 {
4     try
5     {
6         Utility.Log.Info("Starting test: " + ↵
             ↪ TestContext.CurrentContext.Test.FullName);
```

```
 7
 8          var home = new pageHome(driver);
 9          home.Visit();
10
11          home.ClickHelp();
12
13          Utility.VerifyLinksOnPage(driver);
14
15          home.ClickHome();
16          home.ClickLogin();
17
18          var login = new pageLogin(driver);
19          login.Login("Tester", "Tester123");
20
21          var homeTester = new pageTesterHome(driver);
22          homeTester.ClickOther();
23
24          Utility.VerifyLinksOnPage(driver);
25
26          Utility.ReportResult();
27      }
28      catch (Exception exception)
29      {
30          Utility.Log.Error("exception" + ↵
              ↪ exception.ToString());
31          throw exception;
32      }
33 }
```

Line 13 and 24: Calls the Utility function to verify and return broken links on the page.

8.2.3 Executing Tests

Execute the test and you will see an output as shown in Figure 8.2. The test purposely fails due to a missing link on the page.

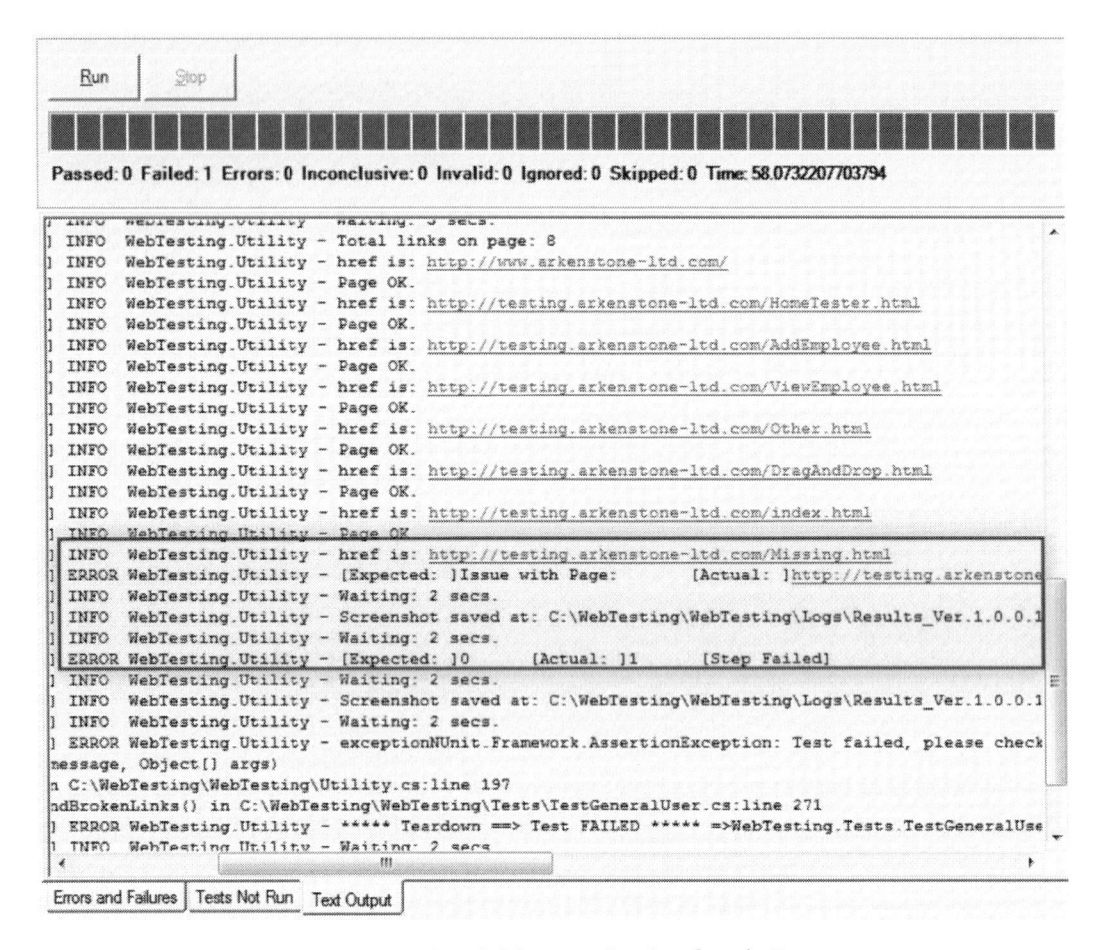

Figure 8.2: Find Missing Links On A Page

8.3 Finding Tooltips

A Tooltip is a small pop-up box that appears near an object when the mouse hovers over it. Tooltips are very helpful for new users to help them understand objects or elements on website pages. A well designed Tooltip system is usually configurable, particularly with regards to the ability to turn them 'on' or 'off'. For our demo purpose, here is a Test Scenario that we will verify:

- Launch the demo website.
- Go to the *Login* page.
- Verify the Tooltip of the User ID entry field.
- Verify the Tooltip of the Password entry field.

8.3.1 Configuration Parameters

Let's add some new configuration variables. Double click on the 'Config.cs' file in the 'Solution Explorer' and add the Listing 8.5 code to it.

Listing 8.5: 'Config.cs' - Parameters for Tooltips

```
1  public const string USERID_TOOLTIP = "Please enter the ↵
       User ID";
2  public const string PASSWORD_TOOLTIP = "Please enter the ↵
       Password";
```

Line 1: Defines a string constant for the User ID Tooltip as displayed in the demo website.
Line 2: Defines a string constant for the Password Tooltip as displayed in the demo website.

8.3.2 Utility Functions

GetTooltip - Gets the Tooltip displayed on the element		
Input Parameters	*driver*	Object driver to control the browser
	by	Mechanism by which to find the element within the browser
Return Value	*tooltip*	Returns the Tooltip

Add Listing 8.6 code to the 'Utility.cs' file.

Listing 8.6: 'Utility.cs' - Code to get the Tooltip displayed on an element

```
1  using OpenQA.Selenium.Interactions;
2
3  public static String GetTooltip(this IWebDriver driver, ↵
       By by)
4  {
5      try
6      {
7          Actions action = new Actions(driver);
8
9          IWebElement elem = FindElementAndReturn(driver, ↵
              by);
10
11         action.MoveToElement(elem).Perform();
12
13         Wait(3);
14
15         return elem.GetAttribute("title");
```

```
16      }
17      catch (Exception exception)
18      {
19          Log.Error("GetTooltip exception: " + ↵
               ↪ exception.ToString());
20          throw exception;
21      }
22  }
```

Line 1: Additional import required to support the new functionality.
Line 7: Initialises a new instance of the **Actions** class for advanced interactions with the browser.
Line 9: Gets a reference to the element.
Line 11: Moves the mouse to the specified element. A **Perform** operation will execute the currently built action.
Line 13: Gives some breathing time for the Tooltip to be visible. You may have to adjust the wait time according to the website you are testing.
Line 15: Returns the Tooltip.

8.3.3 Page Logic

In order to verify the Tooltip, we need to add an additional action to the *Login* page as follows:

Action	Description
VerifyToolTips()	This action will verify the Tooltips on the login page.

Add the additional function to the 'pageLogin.cs' file as shown in Listing 8.7.

Listing 8.7: 'pageLogin.cs' - Code to verify Tooltips

```
1  public void VerifyToolTips()
2  {
3       String toolTipUId = Utility.GetTooltip(driver, ↵
            ↪ By.Name(Repository.Login.txtUserId_ByName));
4
5       Utility.ReportExpectedVsActual(driver, ↵
            ↪ Config.USERID_TOOLTIP, toolTipUId);
6
7       String toolTipPwd = Utility.GetTooltip(driver, ↵
            ↪ By.Name(Repository.Login.txtPassword_ByName));
```

```
 8
 9        Utility.ReportExpectedVsActual(driver, ↵
              ↪ Config.PASSWORD_TOOLTIP, toolTipPwd);
10 }
```

Line 3 and 7: Call the Utility function to retrieve the Tooltip.
Line 5 and 9: Compare the retrieved Tooltip with the expected value and report the outcome.

8.3.4 Creating Tests

Add Listing 8.8 code to the 'TestGeneralUser.cs' file.

Listing 8.8: 'TestGeneralUser.cs' - Test to check the Tooltips

```
 1 [Test]
 2 public void ToolTipCheck()
 3 {
 4     try
 5     {
 6         Utility.Log.Info("Starting test: " + ↵
              ↪ TestContext.CurrentContext.Test.FullName);
 7
 8         var home = new pageHome(driver);
 9         home.Visit();
10         home.ClickLogin();
11
12         var login = new pageLogin(driver);
13         login.VerifyToolTips();
14
15         Utility.ReportResult();
16     }
17     catch (Exception exception)
18     {
19         Utility.Log.Error("exception" + ↵
              ↪ exception.ToString());
20         throw exception;
21     }
22 }
```

Line 13: Call the page logic to verify Tooltips.

8.3.5 Executing Tests

Execute the test and you will see an output as shown in Figure 8.3. The Tooltips are verified as expected.

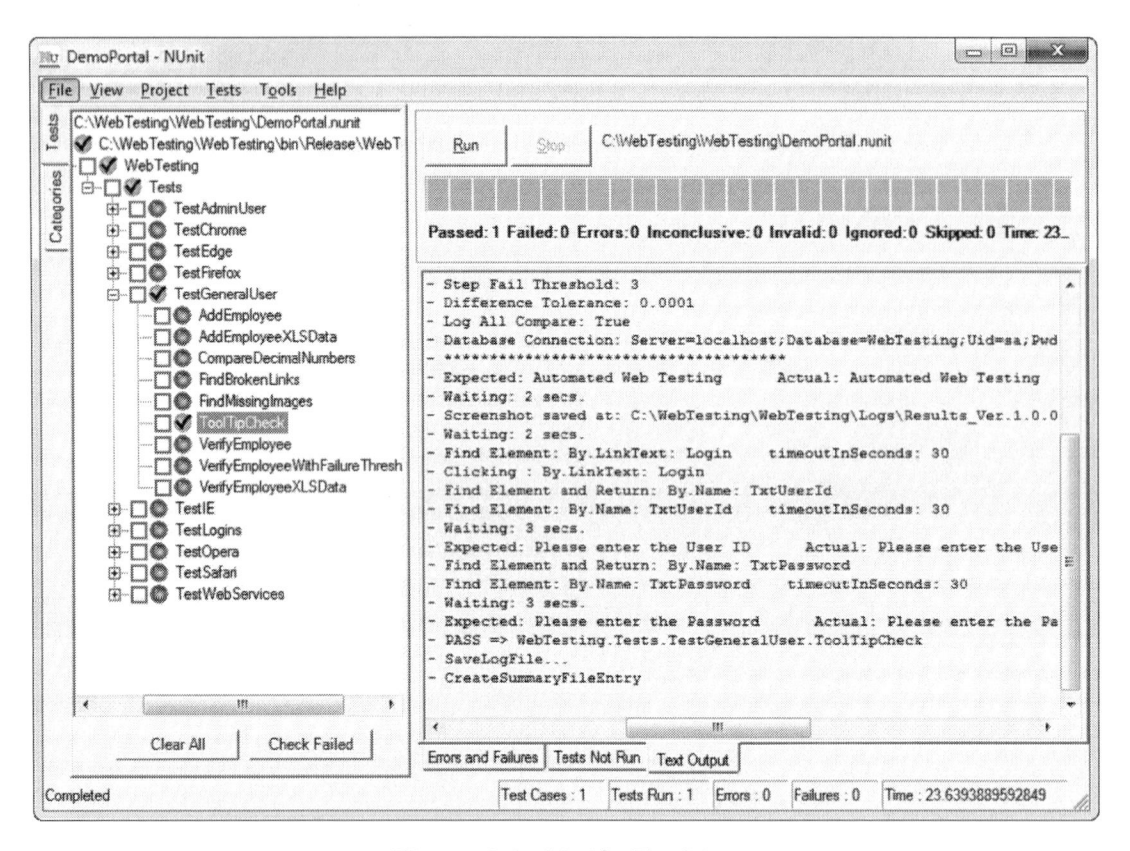

Figure 8.3: Verify Tooltips

8.4 Drag And Drop

'Drag and Drop' is a powerful *Graphical User Interface* concept which makes it easy to perform a number of tasks with the help of mouse clicks. This allows the user to click and hold the mouse button down over an element on the web page, drag it to another location and release the mouse button to drop area. Here is a Test Scenario that we will verify for our demo purpose:

- Launch the demo website.

- Login with the user 'Tester'.

- Click on the *Drag-n-Drop* link.

- Drag the image and drop it to the canvas area as shown in Figure A.9.

8.4.1 Object Repository

First of all, let's build the object repository of our *Drag-n-Drop* page as shown in Figure A.9:

Drag-n-Drop Page Elements			
Element	*Type*	*Attribute*	*Value*
Image For Drag	Image	id	ImgDrag
Drop Area	Div	id	DivDrop

Now double click on the 'Repository.cs' file in the 'Solution Explorer' and add the code for 'DragAndDrop' as shown in Listing 8.9.

Listing 8.9: 'Repository.cs' - Code for Drag-n-Drop page

```
1  public static class DragAndDrop
2  {
3      public static string imgImageForDrag_ById { get { ↵
           ↪ return "ImgDrag"; } }
4      public static string divDropArea_ById { get { return ↵
           ↪ "DivDrop"; } }
5  }
```

We will learn three methods to automate the Drag-and-Drop operation.

8.4.2 Creating Test - DragAndDrop

In this method, a Drag-and-Drop operation is performed from one element to another. The element on which the drag operation is performed is referred to as the *source* and the element on which the drop is performed is referred to as the *target*.

Add Listing 8.10 code to the 'TestGeneralUser.cs' file.

Listing 8.10: 'TestGeneralUser.cs' - Test by DragAndDrop

```
1  using OpenQA.Selenium.Interactions;
2
3  [Test]
4  public void DragDropMethod1()
5  {
6      try
```

```
 7      {
 8          Utility.Log.Info("Starting test: " + ↵
              ↪ TestContext.CurrentContext.Test.FullName);
 9
10          driver.Manage().Window.Maximize();
11
12          var home = new pageHome(driver);
13          home.Visit();
14          home.ClickLogin();
15
16          var login = new pageLogin(driver);
17          login.Login("Tester", "Tester123");
18
19          var homeTester = new pageTesterHome(driver);
20          homeTester.ClickDragnDrop();
21
22          Utility.Wait(2);
23          IWebElement eleSource = ↵
              ↪ Utility.FindElementAndReturn(driver, ↵
              ↪ By.Id(Repository.DragAndDrop. ↵
              ↪ imgImageForDrag_ById));
24          IWebElement eleTarget = ↵
              ↪ Utility.FindElementAndReturn(driver, ↵
              ↪ By.Id(Repository.DragAndDrop. ↵
              ↪ divDropArea_ById));
25
26          Actions action = new Actions(driver);
27
28          action.DragAndDrop(eleSource, ↵
              ↪ eleTarget).Build().Perform();
29
30          Utility.ReportResult();
31      }
32      catch (Exception exception)
33      {
34          Utility.Log.Error("exception" + exception.ToString());
35          throw exception;
36      }
37  }
```

Line 1: Additional import required to support the new functionality.
Line 10: Maximises the browser window.
Line 20: Goes to the *Drag-n-Drop* page.
Line 22: Gives some breathing time for the objects to be loaded. Adjust the wait time according to your website's response time.

Line 23: Gets the source element.

Line 24: Gets the target element.

Line 26: Initialises a new instance of the **Actions** class for advanced interactions with the browser.

Line 28: Performs a Drag-and-Drop operation from the source element to the target.

8.4.3 Executing Test - DragAndDrop

Execute the test and you will see an output as shown in Figure 8.4. The browser window will also show the Drag-and-Drop operation in action.

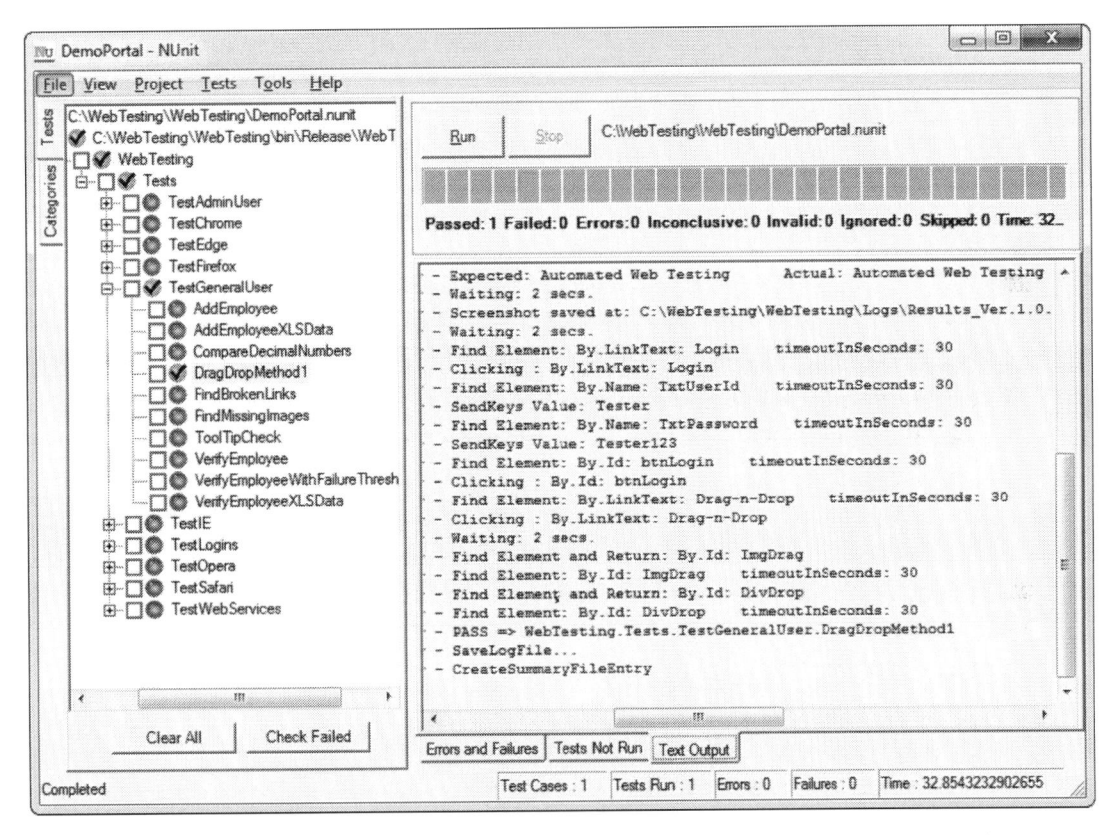

Figure 8.4: Drag And Drop Output

8.4.4 Creating Test - Mouse In Action

In this method, a series of mouse actions are performed i.e. click and hold mouse button down on the *source* element, move the mouse to the *target* element and release the mouse button on the *target* element.

Add Listing 8.11 code to the 'TestGeneralUser.cs' file.

Listing 8.11: 'TestGeneralUser.cs' - Test by mouse in action

```
1  [Test]
2  public void DragDropMethod2()
3  {
4      try
5      {
6          Utility.Log.Info("Starting test: " +
                 TestContext.CurrentContext.Test.FullName);
7
8          driver.Manage().Window.Maximize();
9
10         var home = new pageHome(driver);
11         home.Visit();
12         home.ClickLogin();
13
14         var login = new pageLogin(driver);
15         login.Login("Tester", "Tester123");
16
17         var homeTester = new pageTesterHome(driver);
18         homeTester.ClickDragnDrop();
19
20         IWebElement eleSource =
                 Utility.FindElementAndReturn(driver,
                 By.Id(Repository.DragAndDrop.
                 imgImageForDrag_ById));
21         IWebElement eleTarget =
                 Utility.FindElementAndReturn(driver,
                 By.Id(Repository.DragAndDrop.divDropArea_ById));
22
23         Actions action = new Actions(driver);
24
25         action.ClickAndHold(eleSource).Build().Perform();
26         Utility.Wait(2);
27         action.MoveToElement(eleTarget).Build().Perform();
28         action.Release(eleTarget).Build().Perform();
29
30         Utility.ReportResult();
31     }
32     catch (Exception exception)
33     {
34         Utility.Log.Error("exception" + exception.ToString());
35         throw exception;
36     }
37 }
```

Line 25: Clicks and holds the mouse button down on the source element.
Line 27: Moves the mouse to the target element
Line 28: Releases the mouse button on the target element.

8.4.5 Creating Test - DragAndDropToOffset

In this method, a Drag-and-Drop operation is performed on an element to a specified offset. The element on which the drag operation is started is referred to as the *source* element. We then specify the *horizontal* and the *vertical* offset to which to move the mouse.

Add Listing 8.12 code to the 'TestGeneralUser.cs' file.

Listing 8.12: 'TestGeneralUser.cs' - Test by DragAndDropToOffset

```
1  [Test]
2  public void DragDropMethod3()
3  {
4      try
5      {
6          Utility.Log.Info("Starting test: " + ↵
               TestContext.CurrentContext.Test.FullName);
7
8          driver.Manage().Window.Maximize();
9
10         var home = new pageHome(driver);
11         home.Visit();
12         home.ClickLogin();
13
14         var login = new pageLogin(driver);
15         login.Login("Tester", "Tester123");
16
17         var homeTester = new pageTesterHome(driver);
18         homeTester.ClickDragnDrop();
19
20         Utility.Wait(2);
21         IWebElement eleSource = ↵
               Utility.FindElementAndReturn(driver, ↵
               By.Id(Repository.DragAndDrop. ↵
               imgImageForDrag_ById));
22         IWebElement eleTarget = ↵
               Utility.FindElementAndReturn(driver, ↵
               By.Id(Repository.DragAndDrop.divDropArea_ById));
23
```

```
24        Actions action = new Actions(driver);
25
26        action.DragAndDropToOffset(eleSource, 10, ↵
              ↪ -(eleSource.Location.Y - eleTarget.Location.Y) ↵
              ↪ + 10).Build().Perform();
27
28        Utility.ReportResult();
29      }
30      catch (Exception exception)
31      {
32        Utility.Log.Error("exception" + exception.ToString());
33        throw exception;
34      }
35  }
```

Line 26: Performs a Drag-and-Drop operation on the source element to a specified offset.

8.5 Context Click

'Context Click' is when you right click on a specified element and you get a drop down menu (usually called the *Context Menu*) of certain options, depending on the context of the click. In our demo website let's verify the following Test Scenario:

- Launch the demo website.
- Login with the user 'Tester'.
- Click on *Drag-n-Drop* link.
- Context Click on the image.
- Press key 'o' to *Copy Image Location* to the Clipboard.
- Log the image location from Clipboard.

8.5.1 Adding Necessary Reference

Let's add a new reference to our WebTesting project which is needed to support the new functionality.

- In the 'Solution Explorer' window, right click on 'References' in the WebTesting project and select 'Add Reference'.
- Click the 'Browse...' button and navigate to folder 'C:\Program Files (x86)\Reference Assemblies\Microsoft\Framework \.NETFramework\v4.5.2'.
- Select 'System.Windows.Forms.dll' as shown in Figure 8.5.

- Click the Add button and then press OK.

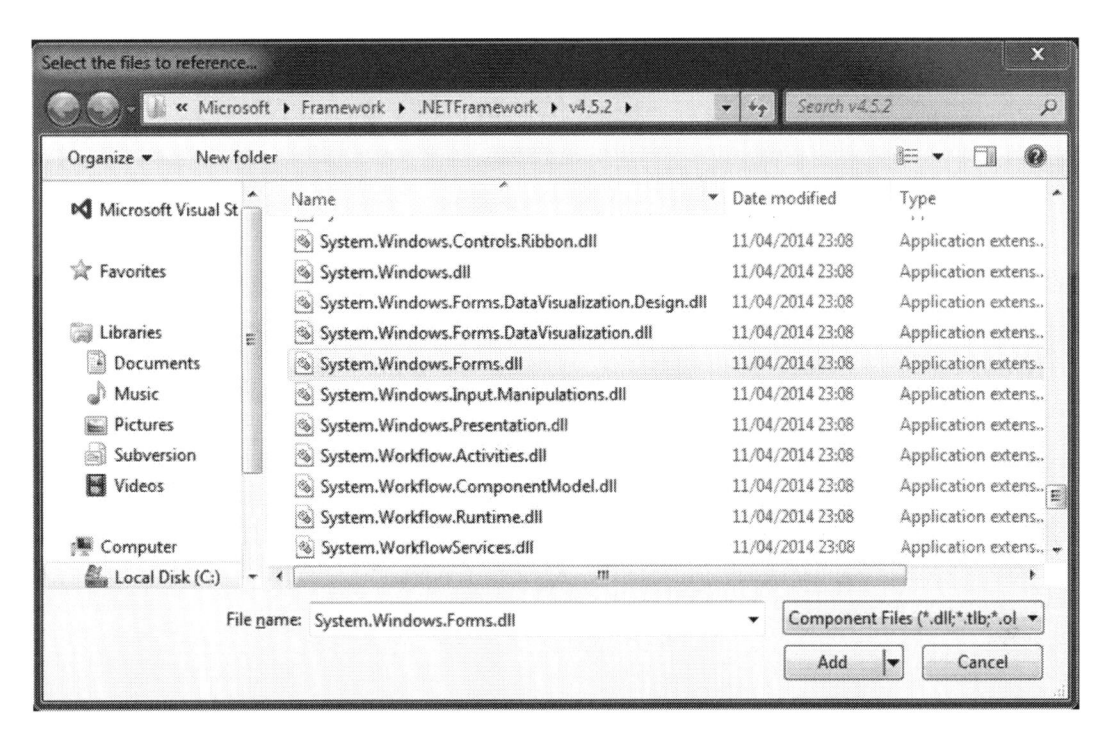

Figure 8.5: Add Windows Dll Reference

8.5.2 Creating Tests

Add Listing 8.13 code to the 'TestGeneralUser.cs' file.

Listing 8.13: 'TestGeneralUser.cs' - Test for context click

```
using System.Windows.Forms;

[STAThread]
[Test]
public void ContextClick()
{
    try
    {
        Utility.Log.Info("Starting test: " +
            TestContext.CurrentContext.Test.FullName);

        driver.Manage().Window.Maximize();

        var home = new pageHome(driver);
        home.Visit();
```

```
15              home.ClickLogin();
16
17              var login = new pageLogin(driver);
18              login.Login("Tester", "Tester123");
19
20              var homeTester = new pageTesterHome(driver);
21              homeTester.ClickDragnDrop();
22
23              IWebElement eleSource =
                    Utility.FindElementAndReturn(driver,
                    By.Id(Repository.DragAndDrop.
                    imgImageForDrag_ById));
24
25              Actions action = new Actions(driver);
26
27              action.ContextClick(eleSource).Build().Perform();
28              Utility.Wait(1);
29              action.SendKeys("o").Build().Perform();
30
31              Utility.Log.Info("Path: " + Clipboard.GetText());
32
33              Utility.ReportResult();
34          }
35          catch (Exception exception)
36          {
37              Utility.Log.Error("exception" +
                    exception.ToString());
38              throw exception;
39          }
40  }
```

Line 1: Additional import required to support the new functionality.

Line 3: Indicates that the COM threading model is Single-Threaded Apartment (STA). This is needed to communicate with the Windows Clipboard.

Line 23: Gets reference to the element we want to context click which is the image in our case.

Line 25: Initialises a new instance of the **Actions** class for advanced interactions with the browser.

Line 27: Right clicks the mouse on the image.

Line 28: Breathing time for the popup to appear.

Line 29: Sends key **"o"** to select the 'Copy Image Location' option.

Line 31: Retrieves the text data from the Clipboard and logs it.

8.5.3 Executing Test

Execute the test and you will see the 'Context Click' pop-up as shown in Figure 8.6.

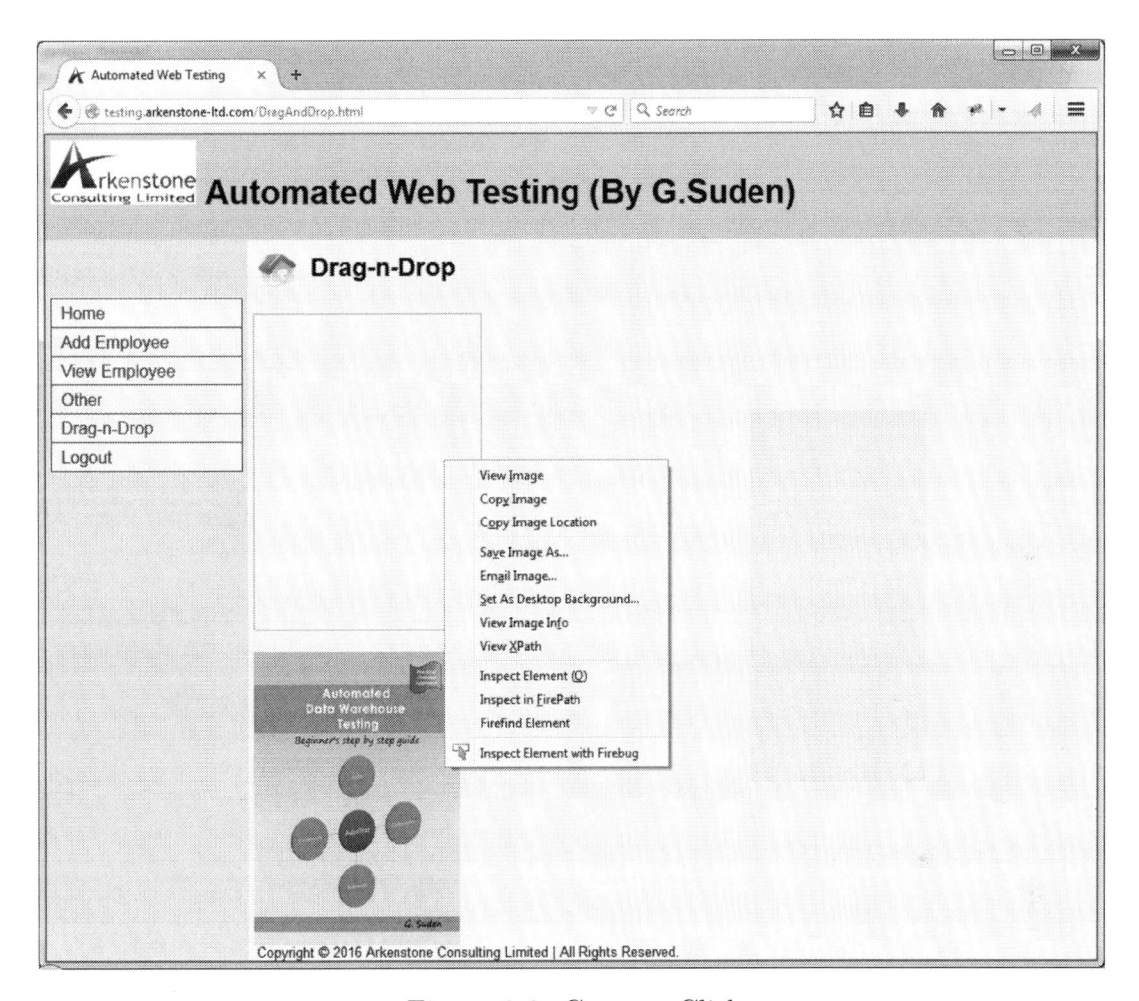

Figure 8.6: Context Click

8.6 Executing JavaScript

There are times when you will need to execute a JavaScript as part of your test. Let's perform the following Test Scenario to demonstrate the use of JavaScript:

- Launch the demo website.

- Login with the user 'Tester'.

- Highlight elements, using a JavaScript, when the data is entered into the data entry fields.

We will use the `IJavaScriptExecutor` interface to execute JavaScript in the browser window.

8.6.1 Utility Functions

FindElementAndSendKeysWithHighlight - Finds an element; sends keys to it with highlight		
Input Parameters	*driver*	Object driver to control the browser
	by	Mechanism by which to find the element within the browser
	val	Data string to be sent to the element
Return Value	void	Returns nothing

Add Listing 8.14 code to the 'Utility.cs' file.

Listing 8.14: 'Utility.cs' - Code to find an element and send keys with highlight

```
public static void 
    FindElementAndSendKeysWithHighlight(this IWebDriver 
    driver, By by, string val)
{
    string ex = "";

    try
    {
        IWebElement elemt = FindElementEx(driver, by, 
            Config.OBJECT_TIMEOUT_SECS);

        String orgStyle = elemt.GetAttribute("style");

        IJavaScriptExecutor js = 
            (IJavaScriptExecutor)driver;

        js.ExecuteScript("arguments[0].style.border='3px 
            solid red'", elemt);

        Log.Info("SendKeys Value: " + val);

        elemt.SendKeys(val);

        Wait(1);

        js.ExecuteScript("arguments[0].style.border='" + 
            orgStyle + "'", elemt);

        return;
    }
```

```
25      catch (NoSuchElementException)
26      {
27          ex += "Unable to Sendkeys " + val;
28          Log.Error(ex);
29          throw new NoSuchElementException(ex);
30      }
31 }
```

Line 7: Finds the required element using the core function.
Line 9: Saves element's original style for later use.
Line 11: Defines the interface through which we can execute the JavaScript.
Line 13: Executes the JavaScript to set the border style to 3px with solid red colour.
Line 17: Sends keys to the element.
Line 21: Executes the JavaScript to set the border to the original style.

8.6.2 Creating Page Logic

Action	Description
LoginWithHighlight()	This action will login a user with the data entry fields highlighted.

Add Listing 8.15 code to the 'pageLogin.cs' file.

Listing 8.15: 'pageLogin.cs' - Code to login with highlight

```
1  public void LoginWithHighlight(string uid, string pwd)
2  {
3      Utility.FindElementAndSendKeysWithHighlight(driver, ↵
              By.Name(Repository.Login.txtUserId_ByName), ↵
              uid);
4      Utility.FindElementAndSendKeysWithHighlight(driver, ↵
              By.Name(Repository.Login.txtPassword_ByName), ↵
              pwd);
5      Utility.FindElementAndClick(driver, ↵
              By.Id(Repository.Login.btnLogin_ById));
6
7      if (uid.Equals("") && pwd.Equals(""))
8      {
9          Utility.ReportExpectedVsActual(driver, ↵
                  Config.USERID_MANDATORY_ERROR, ↵
                  Utility.FindElementAndReturn(driver, ↵
```

```
                    ↪ (By.Id(Repository.Login. ↵
                    ↪ lblUserIDError_ById))).Text);
10            Utility.ReportExpectedVsActual(driver, ↵
                    ↪ Config.PASSWORD_MANDATORY_ERROR, ↵
                    ↪ Utility.FindElementAndReturn(driver, ↵
                    ↪ (By.Id(Repository.Login. ↵
                    ↪ lblPasswordError_ById))).Text);
11        }
12        else if (uid.Equals(""))
13        {
14            Utility.ReportExpectedVsActual(driver, ↵
                    ↪ Config.USERID_MANDATORY_ERROR, ↵
                    ↪ Utility.FindElementAndReturn(driver, ↵
                    ↪ (By.Id(Repository.Login. ↵
                    ↪ lblUserIDError_ById))).Text);
15        }
16        else if (pwd.Equals(""))
17        {
18            Utility.ReportExpectedVsActual(driver, ↵
                    ↪ Config.PASSWORD_MANDATORY_ERROR, ↵
                    ↪ Utility.FindElementAndReturn(driver, ↵
                    ↪ (By.Id(Repository.Login. ↵
                    ↪ lblPasswordError_ById))).Text);
19        }
20 }
```

Line 3 and Line 4: Call the Utility function to highlight the element when entering data in it.

8.6.3 Creating Tests

Add Listing 8.16 code to the 'TestLogins.cs' file.

Listing 8.16: 'TestLogins.cs' - Test to login user with highlight

```
1 [Test]
2 public void LoginWithHighlight()
3 {
4     try
5     {
6         Utility.Log.Info("Starting test: " + ↵
                ↪ TestContext.CurrentContext.Test.FullName);
7
8         var home = new pageHome(driver);
```

```
 9          home.Visit();
10          home.ClickLogin();
11
12          var login = new pageLogin(driver);
13          login.LoginWithHighlight("Tester", "Tester123");
14
15          Utility.ReportResult();
16      }
17      catch (Exception exception)
18      {
19          Utility.Log.Error("exception" + ↵
              ↪ exception.ToString());
20          throw exception;
21      }
22  }
```

Line 13: Calls the page logic function to login with highlight.

8.6.4 Executing Tests

Execute the test and you will see elements being highlighted in red during data entry as shown in Figure 8.7.

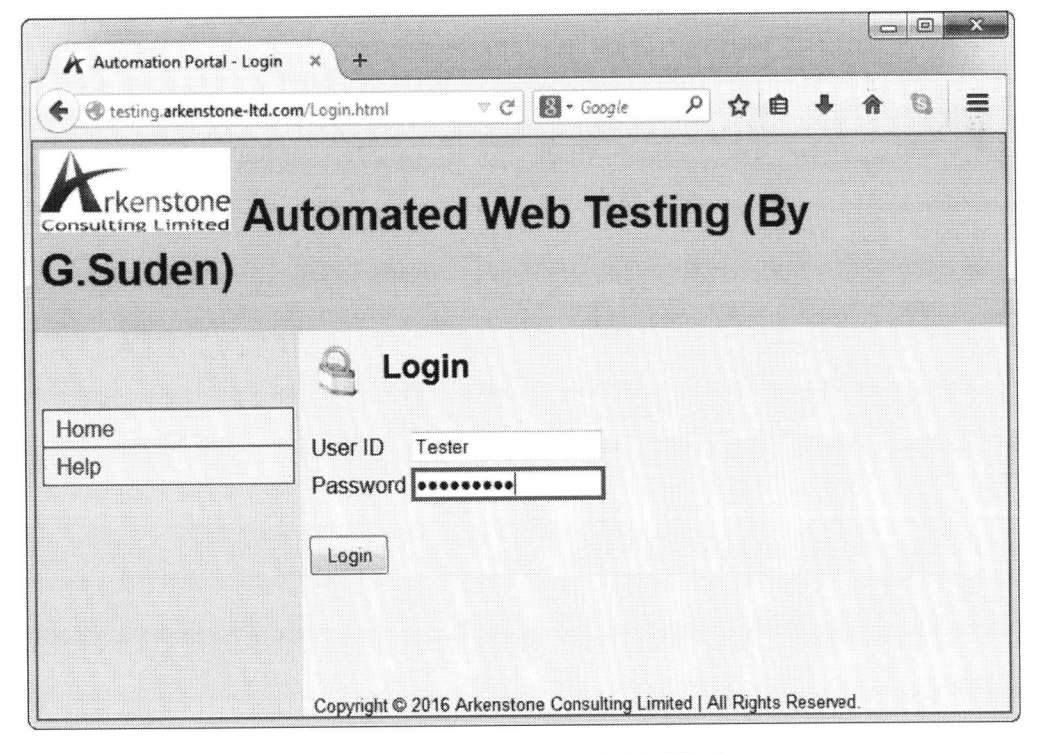

Figure 8.7: Login With Highlight

Hopefully, now that you have learnt about how to automate the testing of our demo website, you are feeling extremely comfortable using this Automation Framework and are now confident enough to be able to apply it to a number of different websites.

Happy Automated Web Testing!

Appendices

A.1 Automation Portal

Home Page

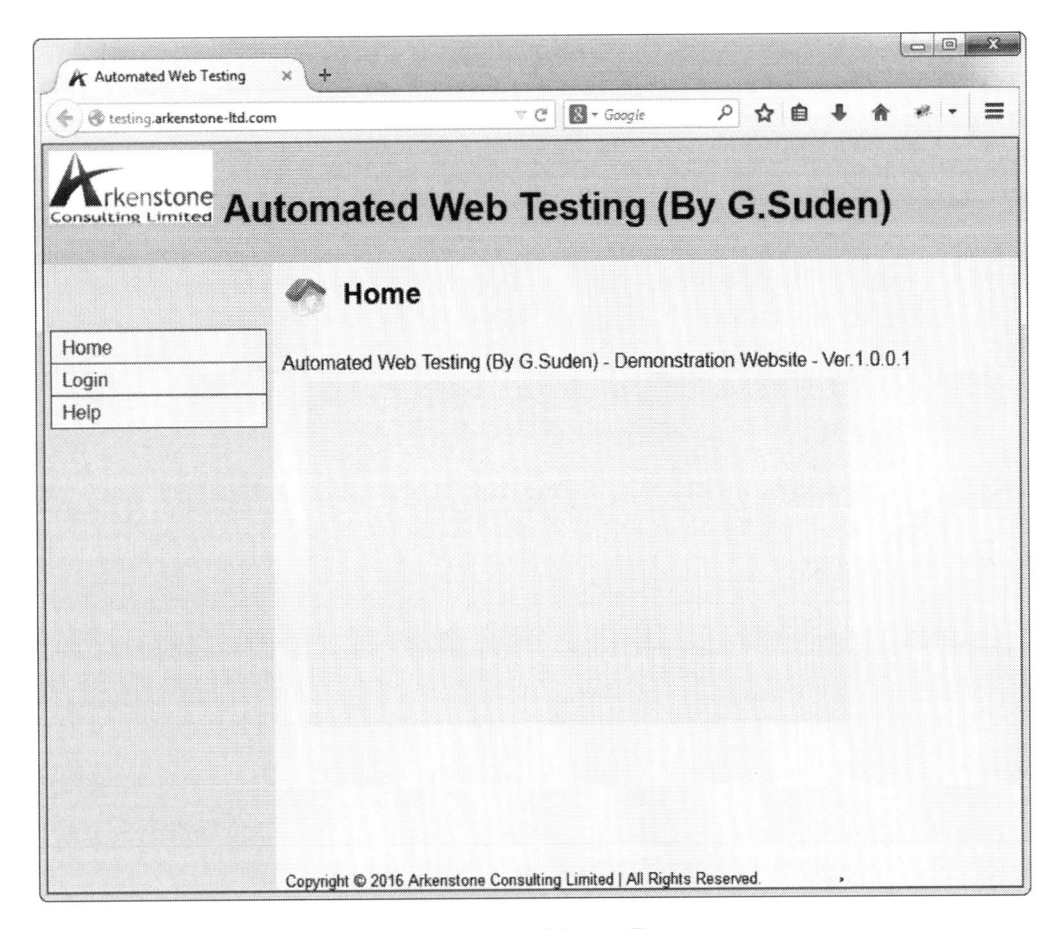

Figure A.1: Home Page

This is the landing page of the demonstration website. There are three links on this page:

- Home - takes you to the *Home* page i.e. this page.

- Login - takes you to the *Login* page.

- Helps - displays the *Help* page.

Login Page

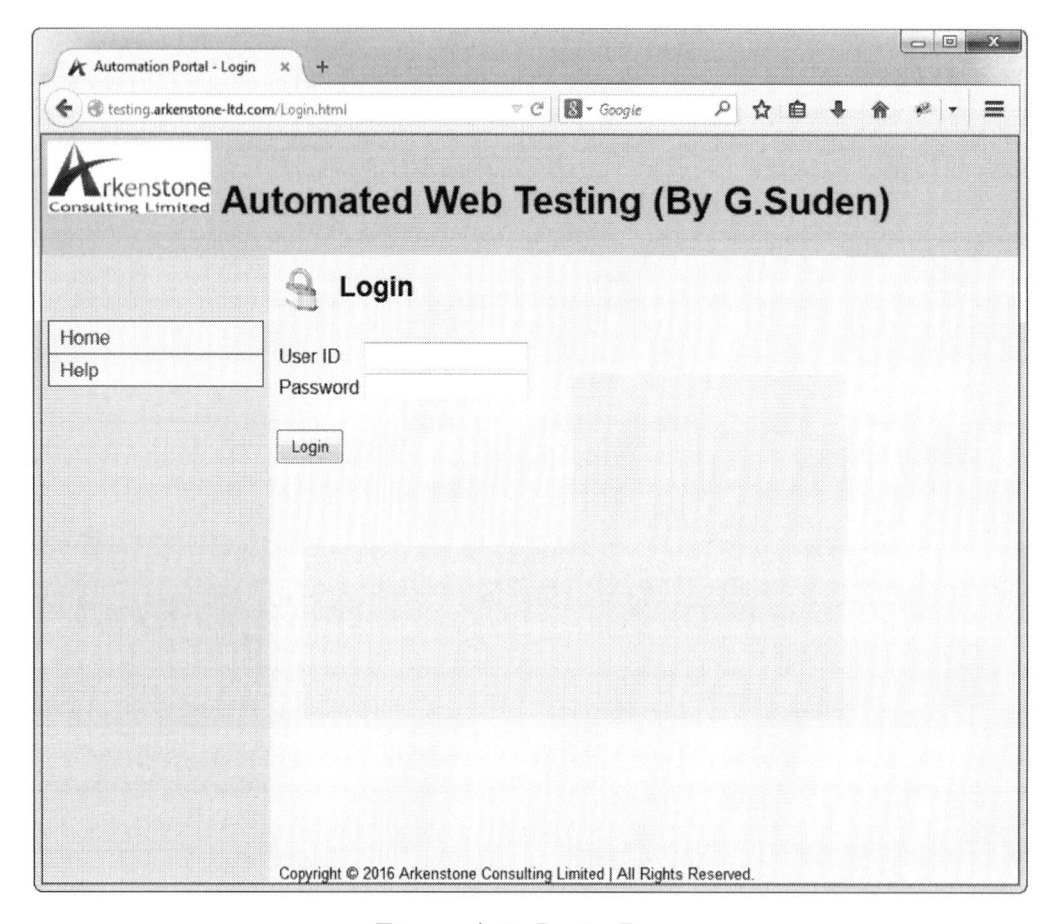

Figure A.2: Login Page

This is the *Login* page of the demo website. Two types of users exist for the demo website:

- A normal or general user with the following credentials:
    - User ID: Tester
    - Password: Tester123

- An administrative user with the following credentials:
    - User ID: Admin
    - Password: Admin123

The credentials are case-sensitive.

Help Page

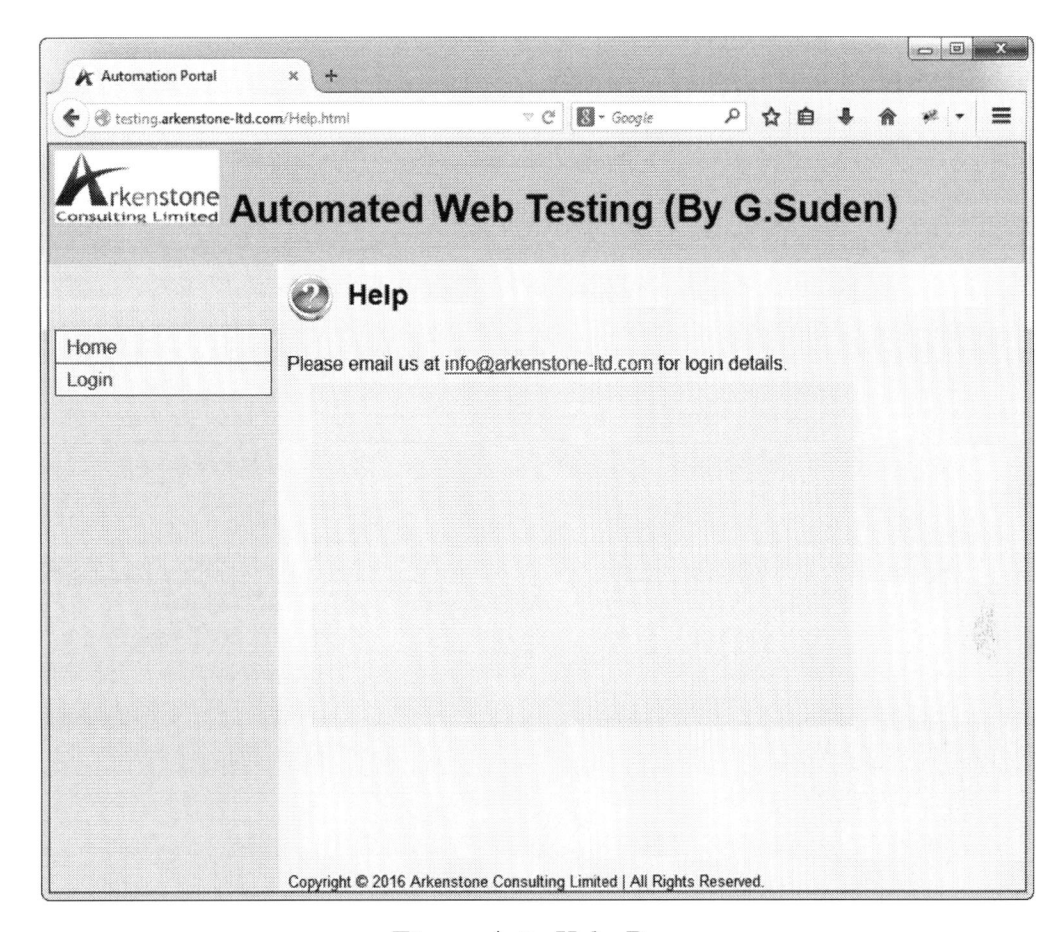

Figure A.3: Help Page

This is the Help page of the demo website.

Tester's Home Page

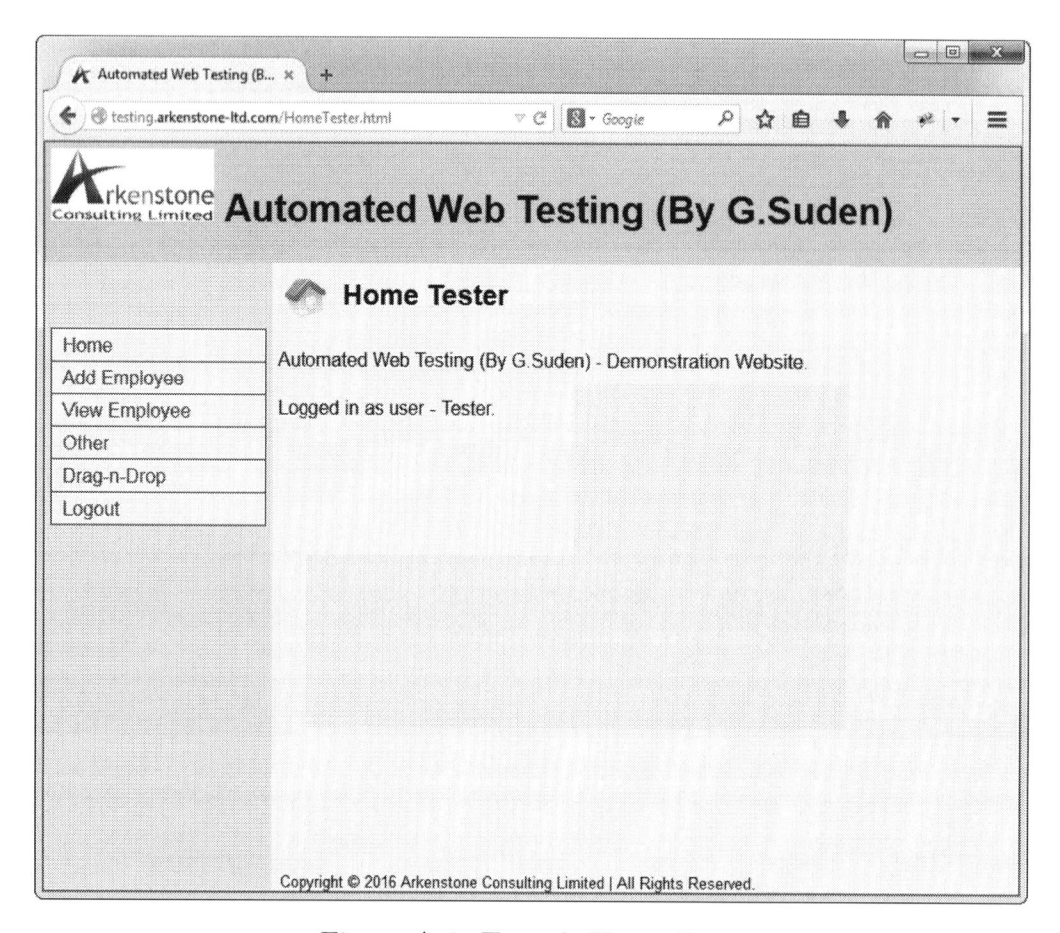

Figure A.4: Tester's Home Page

This is the landing page for a logged in Tester user. There are six links on this page:

- Home - takes you to the Tester's *Home* page i.e. this page.

- Add Employee - takes you to the *Add an Employee* page.

- View Employee - displays the *View an Employee* page.

- Other - displays the *Other* page.

- Drag-n-Drop - displays the *Drag-n-Drop* page.

- Logout - logs the user out and displays the generic *Home* page.

Add Employee Page

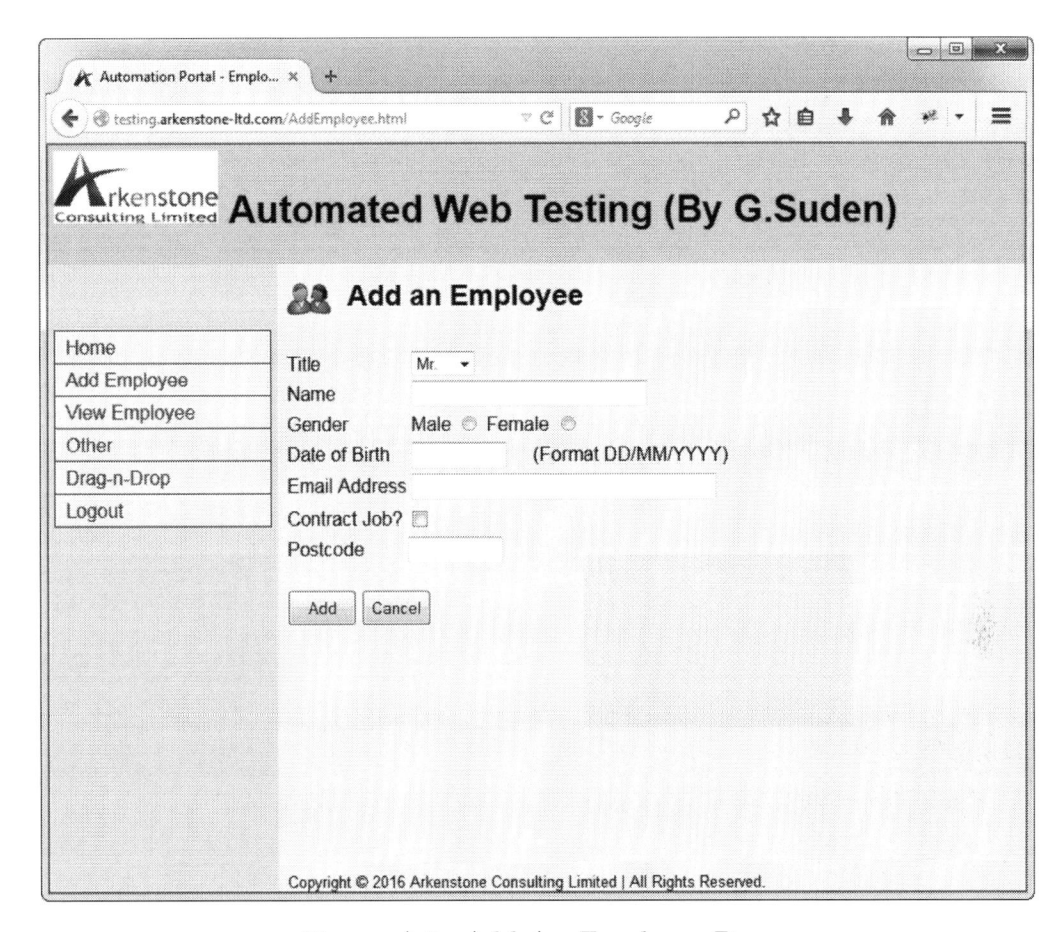

Figure A.5: Add An Employee Page

This page displays controls to add a new employee to the system. Please note that the demo website only mimics the business process without adding it to the database and just gives a success message as shown in Figure A.6 to facilitate our automated testing.

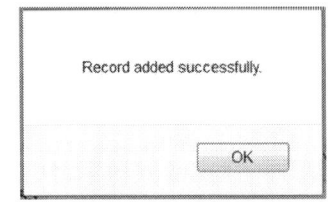

Figure A.6: Success Message

Automated Web Testing

View Employee Page

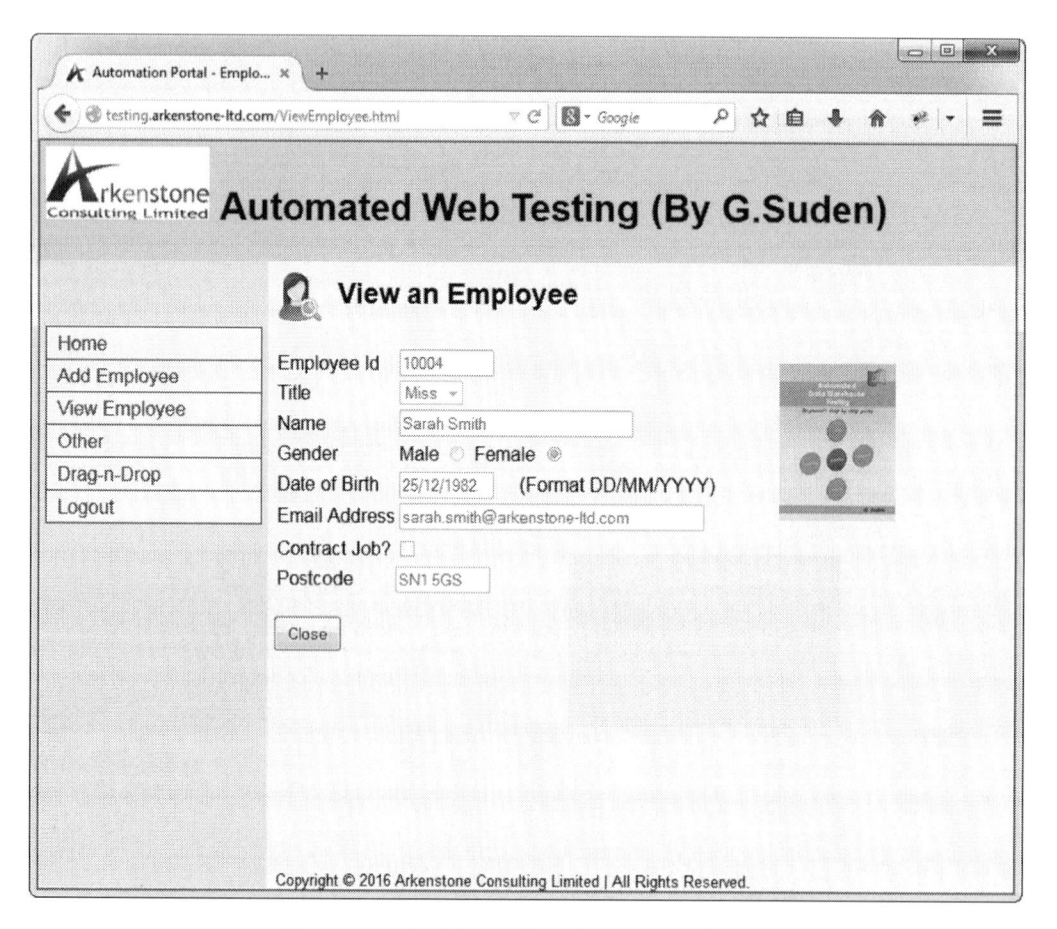

Figure A.7: View An Employee Page

This page displays the details of an employee in a read-only mode.

Other Page

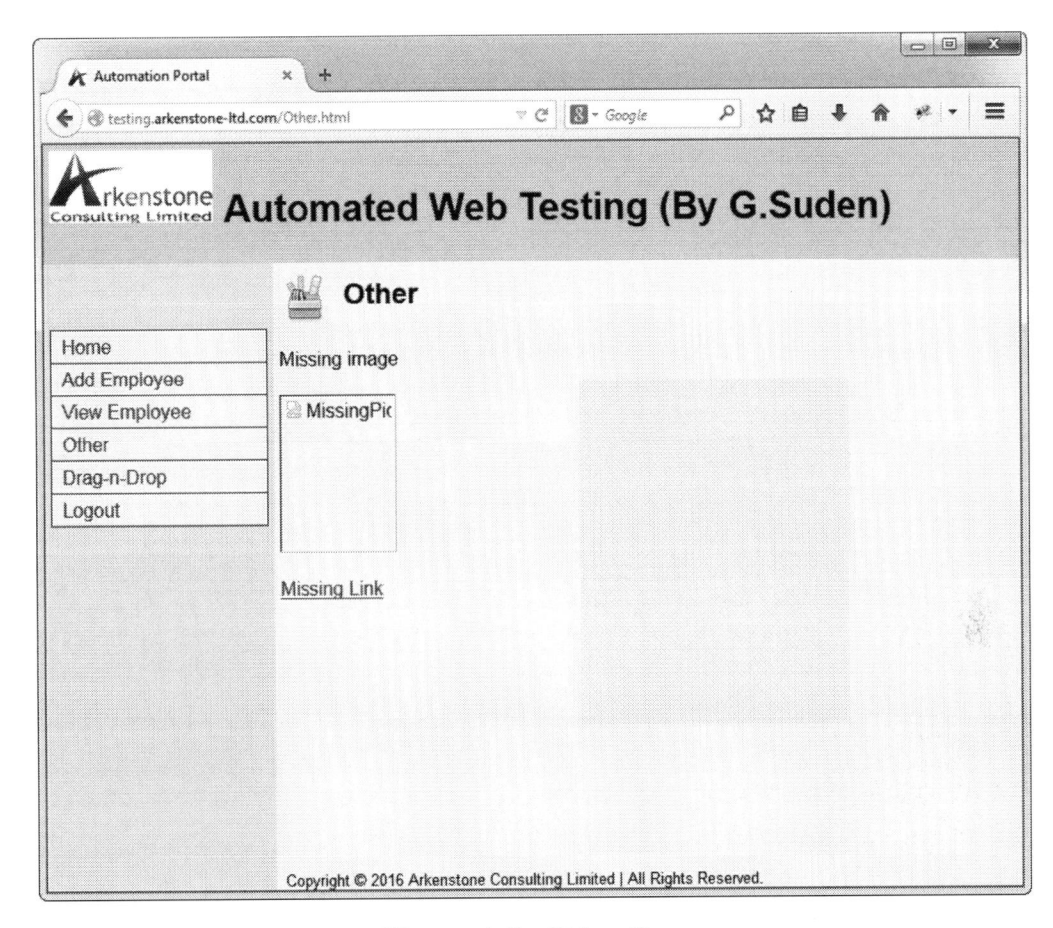

Figure A.8: Other Page

This page intentionally has a missing image and a broken link which we will check via automation.

Drag-n-Drop Page

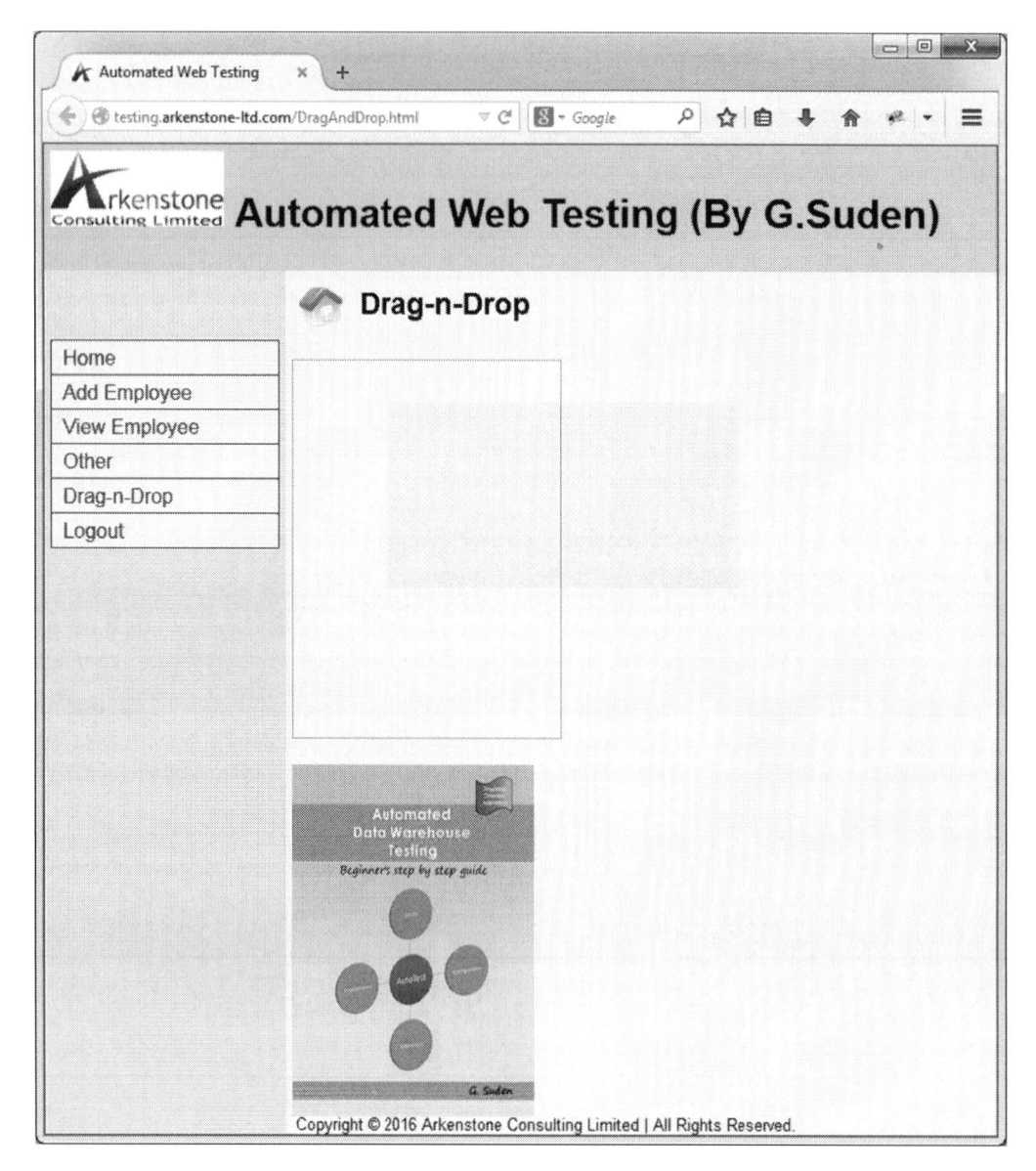

Figure A.9: Drag-n-Drop Page

This page demonstrates the Drag-and-Drop feature. Drag the image and drop it to the canvas area.

Admin's Home Page

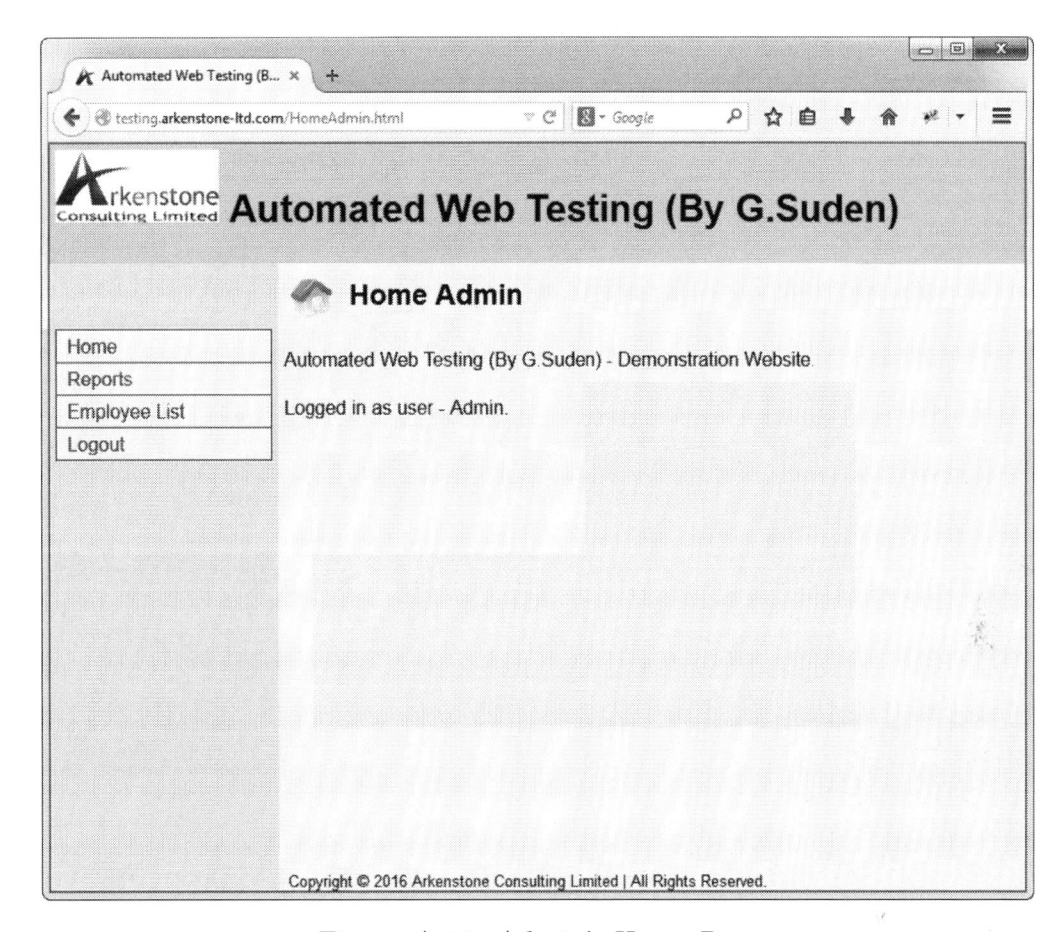

Figure A.10: Admin's Home Page

This is the landing page for a logged in Admin user. There are four links on this page:

- Home - takes you to the Admin's *Home* page i.e. this page.

- Reports - lets the user view reports.

- Employee List - lets the user view details of all the employees.

- Logout - logs the user out and displays the generic *Home* page.

Reports Page

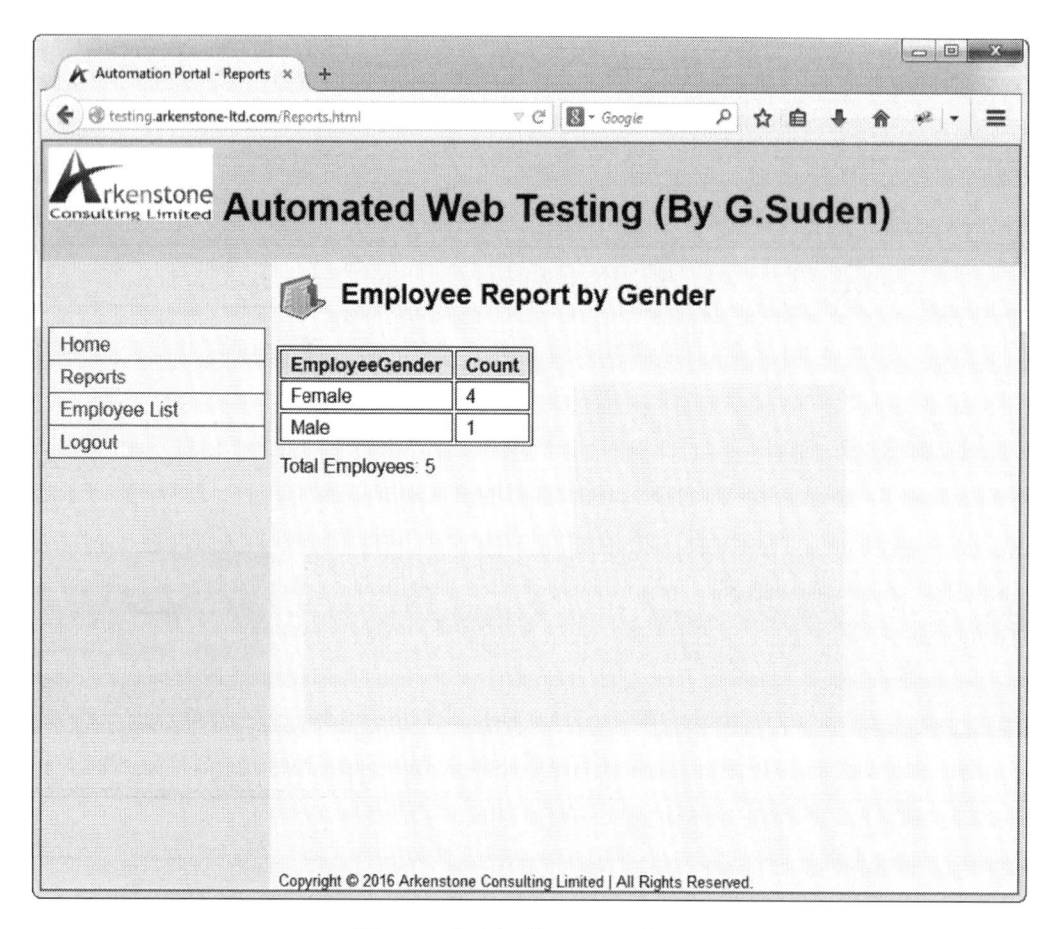

Figure A.11: Reports Page

This page displays a summary report of employee counts by Gender. It also displays total count of all the employees.

Employee List Page

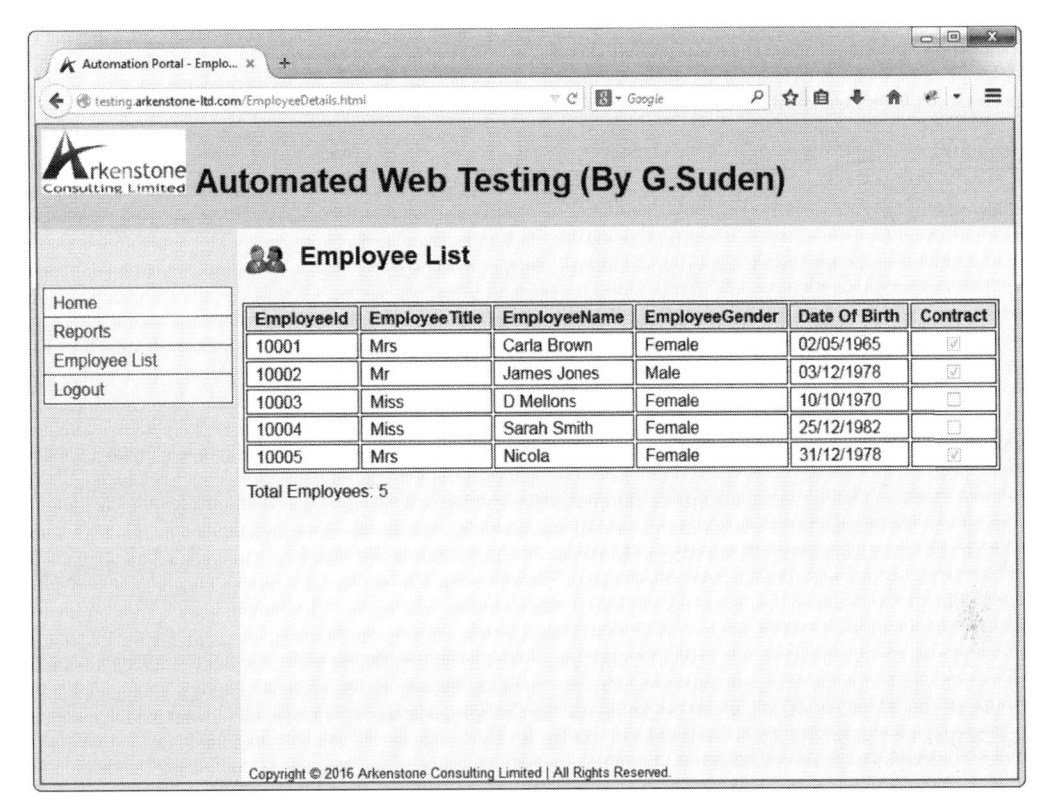

Figure A.12: View All Employee Details Page

This page displays a list of all the employees in a tabular form. It also displays total count of all the employees. Double click on any row to view details of the employee.

Index

3-Tier Web Application Architecture, 15

AddEmployeeXLSData, 172
AddVersionInfo, 260
AddVersionToPath, 260
Apache Log4net, 72
Appender, 79
Automation Framework, 33

CheckFailureThreshold, 187
Chrome, 222
Chrome Driver, 221
Chrome Extensions, 230
Chrome Options, 223, 227
CompareDetails, 131
Config.cs, 47, 89, 115, 130, 142, 155, 187, 193, 195, 201, 221, 232, 237, 243, 248, 254, 258, 259, 309
Configuration File, 33
CreateSummaryFileEntry, 156

DecodeContract, 142
DecodeGender, 142
Demo Portal - Site Map, 22

EmployeeListAdmin, 141
Employees.csv, 128
EmployeeWebService.asmx, 271
EncodeGender, 164
ExcelDateParse, 164

FindElementAndClick, 52
FindElementAndReturn, 90
FindElementAndSendKeys, 54
FindElementAndSendKeysWithHighlight, 322

FindElementEx, 51
FindElementsAndReturn, 115
FindElementsEx, 115
Firefox, 201
Firefox Add-ons, 204
Firefox Preferences, 217
Firefox Profiles, 208, 213
Firefox WebDriver, 201

GetCountOfRecs, 131
GetEmployeeByHttpWebRequest, 285, 286
GetEmployeeByServiceReference, 292
GetEmployeeByWebRequest, 278, 279
GetSelectedRadioButton, 116
GetSpreadSheetXLS, 164
GetSpreadSheetXLSX, 178
GetTooltip, 309

HandleAlert, 105
HomeAdmin, 129

Internet Explorer, 232
Internet Explorer Driver, 231
Internet Explorer Options, 233
IsElementPresent, 303, 304

Layout, 79
Log4net, 20, 72
log4net.config, 79, 81
Logger, 79
LogSysInfo, 260

Microsoft Edge, 238
Microsoft Edge Options, 239
Microsoft Edge WebDriver, 237

NPOI, 20

Opera, 248
Opera Options, 250
Opera WebDriver, 248

Page Files, 34
pageAdminEmpList.cs, 144
pageAdminHome.cs, 133
pageAdminReports.cs, 134
pageBase.cs, 56
pageHome.cs, 57
pageHomeTester.cs, 107
pageLogin.cs, 59
pageTesterAddEmployee.cs, 108

Record and Playback, 12
Reference Files, 34
Regression Testing, 11
Report Overall Test Result, 34
ReportExpectedVsActual, 67, 188, 193
ReportExpectedVsActualEx, 278, 279
ReportExpectedVsActualWithTolerance, 195
ReportResult, 68
ReportsAdmin, 129
Repository - DragAndDrop, 313
Repository File, 34
Repository.cs, 49, 50, 89, 103

Safari, 243
Safari Options, 244
SafariDriver, 243
SaveLogFile, 84
SaveScreenShot, 97
SelectOptionInList, 105
SelectRadioButton, 105
Setup Before Each Test, 34
SetupDriver, 51, 201
SetupSummaryFile, 156

Teardown After Each Test, 34
Test - AddEmployee, 110
Test - AddEmployeeXLSData, 173
Test - CompareDecimalNumbers, 197
Test - ContextClick, 319
Test - DragDropMethod1, 313
Test - DragDropMethod2, 315

Test - DragDropMethod3, 317
Test - FindBrokenLinks, 306
Test - FindMissingImages, 301
Test - LoadDefaultProfile, 208
Test - LoadFirefoxWithFirebug, 204
Test - LoadProfileWithPreferences, 217
Test - LoadSpecificProfile, 213
Test - LoadWithAllowFileAccessOption, 227
Test - LoadWithDisableExtensionsOption, 223
Test - LoadWithExtension, 230
Test - LoadWithOptions, 233, 239, 244, 250
Test - LoginAdminUser, 69, 76
Test - LoginUser, 61, 69, 76
Test - LoginUserXLSData, 169
Test - LoginWithBlankDetails, 92
Test - LoginWithHighlight, 324
Test - LoginWithInvalidPasswordOnly, 92
Test - LoginWithInvalidUserIdPassword, 92
Test - LoginWithInvalidUserOnly, 92
Test - LoginWithValidPasswordOnly, 92
Test - LoginWithValidUserOnly, 92
Test - ToolTipCheck, 311
Test - VerifyEmployee, 120
Test - VerifyEmployeeById, 152
Test - VerifyEmployeeList, 152
Test - VerifyEmployeeListXLSXData, 185
Test - VerifyEmployeeWithFailureThreshold, 191
Test - VerifyEmployeeXLSData, 176
Test - VerifyReportByGender, 137
Test - WebServicesHttpWebRequest, 289
Test - WebServicesServiceReference, 293
Test - WebServicesWebRequest, 282
Test Coverage, 11

342

Test Files, 34
TestAdminUser.cs, 152
TestChrome.cs, 223, 227
TestEdge.cs, 239
TestFirefox.cs, 208, 213
TestGeneralUser.cs, 110
TestIE.cs, 233
TestLogins.cs, 61, 158
TestOpera.cs, 250
TestSafari.cs, 244
TestWebServices.cs, 282

UserData.xls, 168, 171
UserData.xlsx, 182
Utility File, 33

Utility.cs, 52

VerifyEmployee, 278, 279
VerifyEmployeeListXLSXData, 183
VerifyEmployeeWithDB, 148, 286
VerifyEmployeeWithDBRandom, 150
VerifyEmployeeWithFailureThreshold, 189
VerifyEmployeeWithXLSData, 292
VerifyEmployeeXLSData, 175
VerifyImagesOnPage, 299
VerifyLinksOnPage, 303, 304
VerifyToolTips, 310

Wait, 97

29322510R00197

Printed in Great Britain
by Amazon